Byron's
"Corbeau Blanc"

Byron's
"Corbeau Blanc"

THE LIFE AND LETTERS OF LADY MELBOURNE

Edited by Jonathan David Gross

Texas A&M University Press
College Station

DEDICATION

To the memory of my mother,
Selma Gross, Educator

Lady Melbourne, by Sir Francis Cotes
(courtesy Hertford County Record Office)

J am not perhaps an impartial judge of Lady M. as amongst other obligations I am indebted to her for my acquaintance with yourself—but she is doubtless in talent a superior—a *supreme* woman—& her heart I know to be of the kindest—in the best sense of the word.—Her defects I never could perceive—as her society makes me forget them & every thing else for the time.—I do love that woman (*filially* or *fraternally*) better than any being on earth—& you see—that I am therefore unqualified to give an opinion.

—Lord Byron to Annabella Milbanke, February 12, 1814

J willingly accept the office, in which you have install'd me & hope always to be your Corbeau blanc.

—Lady Melbourne to Lord Byron, January 31, 1815

Originally published by
Rice University Press, 1997
First Texas A&M University Press printing, 1998

LIBRARY OF CONGRESS CATALOGING-IN-PUBLICATION DATA

Melbourne, Elizabeth Milbanke Lamb, Viscountess, 1751–1818
    Byron's "Corbeau Blanc": The Life and Letters of Lady Melbourne/[edited] by Jonathan
        David Gross.
    p. cm.
    Includes bibliographical references (p.).
    ISBN 0-89096-672-9 (pbk.)
    1. Great Britain—Social life and customs—18th century—Sources. 2. Melbourne.
Elizabeth Milbanke Lamb, Viscountess, 1751–1818—Correspondence. 3. Byron,
George Gordon Byron, Baron, 1788–1824—Correspondence. 4. Great
Britain—Social life and customs—19th century—Sources. 5. Great Britain—Court
and courtiers—Correspondence. 6. Regency—England—Sources. I. Gross, Jonathan
David. II. Title. III. Title: Letters of Lady Melbourne
DA485.M45   1997
941.07′3—dc21

96-49643
CIP

Cover art: *Elizabeth, Viscountess Melbourne,* engraving after Sir Joshua Reynolds,
Courtesy of British Museum

CONTENTS

ILLUSTRATIONS

Letters

IV: BYRON'S "ZIA," 1814

V: THE MAKING OF A DIPLOMAT, 1817-18

ACKNOWLEDGEMENTS

It is my pleasure to acknowledge the generous financial support of the Huntington Library and DePaul University, which enabled me to complete this work. Mr. Robert Ritchie and Elma Sink made my term as a Mayer Fund Fellow at the Huntington a pleasant and rewarding experience. DePaul University provided two University Research Council grants as well as a Summer Stipend. Special thanks to Stephanie Quinn and Marjorie Piechowski for making this possible. Professor Karl Kroeber, my dissertation director at Columbia University, and Professor Gerald Mulderig, chair of the Department of English at DePaul, were great champions of this project.

I am grateful to the owners of the following collections for allowing me to transcribe and publish material contained in their archives: Melbourne Hall (Lord Ralph Kerr); John Murray, Ltd.; the Huntington Library (San Marino, California); the Chatsworth Collection (Devonshire House); the Lovelace Collection (Laurence Pollinger, by courtesy of the earl of Lytton); the Osborn Collection (Yale University); and the British Library.

Lord Ralph Kerr graciously arranged for me to view the Melbourne Archives at Christie's in the summer of 1993. His generosity and patient response to my detailed enquiries enabled me to include a large number of letters by Lady Melbourne that have not been previously published. Lord Brocket allowed me to visit Brocket Hall at a time when it was not open to the public. Virginia Murray, of John Murray's, Ltd., deserves my special thanks for her advice, guidance, and encouragement. She led me to many important archival discoveries, arranged for the photography of Lady Melbourne's letter that appears in this edition, and nourished me with tea and hospitality. My work at the publishing firm of John Murray will always be one of my fondest memories.

A number of curators aided me substantially. Mrs. Gill Weston responded to numerous inquiries concerning Melbourne Hall and provided important information regarding the location of Richard Cosway's portrait of Lady Melbourne. Howard Usher, also of Melbourne Hall, provided me with photographs of the Albany and Halnaby Hall. His monographs, *Femmes Fatales*; *William Lamb, Lord Melbourne*; and *The Owners of Melbourne Hall* are important sources of information about Lady Melbourne. Kathryn Thompson of the Hertfordshire County Record Office answered numerous requests for photographs and allowed me to photocopy Frederick Lamb's letters to his mother. The staff at the Hertfordshire Record Office was always unfailingly cheerful and helpful, making my work there a pleasure. At the British Library, I also enjoyed the professional attention of a superb staff: R. J. Conway, Chris Fletcher, and the attendants in the North Library deserve my special thanks. Equally helpful in terms of photocopying letters and answering my numerous letters were Peter Day of Chatsworth; R. S. Conway of the manuscripts room at the British Library; the staff of the University of Liverpool; Mr. Woolgar of Broadlands; Robin Harcourt Williams of Hatfield House; and Brett Withers of the Law Library at DePaul University.

Various friends assisted materially in the production of this manuscript. Kerry Mackenzie, a free-lance writer, helped transcribe Lady Melbourne's letters at the British Library in 1992, cracking the code of her difficult hand. Professor Mark Pohlad brought to my attention Sheila Birkenhead's *Peace in Piccadilly,* which became such an important source for the introduction. Professor James Soderholm provided me with a print of Anne Isabella Milbanke and gave helpful advice on procuring photographs. Margot Strickland's beautifully written chapter on Lady Melbourne in *The Byron Women* was the inspiration for this book.

Byron scholars and biographers have been very helpful. Benita Eisler shared her knowledge about Lady Melbourne and wrote generously on my behalf. William St. Clair gained access for me to the British Library in 1991, thus enabling me to see Lady Melbourne's letters for the first time. Mrs. Marsha Manns, secretary of the Byron Society, played a crucial role in bringing this project to fruition through her encouragement and support. Professor Carl Woodring, of Columbia University, provided me with a tutorial on scholarly editing through his patient answers to my numerous inquiries. Professor Peter Graham of Virginia Polytechnic

Institute and State University and Professor John Clubbe of the University of Kentucky read the manuscript in its final stage and suggested numerous improvements. Professor Pascale-Anne Brault of DePaul University assisted me with several French translations. I am grateful to them all for their shrewd advice and for taking time out of their busy schedules to help. Any remaining errors are mine alone.

The illustrations that appear in this book would not have been possible without the expert guidance of Miss Deborah Gage and H. G. Belsey. Miss Gage was of great assistance in guiding me through the collection at Firle Place and suggesting other locations where I might find portraits of Lady Melbourne. Mr. Belsey lent me his rare copy of the Romney painting of Lady Melbourne and Mrs. Julian Salmond allowed me to include Daniel Gardner's *Witches 'Round the Cauldron* in this edition. Katherine Ward of the Prints and Drawings Department of the British Museum supplied numerous engraved portraits that appear in this volume at a time when the collection was being moved. I am grateful for her diligence and perseverance. Miss Lynn Ryut arranged for the superb photograph of Lady Melbourne's second home, Melbourne Hall, London (now Dover House), and Claire Lunness was kind enough to send me her photograph of Brocket Hall. Sarah Wimbush of the Courtauld Institute provided prints of obscure works and obtained permission on my behalf in numerous instances. Miss Costello of *Country Life Publications*, Shane Nelson of the Royal Brighton Arts Council, the staff at the Newberry Library, Chicago, and James Kilvington and Philip Cox of the National Portrait Gallery in London also deserve my thanks for their patient response to my numerous inquiries. Deidre Cantrell of the Art Library at the Huntington generously provided a photograph of Reynolds' portrait of the duchess of Devonshire.

The staff at Rice University Press supported this project through a difficult period. Special thanks to Susan Bielstein, editor-in-chief; Michelle Nichols, textual editor; and Barrie Scardino, production editor.

I would like to thank my friend, Jon Horvitz; my sister, Donna; my father and mother, Theodore and Selma Gross; and my step-mother, Marion Simon, for their loving support. Marty and Mart Russell provided unfailing encouragement during the length of this project.

Jacqueline Russell, my wife, never lost faith in Lady Melbourne's importance. Her careful editing of the introduction improved the final draft. My gratitude to her and to our daughter, Shiri Nicole, for emotional support along the way.

PREFACE

*W*hen Edmund Burke called the eighteenth century the age of extraordinary women,
he could well have had Lady Melbourne in mind. She lived at a time when political
influence was wielded not only in the House of Commons, but at gatherings at
Devonshire House, Holland House, and Melbourne House, Piccadilly. Women were
barred from holding political office. Nevertheless, Robert Southey could write and
believe that England was their "paradise," a place where they enjoyed more privileges than any civilization on earth (Southey 398). Byron called the country he left
behind a "gynocracy," adding that society was "one polish'd horde" that moved at
their behest (Byron, *Don Juan* 16:52; 13:9; in *CPW*). A young politician such as
Charles James Fox, Richard Sheridan, or Lord Byron himself often owed his success
or failure to the active partisanship or benign neglect of the women with whom he
socialized.

Educated privately, like contemporaries of her social class, Lady Melbourne
could read French and compose poetry on occasion. Even as a young girl she
refused to embrace the parochialism of the Yorkshire countryside from which she
sprang, sensing that London was the location best suited to the scope of her talent.
In 1769, only two years after the death of her mother, she accepted an offer of marriage from Sir Peniston Lamb which she had done much to arrange. Soon her every
move was recorded in the London newspapers. Leading painters, including Sir
Joshua Reynolds and Richard Cosway, executed her portrait in oil.

The brilliance of Lady Melbourne's career lies in its seamless wedding of
the personal and the political. At elegant dinner parties she gathered together a
bipartisan group. Wealthy landowners such as Lord Egremont and the duke of
Bedford could exchange opinions with rising men of influence such as Charles Grey

and George Canning. Guests who flocked to Melbourne House, Piccadilly must have found her less judgmental than the tyrannical Lady Holland and more politically mature than her close friend, the effusively sentimental Georgiana, duchess of Devonshire. Certainly the Prince of Wales did. He visited her frequently, traveling by horseback from Carlton House, and sometimes stayed until three or four in the morning. In the early 1780s they became lovers. The thin black velvet band that she wore around her neck in numerous portraits was said to be a symbol of this attachment (Airlie, *Whig* 2). Somewhat tactlessly, the prince even confessed to Lady Melbourne his infatuation for Mrs. Maria Fitzherbert in December 1785. That same month he married the Catholic widow in a secret ceremony.

Lady Melbourne once wrote that few men could be trusted with their neighbors' secrets, and scarcely any woman with her own (Boyle 460). In her letters, as in her life, she often traded on the private lives of well-placed individuals. The comfort she provided to others as their confidante became the political coin she minted when she needed a favor returned. Surrounded by a younger generation in London with more sensibility than sense, she quickly gained ascendancy over them, becoming the trusted adviser first of the duchess of Devonshire, then of Lady Caroline Lamb, and finally of Lord Byron.

Lady Melbourne made use of her political influence in a number of ways. After her love affair with the Prince of Wales subsided into a lifelong friendship, she used her contact with Carlton House to see her husband appointed an Irish viscount (1770), lord of the bedchamber (1784; 1812), and finally, an English peer (1816). In 1791 she agreed to exchange homes with the Prince of Wales' brother (Frederick, duke of York), and the Prince of Wales returned the favor. He lent her his home in Brighton to recover when her eldest son, Peniston, died of consumption in 1805. Through Lord Wellesley, the prince offered her son Frederick a position in the diplomatic line in 1811, and another son, William, a position in the treasury department the following year.

After 1806 Lady Melbourne exerted influence over naval appointments and promotions through her friendship with Thomas Grenville. She was related by marriage to William Huskisson, one of the leading financiers of the age, and could also count on political favors from Charles Grey, having helped him keep his affair with the emotional duchess of Devonshire a relative secret in the 1790s. Her lifelong friendship and affair with Lord Egremont enabled her to influence him politically for decades, especially during the court-martial of Colonel Dick Quentin in December 1815.

Although Lady Melbourne was compared by some to Mistress Overdone in *Measure for Measure,* she was far more than a mere busybody. There seemed to be no field in which she could not succeed once she directed her attention to that quarter. Her achievements in agriculture earned her the attention of Arthur Young, who praised her as one of the first to make use of drill husbandry in the Hertfordshire countryside. During the rage for amateur theatricals in the 1770s, she could be found at the duke of Richmond's theater with her friend Anne Damer. Several decades later, in 1803, she had the pleasure of watching her own children, Peniston, George, and William, perform in amateur productions staged at Lord Abercorn's estate, the Priory.

Lady Melbourne had no radical social program. However, the care she took in her children's education ensured their political success and gave her social ambition a civic dimension.[1] William became Queen Victoria's first prime minister and did much to unite the country after the passage of the Reform Bill in 1830. Frederick accompanied Lord Castlereagh to the Treaty of Vienna, which redivided Europe after the fall of Napoleon, and later became ambassador to that city, a coveted post. George Lamb, Lady Melbourne's son by Prince of Wales, was a lawyer and actor who wrote several plays, including *Who's the Dupe?* and *Whistle for It.* He served with Byron on the Drury Lane committee in 1815. Lady Melbourne's only surviving daughter, Emily, was a complex and stricking figure who followed in her mother's footsteps. She sat on the Ladies' Committee at Almack's that once excluded the duke of Wellington from a fashionable event because he arrived ten minutes late (Airlie, *Palmerston* 40).

It was said of Lady Melbourne that she never saw a happy marriage without trying to destroy its harmony. The marriages she helped to arrange between Augusta and Colonel George Leigh, and between Lord Byron and her niece, Annabella Milbanke, both proved disastrous. She oversaw the marriage of her beloved daughter Emily to the fifth earl of Cowper, but later countenanced her daughter's indiscretions with Lord Palmerston. When Caroline Lamb and Caroline St. Jules proved unfaithful wives to her sons William and George, Lady Melbourne reproved them not for their behavior so much as for the publicity it aroused. Her letters to Lord Byron, which form the heart of this collection, were ostensibly written to end his affair with Caroline Lamb, but more than one contemporary thought it strange that Lady Melbourne would correspond with the very man who was cuckolding her favorite son, William.

Lady Bessborough nicknamed Lady Melbourne "the Thorn" for her sharp tongue. So striking was her repartee that two generations of writers remembered her conversation in their plays and novels. She appears as a deceptively innocent provincial, Lady Teazle, in Sheridan's *The School for Scandal* (1776); as a worldly confidante, Lady Besford, in the duchess of Devonshire's *The Sylph* (1779); as a gothic villain, Lady Margaret Buchanan, in Lady Caroline Lamb's *Glenarvon* (1816); and as a compassionate mother, Lady Pinchbeck, in Byron's *Don Juan* (1818–23). However, Byron reserved his highest compliment for Lady Melbourne in his letters, calling her conversation "champagne" to his spirits (May 14, 1813; *LJ* 3:48).

Lady Melbourne gave to the Regency period the stamp of her personality, an impression she borrowed from the late eighteenth century. Byron only echoed the judgments of others when he called her the most talented woman of her generation, a complex and scintillating personality. She was a remarkable woman, as her son William observed after her death, a devoted mother, but "not chaste, not chaste" (Usher, *Owners* 3).

---

1. Peniston was born in 1770, followed by William in 1779, Frederick in 1782, George in 1784, Emily in 1787, and Harriet in 1789.

EDITORIAL METHOD

*L*ady Melbourne is a compelling stylist. To break up her fluid and well-constructed sentences with numerous punctuation marks would do violence to her gift for unlaboured self-expression. For this reason, I have retained her lengthy sentences and included punctuation in brackets only when the omission of commas and periods would obscure her meaning. My aim throughout these letters has been to retain the freshness of her correspondence. By normalizing the punctuation of politicians and citizens, and leaving the punctuation of writers untouched, we give a false impression of the Romantic writers' relationship to their own time period, a relationship that it is one purpose of this volume to restore.

I have included a larger number of Lady Melbourne's letters than might seem warranted. Letters to Henry Fox, Lady Melbourne's warden at Melbourne Hall, are included because they show her importance as an agricultural innovator, a quality noted by Arthur Young. Letters to Frederick Lamb are included, even when they discuss such mundane matters as a recipe for mince pies, because they show a domestic side to Lady Melbourne that has not always been acknowledged. They also show how often she tried to use her influence with the Prince Regent to advance Frederick's diplomatic career.

One reads Lady Melbourne's letters as much for the light they shed on life in Regency England as for her own opinions and insights. For this reason I have included endnotes to identify the many names that appear in this volume, and have added more extensive biographies of these figures in a glossary. I hope these biographies will be helpful in their own right, for though the *Dictionary of National Biography* provides information on the most well-known figures, it does not include many of the men and especially the women mentioned by Lady

Melbourne. I have tried to avoid canned biographies that include only names, dates, and positions held, and strived to cull more personal anecdotes about these individuals from the works of their contemporaries, including Nathaniel Wraxall, Elizabeth Steele, and Horace Walpole. This is in the spirit of Lady Melbourne's letters themselves, which touch upon personalities as often as they do upon politics.

Many of the endnotes that appear in this volume relate to Byron's letters. Inclusion of quotations from these letters may seem unnecessary to scholars familiar with his correspondence. My purpose in inserting them here—indeed my purpose in assembling Lady Melbourne's letters to begin with—is to show the extent to which the two collaborated in developing their opinions of their contemporaries. To read both ends of the correspondence is to realize how often Byron's literary imagination was first stimulated by the worldly insights offered to him by Lady Melbourne. More practically, Lady Melbourne's correspondence reveals the fact that Byron wrote a number of letters during the period he was in England that have not yet been recovered, if they still exist at all.

The great majority of letters that appear in this collection have not been previously transcribed. In all cases, I have transcribed letters from the original documents housed at the following locations: John Murray Archives; Lovelace Collection, Oxford University; British Library; Hertford County Record Office; Melbourne Hall Archives; and the Huntington Library. Photocopies were consulted from manuscripts at Chatsworth and Yale University.

CONVENTIONS USED IN TEXT

[ ]   Words or letters supplied by editor for words,
                             letters, or names missing in the original manuscript

^   ^   Words that appear in between two lines of the manuscript

< >   Matter unclear in manuscript; uncertain reading

Format: The author and recipient of each letter appear in italics on the upper left-hand corner of each letter, followed in parentheses by the archive in which the letter can be found.

Dates: For convenience, dates of letters are included on the upper right-hand corner of each letter, even if this information is repeated at the bottom of the letter. These dates are placed in brackets when they appear not at the top of the letter, but at the bottom or on an envelope. When a date has been assigned by the curator of a museum, that date also appears in brackets and an endnote is included to that effect.

Envelopes: Written information that appears on envelopes is included at the end of each letter in brackets.

Superscripts: Lady Melbourne's orthography corresponds with that of the duchess of Devonshire, and other contemporaries. For this reason, her superscripts have been retained, along with the marks of punctuation that accompany them. When periods fall below the level of superscripts in the manuscript, they have been maintained at that level in order to be faithful to the manuscript. The most commonly used abbreviations are listed below with their referents:

D^{ss}	Duchess
D^k	Duke
L^d	Lord
L^y, L^{dy}, L$^{dy.}$	Lady
Mor^{ning}	Morning
M^r	Mr
M^s	Miss
P R^t	Prince Regent
s^d	said
y^t	that
y^e	the
y^m	them
y^r	your

In conformance with Lady Melbourne's usage, months are abbreviated as follows:

Jan^y	January
Feb^y	February
Sep^{tr}	September
Oc^r	October
Nov^r	November
Dec^r	December

Paper Size: Lady Melbourne used three sizes of paper (7.1 x 8, 7.1 x 4.5, and 7.1 x 9.1 inches). She allowed the paper size to guide punctuation and would frequently omit end punctuation if her sentence ended at the right-hand margin or if a line break corresponded with the end of a page. At times it would appear as though she ended or even constructed her sentences so they would conform to the size of the paper.

Typography, Punctuation, and Capitalization: Lady Melbourne and her correspondents often use underlining to emphasize certain words. Such underlinings have been replaced with italics in this volume. Underlinings in Lady Melbourne's superscripts, however, do not serve the same purpose and have been retained.

In order to clarify meaning, I have sometimes added punctuation in brackets. To avoid a superfluity of brackets, I have not added apostrophes to possessives or contractions. Thus, "Ms Ossultone[']s" reads "Ms Ossultones" and "dont" and "its" appear here as they do in the letters. I have not added end punctuation when a dash serves the same purpose.

Sometimes Lady Melbourne does not capitalize the first word of a new sentence; at other times she is guilty of comma splices. In both cases, I have left the letters as they are in order to convey a sense of her mixture of erudition and carelessness, and to show that she shared with Byron a lack of concern about punctuation, though she was a gifted stylist.

Dashes: To approximate Lady Melbourne's squiggles, the length of dashes has been adhered to as much as possible, but this is an inexact science. Because the writer's hand moves forward to the right so rapidly, periods sometimes look like dashes. I have used dashes only when the height of the pen mark militates against interpreting the mark as a period or comma.

Abbreviations: Whenever possible, I have retained abbreviations, especially those referring to proper names. On some occasions, I have filled in a name to avoid confusion. The following are some of Lady Melbourne's most frequent abbreviations:

C-	Caroline Lamb
Cow	Lady Cowper, Lady Melbourne's daughter
L B	Lord Byron
L M	Lord Melbourne
L^d E	Lord Egremont
L^y B	Lady Bessborough
P R^t	Prince Regent
W^m	William Lamb

Identification and Spelling of Names: If a name has not been identified, I have left it in abbreviated form with an endnote that reads "unidentified." If the identification is conjectural, I have indicated so by saying "perhaps." The proper spelling of names can be found in endnotes and in the glossary.

Additional Letters: Letters to Lady Melbourne from other correspondents—including Lady Byron, Judith Milbanke, Charles Grey, and the Prince Regent—have been included when they provide a crucial context for understanding Lady Melbourne's response.

CHRONOLOGY

1751   Lady Melbourne baptized on October 15, 1751

1757   Duchess of Devonshire born

1769   Lady Melbourne marries Peniston Lamb, April 12

1770   Birth of Peniston Lamb; sits for Reynolds portrait, *Maternal Affection*

1773   Peniston Lamb's affair with Sophia Baddeley

1774   Duchess of Devonshire's marriage

1779   Affair with Lord Egremont; birth of William Lamb

1780   Affair with Prince Regent (1780-85)

1782   Birth of Frederick Lamb; Duchess of Devonshire still childless; Duchess of Devonshire meets Elizabeth Foster

1784   Birth of George Augustus Lamb, reputed child of Prince Regent; Lady Elizabeth Foster abroad with Duke of Devonshire's illegitimate daughter, Caroline St. Jules

1785   Prince Regent marries Mrs. Fitzherbert in secret ceremony, December 15; Caroline Lamb born, November 12; Lady Melbourne ill with gout

1787   Birth of Emily Lamb, Lady Melbourne's eldest daughter, and the reputed child of Egremont

1788   Duchess of Devonshire reveals debts to her husband in September

1788   Birth of Lord Byron

1791   Lady Melbourne trades houses with Duke of York

1792   Lady Melbourne writes "The Bed"

1802	Death of duke of Bedford, reputed lover of Lady Melbourne
1802	Death of Harriet, Lady Melbourne's youngest daughter
1805	Death of Peniston, Lady Melbourne's eldest son
1805	Marriage of Emily Lamb to Lord Cowper; Marriage of William Lamb to Caroline Ponsonby
1809	Caroline Lamb's affair with Sir Godfrey Webster; George Lamb's marriage to Caroline St. Jules (Caro George)
1811	Frederick Lamb appointed to diplomatic post in Sicily
1812	Byron's maiden speech in House of Lords; publication of *Childe Harold*—famous "overnight"—March 10; Byron's affair with Caroline Lamb; Commencement of Lady Melbourne's correspondence with Byron; Byron's first proposal to Annabella Milbanke rejected; Lady Melbourne solicits Annabella's requirements in husband, forwards them to Byron.
1813	Visit of Madame de Staël, June; Byron publishes *Giaour, Bride of Abydos*; refers to Annabella as "Clarissa Harlowed into an awkward kind of correctness" (September 5, 1813; *LJ* 3:108).
1814	Byron publishes *The Corsair*, February 1
1815	Byron's marriage to Annabella Milbanke, January 2; Lady Melbourne arranges honeymoon at Halnaby and rents their first house at 13 Piccadilly.
1816	Byron departs for continent; *Glenarvon* published
1818	Death of Lady Melbourne, April 6

*E*lizabeth Milbanke was seventeen when she married Sir Peniston Lamb on April 13, 1769 at the bishop of Peterborough's house in Great George Street, St. George, Hanover Square. She was destined to become a famous beauty and a fashionable Whig hostess, Lord Byron's confidential correspondent, and the mother of Queen Victoria's first prime minister.[1] The leading painters of the day paid tribute to her enchanting smile. Tall, beautiful, and intelligent beyond measure, she had affairs with several prominent men, which led her own sister-in-law to compare her to Madame de Merteuil in Laclos' *Les Liaisons dangereuses*. But Lady Melbourne's character was more complex than even a French novelist could suggest. She was a devoted mother who was as comfortable tending her garden at Brocket Hall as she was entertaining the *bon ton* of London society. While her daughter-in-law painted her as a gothic villain in *Glenarvon,* Byron praised her as a loving mother in *Don Juan*.

Lady Melbourne entertained a distinguished company at the Albany and Whitehall in London, spending her summers at Brocket Hall, Hertfordshire and, more rarely, at Melbourne Hall, Derbyshire. She commissioned the building of Melbourne House, later known as the Albany, in Piccadilly, adorning it with silks and frescoes, statues and Venetian art. What secrets were exchanged in the magnificent reception rooms of this London mansion? What family fortunes united in marriages that would consolidate the power of the Whigs? In the early 1780s, even Charles James Fox paid Lady Melbourne court, for that was when her affair with the Prince of Wales was at its height. A disapproving Horace Walpole compared her to the scheming Diane de Poitiers, mistress of Henry II.[2] Certainly, the young woman who arrived in London lived in an elegant manner which would be difficult to surpass, and to which, for good reasons perhaps, we can never return.

***

A painting by George Stubbs entitled *The Milbanke and the Melbourne Families* (figure 1) still hangs in the National Gallery.[3] Peniston Lamb sits on a horse surveying his estate, while Elizabeth's brother and father attend her wearing tricolor hats. They are giving the young woman away, presumably on the day of her marriage. She appears in a pink silk gown and white satin cape, which are "unsuited to her outdoor surroundings and betray the little 'provinciale'" (Airlie, *Palmerston* 3). She nevertheless dominates Stubbs' portrait, as she sits in a timwhiskey, drawn by a single white pony whose reins she grasps with both hands. Nine years later, her sister-in-law, Judith Milbanke, registered a similar impression, describing Lady Melbourne as "very much too good for her *Lord & Master*" (January 1778; Elwin, *Wife* 52).

Stubbs' *The Milbanke and the Melbourne Families* captures the extent to which an eighteenth-century marriage was a "Smithfield bargain," to use Lydia Languish's term for such unions.[4] Sir Peniston Lamb received £5,000 from the Milbankes and an additional £5,000 as his wife's dowry (Newman 3). He later boasted that he gave the whole of his wife's fortune back to her in diamonds (Steele 1:89). Peniston's sister, Lady Fauconberg, had been the first to introduce the young girl to her eligible brother. After several meetings, the couple was married at the bishop of Peterborough's house in Great George Street, St. George, Hanover Square (*Peerage* 8:634).

Despite the great wealth of the Lambs, which was acquired from Peniston's father, Matthew Lamb, the Milbankes were senior to them in rank. Baptized on October 15, 1751 at the parish of Croft-on-Tees in North Yorkshire, Elizabeth Milbanke was the only daughter of Sir Ralph Milbanke of Halnaby Hall, Yorkshire, fifth baronet of a title that dates back to 1663 (Elwin, *Wife* 13).[5] She could trace her lineage back to Ralph Milbancke, cupbearer to Mary Queen of Scots (Airlie, *Whig* 1). Her mother, Elizabeth Hedworth, was the daughter of John Hedworth, a Whig M.P. for Durham who apparently attended Oxford University but about whom little else is known. Lady Melbourne's mother died in 1767, only two years before her daughter's wedding. In marrying this second baronet of a parvenu family, Lady Melbourne succeeded in trading the provincial north for London high society. When she arrived in London, moving into her husband's bachelor residence in Sackville Street, she became known as much "for her vivacity as her beauty" (*BBI* 56).

Her husband was another story. Over the course of two decades in Parliament, he distinguished himself only by voting silently in the interests of Lord North, the prime minister largely responsible for the loss of the American colonies. When not uncovering fox holes on his Hertfordshire estate, Peniston could be found at the "Star and Garter" in Pall Mall, where the Dilettanti Club held dinners for artists and their patrons (Graves 1:251; Torrens 1:19). A boon companion of the Prince of Wales, he contrived to appear "drunkish" even when he was not, his daughter Emily wrote, and he became known in 1812 as the "Paragon of Debauchery" (Airlie, *Palmerston* 1:2). Though generous and amiable, he was a passive man easily led by his wife and mistresses. The latter included Harriet Powel, with whom he lived before he met Lady Melbourne (Steele 5:151);[6] Madame de la Tour, on whom he spent lavish sums (Quennell 73); and, most notoriously, Mrs. Sophia Baddeley, who remembered him in her *Memoirs*.[7] Clearly, he was no match for his wife, whose correspondence and conversation fascinated the duchess of Devonshire, Richard Sheridan, and Lord Byron. With her superior education and attention to detail, Lady Melbourne quickly took charge of her husband's affairs. She invoked his name in letters to the warden at Melbourne Hall, even as she gave explicit directions that far exceeded her husband's insights or abilities. She encouraged him to invest in the Cromford Canal, supervised the deforestation of the Melbourne estate in Derbyshire, and dispatched other business matters in a responsible and profitable manner.

Due in large part to his wife's influence, Peniston became an Irish peer on April 10, 1770 and took his title from Melbourne Hall.[8] "It's very agreeable to me as I look upon it as a step to an English Peerage in some future time," he wrote to his steward (Usher, *Femmes* 2). On May 3, 1770, Lady Melbourne gave birth to a son, Peniston. The following year, on April 1, 1771, the couple purchased Lord Holland's house in Piccadilly for £16,500, but it would be several years before the decorations were completed to Lady Melbourne's satisfaction and the family could move in.

William Chambers, George III's own architect, was commissioned to build a new house on this site for £21,300, though the costs spiraled to approximately £40,000 before the mansion was completed (Birkenhead 6). Lady Melbourne's plan was to build a grand residence to which the fashionable world would flock (figure 2), and Chambers did not disappoint her. Set a hundred feet back from Piccadilly and directly to the east of Burlington House, Melbourne House, Piccadilly was protected by a high wall surmounted by ornamental lamps (figure 2), with two gates leading into a great court (figure 3 and 4). On the left were coach houses and stables; on the right, a porter's lodge and kitchen (Birkenhead 6). Perhaps the most successful addition was Chamber's staircase with a cast-iron flyer, "designed with spatial ingenuity in a square top-lit well" (Harris 227),[9] but there were other brilliant touches as well (figure 5).[10] Anne Damer contributed significantly to the building's interior design. On August 14, 1773, Thomas Chippendale supplied sofas and mirrors for the boudoir on the first floor, as well as general designs for the furnishing of the rooms. Chambers wrote to Lord Melbourne that the brilliant gilding in the boudoir would "set the plainess of the rest off to perfection" (October 22, 1774; Harris 227).[11] Francis Wheatley designed the garden, which looked out on Savile Row; Giambattista Cipriani adorned the fifty-two-foot saloon ceiling with nymphs and cherubs (figure 6); and Biaggio Rebecca contributed several humorous frescoes (Torrens 1:18). William Marlow executed two paintings, "probably architectural landscapes," which were set in stucco frames in the eating room (Harris 226). In a letter to Lord Byron in 1814, Lady Melbourne remembered Melbourne House, Piccadilly as the place "where most of my happiest days were pass'd,— whilst I lived in that House, no Misfortune reach'd me, & I should not have disliked to be an appendage to ye Lease to live in it again" (April 1, 1814). Lady Melbourne's brother, John Milbanke, married Chambers' daughter, Cornelia, in 1775, a year after the project was completed.

Lady Melbourne also oversaw the decorations at Melbourne Hall, Derbyshire and Brocket Hall, Hertford. The first of these estates had been owned by the bishops of Carlisle and the Coke family since 1133. Matthew Lamb inherited the property at the death of his wife's brother in 1751 (Tipping 21). Though rarely used by Lady Melbourne in her lifetime, Melbourne Hall (figure 7) boasted gardens laid out by Sir Thomas Coke and Henry Wise, a pupil of Le Nôtre.[12] Philip Ziegler has recently called it "one of the most exquisite of the smaller stately homes of England" (14). The second estate, Brocket Hall, was a favorite retreat of the family (figures 8 and 9).[13] Peniston Lamb's father, Matthew Lamb, tore down the old manor house that he bought from the Reade family in 1746 and built the red-brick estate that exists today from designs by James Paine (Paine 15) (figure 10). Situated on a hill that slopes down to a park, the house overlooks the River Lea and can still be found only twenty miles or so from London. Paine added a bridge and several ornamental lakes, and Lord Egremont advised Lady Melbourne in laying out the remaining grounds. One of the more memorable rooms in the house is the great drawing room, which boasts a ceiling with the twelve signs of the zodiac, the four seasons of the year, and Morning, Evening, Noon, and Night (figure 11) (Airlie, *Palmerston* 7). This was executed by John Hamilton Mortimer, who was advised by Giambattista Cipriani.

As Lady Melbourne improved her husband's estates, Peniston Lamb was in the throes of an affair with Mrs. Sophia Baddeley, a celebrated actress whose notice was "sufficient to give credit and *eclat* to a man of the *ton*" (Steele 1:76). A portrait by Sir Joshua Reynolds (figure 12) captures the charm of this coquettish woman, whose lovers included William[14] and John Hanger, Lord Sefton, Lord Palmerston, and the duke of Queensbury, among others (Steele 1:26). When Peniston met her in 1770, he was only twenty-five and had been married for just ten months.

Their courtship was an awkward one. After struggling unsuccessfully to meet her at the gardens at Ranelagh, Peniston persuaded a friend to deliver to Baddeley a letter, which contained a £300 note. Shortly afterwards, he made his way to her lodgings at King's Street, Chelsea for a more personal interview (Steele 1:79). Baddeley's friend, Elizabeth Steele, found them together and remonstrated with the actress about the propriety of such visits. "His Lordship, who overheard me, and fearing an attack upon him personally, threw up the parlour window, and precipitately leaped out" Steele remembered (1:82). Before departing, he left behind £200 in a teacup as an apology for his intrusion. The following day he sent a note requesting that Baddeley and her circumspect friend meet him in the poet's corner of Westminster Abbey (Steele 1:82-84). After that, the affair began in earnest. Lord Melbourne hired hackney coaches to visit his mistress undetected. Soon he became the most generous of her lovers, offering to support her on the condition that she give up the theater and become his exclusive mistress.

Elizabeth Steele provided Baddeley with free lodging and tried to persuade her to return to the stage and give up the life of a courtesan. When she published her friend's *Memoirs* in 1782, Steele had her revenge on Lord Melbourne by including his illiterate letters as an appendix to the first volume. "I should be happey in seeing my love every minnit, with sending you a thousand kisses," one of these begins (Steele 1:203). Critical though she was of Melbourne's grammar, Steele could not gainsay his generosity. He bought Baddeley diamond earrings and supplied her with a regular allowance, something her previous lovers had never done. Meddling journalists began to circulate false rumors about the affair. One paper described how a jeweller mistakenly delivered a diamond necklace intended for Mrs. Baddeley to Peniston's Piccadilly address. Lady Melbourne supposedly thanked him for the present, which surprised and alarmed him. When she read this account in the newspapers, Lady Melbourne only smiled at such gossip, noting that "the paper might have been better employed" (Steele 1:140).

But Lady Melbourne was not completely neglected. Lord Melbourne would frequently accompany his "Betsy" to the theater or on shopping sprees in London and vacations in Bath. In March 1771, he presented her with a complete dinner service he had ordered from the famous factory in Sèvres, France. It was adorned with musical trophies and emblems of the arts and love to celebrate his beautiful wife's gifts (Gage 1329) (figure 13). Too shrewd to lose her composure with such a generous and easily managed husband, Lady Melbourne turned a blind eye on his foolish affair. Steele remembers how the couple attended a ridotto at the opera house "arm in arm, and walked together the whole evening; but his Lordship did not omit to give Mrs. Baddeley many pleasant looks; and even Lady Melbourne bestowed a smile upon her" (Steele 4:144). This smile became a defining characteristic. "Life is a tragedy to those who feel and a comedy to those who think," Lady Melbourne was fond of saying (Cecil, *Lord M* 20). The epigram was a guiding principle in her life and the core belief she returned to most often in her correspondence. Clearly the strategy paid off, for Baddeley began to feel guilty about duping a woman as prominent and respected as Lady Melbourne. The affair came to an end when the actress spent an extended weekend with a Colonel Luttrell in Ireland, thus breaking the terms of her "contract" with Lord Melbourne (Steele 5:155). "I see the errors of my ways and have done," he wrote (Strickland 95).

Lady Melbourne's portrait was first painted by Reynolds in 1770, only a few months after her husband's affair with Baddeley had begun.[15] Reynolds shows her wearing a light-blue cape lined in ermine, which covers a white evening dress. She wears a pearl necklace entwined with a tress of her hair and rests her right arm on a table while posing in front of a red curtain (figure 14). The strand of pearls that weaves liberally through her hair seems like a price exacted from her husband for her beauty and virtue, a point underscored by the inscription beneath the oval canvas: *Virtute et Fide*. The motto would have an unintended ironic application in a few years, when Lady Melbourne's son George knocked Scrope Davies down for calling his mother a whore (R. G. Thorne 4:354). Before that untoward event, and shortly after the birth of her first son, Peniston, Reynolds again painted Lady Melbourne's portrait. This work, incongruously titled *Maternal Affection*, shows Lady Melbourne peering straight out from the canvas as she removes her child from the cradle (figure 15).[16] Between 1770 and 1773, when Lady Melbourne sat for this painting, Reynolds successfully captured her driving ambition, which was now put in the service of her family's social advancement. When Reynolds depicted the duchess of Devonshire a few years later, by contrast, Reynolds showed her completely engaged by her infant, whom she lovingly bounces on one knee (figure 16).[17]

In her first decade of married life, Lady Melbourne became known for her refinement and elegance. Nathaniel Wraxall, the diplomat, paid tribute to her "commanding figure, exceeding the middle height, full of grace and dignity, an animated countenance, intelligent features, captivating manners, and conversation; all these and many other attractions, enhanced by coquetry, met in Lady Melbourne" (Wraxall 5:371). So striking was her appearance that she and Lady Salisbury were continually named in the newspapers as "the most elegant equestrians" in Hyde Park (Birkenhead 25).[18] Dining at six, she would attend the opera or theater, and play faro or whist until two or three in the morning.

On April 30, 1772, Lady Melbourne attended a masquerade with the duchess of Ancaster and Mrs. Damer (figure 17) in which she "appeared as masculine as many of the delicate maccaroni things we see everywhere—the 'Billy Whiffles' of the present age" (T. Taylor 1:433; in Graves and Cronin 2:637). She was no less fashionably attired at the French ambassador's ball, where Horace Walpole spotted her dancing with Lord Robert Spencer, Mr. Fitzpatrick, Lord Carlisle, and another man. "The quadrilles[19] were very pretty: Mrs. Damer, Lady Sefton, Lady Melbourne and the Princess Czartoriski in blue satin, with blond [lace] and *collets montés à la reine Elizabeth*" (March 27, 1773; Walpole 32:111).

In four short years, Lady Melbourne had become one of the leading Whig hostesses in London. Married to a husband whose wealth was too recently acquired, however, she was never fully accepted by other women of her rank (Strickland 97). On June 5, 1774, an important event occurred that would change all that. Georgiana Poyntz married the fifth duke of Devonshire, whose family had resisted royal tyranny in the Glorious Revolution of 1688.[20] Lady Melbourne shrewdly befriended the young girl, who was destined to become the leading figure in Whig society.

During the next two years, Lady Melbourne, the duchess of Devonshire, and Anne Damer took London by storm. All three women enjoyed attending private theatricals, *tableaux vivants,* and "other dramatic entertainments" (Boyle 475). Damer performed frequently at Lady Melbourne's residence at Brocket, and later at Whitehall (Boyle 476). At the outset of their friendship, she had Daniel Gardner execute a sketch of herself and her friends, titled *Witches 'Round the Cauldron* (July 1775; Boyle 475-77).[21] "Has Lady Greenwich told you of the Duchess of Devonshire, Lady Melburn, and Mrs. Damer all being drawn in one picture in the Characters of the three Witches in Macbeth?" Coke asked an unnamed friend that summer. "They have chosen that Scene where they compose their Cauldron, but instead of 'finger of Birth-strangled babe, etc.' their Cauldron is composed of roses and carnations and I daresay they think their charmes more irresistible than all the magick of the Witches" (July 14, 1775; Birkenhead 13) (figures 18 and 19).[22] In choosing this subject from *Macbeth,* Damer seemed determined to define femininity on her own terms. She implicitly rejected the "precarious, tottering stances" of society women Sir Joshua Reynolds had popularized in his portraits (figure 20).[23] She knew that female virtue was not the only value for women to uphold in late eighteenth-century society, nor motherhood their sole purpose.

The following year, these enchanting witches amused themselves at Ranelagh. They would puff out their cheeks and let their friends strike them on each side to bring them to their natural form. "The *bon ton* are still in Town, Duchess of Devonshire, L^y Melburn, Mrs. Damer etc., they have dinners, suppers, etc., and live much together," Mary Coke observed (July 6, 1776; Birkenhead 17).[24] Coke took an almost microscopic interest in Lady Melbourne, noting that she enjoyed her food and drink "in a very unusual manner," though "her spirits were just as equal after dinner as before" (November 23, 1783; Birkenhead 15). The Tory *Morning Post* was no less attentive. In an elaborate grid, Lady Melbourne's virtues and defects were contrasted with those of her contemporaries (figure 21). She scored higher for principles than for wit, though this perception would be precisely reversed in a few short years.

On August 15, 1776, tragedy struck. Anne Damer's husband, John, had run into considerable debt. His father, Lord Milton, refused to pay for his son's extravagance, suggesting instead that John's two older brothers leave for France and take Mrs. Damer with them. On a Thursday evening, "Mr. Damer supped at the Bedford Arms in Covent Garden with four common women, a blind fiddler and no other man," Horace Walpole later wrote to a friend. "At three in the morning he dismissed his seraglio, bidding each receive her guinea at the bar, and ordering Orpheus to come up again in half an hour. When he returned, he found a dead silence, and smelt gunpowder. He called, the master of the house came up, and found Mr. Damer sitting in his chair, dead, with a pistol by him, and another in his pocket!" Suicide was suspected because the act seemed premeditated. The balls he bought were too large for his pistol, "upon which, as it was found afterwards, he had sat down and pared them with a pen-knife till he had made them fit" (September 5, 1776; Birkenhead 18; *DNB* 5:450).

Anne Damer was returning to London for a Friday departure when she encountered Charles James Fox on the road. He did not have the heart to break the news to her himself, but warned her to return to her husband's house as soon as possible. It turned out that Lord Milton blamed the entire event on his daughter-in-law. He sold her jewels, "her furniture, carriages and *everything* . . . to pay the debts with, and he abused her for staying *in another man's house* (for she stay'd a few days there before she went to the country, and the house is another's being seiz'd)" (September 21, 1776; Birkenhead 19). Insulted by her father-in-law, Damer chose to leave her deceased husband's house in a hackney coach. According to Lady Sarah Lennox, she took with her only an "ink-stand, a few books, her dog, and her maid" (Ilchester and Stavordale 1:251-52).

To help her friend recover from her grief, Lady Melbourne encouraged her to perform at the duke of Richmond's private theater. There Damer appeared alongside Lady Buckinghamshire, Lord Fitzgerald, and the duchess of Richmond in *The Way to Keep Him* and *The Jealous Wife* (*BBI* 258:330). Charles James Fox, Richard Fitzpatrick, and Richard Sheridan participated, as did "all the young men of talent or of *ton*" (Torrens 1:325). Though not remembered as a performer herself, Lady Melbourne did not go unnoticed. "I hear much of L^y Melbourne who is a great friend of the D^ss of Richmond, & comes to Goodwood every year," Sarah Napier wrote. "I find she is liked by everybody high & low & of all denominations, which I don't wonder at, for she is pleasing, sensible, & desirous of pleasing, I hear, which must secure admiration" (November 20, 1777; Ilchester and Stavordale 1:261). Unable to keep up with her friend's lavish lifestyle, Anne Damer retired to the country to limit her expenses.

On May 8, 1777, Lady Melbourne attended the opening performance of Richard Sheridan's *The School for Scandal,* which celebrated the witty repartee displayed by members of the Devonshire House circle.[25] Nicknamed "the Thorn" by Lady Bessborough for her sharp tongue, Lady Melbourne would have agreed with Lady Sneerwell that it is impossible to be "witty without a little ill nature" (Masters 65). Her cynical view of marriage is strongly recalled by Lady Teazdale, the heroine, who informs her husband that "women of fashion in London are accountable to nobody after they are married" (Masters 64). Both Lady Melbourne and Lady Teazle hail from the provinces and quickly learn to gain the upper hand over their husbands, who seriously underestimated their abilities.

Lady Melbourne's friendship with the duchess of Devonshire survived Sheridan's friendly caricature. At a party held at Mrs. Lloyd's on June 7, 1777, the duchess came in "leaning on Lady Melburn's arm." Lady Melbourne was pregnant with twins at the time, and Lady Mary Coke registered her surprise, "thinking as they [the Melbournes] had spent the greater part of their fortune, it was happy they had but one Child, but it seems they are of different opinion" (July 1777; Birkenhead 21). There was occasion for further surprise when rumors circulated that Lord Egremont (figure 22) was the father. A month later, the Melbournes continued to entertain "all of the *bon-ton* who remain in Town. I hear of parties and suppers frequently: her Ladyship lies inn in December," Coke observed. On October 25, a premature delivery resulted in the death of first the son, and then the daughter. The Prince of Wales told Lord Egremont's mother "he was sorry her Grandson was dead" (October 25, 1777; Birkenhead 21).

The following year, on May 12, 1778, Lady Melbourne attended a fashionable party at Mrs. Meynel's after the opera. Horace Walpole spotted her "standing before the fire, and adjusting her feathers in the glass, says she, 'Lord! they say the stocks will blow up: that will be very comical'" (Walpole 28:391). The frivolous remark disturbed him enough to return to it in a subsequent letter. "Everybody seems to think like Lady Melbourne, that if we are blown up it will be very comical," he wrote (28: 394).

In the summer of 1778, Lady Melbourne and her circle gathered at Tunbridge Wells, a fashionable watering place (figure 23). Several scandals had already occurred: Lady Clermont had had an affair with Mr. Marsdan, an apothecary, and miscarried. Lady Derby had left her marital home to live with the duke of Dorset, a notorious womanizer, and was ruined as a result. When Lady Spencer became concerned about her daughter's company, Georgiana told her mother that Lady Melbourne's friendship would be too "terrible for me to break off" (n.d.; Masters 74, 82).

The following year Lady Melbourne shared a box with the duchess for the opening performance of Sheridan's *The Critic* (Masters 77). Later that year, she attended a country dance with Georgiana. "Here the fat dame with hair of shining black / With pucker'd bonnet and with linnen sack / Swims down the dance, whilst her pert ensign's run / Has finished ere his partner had begun," Georgiana remembered ([October 7] 1779; Bessborough 41). Lady Melbourne may well have shared her friend's sentiments in preferring London society to the provincial Yorkshire lifestyle she had left behind a mere ten years before.

In 1779 Fanny Burney's *Evelina* and the duchess of Devonshire's *The Sylph* were published anonymously.[26] One took two years to write, the other two months. The first was a literary masterpiece about the foibles of a young girl coming out in society; the second, a roman à clef that surveyed the duchess' unhappy marriage and the life of the *bon ton*. Only six weeks after this joint publication, Lady Melbourne gave birth to William Lamb, the offspring of her affair with Lord Egremont. The duchess must have had Lady Melbourne's views on marriage fresh in mind when she depicted her friend as Lady Besford. The passage is worth quoting at length for it gives us the most intimate view of Lady Melbourne's ideas and opinions at the time.[27]

> "Are you not happy?" I asked [Lady Besford] one day. "Happy! why yes I probably am: but you do not suppose my happiness proceeds from my being married, any further than that I enjoy title, rank and liberty, by bearing Lord Besford's name. We do not disagree because we seldom meet. He pursues his pleasure one way, I seek mine another, and our dispositions being very opposite, they are sure never to interfere with each other. I am, I give you my word, a very unexceptionable wife and can say, what few women of quality would be able to do that spoke truth, that I never indulged myself with the least liberty with other men, till I had secured my lord a lawful heir." I felt all horror and astonishment. "Come don't be so prudish," said she: "my conduct in the eye of the world is irreproachable. My lord kept a mistress from the first moment of his marriage. What law excludes a woman from doing the same? Marriage now is a necessary kind of barter, and an alliance of families;—the heart is not consulted:—or, if that should sometimes

bring a pair together—judgment being left far behind, love seldom lasts long. In former times, a poor foolish woman might languish out her life in sighs and tears for the infidelity of her husband. Thank heaven! they are wiser now; but then they should be prudent. I extremely condemn those who are enslaved by their passions, and bring a public disgrace on their families by suffering themselves to be detected; such are justly our scorn and ridicule; and you may observe that they are not taken notice of by anybody. There is a decency to be observed in our amours; and I shall be very ready to offer you my advice, as you are so young and inexperienced. One thing let me tell you; never admit your *Cicisbeo* to an unlimited familiarity; they are first suspected. Never take notice of your favourite before other people: there are a thousand ways to make yourself amends in secret for that little but necessary sacrifice in public" (*The Sylph* 1:135-38).

It is in her capacity as adviser that we can best understand the influence Lady Melbourne came to exert over Georgiana. In *The Sylph,* Lady Besford obtains a fashionable hairdresser for her protégé, Julia Stanley.[28] In her correspondence Lady Melbourne was no less helpful, and she soon earned the name of "Themire," goddess of justice, which the duchess bestowed upon her. She advised Georgiana to reject the advances of the libertine duke of Dorset (45548, f.3) and accept those of the more serious and scholarly Charles Grey. She even found a maidservant to attend the duchess during her lying in (45548, f.4). Lady Melbourne's guidance was morally expedient, if not morally sound. The duchess seemed to sense this, for she included an epigram in *The Sylph* that might have stood as a caveat to her friendship with Lady Melbourne: "More women are seduced from the path of virtue by their own sex, than by ours" (*The Sylph* 2:22).

Both women learned to guard each other's secrets. During the Gordon riots in 1780, Lady Melbourne allowed the duke of Devonshire's illegitimate daughter, Charlotte Williams, to stay at Brocket Hall without explanation. "L^y. M[elbourne] thinks she [Charlotte] is a relation of mine," Georgiana explained to her mother. "I was in a great hurry and fright about it or I should have sent her to Wimbledon"

(Bessborough 47). By the same token, Georgiana silenced gossip about Lady Melbourne's affair with Lord Egremont. Egremont had suddenly and inexplicably broken off his proposed marriage to Lady Charlotte Maria Waldegrave. "I was dancing with Mr. Edward Vernon,[29] who asked if I was . . . in town when L[d] E's match went off," Georgiana wrote to Lady Melbourne. "I said no—he then said Egremont deserv'd to be hang'd & ask'd me what reason people gave for it & then he said quite loud, 'It proves that L[y] Mel is very handsome'" (1780; 45911, f.1). Georgiana denied that her friend's appearance had anything to do with the broken engagement, but she could not stop wagging tongues. "No reason can be assign'd, as the young lady was unexceptionable by all I can hear, but the dominion he is under of a great lady (L[ad]y M-l-b-e) who has long endeavoured to prevent any other engagement and it is suspected she has *forbid the banns*," Mrs. Delany wrote (August 7, 1780; Delany 6:553; *DNB* 21:1159). Protective of his niece, Horace Walpole described Egremont as a "pitiful object on whom her merit would have been deplorably thrown away" (August 8, 1780; Walpole 29:72). Some time afterwards, Lady Melbourne visited Walpole and sat underneath a Reynolds portrait of the three Waldegrave sisters. Walpole was delighted to note her discomfort (August 5, 1783; Walpole 39:403-4 n.11) (figure 24).

In choosing Lord Egremont as a lover, Lady Melbourne was selecting not only a companion for herself, but also a man who could provide her with talented children. Writing to Lord Holland, Egremont remembered that "there was hardly a young married lady of fashion, who did not think it almost a stain upon her reputation if she was not known as having cuckolded her husband; and the only doubt was who was to assist her in the operation" (G. Ilchester 205). Lady Melbourne chose wisely. Egremont was one of the principal landholders in Sussex, a man whose political opinions were respected by Fox, and whose magnificent country house at Petworth was immortalized by William Turner. "I suppose Egremont is with you, talking the *best of prose*" (45911, f.8), Georgiana wrote to her on one occasion. Egremont visited Melbourne House frequently from his London residence at 94 Piccadilly, sharing a box with Lady Melbourne at the opera (Coke, *Letters* 3:66).

Biographers believe that Lady Melbourne had two children by Egremont:

William, born in 1779, and Emily, born in 1787.[30] In doing so, she observed the unwritten code of female conduct in late eighteenth-century society. This declared that a wife was not to deceive her husband until she had first provided him with an heir. Legitimacy had to be ensured, for under the system of primogeniture the eldest son inherited the fortune, houses, and estates (Birkenhead 20). Peniston was Lady Melbourne's firstborn son, but when he died of tuberculosis in 1805 it was William who inherited the title and estates. Even after he became prime minister, however, William found his legitimacy questioned. When viewing the pictures at Brocket Hall, the animal painter Sir Edwin Landseer stopped at Egremont's portrait and scrutinized William's features more carefully. "Ah, so you've heard that story, have you?" William responded. "It's a damned lie for all that." And then, after a short pause, "But who the devil can tell who's anybody's father?" (Ziegler 17).

Lady Melbourne loved her eldest son, Peniston, but had less in common with him than with the more politically inclined William. The eldest and favorite child of Lord Melbourne still peers out at us from the canvas of Ben Marshall, freshly dismounted from his horse, Assassin, and admired by his black-and-brown dog, Tanner (Boyle 324).[31] Twice a week, Lady Melbourne would visit Peniston at Eton (August 8, 1782; Ilchester and Stavordale 2:34), where the Prince of Wales was a gentleman commoner (Airlie, *Whig* 5). Mixing business and pleasure, she often threw dinner parties there which this illustrious guest attended. By March 25, 1783, Lady Sarah Napier noted that the prince is "*desperately* in love with L.ʸ Melbourne, & when she don't sit next to him at supper he is not commonly civil to his neighbours: she *dances* with him, something in the cow stile, but he is *en extase* with admiration at it" (August 8, 1782; Ilchester and Stavordale 2:34, 36).

By the end of that year, the prince's infatuation already had political repercussions.[32] Lady Mary Coke noted that "Mr. Fox pays her great attentions in consideration of her high favour" (November 23, 1783; Birkenhead 24). When the prince moved into Carlton House that year, he appointed Lord Melbourne as lord of the bedchamber, "which no doubt is procured him by his Lady," Coke observed (June 13, 1783; Birkenhead 24). George was born the following year, on July 11, 1784 (Usher, *Femmes* 3), when Lady Melbourne was thirty-one and the Prince of Wales twenty-two. Publicly, the prince served as godfather, but privately, George

Lamb was treated as the illegitimate offspring of the father whose name he shared.[33]

Lady Melbourne's affair with the Prince of Wales followed his attachment to Lady Augusta Campbell and preceded his close friendship with the duchess of Devonshire (Wraxall 5:369f). Satirists linked Lady Melbourne and Lady Jersey with the prince for the first time in February 1782 (Aspinall, *Correspondence* 5:644). Four months later, she was depicted sharing the attentions of the Prince of Wales with Lady Salisbury and the actress Mrs. Robinson in a cartoon titled *Monuments Lately Discover'd on Salisbury Plain* (June 15, 1782) (figure 25).[34] Two political cartoons on a related subject appeared the following year. The first, aptly titled *The Political Churchyard* (August 9, 1783), portrayed Fox and other Whigs as self-destructive supporters of the prince in his dispute with his father, George III (figure 26). The second, *The Ladies Church Yard* (September 22, 1783), suggested that Lady Melbourne and the duchess of Devonshire's contact with the Prince of Wales had damaged their reputations (figure 27). The sexual politics of both women had their price, and Lady Melbourne's fawning behavior with the Prince of Wales did not go unnoticed. The Prince of Wales' tomb appears adorned with ostrich plumes. Flanked on either side are the headstones of Lady Melbourne and the duchess of Devonshire (September 1783). "Here lieth L—y M—B—E," Lady Melbourne's tomb reads. "Tho on my back Death / Has me laid / I might remain / For him A Maid." The duchess of Devonshire's epitaph contains a less personally insulting reference to her promiscuity: "Here lies the D-s of D-re / Cease Kissing Death / You stop my Breath." The prince was attached to both of these women, Wraxall observes, though it is difficult to know what "attached" means (Wraxall 5:370-72).

By the time *The Cock of the Walk, Distributing his Favour's* appeared on May 31, 1786, Lady Melbourne's affair with the first gentleman of Europe was already in decline. Portrayed as a bird with three tail-feathers, the Prince of Wales is accompanied by his libertine companion George Hanger, who distributes the feathers to Lady M—ne, with others inscribed to Lady M—d, the D-ss of D—e, and Miss Van—k.[35] The fickle prince had already become enamored with Mrs. "Perdita" Robinson[36] and Mrs. Armistead, before marrying Lady Maria Anne Fitzherbert in a secret ceremony on December 15, 1785.[37]

Before their affair ended, Lady Melbourne and the prince exchanged portraits. She gave him a painting of herself by Richard Cosway (figure 28), which he hung in his private bedroom at Carlton House.[38] Lady Melbourne appears fashionably attired in seventeenth-century costume, her sensuality suggested by her exposed neck. She holds a book half-open in her hands, as if recollecting an amusing thought, and this, along with her mischievous eyes glancing away from the viewer, betrays her wit and intelligence.[39]

The prince gave Lady Melbourne a Reynolds portrait of himself (figure 29). He is depicted standing by his charger in a grandiloquent martial pose that bore little relation to the overweight dandy he had already become. "The Prince of Wales looks too much like a woman in men's clothes," the duchess of Devonshire confided to her journal at about the same time (1784?; Masters 130). But Lady Melbourne was more enamored by the prince's social position than was her well-heeled friend. She hung this painting of her lover directly next to *Maternal Affection* at Brocket Hall, never, perhaps, noting the contradiction.[40]

The same year in which Lady Melbourne's affair with the Prince of Wales was lampooned in the press, Reynolds idealized her family life in another painting, *The Affectionate Brothers* (figure 30).[41] Here the eldest son, Peniston, is incongruously dressed in a formal suit of black silk as he encourages his brothers to play in the woods. William wears a buff jacket and Frederick a white, back-fastening muslin frock, as well as a hat with ostrich plumes (Penny 305). Lord Melbourne must have felt the horns of cuckoldry sprout from his scalp as he realized that he had only one legitimate son represented in this painting. He returned the portrait to Reynolds, explaining that it did not "give satisfaction" (Boyle 441).

George III laid much of the blame for his son's libertine lifestyle at the door of Charles James Fox. Unbeknownst to his father, the prince encountered Fox regularly at Lady Melbourne's dinner parties, along with other wits and wags of the Opposition party, including Richard Fitzpatrick, George Selwyn, James Hare, and Francis Russell, duke of Bedford (Torrens 1:24). Lady Melbourne escaped the king's censure by rarely associating with Fox directly. During the Westminster election campaign of 1784, the king used all his power to unseat Fox, his most vocal critic. The duchess of Devonshire, her sister Lady Bessborough, and Anne Crewe campaigned vigorously for Fox, subjecting themselves to newspaper attacks for trading kisses for votes (figure 31).[42] Lady Melbourne played a less prominent role. She was intent on gaining access to royal patronage, not shutting her family off from it.

A fellow campaigner, Anne Damer, returned to London to lease a house that was practically in the Melbournes' backyard.[43] At about this time, Lady Sarah Lennox remembered that Damer's learned conversation lacked humility: "She is too *strictly right* ever to be beloved" (Masters 49). But Damer was a talented woman whose independent lifestyle inspired envy. She sculpted busts of Lady Melbourne and Lady Elizabeth Foster, Georgiana's friend and protégé. Erasmus Darwin commemorated Damer's work in the poem "Economy of Vegetation":

> Long with soft touch shall Damer's chisel charm,
> With grace delight us and with beauty warm;
> Foster's fine form shall hearts unborn engage,
> And Melbourne's smile enchant another age. (2:113)

One day, David Hume inspired Damer to pursue sculpture as a career by suggesting that women were capable only of pencil sketches and occasional verse, the customary pursuits of women of her social background. The next day she proved him wrong by presenting him with a bust in wax. Afterwards, Damer studied anatomy with William Cumberland Cruikshank and the modeling of clay with Giuseppe Ceracchi.[44] She executed busts of her heroes—Fox, Nelson, and Napoleon—acquiring in return an engraved snuffbox from the future emperor of France.

Just as her closest friend's distinguished career as an artist had begun, Lady Melbourne found that her own five-year flirtation with the Prince of Wales had brought her into disrepute. The same reporters who once praised her charm now focused on her dissipation. "Lady Melbourne is doing all she can to keep off the gout,—and her noble Lord, though without designing it, is deeply engaged in bringing it on," the *Times* reported. "The Autumn, perhaps, will discover the success of their mutual endeavours" (August 17, 1786). Journalists recalled the "huge cloth shoe" she had been forced to wear in public and sneered at the frivolous conduct that had brought on the disease (November 5, 1786; *Times*). "What a lesson is here for youth and beauty," wrote one (October 19, 1786; *Times*).

Lady Melbourne was often linked with the duchess' worst extravagances, though the two women were not as close as they had been. In one sense, Lady

Melbourne no longer needed the duchess to consolidate her social position. Perhaps Lady Melbourne's feelings were injured when she read what her friend thought of her in *The Sylph*. "That horrid Lady Besford!" the heroine's sister exclaims. "I am sure you feel all the detestation you ought for such a creature" (1:146). It is more likely that the interests of the two women changed. Lady Melbourne never evinced a passion for gambling and consequently had little advice to give when, by 1789, the duchess' debts had exceeded £50,000 (Masters 158). A further rift may have been created by Georgiana's need to produce a male heir for her husband, which Lady Melbourne had done the first year of her marriage. The duchess was filled with self-loathing at the time and confessed to the Prince of Wales that she felt "only a burden and plague to all my friends" (Masters 161).

As early as June 1782, the duchess began consorting with Elizabeth Foster (figure 32). The two were closer in age, and Foster inspired Georgiana's pity, whereas Lady Melbourne seemed to arouse her fear. Foster's husband had abandoned her in 1780 and claimed custody of their two children. Georgiana invited Foster to spend the summer at Plympton with her and her husband. The three became so intimate that they established the nicknames of "Canis," "Rat," and "Racky," and were soon believed to be involved in a ménage à trois.[45] Strikingly beautiful, Foster awakened feelings long dormant in the fifth duke (figures 33 and 34). Shortly after that, on July 12, 1783, the duchess was able to conceive her first child, Georgiana Dorothy. A second daughter, Harriet, was born on August 30, 1785 (Masters 140).

When Georgiana became pregnant with a third child five years later, rumors circulated that the duchess would swap babies with Foster in order to produce a son and heir. Lady Melbourne asked her to visit them in Belgium to dispel these accusations. "You will be another witness of the reality of her being pregnant, my not being so, and of the sex of the child when born," Foster wrote (Masters 181).[46] On May 21, 1790, the duchess of Devonshire gave birth to the marquis of Hartington, but rumors about a swapping of babies circulated nevertheless. In 1817 Elizabeth Foster was assumed to have had a deathbed conversion to Catholicism in which she related the entire story. "Nothing can be more foolish than crediting one word of it," Lady Melbourne declared in a letter to her son Frederick (February 17, 1818).

No sooner had the thirty-four-year-old duchess provided a legitimate heir for her husband than she followed contemporary fashions in finding a lover. She chose Charles Grey, a handsome young orator who had admired her ever since she helped Fox win the famous Westminster campaign of 1784 (figure 35). Seven years her junior, Grey helped manage the impeachment of Warren Hastings as a Whig M.P. from Northumberland in 1786. He would go on to oversee the abolition of the slave trade after the death of Fox in 1806 and the passage of the Reform Bill in 1832. As a young man, however, he could be a "fractious" and "exigeant" lover (E. Holland, *Journal* 1:98; Villiers 114), with a "violent temper and unbounded ambition" (E. Holland, *Journal* 1:100).[47] Lady Melbourne urged Georgiana to avoid compromising her reputation by pursuing a public liaison.[48] "I cannot express how grateful I feel to you my Dear Love for letters which are so kind & satisfactory," Georgiana responded, "—& so reasonable they have made even *me* reasonable" (45548, f.6).

But Georgiana was difficult to make reasonable, especially after she succumbed to the literary charms of Jean-Jacques Rousseau and Choderlos Laclos (October 24, 1782; Bessborough 54). The duke of Devonshire confronted his wife about her affair in 1791, when she was six months pregnant with Grey's child. "I find you are not to be told any thing," Lady Bessborough (figure 36) wrote to Lady Melbourne, because "it is of the greatest consequence it should not be suspected he is distress'd" (November 1791; 45548, f.44). When the duke finally banished her, the duchess traveled throughout Italy, Switzerland, and the south of France for almost two years, accompanied by her mother, Lady Spencer, and her sister, Lady Bessborough. Doctors Warren and Fraser preserved what was left of appearances by announcing that Lady Bessborough's mild stroke, which had occurred in February 1791, was the reason for the family's departure.[49]

From November 1791 until September 18, 1793, Lady Melbourne became the duchess of Devonshire's only confidential correspondent. Georgiana begged Lady Melbourne to "write constantly, otherways in the state of mind I am in I shall think you are angry with me or do not Love me" (undated letter; 45548, f.12).

When the duke refused to send money to support his wife, Lady Melbourne struggled to explain his inscrutable motives. "There never was anything so amiable & so good as you are about writing," Lady Bessborough informed her. "It makes me feel we are not quite forgot, by every thing we have left in England" (December 11, 1791; 45548, f.48). Lady Melbourne must have relished the irony of knowing more about Georgiana than members of her own family. Lady Bessborough thought her sister was distressed because of the duke's refusal to send money, but Lady Melbourne knew that Georgiana was more disturbed by Charles Grey's cold letters. "Why will people be harsh at such a distance," Georgiana asked her worldly confidante (December 10, 1791; 45548, f.10).

Lady Melbourne had risen to such a prominent position in the duchess' absence that she had begun to inspire the envy of the royal family. At one of her elegant receptions, perhaps the "Grand Concert" she gave at her house in Piccadilly on June 19, 1791 *(Times)*, the Prince of Wales told her that his brother, the duke of York, longed to live in a house like hers.[50] Lady Melbourne joked that she would willingly exchange the chimes of St. James for those of Westminster Abbey (Torrens 1:34).

The jest was well timed, for the lavish lifestyle of the Melbournes had already caught up with them. Lord Melbourne took out two mortgages on his Piccadilly residence a year after its restoration was completed, and had still not paid his architect, Sir William Chambers, by 1791.[51] That fall, he pursued the duke of York's suggestion in earnest. "The Melbournes I think have made an excellent bargain about their House," Thomas Noel informed Judith Milbanke, "& I hear have secured the payment by *the D. of B*. lending H.R.H. the money" (Elwin, *Noels* 404). The duke of Bedford, whose name was now italicized as one of Lady Melbourne's admirers, lent the duke of York £30,000 to facilitate his purchase of Melbourne House, Piccadilly (Elwin, *Noels* 407).

The swapping of houses was celebrated at York House on December 8, 1791 (figures 37, 38, 39). The following day, the duke and duchess of York came to Melbourne Hall, Piccadilly accompanied by the Prince of Wales, the duke of Bedford, and the duchess' ladies of the bedchamber. "His Highness was received by Lord Melbourne at the door, who conducted his illustrious visitors into the

Breakfast Room, where a profusion of hot and cold dishes, besides teas, coffee, chocolate, &c. awaited their arrival." Lady Melbourne's obsequious manner did not go undetected. "The noble host and hostess" were "so anxious . . . to do honour to their Princely guest, that they each brought in a dish," a *Times* reporter observed (December 10, 1791).[52]

Shortly after exchanging homes, Lady Melbourne published a poem in the same newspaper. This poem, titled "A Bed," gives us some insight into her worldly morality:

> Form'd long ago, yet MADE to-day,
> Most employ'd when others sleep;
> What few will dare to GIVE AWAY,
> Yet none can wish to keep!" (October 5, 1792; *Times*)

Lady Melbourne was fond of such riddles, and must have bantered with her dinner guests at Whitehall to display her verbal facility. The poem proceeds through a series of double-entendres—"form'd," "Most employ'd," "give away," and "keep"— that remind us of nothing so much as the poet's own compromised reputation. Lady Melbourne smiled chastity away through such clever wordplay by taking her own worldly outlook for granted.

In September 1793, a penitent duchess of Devonshire returned to England to find Lady Melbourne in a new residence.[53] The two correspondents renewed their friendship once again, and Lady Melbourne attracted even more attention than before. "Our parties at Devonshire House were delightfully pleasant," Lady Holland noted. "Lady Melbourne is uncommonly sensible and amusing, though she often put me in mind of Madame de Merteuil in *Les Liaisons Dangereuses* . . . the Duke of Bedford is attached to her; he is quite brutal in the *brusquerie* of his manner . . . Mr. Grey is the *bien aimé* of the Duchess" (October 1793; Villiers 114).

Lady Holland's discreet reference to Lady Melbourne's "attach[ment]" to the duke of Bedford is not surprising, for he moved in the same circles as Lady Melbourne[54] and shared her love of agriculture (figure 40). The duke of Bedford's experiments on the South Down and new Leicestershire breeds of sheep would have caught her attention, for she was fond of innovation. He also owned the same chaff-cutter as her, one that could be worked by men, horses, or water. His practice of irrigation brought unused land into a high state of cultivation, as did his enclosure of common fields *(DNB)*.

Lady Bessborough, a member of the pampered *beau monde*, once ridiculed Lady Melbourne for turning a profit on her own garden at Brocket. In a more generous mood, however, she informed her lover, Lord Granville Leveson-Gower, of "all the wisdom I have been gathering from L^y. Melbourne, whose farm and Garden I went all over inch by inch, my eyes and ears wide open to learn all I could" ([September 5] 1811; G. L. Gower 2:394). Arthur Young singled out Lady Melbourne's garden for special praise in his account of agricultural innovations in the Hertfordshire countryside.[55] He found the rows of vegetables at Brocket Hall "straight, the land clean, and the husbandry, upon the whole, practised with intelligence and success." Young stressed the technological sophistication evident in Lady Melbourne's approach to planting. She owned one of Salmon's Woburn chaff-cutters, a device that could bruise oats or beans at the same time (Young 40), and introduced drill husbandry to the Hertfordshire countryside *(Europa)*.

Lord Egremont, Lady Melbourne's other admirer, was probably an even more valuable fount of agricultural information than the duke of Bedford. He owned one of three threshing machines in the county of Sussex and used oxen in place of horses on his estate.[56] This oddity was remembered in sketches by William Turner. Egremont had always believed that agriculture was an art, and Turner gained his generous patronage, in part, by reflecting that belief. *The Forest of Bere*[57] depicts workers stripping the bark off chestnut trees, uniting the two endeavors in a manner that would have pleased Egremont. Egremont's estate at Petworth became a kind of artist's colony. Sculptors such as John Flaxman and painters such as Thomas Phillips, Charles Leslie, and Turner himself consulted Egremont's collection of Old Masters while living at the country house. They commemorated the magnificent estate in a series of paintings, of which Turner's *Fighting Bucks* is a representative example. In this painting one can spot the most prominent of Egremont's agricultural improvements, the conversion of a large stag park into arable land.

While Lady Melbourne was cultivating her garden, Lord Melbourne gave up his seat in Parliament to make room for his son. After graduating from Eton in 1786, Peniston had lived a lavish lifestyle at the court of Montbeliard for less than a year before returning home in 1788. Described as "handsome and indolent," he failed to attend the first meeting of the House after he was elected M.P. for Newport, Isle of Wight on March 6, 1793.[58] Opposition members charged that he "neglected Parliament while in it, was fonder of racing, opera, and theatricals," and was "only known at the Pic Nic and at Boodles." He once asked how many quarter sessions there were in a year. Frederick Lamb complained of Peniston's conduct to his mother. "The staying away I really think a disgrace to any man's character," he wrote (R. G. Thorne 4:357).

Thankfully, Peniston was not the only outlet for Lady Melbourne's political ambitions. William Lamb, her son by Lord Egremont, entered Lincoln's Inn as a law student on July 21, 1797 (Torrens 1:36). Egremont wisely preferred this path to the clergy, which Lady Melbourne had briefly considered. Fox honored William as a "rising genius" at Holland House and quoted Lamb's Cambridge prize oration, "On the Progressive Improvements of Mankind" (1798), in the House of Commons (Torrens 1:36). The same year that he was noticed by Fox, William Lamb wrote the epilogue to Sheridan's adaptation of *Pizarro* (1798) from Kotzebue. Elizabeth Foster noted that it was "pretty," but "wanted strength." "I dined yesterday at Richmond House with the Melbournes, and there it had a grand discussion," she wrote (December 27, 1799; Foster 162).

Having graduated from Lincoln's Inn, William Lamb studied at Glasgow University with his brother for two years (1799-1801) under Professor John Millar.[59] Millar had written *An Historical View of the English Government*, which Fox had praised, and was a friend of Lord Egremont, who may well have had a hand in the decision. Frederick described the daily routine: "There is nothing heard of in this house but study," he wrote to his mother (n.d.; HRO). Millar was resolutely opposed to the arts, calling poetry "a mere jingle which proves no facts" (E. Holland, *Journal* 2:100). William mocked the seriousness of some of his fellow students, but returned from the experience praising Scottish educational methods. The "Scotch have outdone in moral philosophy and ethics all who have gone before them," he said to Lady Holland (E. Holland, *Journal* 2:100).

On May 15, 1800, during one of William's vacations from his academic regime, George III was almost assassinated by a man named Hatfield. The Prince of

Wales was dining at Melbourne House when he heard the news. He pretended not to believe the rumor, but Lady Melbourne insisted that he attend to his father as a public gesture. She provided him with her own coach for the purpose, and sent her son William to accompany him. Afterwards, William was remembered fondly by the king and invited to Carlton House more frequently (Torrens 1:41).

Despite these royal connections, William and Frederick seem to have taken a turn for the worse after their trip to Glasgow. Lady Holland commented on William's "love of singularity" and his affected lisp. A similar reaction was registered at Devonshire House. "On Sunday we went to a sort of Assembly at Lady Melbourne's," Georgiana's critical daughter, Hary-O, wrote.[60] "It was not pleasant. The two Lambs, William and Frederick, had dined out and were very *drunk*, and the former talked to me in a loud voice the whole time of the danger of a *young womans* believing in *weligion* and *pwactising mowality*" (January 1803; *Hary-O* 44).

Lady Melbourne's efforts to keep her sons in the right circles also exacted its price on the family's finances. "A Great House makes a bad Figure without Suitable Living," her ever compliant husband informed his lawyer, Thomas Hill, shortly after the birth of George in 1784 (Usher, *Owners* 34-35). Sixteen years later, Lord Melbourne was selling off several estates in order to maintain his family's lavish lifestyle. Most of these were entailed to each of his children by his marriage settlement. Those that were not were quickly dispatched, including Bolsterstone and Langsett in Yorkshire and Wilsford in Lincolnshire. In 1802, the enclosure of Chellaston provided him with an opportunity to sell his significant holdings there (Usher, *Owners* 35).

While Lord Egremont took an interest in the education of the elder Lamb children, Lord Melbourne asserted his will with regard to his younger sons on only two recorded occasions. He faulted William for following the fashion of wearing short hair, and questioned a courtesan's taste in preferring the wealthy Lord Craven to his son Frederick. "Not have my son, indeed," he said, "six foot high and a fine strong handsome able young fellow. I wonder what she would have" (Cecil, *Young M* 33). Harriette Wilson ridiculed this odd outburst of indignation,[61] but lived with Frederick for three months when he was stationed with his regiment in Hull, Yorkshire. Frederick was serving as aide-de-camp to General Mackenzie, and dined "on every imagined luxury . . . without a thought or care whether I had bread and cheese to satisfy hunger," she remembered (Wilson 1:33). He cut a rather ridiculous figure reading Shakespeare to her in a singsong voice, waylaying her after she abandoned him for his friend and rival the duke of Argyll (1:223). When she found herself penniless later in life, Wilson asked him for financial assistance, and even threatened him with the publication of her memoirs, which included an account of how he once strangled her when she refused his entreaties (1:129). Frederick, who preferred embarrassment to blackmail, saw the book go into thirty editions in 1825.

If Lady Melbourne had trouble bringing her boys to what she liked to call "polish," she suffered no loss of prestige herself during those years (October 15, 1802; Airlie, *Whig* 72). In 1800 she was forty-eight and could still attract the notice of young men (figure 42). "When you see Lady Melbourne which I suppose will often happen [at Brocket]," Henry Luttrell wrote to the fifth earl of Cowper, "keep me alive in her recollection. I like her, as we are told we should love God, with all my heart, mind and strength" (Strickland 101). Even those who disapproved of her could not fail to note her influenece. Hary-O observed that "Though Lady Melbourne was old and fat, yet the number of admirers had rather increased than diminished—and to one and all she was haughty and distant" (*Hary-O* 165). Robert Adair, who would later serve as minister to Austria (1806-8) and Turkey (1808-10), became so infatuated that he traveled to Constantinople "for no other purpose" than to forget her and "despair'd of being cured" (September 14, 1802; G. L. Gower 1:356). "I was looking at Lʸ. Mel. from time to time," Lady Bessborough wrote to Granville Leveson-Gower, "and she certainly is fatter even than me, and a good deal older, and tho' very Clever, yet she treats him [Adair] with disdain instead of love" (September 1802; G. L. Gower 1:356). Other women were equally critical. Lady Melbourne "never comes . . . but at hurried moments," Anne Damer noted, "commonly while I am at dinner" and then only because of her

> wish to stay and [confide] something or other . . . in a safe ear. She
> is, to be sure,—no, not a *comedy,* for she often makes me reflections
> too serious for that sort of *Drama;* but thank heaven they no longer
> affect me. To-day she wanted to look over the plates of Devon's
> *Aegypt* which Sir J[oseph]. Banks has lent me and stayed below

with her daughter looking at them, while we were dining above;
but all this is by the bye.

"Well," I said, "tell me something before I go up to them." "Oh,"
she replied, recollecting herself, "the negociation with Pitt is entirely
over."[62]

Mrs. Damer apparently thought Lady Melbourne was something of a curiosity,
but she did not doubt "the truth" of her political information (April 17, 1803;
Melville 134).

There seems to be only one recorded moment in which a contemporary of
Lady Melbourne's knew more than she did. Lady Melbourne had hoped to forestall
the duke of Bedford's marriage long enough to make him useful to the Whigs.
Without her knowledge, the duke proposed to Georgiana, the youngest daughter
of the duchess of Gordon (Airlie, *Whig* 29), forming a Tory connection that might
color his future political allegiance. "No possible event could have so thoroughly
overthrown the habits of our Society as this," Georgiana wrote to Lady Melbourne
in consolation (Watermark, 1799; 45548, f.26). The crisis of "Loo's" marriage, as he
was called in their circle, came to nothing, for the duke died of a strangulated
hernia on March 2, 1802, before the marriage ever took place (*BBI* 955:349).[63]

In the next three years, members of Lady Melbourne's immediate family
would have their own brushes with mortality. Her youngest daughter, Harriet,
became ill with consumption in 1803. Although doctors recommended a journey
on the continent to escape the fogs of Hertfordshire, Lady Melbourne used the
excuse of the Napoleonic wars to ignore the advice, for she seems to have been
more preoccupied with maintaining her London connections. "Looking at Europe
now is like looking at a lady in *déshabillé*," Henry Luttrell reassured her from
Rome. "One should wait until she is dressed and fit to be seen" (January 1803; Airlie,
Palmerston 12). Six months later, it was too late. Harriet died on June 7, 1803 and
Frederick and Emily regretted that more had not been done to save her. She was
only fourteen and "promised much," her brother William remembered. Harriet's
merry disposition is captured in a painting by Sir Thomas Lawrence, in which she
smiles as her sister Emily has just stolen her white cap. (figure 42).[64] Lady
Melbourne was "miserably affected" by Harriet's death, which she may have attrib-

uted to her own selfish decision to remain in London. She "has certainly a good heart and strong feelings," her friend Anne Damer wrote (June 12, 1803; Berry 281).

In the years since he returned from the continent, Lady Melbourne's eldest son, Peniston, had become a "capital shot" who could ride "well to hounds" (Boyle 321) (figure 43). He was a great aficionado of the horse races at Lewes, where he enjoyed the company of the celebrated equestrian Mrs. Dick Musters. Though not suited to a parliamentary career, he became an accomplished amateur actor and recited an epilogue of his own composition to his brother George's play *Who's the Dupe?* (January 25, 1803; *Hary-O* 48). Unfortunately, Peniston was soon stricken with the same disease that took his sister Harriet. Two previous attacks in 1803 and 1804 had weakened his condition. "I am alarm'd & frightened more than I ever tell & every move & alteration of his countenance has an effect upon me that I cannot describe" (January 1805), Lady Melbourne wrote to Frederick. Peniston died on January 24 in the arms of Mrs. Musters, his lover from Colwick, near Nottingham, whom Lady Melbourne had considerately and somewhat boldly invited to be present (Usher, *Owners* 37). The grieving mother convalesced at Brighton Pavilion at the invitation of the Prince of Wales.

That same year Lady Melbourne could announce happier news. Her son William married Caroline Lamb on June 3, 1805 and her daughter Emily married the fifth earl of Cowper the following month, on July 20 (figures 44, 45, 46, and 47). Both receptions took place in the great drawing room at Whitehall; neither event occurred without careful planning on Lady Melbourne's part. Only two years before, Emily had turned down an offer of marriage from Lord Kinnaird (Airlie, *Whig* 79). Lady Melbourne may well have had her eye on another eligible bachelor as early as 1801. The fifth earl of Cowper owned Panshanger Hall, only ten miles or so from Brocket, and was a prince of the Holy Roman Empire (Airlie, *Palmerston* 15). During his travels through France, Switzerland, and Italy—made possible by the Peace of Amiens in 1802—Cowper received numerous letters from Lady Melbourne that were filled with the political news of the day. An erstwhile correspondent himself, Cowper wrote only a handful of letters in response.[65] One of these describes the brilliant conversation of Talleyrand and records Napoleon's rhetorical flourish upon transporting a dissident writer: "Il s'amuse assez bien avec la plume. Nous verrons comment il s'amusera avec la bayonette" (n.d.; 45549, f.1).[66]

Upon his return, Lord Cowper proposed to Emily, precisely as Lady Melbourne had hoped he would. Emily thanked her mother for her role in facilitating the match, drawing a sketch of a wedding ring with her new initials inside to celebrate the union. "I begin to believe that he does really love me & therefore dear Mama you will never be again obliged to spend so much breath on that subject," she wrote. "Is not this a relief" (July 20, 1805; 45549, f.8). The couple settled in George Street, Hanover Square, maintaining their country house at Panshanger. Visits to Devonshire House followed shortly afterwards, and Emily could not conceal her hope that she was pregnant. "They really do announce any events of that sort very soon in the Melbourne family," Hary-O wrote (*Hary-O* 118). On June 26, 1806, Emily delivered a son and heir, George Augustus Frederick (later Lord Fordwich). Her other children's names suggest that they were the offspring of Lord Palmerston (figure 48): Emily Caroline Catherine Frances ("Minnie") (1808); William Temple Cowper (1811); George Spencer Cowper (1816); and Frances Elizabeth ("Fanny") (1819).

William's marriage to Lady Caroline Lamb had a longer history. From the age of sixteen, William had been in love with Caroline Ponsonby, the wayward child of Frederic Ponsonby, third earl of Bessborough. He could not propose marriage, however, until he could sustain her in a suitable lifestyle. After his elder brother Peniston died in 1803, William came into a considerable inheritance. Nevertheless his father allowed William only £2,000 of the £5,000 per annum that his legitimate heir, Peniston, had enjoyed. Lady Melbourne protested this arrangement, but it was to no avail. She must have been pleased, then, when William chose to marry Caroline. The marriage would not make her son rich, for Lady Melbourne knew that the Bessboroughs had lost much of their fortune through bad investments in a shipping business, but it would consolidate the family's ties to Devonshire House. A week after the wedding, however, Lady Melbourne was careful not to appear too pleased. "The *Thorn* (William's mother), tho' she seem'd delighted with the marriage, has throughout had a degree of sharpness towards me that is very unpleasant," Lady Bessborough wrote to Lord Granville Leveson-Gower (figure 49). "Yesterday, after various very unpleasant *cuts*, she told me she hoped the Daughter would turn out better than the Mother, or William might have to repent of his choice, . . . I . . . only said I hoped and believed she would prove much better—'especially (I added) with the help of your advice' (I would not say example)" (June 12, 1805; G. L. Gower, 2:81). Lady Melbourne was no doubt alluding to the fact that Lady Bessborough bore at least two children by Lord Granville Leveson-Gower, Harriette and George Stewart.[67] Lady Melbourne only improved upon Lady Bessborough's "example" by being more discreet.

But Lady Bessborough was not the only person to rebuke Lady Melbourne for her sharp tongue. "Everybody has foibles from which no quarantine can purify them," William wrote to his mother on one occasion. "No resource remains but to make up your mind to put up with them. As to . . . laughing people out of them, which by the way you are . . . inclined . . . it only confirms them—makes the person ridiculed hate you into the bargain" (Strickland 104).

Despite these tensions between the recently united families, the year of the marriage was a happy one. In December 1805, William played Captain Absolute in Sheridan's *The Rivals* alongside his close friend, the future Tory prime minister Lord Aberdeen (Ziegler 48). Frederick criticized his mother for continuing to attend amateur theatricals held by the overbearing marquis of Abercorn. "What, is it possible you can so much have demeaned yourselves as to go to the priory after the contempt and neglect with which they have treated you," he wrote. "If so you must hereafter rank with his Irish members, servants of a Servant" (circa 1805; HRO). But Lady Melbourne knew the importance of overlooking slights and maintaining good connections.

As Lady Melbourne's children married into the Devonshire House circle, Georgiana found herself increasingly overwhelmed by gambling debts. In 1785 she made the mistake of turning to Thomas Coutts for assistance, which only compounded her problems. Soon her health gave way. In October 1796, after two very painful operations, she lost the use of one of her eyes, becoming increasingly shy about her disfigurement (Calder-Marshall 82, 126). "Her figure is corpulent, her complexion coarse, one eye gone, and her neck immense. How frail is the tenure of beauty!" Lady Holland wrote (E. Holland 1:224).

Not surprisingly, Georgiana rarely ventured out in public after this point, though she maintained a warm correspondence with Lady Melbourne. "I will do nothing without telling you," she wrote concerning the replacement of a governess (n.d. 45548, f.3). Both women still hoped Fox might attain office, which he did for the first six months of 1806, when he served as Grenville's foreign secretary. On June 10, 1806 Fox set in motion legislation abolishing the slave trade. Who knows what other accomplishments this man might have achieved had he been born at a different time? As it was, he found his patriotism questioned as he bravely defended a number of unpopular causes: the independence of the American colonies, the French Revolution,[68] and, worst of all, peace with Napoleon Bonaparte. Fox's coalitions with Tory opponents, especially Lord North and the duke of Portland, opened him to the charge of hypocrisy, but Lady Melbourne agreed with Georgiana that his career "has been perfect" (45548, f.30). His brief moment of political triumph coincided with Georgiana's death on March 30, 1806. She was forty-nine years old. Six months later, on September 13, 1806, Fox died at the age of fifty-eight (*DNB* 543, 550).

Lady Melbourne was deeply affected by both deaths, but especially by the passing of her protégé. She must have sensed that an era had passed away. "Pray let me know how you go on," the duke of Richmond wrote, "for with all Your Philosophy and your sense you have a Heart that must suffer dreadfully on such occasions and makes the best Health feel its consequences" (Airlie, *Whig* 94). Always prone to keep her own counsel, Lady Melbourne asked the duke of Richmond to comfort Lady Elizabeth Foster instead. She knew that power and influence would now lie with Foster, the next duchess of Devonshire.

That year, the Melbournes continued to visit Devonshire House, where they helped "disperse the gloom of a long evening." They "are much more gentle and comme il faut than usual," Georgiana's daughter, Hary-O, observed. After supper one night, they played chess and discussed George Lamb's support for Sheridan in the upcoming election. Lady Melbourne wore a turban and her daughter appeared in a "dirty gown and pearls, graceful and cold" (November 10, 1806; *Hary-O* 158). As this uncharitable remark suggests, some rivalry existed between Lady Melbourne's daughter and the youngest daughter of the duchess of Devonshire. Hary-O was now stuck in a house in which her father's mistress,

Elizabeth Foster, acted as her stepmother. At twenty-three, Hary-O may have envied the comparative freedom of Emily, who was already married and beginning her own family, though two years younger.[69]

Where Emily inspired Hary-O's jealousy, the red-haired and boisterous George Lamb was the delight of all. As a young child, George was portrayed allegorically as *The Infant Bacchus* by Maria Cosway (Torrens 1:29). He more than lived up to the name, for he ate too much supper and drank too much wine, but his talents and sense of humor more than compensated for his vices. He composed prologues to the revivals of old English plays and saw his comic opera, *Whistle for It,* produced at Covent Garden. Harriette Wilson described him as "one of the frankest men I ever met with" (Wilson 234), and his appealing personality soon attracted the notice of Caroline St. Jules (figures 50 and 51).

Pleased as she was to have a further connection with the Devonshire House circle, Lady Melbourne worried about Caroline's financial prospects, for she was the illegitimate daughter of Elizabeth, duchess of Devonshire. "Hang these marrying fellows," Frederick wrote to his mother in 1806. "Think only what it would be for him at two and twenty to be set down with a great fubsy breeding wife to all eternity to be provided for by his own exertions" (n.d.; F7 D/Elb HRO). The marriage was delayed for financial reasons, while George eked out a living as a lawyer on the northern circuit, earning only £20 in five months. "His heart is in Drury Lane," his sister Emily noted, "and he thinks of nothing but plays and epilogues and prologues" (R. G. Thorne 4:354). When the duke of Devonshire married Elizabeth Foster—finally making official their liaison of more than twenty years—Caroline St. Jules came into a sizable inheritance. On May 17, 1809, George was finally able to marry Caroline with his mother's blessing.[70]

Meanwhile, in October 1807, General Andoche Junot had marched into Portugal with an army of thirty thousand men and occupied parts of northern Spain. The Portuguese royal family fled, sailing to Brazil, and Godoy persuaded the king of Spain, Charles IV, to abdicate.[71] At Whitehall, "many of the company were not away till near three, and the Prince of Wales and a very few persons supped below in Lady Melbourne's apartment and were not gone till past six, Sheridan of the number who was completely drunk" (1808; Berry 2:346). Egremont criticized the prince for his profligacy at a time of national crisis. At another party, a guest named Vernon disagreed with Lord Egremont and Lady Melbourne that England could conquer Napoleon's army in Spain.[72] "To Lady Melbourne he said he hoped she was not John Bull enough to believe that we could fight the French with such inferiority of numbers. She said she longed to see him again to triumph over him" (August 14, 1809; Foster 335). Lady Melbourne and her lover did not have to wait long to be vindicated. Wellington proved victorious at the Battle of Talavera on July 27-28, 1809, though news of the battle did not reach England until more than two weeks later.

During this time Caroline's marriage to William had begun to falter. To save expenses, the couple had occupied the second floor of Melbourne Hall immediately after their wedding. Many of the troubles that arose between Caroline and Lady Melbourne—two strong-willed women—stemmed from this unfortunate arrangement. Further pressure was put on the marriage when Caroline suffered two still-born deliveries. On August 11, 1807, she gave birth to George Augustus Frederick (Torrens 1:72). The child was named by the Prince of Wales, who attended his baptism. He was later discovered to be autistic.

Though her favorite son's marriage was in trouble, Lady Melbourne refused to air her own differences with Caroline Lamb in public. "I went to see Lady Melbourne yesterday," Hary-O wrote to a friend, "and found her looking quite well though kept in town much against her inclination by the remains of a terrible cold and cough she has had for some time.

> Corise[73] was with me, in one of her humours, in which she constantly says everything she ought not, and amongst others she contrived entirely to forget that Caroline Lamb was in any way related to Lady Melbourne, began abusing her for her violence and *whims*. Lady M., though the first person to say this herself, is the last to hear it from anybody else, and if I had not by dint of winking and kicking, recalled Corisande's scattered senses, there would have been a second edition of the Argyle Street quarrel (November 25, 1807; *Hary-O* 257).

Lady Melbourne's defense of her daughter-in-law would come to an abrupt end by 1810, when Lady Caroline Lamb had a brief flirtation with Sir Godfrey

Webster. "I dare not meet y^r eyes," Caroline wrote to Lady Melbourne (n.d.; 45546, f.23). Apologies were followed by self-justifications, explaining how William had corrupted her morals with his worldly reading. "He instruct[ed] me in things I need never have known," she wrote (45546, f.13). Lady Melbourne asked her daughter-in-law to desist from mentioning a topic that had become hateful to her, but she had never had a very optimistic view of marriage. When Lord Henry Petty visited Brocket Hall in 1808, Lady Melbourne asked him to guess the following riddle about marriage: "mon premier est un Tyran, mon second est un Monstre, mon tout est le Diable." He said he would not only guess it but answer it by another— "Quand on aime son premier on ne craint pas son second et le tout est la félicité suprême" (*Hary-O* 280).[74]

Caroline Lamb's dalliance with Godfrey Webster paled beside her more notorious affair with Byron. Byron had returned from a two-year tour abroad in 1811 and published the autobiographical *Childe Harold's Pilgrimage* in the spring of 1812 to immediate acclaim. Caroline set out to meet the author of this overnight success. "If he bites his nails and is as ugly as Aesop, I must know him," she told Samuel Rogers after reading the poem. An introduction was arranged at Lady Westmoreland's. Seeing Byron surrounded by servile flatterers, Caroline spurned him. That same night she wrote in her diary that he was "Mad—bad—and dangerous to know." On another occasion, she predicted that his "pale face" would be her "fate." Both predictions proved accurate (Marchand, *Portrait* 118).

The Princess Lieven introduced the waltz to London society in 1812, and Caroline persuaded Lady Melbourne to let her use the great drawing room at Whitehall for this purpose. "All the *bon-ton* assembled there continually," Caroline later wrote. "There was nothing so fashionable" (Torrens 1:105). Byron was impressed. He liked being spoken of as a favored guest at Whitehall, and Caroline Lamb's attraction to him was flattering to his self-esteem (Torrens 1:105, 107). But Byron was a jealous lover. Lame from a club foot, he would not allow Caroline to waltz, despite her great facility. As their affair progressed, he demanded to know if she loved him more than her husband. When she hesitated, he told her, "My god, you shall pay for this, I'll wring that little obstinate heart" (Marchand, *Portrait* 123).[75]

By mid-May, the public nature of Byron's affair with Caroline Lamb embarrassed the poet. "People talk as if there were no other pair of absurdities in London," he wrote to Caroline. "We have both had 1000 previous fancies of the same kind, & I shall get the better of this & be as ashamed of it according to the maxim of Rochefoucauld" ([May 19, 1812?]; 2:177). When Lady Melbourne and Caroline's mother, Lady Bessborough, suggested that Caroline take a trip to Ireland to separate the couple, Byron did not object.[76]

From the Bessborough estate in Kilkenny, Caroline Lamb wrote confessional letters to her mother-in-law. Lady Melbourne sent many of these to Byron, with whom she had now established a regular correspondence. When the Prince of Wales heard this story from Lord Melbourne, he professed to be shocked at this traffic in letters. "I never heard of such a thing in my life," he said, "taking the Mothers for confidantes! What would you have thought of my going to talk to Ly. Spencer in former times!" (Airlie, *Whig* 147).[77] But Byron could not help himself. Though he had first turned to Lady Melbourne to "get the better" of his affair with Caroline, he soon found the older woman's comments on female psychology interesting in their own right ([May 19, 1812?]; *LJ* 2:177). "When I do see a woman superior not only to all her own [sex] but to most of ours I worship her," he explained (September 25, 1812; *LJ* 2:208).

That fall, Byron confessed his interest in marrying Lady Melbourne's niece, Annabella Milbanke. He asked that she advance the proposal, suggesting his true motive "would be the pleasure of calling you Aunt!" When Annabella quickly, if somewhat regretfully, declined the offer, Lady Melbourne asked her to list her requirements in a husband. The older woman corrected this list upon receiving it, reproving her priggish niece for standing upon "Stilts" (October 25, 1812).

Annabella was now courting the company of her worldly aunt, and a friend of the Milbankes registered his alarm. "She is in Many essential points unworthy of you," a certain Dr. Fenwick wrote, "& tho She may in some instances exhibit the Appearance of Sincerity, You Must Not forget that she Can deceive, & has been in the habit of deceiving" (November 26, 1812; Elwin, *Wife* 158). Ignoring Fenwick's prudent warning, Annabella dined with Lady Melbourne on several occasions and found that her talkative aunt could be as much of a hin-

drance as she was a help in pursuing Lord Byron (December 8; Elwin, *Wife* 157).
"You sat between Lady Melbourne and me, but conversed only with her,"
Annabella complained to him two years later, during their engagement (September
29, 1814; Elwin, *Wife* 216).

But other events closer to home were occupying Lady Melbourne's attention at this time. Caroline's affair with Byron had so distracted William that in 1812
he was left without a parliamentary seat. He refused to spend his father's money to
purchase one, for he was determined to find out what value the Whigs placed upon
his services.[78] Lady Melbourne dismissed her son's scruples, assuring him that he
could gain a seat at St. Albans for less than he believed. Meanwhile, Lady
Bessborough approached Earl Fitzwilliam, who shared William's opposition to parliamentary reform, but Fitzwilliam chose a Tory candidate. In the end, William
remained out of office that fall, along with such illustrious company as George
Tierney, Samuel Romilly, Francis Horner, and Henry Brougham. Addressing his
remarks to Lord Grey at a dinner in November 1812, William complained about the
lack of party support. Lady Melbourne was disappointed by her son. "There is no
use in thinking about a person who will not think for themselves," she wrote to
Lady Holland (R. G. Thorne 4:363).

In June 1813, Madame de Staël arrived in England, where she was enthusi-
astically received by the Prince of Wales, the queen, the duchess of York, and the
duke of Gloucester. "To meet a cabinet minister," wrote Miss Berry, "one had to go
to Madame de Stael's" (Herold 419). Sir James Mackintosh, the Scottish publicist,
was her guide, and Byron met the French author on the very night of her arrival in
London, at a ball held at Lady Jersey's (Byron, *Complete Prose* 184). Lady
Melbourne disliked de Staël's manners, deploring her tendency to cause "tracasseries." She wrote to Byron, telling him how "Monk" Lewis quarreled with the
opinionated opponent of Bonaparte's regime at the duchess of York's residence in
Oatlands. De Staël "talk'd loud, so did he, & the Singers at the other end of the
room could not hear one another & were obliged to Stop—I wish I had seen it"
(January 16, 1814).[79] Byron thought de Staël a "sort of Caroline in her senses"
(August 8, 1813; *LJ* 3:87), and anticipated her histrionic response to the death of
her only son, Albert, in a duel. "You judge her quite truly, about her wish to shew

off," Lady Melbourne wrote (August 8, 1813). By the following year, Byron's impression was even more negative. "Her books are very delightful—but in society I see nothing but a very plain woman forcing one to listen & look at her with her pen behind her ear and her mouth full of *ink*.—So much for her" (January 8, 1814; *LJ* 4:19). While the Whigs needed no magnifying glass to find Madame de Staël's faults, Tory ministers did their best to cultivate her acquaintance, hoping she would use her "powerful pen" to denounce Napoleon (January 31, 1815; Lovelace 377).

United by their dislike of Madame de Staël and other sundry opinions, Lady Melbourne and Byron corresponded feverishly for the next two years. From 1812 to 1814, Lady Melbourne learned more than she probably wanted to know about the poet's affairs with Lady Oxford, Lady Frances Webster, and Augusta Leigh (figure 52). Byron had begun to treat her like a mother, his own having died shortly after his return to England. At the same time, there was no small amount of flirtation between the two correspondents, especially when the poet considered traveling abroad with Lady Oxford. "Why won't *you* go off with me?" he asked Lady Melbourne. "I am sure our elopement would . . . cause a 'greater sensation' as our Orators say—than any event of the kind—since Eve ran away with the Apple" (June 21, 1813; *LJ* 3:66). At one point they exchanged rings, and Byron wrote that he hoped "you will not reject the only thing I ever dared to present you" (Strickland 111).

Alone at Seaham, Annabella began to wonder if she had made a mistake in rejecting Byron's proposal too resolutely (figures 53 and 54). Had she lied by allowing Byron to believe she was engaged to George Eden? To correct the fault, she wrote to Byron directly, requesting his secrecy. "In particular I would not have it known to L^y Melbourne," she confessed (August 22, 1813; Elwin, *Wife* 167). This was the wrong strategy. Byron responded with an oath of allegiance to his closest confidante, describing her as "the best friend I ever had in my life, and the cleverest of women" (November 17, 1813; *LJ* 3:209). By the following year, Annabella was also praising her aunt, if only to please Byron. "I am sensible of many excellencies in Lady Melbourne," Annabella wrote dutifully. "Your opinion will incline me to look for more" (February 10, 1814; Elwin, *Wife* 186).

Annabella's relationship with Byron was improving, but Lady Melbourne was made "melancholy" by learning details about Byron's incestuous affair with his half-sister, Augusta. Her correspondence with Byron lapsed in November and December 1813, at the precise moment when he was again contemplating eloping with Augusta. By June 1814, it was too late. The couple may well have had a child, Medora, and Lady Melbourne wrote that "I am shock'd at some of the things you sd to me last Night" (June 10, 1814; Murray). Byron responded to Lady Melbourne's letter that same day. "Who ever said or supposed that you were not shocked and all that?—you *have* done every thing in your power—& more to make me act rationally" (June 10, 1814; *LJ* 4:123). No letters were sent between Lady Melbourne and Lord Byron during July and August of that year, the crucial months in which Byron's marriage to Annabella was arranged. Augusta was with Byron at Newstead Abbey at the time and remembered him repeating "the prejudicial opinions Ly Melbourne had given of [Annabella's] character, particularly of [her] self-willed dispositions & over-strained notions of propriety" (Elwin, *Wife* 207).[80]

Before his proposal was accepted, Byron asked Lady Melbourne's approval, which was given. The engagement was nevertheless in jeopardy more than once. "What? a chance still of my not being a Zia," Lady Melbourne wrote to Byron on one of these occasions (November 18, 1814). She warned him that his delays in visiting his bride in Seaham were inexcusable, and that his reasons would be "pooh pooh'd out of Court" (October 19, 1814). Generally, she played a more active role in bringing about the marriage—which took place on New Year's Day 1815—than has been recognized (Marchand, *Portrait* 188-89). She helped them choose her own birthplace, the Milbankes' home at Halnaby, as the location for their honeymoon (Lovelace 92, f.52, 54),[81] and seemed to exist as a ghostly presence during those first few weeks. During one dark evening, when the ground at Halnaby was covered with snow, Byron pulled a letter from Lady Melbourne out of a red portfolio. It warned him against committing an "atrocious crime," alluding to his affair with Augusta. Annabella remembered how Byron expressed "his admiration of [Lady Melbourne] for having written it, and his sense of her friendliness. "'She is a good woman after all,'" he said, "'for there are things she will stop at'" (Elwin, *Wife* 268-69).

No sooner had the Byrons returned from their "treaclemoon," as Byron termed it, than Lady Melbourne was asked to rent their first home in London. Unwisely, she chose the overpriced mansion of her old friend Elizabeth, duchess of Devonshire. Fashionably located in Piccadilly, the residence was too large for Byron and Annabella.[82] Byron soon found himself short of ready cash, and bailiffs were in the house by November 1815 (Elwin, *Wife* 324).[83] Anxieties about economizing put a strain on the marriage. When he wasn't drinking brandy and behaving strangely, Byron could be found with Susan Boyce and Mrs. Mardyn, two actresses with whom he had affairs. His wife began to refer to him as the "Manager . . . always trottin about behind the Scenes" (October 5, 1815; Elwin, *Wife* 319) and visited him accompanied by Lady Melbourne, determined to arrest the fatal course of his "disease."[84]

Frightened by her husband's irascible temper, Annabella left Byron after the birth of their first child, Ada. Judith Milbanke quickly blamed Lady Melbourne for the failed marriage.[85] "*Buy* and *read* the Book entitled, Les Liaisons dangereuses," she wrote to her husband (figures 55 and 56). "You will *there* find *the Viscountess* depicted exactly in *La Marquise*" (February 2, 1816; Elwin, *Wife* 387). She instructed her daughter "to *break* with her, that is *cut her intirely*" in order to "*contradict* the *Lies* and aspersions She has held out *lately*" (March 15, 1816; Elwin, *Wife* 443). Annabella promised to comply (March 17, 1816; Elwin, *Wife* 443). Byron often alluded to the fact that his correspondence with Lady Melbourne would come to an abrupt end. It did so on April 25, 1816, when he set sail for the continent. The day after his departure, Judith Milbanke still hoped that her sister-in-law's villainy would be exposed. "Lady Melbourne is in a fright," she informed her husband. "She is sure that Lady Byron has seen some of her letters to Lord Byron, for Caroline Lambe has quoted some passages to her" (April 26, 1816; Elwin, *Wife* 448).

In *Dangerous Liaisons,* Madame de Merteuil is forced to leave Paris after her role in Valmont's seduction of Cecile Volanges and Madame de Tourvel is exposed. Scarred by smallpox, she finally reflects outwardly her monstrous morality. Lady Melbourne escaped this fate. Through a remarkable epistolary campaign, she won back a reluctant Annabella, inquiring after her child. Her position on the separation had changed so dramatically that Annabella was led to write to her mother in triumph. "You have great reason to be satisfied,—even with *ma Tante*, who is *now* become my panegyrist!" (March 28, 1816; Elwin, *Wife* 458).[86]

Unlike Lady Melbourne, Byron had no reason to alter his loyalties (November 27, 1816; *LJ* 5:136). Writing from Venice, he remembered his favorite correspondent as Lady Pinchbeck and contrasted her with the sanctimonious mother of his own wife.

> I think you'll find from many a family picture
> That daughters of such mothers as may know
> The world by experience rather than by lecture
> Turn out much better for the Smithfield Show
> Of Vestals brought into the marriage mart
> Than those bred up by prudes without a heart.
>
> (*Don Juan* 12:46)

Ironically, Byron's narrator suggests, it was precisely Lady Melbourne's transgressions that made her a more successful mother. Annabella inherited her mother's tendency to approach the world by "lecture" rather than "experience." "What a grave ass Annabella is," Frederick wrote to his mother at the time of the separation (March 9, 1816; 45546, f.145). Annabella mistakenly believed she could reform Byron, but Lady Melbourne's own daughter, Emily, overlooked her husband's indifference[87] and encouraged the attentions of her next husband, Lord Palmerston. Whereas one woman was living the lonely life of a single mother, the other had become a leading figure in Whig society, controlling the guest list at Almack's.[88]

Lady Melbourne's family benefited materially from her indiscretions in other ways as well. "Whilst I live," the Prince of Wales promised, "I never will neglect an opportunity in which I can be of use to any of you or in which I can forward any wish of yours, or Melbournes" (November 30, 1803; 45548, f.109).[89] The prince reappointed her husband lord of the bedchamber in March 1812[90] and finally succeeded in having him named a peer of the United Kingdom in 1816.[91] A satire of 1812, titled *The Court of Love,* criticizes him for being a false friend of the Prince Regent (figure 57). "As for me," Peniston announces proudly, with a woman on each arm, "My name is sufficient, / I am known by the title of the / Paragon of Debauchery and / I only claim to be the ——s Confidential Friend."

But the prince did not grant his favors only to Lady Melbourne's sottish husband. William was offered a position on the Board of Treasury, which he turned down on February 26, 1812, citing his differences with the Tory inclinations of the prince's ministry. Then a post in the Prince of Wales' coalition government was offered, but failed to materialize. The coalition was to include Charles Grey and George Canning, but the prince seemed "more anxious to strengthen the Ministry, than the Ministry are to strengthen themselves," William explained to his mother (July 28, 1812; 45546, f.2).

Frederick Lamb's career was also aided by his mother's relationship with the prince. After he left Glasgow, Frederick attended Trinity College, Cambridge, where he finished his degree in 1803. He joined the Household Cavalry and became a cornet in the Royal Horse Guards. After this he served as aide-de-camp to General Mackenzie, who commanded the garrison at Hull. Frederick preferred the fashionable life of London to the country, however, and the Prince of Wales thus advised him to leave the Blues, where he would be quartered at Windsor, and raise a troop for the 10th Hussars, the Prince of Wales' own regiment. There he "would get more leave to London" (Airlie, *Palmerston* 13) and have a greater chance of promotion (45548, f.112). As a young man, Frederick was reluctant to have his mother use her political influence too visibly. "None o' your sniggering my Dear mother," he wrote. "Nobody doubts your ability in that way but power restrained is more honourable than power employed" (n.d.; F7 D/Elb HRO).[92]

Dissatisfied with the army as a profession, Frederick began to look to diplomacy as the field in which to satisfy his ambitions. In 1811 he accompanied Lord William Bentinck to Sicily on a "semi-military, semi-diplomatic expedition" (Airlie, *Palmerston* 18). A year later he became a secretary of legation, though still in the army. Lady Melbourne wrote to the Prince of Wales on February 4, 1811 to fight this appointment, for she did not wish to have her son stationed abroad for any length of time. Through Lady Holland, she sounded out Lord Grey about the matter, asking him about his illegitimate daughter and apologizing for writing with all the freedom of an old friend. Grey acknowledged his debt to Lady Melbourne, who had protected him during his affair with Georgiana, duchess of Devonshire, but informed her that "in the Foreign Office there is really nothing but appointments abroad, that I could at present propose to him" (February 24, 1811; F9/2 D/Elb HRO). Lady Melbourne only agreed to let Frederick depart for a post in the Two Sicilies under the prince's express promise that a position would be offered to him at home at the first opportunity. It never was.

For the next four years, Frederick painted a grim picture of diplomatic life (F9/2 D/Elb, HRO). His expenses exceeded his salary, and his social life depended upon the public parties of English aristocrats living abroad. Inheriting his father's taste for liquor, he developed an obstinate case of gout and followed a conservative regimen of early hours, abstinence, and "magnesia lozenges" to combat the disease (November 28 [1816]; 45546, f.169). His mother would often send him books on the subject during his cold winters in Frankfurt, and he was equally generous in his gifts. On November 5, 1814, he sent her "a parcel of sable fur" he had ordered from Russia. "I think it may save you many colds for many winters coming out of the Opera house . . . only don't be stingy of it but have a good pelisse lined with it as they do here" (November 5 [1814]; 45546, f.132).[93] What he really missed in Frankfurt, though, was his mother's company. "I'm not a bit sleepy—but wish you was here to sit and talk till three in the morning" (November 28 [1816]; 45546, f.169), he wrote.

By 1816 George's marriage to Caroline St. Jules was in shambles. George never consummated the union and would retire to bed early to avoid sleeping with her. Caroline's discussion of this with Lady Elizabeth Foster angered Lady Melbourne. "The mother, which is certainly odd, has been less kind to me, since she has known it, and I have never ceased regretting that she was told," Caroline wrote. Caroline's mother thought that the worst aspect of her daughter's situation was that George did not seem to be bothered by it. "Insensible to joy or passion he is to leave her to her solitary bed," she wrote. "I look upon him as a kind of monster" (Masters 300). By 1816 Caroline George Lamb and Henry Brougham (figure 58) had had an affair on the continent. Lady Melbourne rebuked her daughter-in-law for her conduct, but Caroline George explained how her husband had neglected her and found her a distraction from his work in the theater.

Throughout her life, Lady Melbourne learned to make a friend out of a potential enemy. For that reason it is not surprising to find Henry Brougham's name among the company listed for a Christmas party at Brocket Hall in 1816. Other guests included Lord Palmerston and William Huskisson, who talked "to Lady Melbourne about public affairs, believing that Canning would join the Government." He hoped William would enter the House of Commons and arrangements were made through the Damers for this to be effected (Torrens 1:115). Canning became president of the Board of Control (Torrens 1:118), and William served as M.P. for Peterborough (Ziegler 70).[94]

Just as George's marriage seemed to be on the mend, an incident occurred that rocked Whig society to its foundation. On May 9, 1816, William Lamb's wife published *Glenarvon*. In this roman à clef, Lady Caroline Lamb exposed her mother-in-law's villainous role in corresponding with Byron while Caroline was in Ireland in 1812. A paragraph from the novel may serve to explain why Lady Melbourne was so disturbed to see herself depicted as Lady Margaret Buchanan, who

> was not much liked by Mrs. Seymour, nor by many other of the guests who frequented the castle. Her foreign domestics, her splendid attire, her crafty smiles and highly polished manners,—all were in turn criticised and condemned. But neither prejudice nor vulgarity received from her lips the slightest censure. She did not even appear to see the ill will shewn to her. Yet many thought the discords and disasters which occurred after her arrival in Ireland, were the fruits of her intriguing spirit, and all soon or late regretted her presence at the castle, till, then, the seat of uninterrupted harmony and almost slumberous repose. (*Glenarvon* 22)

Caroline Lamb's view of Lady Melbourne as a foreigner betrays the sharp contrast in manners that marked the Devonshires and the Lambs. Though they intermarried, loyalties were retained.[95]

In a letter to Annabella, Lady Melbourne confessed that she had "only read y[e] first Vol. [of *Glenarvon*] & it is so disagreable to me that I do not feel as if I had courage to proceed, I never can excuse y[e] falsehoods she tells about Will[m] & y[e] acc[t] she gives of a Society in which she had lived from her Childhood" (June 29, 1816). Had she continued reading, however, she would have discovered that William did not come across negatively at all in *Glenarvon*. Remembered as the handsome and warm-hearted Lord Avondale, William found it easier to forgive Caroline for the surreptitiously published novel than did his mother.

Nor did Byron have much reason to complain. The gothic villain modeled on him exhibits a commitment to Irish nationalism that is commendable.[96] Others did not fare so well. Lady Holland, who called the novel "a strange farrago" (*Creevey* 163), was parodied as the imperious princess of Madagascar; Lady Oxford as Lady Mandeville; the duchess of Devonshire as Lady Augusta Selwyn; and Samuel Rogers as "a poet of emaciated and sallow complexion" (Lamb, *Glenarvon* vi). If Lady Caroline Lamb portrayed her mother-in-law as "bigotted and vulgar," as Lady Holland observed to Mrs. Creevey (May 21, 1816; *Creevey* 163), Lady Caroline Lamb did not exempt herself from self-criticism. More than a mere portrait of Byron, *Glenarvon* is Caroline Lamb's best autobiography, and offers trenchant observations about mores and manners of the English aristocracy by a talented woman who rejected both.

Fearful that she would be permanently ostracized, Lady Caroline Lamb wrote an effusive letter to her mother-in-law, apologizing for the novel. In other letters, however, she declared her intention to "renounce all intercourse with an Aunt who can so coldly & so cruelly attempt what Lord Westmoreland unfortunately attempted against his wife" (45548, f.141). Lady Melbourne hoped to prove Caroline Lamb mentally unstable and obtain a separation between her and William. When the papers were brought to the couple to be signed, however, William was found with Caroline Lamb on his lap, feeding her bits of buttered bread (Airlie, *Whig* 185). Once again, Lady Melbourne had been outwitted by her witless daughter-in-law.

That fall, Emily Cowper traveled throughout Europe with her husband and children. She was taking advantage of the peace offered by the fall of Napoleon, and hoped also to curb expenses and avoid the economic dislocation that beset England at this time. In Paris she went shopping with Lady Melbourne's friend,[61] Madame de Coigny, but delayed purchasing "a Gown of épingle Velvet" for her mother because she was short of money. Instead, she sent "a little Fan just that I may not leave Paris without sending you something" (September 8, 1816; 45549, f.79). She traveled through Geneva. There she heard that Byron was accused of consorting with another mistress (Claire Clairmont) while seeking a reconciliation with his wife. Emily prematurely informed her mother that the rumors were not true. "The English here I believe avoid seeing him but he is a great favorite with Madame de Staël who takes his part very much and has got L^d & L^y Jersey to go & dine with him today at his House near Geneva" (September 24, 1816; 45549, f.90). In Geneva Emily encountered her own admirer, Lord Palmerston, whom she sent home with several letters. Seven English carriages were robbed in Italy (September 24, 1816; 45549, f.90), but Emily made the journey through the Simplon pass anyway, armed with her mother's recipe for "Portable soup" (October 20, 1816; 45549, f.101). After a short stint in Venice and Rome, she and her husband went to Germany and visited Frederick, who impressed her with his domestic arrangements. "I am really come here to *learn*!!" (n.d.; 45549, f.214), she wrote to her mother.

During her voyage, Emily read Maria Edgeworth, Walter Scott, Thomas Moore, and Byron, whose "Manfred" she thought too "wild." She closed her letter of July 26, 1817 with a reference to Henry Brougham's attack on Lord Castlereagh for suspending *habeas corpus*, submitting to the Piedmontese demands in Italy, and levying undue taxes on the manufacturing industry (July 11, 1817; *London Times*). Emily's Whig principles competed with her sense of family loyalty, for she never lost an opportunity to criticize Brougham after his affair with Caroline George. "I am amused at the Viper Brougham keeping all his venom for the last day tho Ld C[a]s[tlereag]h well deserves it," she wrote (45549, f.224).

On her way back to England, Emily met Maria Fitzherbert[97] at Spa, who reported that Lord and Lady Melbourne were "looking very well" (August 11, 1817; 45549, f.229). Emily had been in England several months when she returned to Brocket Hall to find her sister-in-law, Caroline Lamb, as much of a nuisance as ever. "I am quite sorry the Devil begins so quick to torment you," she wrote to her mother. "[F]or my part I would much rather live near a soap manufacturing, or the gas light Company, or an eternal going Mill which does not make half the noise she does in a House" (November 4, 1817; 45549, f.239).

In addition to sending more than ninety letters to her daughter from 1816 to 1817, Lady Melbourne had been writing regularly to Frederick since his departure for Germany (figure 59).[98] He assured her he would receive his appointment at Munich from Castlereagh without her influence. "Preach perfect indifference and noninterference if possible even to forgetfulness," he wrote. "I think you will see the reason and wisdom of this and if you don't take my word for it" (October 4, 1815; 45546, f.143). He faulted his mother for doubting his decision to accompany Castlereagh to Vienna and Chatillon, and reminded her of the "half cutting letters" she wrote on these subjects, "which I had temper enough never to take the least notice of." The Prince of Wales could see through her self-interest, he argued, and she was doing his cause more damage than good by meddling. "What I want of you," he wrote, "is not to suppose that you at 200 miles off know better than me upon the spot" (October 4, 1815; 45546, f.143).

Despite this admonition, Lady Melbourne was now reaping the rewards for her careful consideration of her family's self-interest. Emily seemed content with her husband, and George's marriage to Caroline St. Jules had worked out after all. William's best accomplishments lay ahead of him, though he was already being considered for the position of leader of the Whig party in 1817 when George Ponsonby vacated the post (Torrens 1:130; R. G. Thorne 4:364).[99]

As for Lady Melbourne's friends, they formed an ever-diminishing circle. Those who survived were barely recognizable. The Prince of Wales had become a fat dandy and a cruel father. In 1816 he tried to force his daughter to marry the Prince of Orange and live in Holland. When Charlotte overcame her father's objections and married Prince Leopold the following year, the English people rallied to her side. Lady Melbourne admired Charlotte's heroic resistance to her father's tyranny and defended her at numerous dinner parties at Whitehall. Princess Charlotte's quiet life in the country with her husband seemed to prove that domestic felicity was still possible (figure 60).

For this reason, Charlotte's death in childbirth on November 6, 1817 constituted a national tragedy. So great was the public pressure brought on her obstetrician, Richard Croft, that he committed suicide the following year.[100] "The greatest gloom has taken place for all ranks of persons feel it as a personal Misfortune to themselves," Lady Melbourne wrote. "Every one wishes to avoid even the appearance of a party" (November 14, 1817).[101]

Contemplating the princess' death must have led Lady Melbourne to consider her own mortality. In January 1818 she was suffering from the effects of rheumatism and an unforgiving winter. Bedridden, Lady Melbourne followed Dr. Warren's prescription for long baths, but this did little to relieve her pain. In her final days at Melbourne House, Whitehall, she was surrounded by members of her family—except for Frederick, who was still stationed in Germany. Her illness "had been a very painful one," Caroline George Lamb wrote to Annabella Milbanke after Lady Melbourne's death on April 6, "and the patience and invariable sweetness of temper with which she bore it, interested me much in her favor." Caroline George had taken Annabella's side in the separation with Byron, but could not help sympathizing with Lady Melbourne during her final illness. "It is impossible to see a person so loved and so regretted & not to feel that they must have had great merits to counteract their faults," she wrote (April 8, 1818; Lovelace). William, who knew his mother's faults as well as anyone, attributed his political success to her shrewd guidance. "My mother was a most remarkable woman," he said long after her death. "Not merely clever and engaging but the most sagacious woman I ever knew. She kept me right as long as she lived" (Torrens 1:135).

Though Lady Melbourne died in relative tranquillity, her correspondence soon became the subject of anxious speculation long before she was buried at Hatfield Church on April 14, 1818. Caroline George wrote to inform Lady Byron that "Hobhouse wrote . . . a most disgusting letter, asking for L[or]d. B[yron].'s letters[,] . . . I . . . do not know that she kept any, indeed the probability is that they were all burnt" (April 8, 1818; Lovelace). But Lady Melbourne did not burn Byron's letters. They were first assembled by Thomas Moore in his biography of the poet, further edited by E. H. Coleridge, and most recently published by Leslie Marchand.

Lady Melbourne's own correspondence with Byron fell into relative neglect, though Byron had joked that their abbreviations would "puzzle posterity when our correspondence bursts forth in the 20th century" (November 6, 1812; *LJ* 2:240). He was referring to their coded references to scandals that are now long past, affairs long forgotten—the use of "+" for Augusta, "P." for the Prince Regent, and "my A." and "your A." for Augusta and Annabella. Three years before this century closes, Byron's prophecy has turned out to be correct. Like characters in Henry James' *Aspern Papers*,[102] we read the letters of this remarkable woman as if for the first time, decoding hieroglyphics scratched out in a crimped and hasty hand. And after almost two centuries, Lady Melbourne's smile shines forth once again to enchant another age.

Notes: Introduction

1. William Lamb served as Whig prime minister from July 16 to November 14, 1834 and again from April 18, 1835 to August 30, 1841.

2. Noted for her beauty, Diane de Poitiers (1499-1566), duchess of Valentinois, was much older than Henry and continued to influence him until his death in 1559. She remained friendly with the queen, Catherine de Medici, "while completely eclipsing her." In court intrigues between Anne, duc de Montmorence, and the Guise family, Diane de Poitiers took sides with the more powerful party at the time. Lady Melbourne adopted a similar strategy, remaining on good terms with the royal family while entertaining the more radical members of the Whig party (*Columbia* 758).

3. The painting was exhibited at the Society of Artists in 1770 (B. Taylor 133). The sitters, from left to right, are Lady Melbourne; her father, Sir Ralph Milbanke; her brother, John Milbanke; and her husband, Lord Melbourne (209). Lady Melbourne's mother, Elizabeth Hedworth, was the daughter of John Hedworth's second marriage. She died two years before Lady Melbourne's marriage (Elwin, *Noels* 60). Sir Peniston's father died in 1768, and his mother passed away in 1751, when he was only a young boy (Airlie, *Palmerston* 2).

4. Sheridan, *The Rivals* 5:1.

5. A letter to the author, dated October 1, 1996, from M. Y. Ashcroft, county archivist for North Yorkshire County Council, confirms that Lady Melbourne was baptized at Croft on October 15, 1751, as opposed to birth dates of 1752 and 1753 that are cited elsewhere.

6. Steele observes that Powel enjoyed a settlement from Lord Melbourne even after his marriage, something that Sophia Baddeley was unable to obtain.

7. Baddeley's *Memoirs* (1782) were written by her friend Elizabeth Steele.

8. As a follower of Lord North, he was created Lord Melbourne, Baron of Kilmore, County Cavan (Ireland). On January 11, 1781, he was appointed Viscount Melbourne of Kilmore, County Cavan (Ireland). He was a gentleman of the bedchamber (1783-95) to the Prince of Wales and a lord of the bedchamber (1812-28) until his death (White 8:635). On August 11, 1815, he was created Baron Melbourne of Melbourne, County Derby (United Kingdom).

9. Unfortunately, this staircase (figure 6) was torn down by Henry Holland when he redesigned the premises and converted them into the bachelor apartments known as the Albany.

10. The first Lord Holland, father of Charles James Fox, had planned to rebuild his house in Piccadilly from designs by Adam, but elected instead to sell it to Lord Melbourne. As paymaster-general, Lord Holland accumulated a fortune, which his third son, Charles James Fox, quickly dissipated (Harris 227).

11. The building can still be found today, around the corner from the neon lights of modern London and as well located as ever. It was sold to the duke of York before being transformed into the Albany, where Byron, Canning, Macaulay, and other bachelors lived.

12. André Le Nôtre (1613-1700) created French landscape gardening. He designed the gardens at

Versailles and laid out St. James' Park in London. Coke, who visited France and Holland in his youth, had the garden at Versailles in mind when he took possession of the property in 1696 and put his ideas into practice from 1696 to 1700. The gardens sport numerous statues, a vase by Samuel Watson, an urn of the four seasons by John Van Nost, and an iron arbor designed by Robert Bakewell in 1706 (Kerr 497).

13. Love Reade inherited the property from Sir John Brocket, who died a bachelor of twenty-two in 1712. Reade possessed Brocket Hall with her husband, Thomas Winnington, after whose death in 1746 it was bought by Matthew Lamb (Tipping 20).

14. William Hanger commissioned the portrait in 1772 (T. Taylor 1:429), but had the misfortune to see himself supplanted in Baddeley's affections by his brother, John Hangar, who used to beat Baddeley (Steele 1:82).

15. This painting, which was engraved by John Finlayson (August 16, 1771), appeared in the British Institution's exhibition of 1843 (Graves and Cronin 637).

16. The painting is titled *Maternal Affection* and is described as *Lady Elizabeth Melbourne with her Son, the Hon. Peniston Lamb* in the Graves and Cronin catalogue (2:637). The child, born May 3, 1770, sat for the painting in November 1770. Lady Melbourne sat in 1770 and 1773, showing that the picture was in progress for three years. It was exhibited by the Royal Academy in 1773 (no. 235) and at the British Institution in 1813 (no. 14) as *Lady Melbourne and Child*, by Viscount Melbourne. It was engraved by Thomas Watson (Graves and Cronin 2:637-38). "I *must* see you at Sir *Joshua's*," Byron wrote, "though I don't much like venturing on the sight of *seventeen*—it is bad enough *now*—and must have been *worse then*—the painter was not so much to blame as you seem to imagine by adding a few years—he foresaw you would lose nothing by them" (May 7, 1813; *LJ* 3:46). Baptized on October 15, 1751, Lady Melbourne was not seventeen but at least nineteen when she first sat for the painting. Either she lied about her age or the dates provided by Graves and Cronin are incorrect.

17. Lady Melbourne entrusted the early upbringing of Peniston and her subsequent children to an old and petulant woman from Jersey whom they detested and whom Lady Melbourne inexplicably admired (Ziegler 17).

18. Lady Salisbury, whose politics were Tory, provided balance to the report.

19. The quadrille, a square dance designed for four couples, was fashionable during the late eighteenth and the nineteenth centuries.

20. The Glorious Revolution deposed the Catholic King James II with a minimum of bloodshed and secured great fortunes for Whigs as supporters of William of Orange (Foster 99).

21. Boyle mistakenly attributes this sketch to Damer (475). More than one copy of the pastel sketch exists and perhaps all three women received their own copies. One version is owned by the Salmond family and another can be found in George C. Williamson's *Daniel Gardner* (44).

22. Williamson (without knowledge of the actual sitters or the number of versions) writes that the sketch was done for the family of Sir Philip Grey Egerton. He assumes that one of the sitters was a sister of Lord Grey de Wilton (44). *Christie's Sales Catalog* and Ian Ritchie of the National Portrait Gallery indicate that the group portrait was of Lady Melbourne, Anne Damer, and the duchess of Devonshire. No mention of Egerton as patron is given.

23. Bram Dijkstra, *Idols of Perversity: Fantasies of Feminine Evil in Fin-de-Siecle Culture* (Oxford: Oxford University Press, 1986), 44 contains an interesting account of Reynolds' representation of women.

24. Lady Melbourne was connected to the Coke family through her father-in-law's marriage.

25. The gambling debts and jovial nature of Charles Surface in *The School for Scandal* recall Charles James Fox, who used to refer to the hall outside of Brooks' Club as the "Jerusalem Chamber."

26. *Evelina* was first published in 1778 by T. & W. Lowndes, but was sold and advertised with *The*

Sylph in January 1779 (Calder-Marshall 38; Masters 70).

27. The duke of Devonshire appears as Sir William Stanley; the duchess as Julia Stanley; and Georgiana's mother and sister are recalled in the character of Julia's sister, Louisa.

28. She recommends "a French frizeur of the last importation, who dressed hair to a miracle *au dernier gout*" (1:61).

29. The Honorable Edward Vernon, bishop of Carlisle.

30. Throughout his life, William Lamb reflected the enlightened conservatism of his natural father. Egremont once wrote that "Almost every great improvement in society is counterbalanced by some evil arising from it, which is not thought of till it happens" (Usher, *Femmes* 3). William Lamb's support for laissez-faire economic programs reflects Egremont's views. Emily also displayed Egremont's political gifts (3). He lent her his summer house at Brighton when she vacationed there with her child.

31. Peniston was also painted by Maria Cosway and George Romney. In the portrait by Romney, he wears a tawny coat and white cravat (Boyle 320).

32. Fashionable ladies who wished the prince to attend their parties would approach him through Lady Melbourne (November 2, 1783; Birkenhead 24).

33. The Prince of Wales' full name was George Augustus Frederick.

34. In the foreground, the Prince of Wales, wearing a ribbon and a star, is accompanied by Lady Salisbury and Mrs. Robinson, the actress known as "Perdita" (1758-1800). Other women who the prince had "flattered with his attention," including Lady Melbourne herself, are to the left, dancing in a circle. The husband, James, sixth earl (afterwards first marquis) of Salisbury (1748-1823), exclaims, "Zounds so leave my Wife alone or I'll tell the Old Wig [George III]" (Aspinall 5:644).

35. George Hangar, a dandy, remained in the Melbourne circle as late as 1806. Lady M—d was possibly the wife of Viscount Maitland, one of Fox's supporters. Miss Vanneck, the third daughter of Sir Joshua, first baronet, was mentioned by Walpole on August 25, 1795 as one of the prince's companions at Brighton.

36. Mary "Perdita" Robinson (1758-1800) was named after the part she played in *The Winter's Tale*. The Prince Regent's affair with her began in 1779, when he was seventeen (*Chambers* 1139).

37. Lady Fitzherbert had rejected the prince's advances until he agreed to marry her. One night he staged a suicide attempt. He summoned the duchess of Devonshire to witness him giving Mrs. Fitzherbert his ring, but only obtained Mrs. Fitzherbert's consent to marry him. The marriage occurred in a secret ceremony on December 15, 1785. The Melbournes may have been privy to the information of the marriage, for the *Times* reported that the prince would pass a few days during Christmas at Lord Melbourne's, only eleven days after the marriage had taken place (December 26, 1785). Cecil notes that the prince was annoyed by Lady Melbourne for a year or two because she continued seeing Maria Fitzherbert after he had quarreled with his secret wife (Cecil, *Young M* 53). In 1795 the prince married Caroline of Brunswick, in part to liquidate his debts.

38. Richard Cosway (1742-1821), the famous miniaturist, was a companion of the Prince Regent's.

39. The book was added to the painting to compensate for the painter's difficulty in portraying her hands (Lloyd 30).

40. The portraits were later moved to opposite sides of the room.

41. Aileen Ribeiro notes that this painting illustrates the three costumes worn by boys at the end of the eighteenth century. The dating of the painting coincides with the boys' birthdates. William was born nine years after Peniston on March 15, 1779; Frederick on April 17, 1782; and George, who does not appear in the painting, on July 11, 1784 (Usher, *Femmes* 4; Penny 305).

42. Fox was opposed by Lord Hood and Cecil Wray. Lady Melbourne and Anne Damer also supported Fox, though less visibly. The election turned on the king's hatred for Fox, who had helped to corrupt his son, the Prince Regent. Three groups predominated at the time of this election: the duke of

Bedford led a contingent that was determined to increase their revenues; Lord Shelburne sought parliamentary reform; and the Rockinghams, including the dukes of Portland and Richmond, stood for traditional Whiggism and the principles of 1688. Fox sided with Lord Rockingham and thus showed his exaggerated respect for landed families. By the 1784 election, he still retained this reactionary position, proclaiming the powers of Parliament greater than the rights of the people. The House of Commons, he argued, was the more important check on royal tyranny (Masters 114). The final numbers were Lord Hood, 6, 694; Fox, 6,234; and Wray, 5,998 (*DNB* 544).

43. Damer's house was adjacent to the east side of the garden at Melbourne House. A deed dated 1784 makes clear "Lord Viscot Melbourn's Agreement to Lett the Honoble Mrs. Damer have a Door through the Garden Wall and a window looking into it" (Birkenhead 25).

44. Dr. William Cumberland Cruikshank (1745–1800) was a surgeon and anatomist in London who attended Dr. Johnson in his final illness.

45. To dispel these rumors, Foster took the duke's illegitimate child, Charlotte Williams, abroad and served as her nanny from December 1782 to June 1783. Foster had two children of her own by the duke: Caroline St. Jules was born on August 16, 1785 in Vietri, Italy, and Augustus William James Clifford was born in Rouen on May 26, 1788. The duke was nicknamed "Canis" for his love of dogs, the duchess "Rat" for reasons that have been forgotten, and Foster "Racky" because of her cough (Masters 95).

46. Lady Melbourne got along well with Elizabeth Foster, perhaps because they were both intelligent, capable, and practical (Stokes 147).

47. Grey's relationship with the king he served was complex and mediated by the amorous intrigues that always surrounded Devonshire House. On one occasion the Prince Regent visited the duchess of Devonshire and was not admitted. Preparing to leave, he saw Grey peering out her window. It is assumed that his lifelong dislike for Grey dates from that incident (Masters 191).

48. An anonymous source had already sent Lady Spencer a letter informing her of her daughter's affair.

49. A child, Lady Elizabeth Courtney, was born abroad in 1792 and brought up by Grey's parents. The duchess' close friendship with Grey continued well past 1794 to 1804 (45546-45549).

50. Privately, the prince wrote to his brother that the trade was advantageous, but that the house "is dirty and nasty, & the furniture so worn yt. it wd. be ridiculous of you to pretend to buy it, as they think it totally unfit to produce it any longer" (Aspinall 2:197).

51. Lord Melbourne mortgaged Melbourne House in 1775 for £8,000 and later for a further £2,000. These mortgages were never paid off and he was paying interest on them. Lord Melbourne received £23,571 for exchanging his house with that of the duke of York (Birkenhead 30).

52. Though the couples took possession of each other's homes on December 25, 1791, due to complicated legal arrangements York House only became known as Melbourne House, or Whitehall, on October 31, 1792 (Usher, *Owners* 4). Located between the Horse Guards and the Treasury Office, Whitehall is now named Dover House and functions as the Scottish Office (4). During the three years that it was owned by the duke of York, the structure was redecorated by Henry Holland, the Prince of Wales' architect at Carlton House. The "courtyard was converted into a huge, circular domed hall entered from a portico in Whitehall" (Birkenhead 31). John Yenn, architect of the King Mews, repaired and altered it when the Melbournes took possession, taking down the Old Lottery Office and erecting a coach house. The Melbournes settled into their new residence free of mortgages and with £10,000 in ready cash.

53. It was only after two years that the duke of Devonshire forgave his wife and permitted her to return to their estate at Chatsworth.

54. In December 1795 he was one of two bachelors attending the Prince of Wales on the occasion of his unhappy marriage to Princess Caroline of Brunswick.

55. Young was the author of *A General View of the Agriculture of Hertfordshire* (1804).

56. So successful a horse breeder was Lord Egremont that he won the Derby and Oaks five times, an honor shared only by Aga Khan.

57. Egremont purchased this painting in 1808.

58. He later served as M.P. for Hertfordshire (1802-5).

59. The "Grand Tour" on the continent was no longer possible because of Great Britain's battles with Napoleon in Italy and Austria (Airlie, *Palmerston* 13).

60. The Devonshires adopted their own peculiar method of pronunciation, which turned "Harriet" into "Harriot" (Masters 140).

61. "Lord Melbourne [was] not one of your stiff-laced moralising fathers, who preach chastity and forbearance to their children," Wilson remembered (Wilson 1:6).

62. The ministerial negotiation between Addington and Pitt.

63. In delivering a deathbed letter to the duchess of Gordon's daughter, Lord John (the duke of Bedford's younger brother), fell in love with her. In 1803 she was married after all, but it was to the sixth rather than the fifth duke of Bedford (Airlie, *Whig* 35).

64. Emily remembered "romping on the floor" at Brocket Hall with Harriet, "who had just snatched her cap off her head, when the door opened, and their mother came in accompanied by a gentleman [Sir Thomas Lawrence] in black, who was very kind, and said, 'Nothing can be better than that;' and he painted the little girls just as he had found them" (Boyle 322). In the painting, however, Emily still wears her hat (figure 42).

65. Henry Luttrell, Cowper's traveling companion at the time, was a more faithful correspondent. He wrote Lady Melbourne long letters about the dark theaters in Italy and the dirty hotels in southern France (November 24, 1802; 45548, f.106).

66. He amuses himself well enough with a pen. We will see how he amuses himself with a bayonet.

67. In December 1809, Gower married Lady Harriet Cavendish (Hary-O), the youngest daughter of the duke of Devonshire. Harriet's aunt, Lady Bessborough, had borne Gower two children and loved him "passionately for seventeen years," but agreed that, at the age of thirty-six, he should marry Hary-O (Surtees 11).

68. On July 30, 1789, after hearing of the taking of the Bastille, Fox wrote to his constant friend and companion, Richard Fitzpatrick: "How much the greatest event it is that ever happened in the world! and how much the best!" (*DNB* 7:547).

69. "She has taken coming to St. George's Church and talks to me of nothing but morality, the misery of being with people of bad character," Hary-O wrote of Emily (Lever 160). Lady Bessborough confirmed Hary-O's suspicions regarding Emily's hypocrisy. "[Emily] flatters Harriet violently to her face and takes every opportunity of cutting at her," she wrote to Lord Granville Leveson-Gower (December 1806; G. L. Gower 2:229).

70. The duke of Devonshire gave Mrs. Lamb a marriage portion of £20,000, together with an annuity of £500 for her and Lamb's joint lives (Thorne 4:354).

71. On March 17, 1808, a revolt was organized by the "Fernandista" faction. Godoy was dismissed and Charles IV's son, Ferdinand VII, was placed on the throne.

72. Overcoming several revolts, Napoleon placed his brother, Joseph, on the Spanish throne in 1808. British forces landed in Portugal on August 1, 1808, quickly achieving success. They conquered Lisbon and forced the French from Portugal on August 30, 1808. Wellington was victorious at the Battle of Talavera on July 27-28, 1809, but was soon forced to retreat into the country around Lisbon. He defeated Marshal Jean-Baptiste Jourdan at the Battle of Vitoria on June 21, 1813, and Ferdinand

VII resumed the throne in March 1814. The guest referred to as "Vernon" may be George Granville Venables Vernon.

73. Lady Ossulstone, née Corisande Sophie Leonice Helene Armandine.

74. "First, I am a tyrant; Second, I am a monster; All in all, I am the devil. Who am I?" Lady Melbourne asks. Lord Henry not only answers the question ("a husband"), but provides another riddle, suggesting how a woman might escape such tyranny through discreet extra-marital affairs. "What is it when a woman loves her first, doesn't dread her second, and all is utter bliss?" (translations courtesy of Professor Pascale-Anne Brault).

75. In *Don Juan*, Byron portrayed William Lamb as Lord Henry Amundeville, "a cold, good, honourable man" who lacked "soul" (14:70-71). No doubt, Byron's affair with Lamb's wife contributed to his jealous assessment of William's character. A club-footed impoverished aristocrat whose own political career had sputtered before being extinguished in the House of Lords, Byron was jealous of the "well / Proportioned" Lamb, who had more common-sense, if less brilliance, than Byron.

76. This decision to end the affair did not occur before one last embarrassing escapade. On August 13, 1812, Lord Melbourne faulted Caroline for her behavior with Lord Byron. She ran away, threatening to travel to Europe and never return. Pretending to be her brother, Byron found her and returned her to Whitehall. A four-way correspondence developed between Lady Melbourne, Lady Bessborough, Lord Byron, and Caroline Lamb.

77. Lady Spencer was the mother of Georgiana, duchess of Devonshire. The prince was infatuated with Georgiana in the 1780s, but they referred to each other in their letters as brother and sister.

78. William turned down the Prince Regent's offer of a position on the Board of Treasury as a matter of principle. On February 26, 1812, his father enclosed the spirited rejection with a note: "I very much lament that he [William] is so involved at present, by the line of politicks he has followed for so many years" (Aspinall, *Letters* 1:28). William worried that his father's reinstatement as lord of the bedchamber in March 1812 would make William appear to be more of a Tory than he was.

79. We have no evidence that Lady Melbourne read de Staël's works, although a copy of the publication that made her famous, *Letters on the Works and the Character of J. J. Rousseau* (1789), can still be found at Melbourne Hall, Derbyshire and was evidently owned by the family. On July 15, 1817, Emily Cowper wrote to say "I have been reading M de Stael's account of *L'Allemagne* again it is so exact and so true that I do not wonder they abuse her and are so angry at it" (45549, f.217). Napoleon had banned the book in France for being pro-German.

80. Annabella was aware of this criticism and remembered it specifically. She suspected that Lady Melbourne's influence inspired Byron "to correct me as a spoiled child" (Elwin, *Wife* 207, 264). On February 2, 1816, Judith Milbanke wrote to her husband, Sir Ralph: "I have further to add that Lady B. saw—Ld B. shewed it her—a letter from the Viscountess written to the Lord, in which are these Words, after speaking well of Lady B. She adds—'but She has always been used to have her own way and has been flattered into a high opinion of herself—but *You* must break her of *this and subdue her*'" (February 1, 1816; Elwin, *Wife* 387).

81. The country house in Hampshire belonging to Hanson, Byron's solicitor, was not available (November 6, 1814; *LJ* 4:230).

82. Biographers have mistakenly assumed that John Cam Hobhouse rented Byron's matrimonial home from Elizabeth, duchess of Devonshire (Marchand, *Portrait* 196), but Lady Melbourne selected the costly residence. "At Lady Melbourne's suggestion, Lord Byron took inconsiderately at a high rent, the Duchess of Devonshire's house in Piccadilly Terrace—far too large,—it has since been altered," Annabella remembered (Elwin, *Wife* 289). She wrote this in 1851, but failed to add that it was she who asked her aunt to find a house for them, telling Lady Melbourne that Byron desired "Space" (Elwin, *Wife* 289).

83. Byron was unable to sell his Rochdale estates or Newstead Abbey.

84. "So far from considering my own tastes," Annabella wrote to Augusta, "if I find that the disease is making a progress I will court Lady M[elbourne]'s Society for him, or any thing in the world to arrest its *fatal* course" (Elwin, *Wife* 323).

85. Judith Milbanke seemed to believe that "the Viscountess never forgave Annabella the involuntary Act of coming into the World—which injur'd her dearly beloved Brother & Nephew—and it has been a regular Wish to *injure* her ever since" (Elwin, *Wife* 387).

86. Mrs. George Lamb informed Annabella that "whatever she MAY have said, [Lady Melbourne] has *now* changed her tone" to conform with the winning side (April 8, 1816; Elwin, *Wife* 462).

87. Hary-O thought Lord Cowper "very inattentive" to his wife. "She says he loves her excessively but he is always away from her" (January 1806; *Hary-O* 148).

88. Named after William Almack (d. 1781), Almack's included the duke of Portland and Charles James Fox among its original twenty-seven members. The club still survives as Brooks'. Weekly subscription-balls were held for the first twelve weeks of each London season. Tickets were distributed at a price of 10 guineas by a committee of Lady patronesses—"a feminine oligarchy less in number but equal in power to the Venetian Council of Ten" (*DNB* 1:339).

89. This letter is not included in Aspinall's collection of the letters of George IV.

90. Melbourne held this position in 1784, before the Regent's allowance was restricted in 1795. His appointment as lord of the bedchamber was announced on March 10 and placed his Whig sons "in an uncomfortable situation." George Eden informed his father, Lord Auckland: "George Lamb told me of the appointment with much regret this morning, and at the same time let me know (in confidence) that he had written the fable of the 'Hare who abandoned his friends,'" which was published in the *Morning Chronicle* (Aspinall, *Letters* 1:28). In 1812 the prince was accused of abandoning his Whig friends because he would not replace his father's Tory ministers when he came to power as Regent.

91. For Viscount Melbourne's impatience concerning this appointment, after Lord Whitworth had been made a peer, see his letter to the Prince Regent (June 20, 1813; Aspinall, *Letters* 262).

92. Internal evidence and Airlie (*Palmerston* 14) suggest that this letter was written in January 1804. Frederick seemed to doubt that the Prince of Wales had as much power as he pretended. "He has not even the power of recalling me without applying through the Adjutant General's office to the Duke of York and I am not sure whether upon this subject a counter application from M[ackenzie] wouldn't carry it against him, so that I couldn't avail myself of this scheme if I wished it" (n.d.; HRO).

93. In 1818 Frederick sent six shawls to his mother, "one red for yourself because you're supposed to like it best, a yellow one for Ly Holland with my love . . . four others out of which you, Emily and the two Caros are to choose" (Strickland 106).

94. William Lamb represented Haddington Burghs (1806-7), Portarlington (1807-12), Peterborough (1816-19); Hertfordshire (November 29, 1819-26), Newport, Isle of Wight (April 24-29, 1827), and Bletchingley (May 7, 1827-July 22, 1828) (Torrens 5).

95. This is also evident in the caustic remarks of the duchess of Devonshire's daughter, Hary-O, regarding the Lamb family. "I saw William for a moment," Harry-O wrote. "He looked very ugly and was as cold to me as she was kind which, as I really do love her, and don't care a fig for him m'était a peu près égal" (*Hary-O* 118).

96. "As for the likeness, the picture can't be good—I did not sit long enough," Byron wrote of the novel to Thomas Moore (December 5, 1816; *LJ* 5:131). For the political context of *Glenarvon*, see articles by John Clubbe, "*Glenarvon* Revised—and Revisited," *Wordsworth Circle* 10 (1979): 205-17, and Malcolm Kelsall, "The Byronic Hero and Revolution in Ireland: The Politics of *Glenarvon*," *Byron Journal* 9 (1981): 4-19. Peter Graham discusses *Glenarvon* in relation to *Don Juan* in his important and illuminating study, *Don Juan and Regency England*, 104-8.

97. Mrs. Fitzherbert's secret marriage with the Prince of Wales took place on 1785 but was invalid under the Royal Marriages Act. When he married Caroline on April 8, 1795, she ceased to live with him, but resumed doing so on the advice of her confessor, who received his instructions from Rome. She and the Prince of Wales were continually short of money, and he began to see other women. Finally, at a dinner given to Louis XVIII at Carlton House, he instructed her to sit "according to her rank," without being recognized as his wife. She retired from the court on an annuity of £6,000 a year, but the prince remained attached to her until the end of his life, when he died with her portrait around his neck (*DNB* 7:171).

98. The present edition updates the important work of Airlie's *In Whig Society*. Airlie writes that "No letters from Lady Melbourne can be found after the year 1816" (196).

99. Henry Brougham was a vocal critic and Lamb's vote for a renewed suspension of habeas corpus on June 27, 1817 hurt his prospects. On February 17, 1818, William Lamb opposed an inquiry into unjust detentions on the part of the government, and Tierney and Grey questioned his loyalty to the opposition party. On June 2, 1818, he opposed Burdett's proposal for parliamentary reform. William's younger brothers, Frederick and George, were more liberal than he was (Thorne 4:364).

100. Croft was unjustly accused of endangering Princess Charlotte's life by not using a timely forceps delivery (Corbett 7).

101. Byron inserted six verses about Princess Charlotte in the fourth canto of *Childe Harold's Pilgrimage*. "The death of the Princess Charlotte has been a shock even here," Byron wrote to John Murray from Venice, "and must have been an earthquake at home" (December 3, 1817; *LJ* 5:276).

102. *The Aspern Papers* is loosely based on Byron's affair with Claire Clairmont, who survived long enough to have made an impression on Henry James. Byron had an affair with Clairmont or, to put it more precisely, she had one with him, and in 1816 he fathered a child, Allegra, by her (James, *The Aspern Papers*, introduction xi)

PART I

Georgiana's Rival, 1770–1804

ive years after she had arrived in London at the age of seventeen, Lady Melbourne won the confidence of Georgiana, duchess of Devonshire, one of the most important figures in Whig society. In a letter that opens this collection, Lady Melbourne informs Georgiana of some witty lines written in her honor, and dismisses the duke of Richmond's suggestion that they were "two rival queens" competing for the Prince of Wales' attention.

Other letters in this chapter allude to the threat of invasion by France in June 1780. A royal proclamation issued on July 9 commanded horses and cattle to be driven from the coasts. Citizens fled to the interior, increasing the panic. That same month, London was in the midst of the Gordon riots. On this occasion, Lady Melbourne agreed to look after the duke of Devonshire's illegitimate daughter, Charlotte Williams, until the danger had passed.

Lady Melbourne's affair with the Prince of Wales took place during the next five years. On July 10, 1795, the prince was forced to terminate her husband's position as lord of the bedchamber when he found his allowance restricted by Parliament. She promised him her husband would work without compensation.

Lady Melbourne's intimacy with Carlton House and Whig society contrasts strikingly with Judith Milbanke's more parochial lifestyle at Seaham. The two women had a falling out after the birth of William Lamb in 1779, when Lady Melbourne's affair with the third earl of Egremont became public knowledge (Elwin, *Wife* 53). After that point, visits between the two practically ceased. While Judith Milbanke accused her sister-in-law of observing only "the appearance of civility" (Elwin, *Wife* 54), Lady Melbourne faulted Judith for thwarting her brother Ralph's political success. When he was elected to Parliament in 1791, Ralph Milbanke was anxious to make use of his sister's political connections and complained about the coolness that had developed between the two women. Lady Melbourne denied the charge in a masterful letter written from Brocket Hall.[1]

In 1799 Lady Melbourne's younger brother John, who had been architect and contractor of His Majesty's Works, was on his deathbed. His son, afterwards Sir John Milbanke, seventh baronet, had married Eleanor, the daughter of Julius Hering. The couple was in debt and Lady Melbourne took it upon herself to extricate her nephew from difficult circumstances (Airlie, *Whig* 17).

Throughout her life, Lady Melbourne took the part of indigent women who had few other courts of appeal. She was sympathetic but never sentimental. When her housekeeper, Mrs. Guidon, died, she wrote to Guidon's friend describing it as a "happy release" in one sentence, and replaced her with Mrs. Howe in the next (September 23, 1801). Her business acumen is shown by her interest in the successful construction of a waterway, the Cromford Canal, which connected Hertfordshire to businesses in the surrounding countryside. Lord Melbourne's name appears on the list of subscribers. His wife may have discussed the subject with Lord Egremont, who invested in canals throughout his life.[2]

Lady Melbourne maintained her estate in Derbyshire in a manner that betrays her knowledge of agriculture. She kept an eye out for poachers, particularly a notorious man named Jackson who was in Derby jail, and instructed her warden, Henry Fox, to thin the trees every two or three years in order to reap a profit while maintaining the timber. Sixty years later, the house would be occupied by two Victorian prime ministers: Lord Melbourne, her son, and Lord Palmerston, who married her daughter Emily.

Lady Melbourne to the duchess of Devonshire (Chatsworth 136.1)
Aug. 1776

Je veux vous écrire ma charmante Amie, pour vous remercier du petit mot que vous m'avez envoyé et pour vous rappeller la promesse que vous m'avez faite de m'écrire au plutot.[3] I have been in Town again with M^rs. Damer.[4] She is better & is gone to Park place.[5] She intends living this Year with L^y Alisbury[6] as by that she will have it in her power to pay some of M^r. Damers Debts which she wishes much to do, & the more so as Ld Milton[7] has refused to contribute any thing towards Satisfying any of the Creditors. The D^k. of Richmond[8] came to her & Staid a Week with her in Town which [was] of great use to her for you can not immagine how low Spirited she has been. If ever I found her alone I was certain to find her Crying; but I hope she will be better now as she has changed the Scene, for her own House was certainly ye worst place she could be at. I hear Ld Edward[9] left you with an intention of going to York Races but that he only dined in ye Town & went on directly which affronted ye people there very much. I have been seeing Madame de Seymour,[10] & she has been here; She is very Big with Child & complains much qu'elle est si lourde que ca l'empeche de profiter de son voisinage autant qu'elle le voudrait,[11] I am sorry too for I like her vastly; I hear L^y Harris[12] goes to Newmarket next Tuesday & that they stay there almost all ye Month, we are to be at S^r. Charles Bunbury's just before the first October meeting. I have some Idea you are to be at Newmarket then pray write me word if it is so because I will endeavour to per-suade L^d M[elbourne] to Stay there till that time; If you was inclined to be compas-sionate you would come to S^r. C[harles] B[unbury's] too for you know how happy it would make him.

I hear L^d & L^y Spencer[13] & all the Party I saw at Brighthelmstone[14] went afterwards to Portsmouth & I had an Uncle[15] there & they went on Board his Ship[.] [H]e came here a few Days ago & complained that there came a whole Boat full & that he did not know the name of any one of them & Baron C- distressed him par-ticularly for he asked him what War the Sailors wished for & as he did not know where he came from he was affraid of telling him, for fear he should hit upon his own Country———.

Ecrivez moi au plutot je vous en prie, adieu ma chere Duchesse.[16]

Lady Melbourne to the duchess of Devonshire (Chatsworth 401.1)

1780

If you want news my D^r D^ch I must send you a list of all ye people y^t are sick, for y^t is ye only News in town & unless you have ye same disorder going about at Bath, I advise you & ye Duke to remain there till this Vile Nasty influenza eases. People are seized with a violent pain in their Bones, violent Head Ach's & some have a good deal of fever. L^d M[elbourne] is at present quite ill & nobody escapes. I have a cold in my head which I am told is a beginning but I dont intend to have it any worse tho' it might perhaps be an advantage to me as it would take off some of my Fat. I am told by some people y^t. I shall be as big as L^y Powis, & by others y^t nobody is so fat except M^rs S^t. John.[17] All these speeches come from Men as ye Women say they dont see it by way of encouraging me I suppose to eat & drink heartily y^t. I may grow still fatter—Powis told me this Mor^g y^t I looked like a Rose. What idea does y^t Speech from her to me give you of my looks. <Piste> has just been to see me. She look'd sick but vastly pretty & was very gracious. The D^e of Richmond has also been here & told me you & I were two rival queens, & I believe if there had not been some people in ye room who might have thought it odd y^t I should have Slap'd his Face for having such an idea & he wish'd me joy of having ye P[rince]. to myself.[18] [H]ow odious people are, upon my life I have not patience with y^m. I believe you & I are very different from all ye rest of ye World as from their ideas they would do such strange things in certain situations or they never could suspect us in ye way they do—you will perceive y^t I am not in ye best of humours, adieu my Dr Love

[P.S.] Since I wrote this I have got y^r Letter—and will do what you desire.[19]

Lady Melbourne to the duchess of Devonshire (Chatsworth 304.1)

27th June

[1780]

My Dearest Duchess

      I wish you was here just to see the Bustle People are in every Body thinking it incumbent upon them to go & fight immediately tho' there is yet nothing to fight, every Creature is going into ye Militia[,] even Mr. Meynell[20] has offered his Services. There is a Bill brought into ye House of Commons which it is thought will pass to Double the Militia in Every County.[21] Ld Spencer has help'd very much to increase this Spirit by writing word to Ld Clermont[22] yt he could get no Horses as they were all employ'd upon ye Brest Road. This occasion'd many Conjectures, which only serv'd to prove to every Body that it was necessary for them to put on a Red Coat directly[23]—however I hear few certain that Sr Charles Hardy[24] has fighting orders so I hope ye beating of ye French fleet will put an end to all this Fuss. The two generals yt are to eat us up are Monsr de Vaux & Monsieur de Beauvaux.[25] There were some ridiculous verses made upon you by ye Chevalier de Boufless[26] which I will write in case you don't know them. Si Monsr de Vaux, etait un peu plus Beau, et Monsr de Beauvaux un peu moins beau, Monsr. de Vaux, serait un beau veau, et Monsr de Beauvaux, ne serait qu'un Veau.[27] If Lady Clermont should be with you tell her there is some good News come from Virginia such as an expedition there having succeeded in destroying a great many Stores, sent from France & two Ships, & taking a quantity of Tobacco—mind this is for Nobody but her.— Mrs. Damer is gone to day to Park Place.[28] She desired I would tell you yt. I have been going on in a strange way which she will tell you when she sees you as it can not be explained by Letter. She says Mr. G had better have taken some agreeable wall for confidant as yt would have told him as much & heard him as well as ye person he has chose—Ld Malde<ar>[29] is trying to marry Ldy Betty Compton,[30] he is with her every where. I dont know whether he has any chance of succeeding, perhaps yt. may prevent him going to Spa. The Duke of Rutland[31] has offered to raise a Regiment & so has Ld. Derby,[32] the offers are not yet accepted but it keeps you in Town. We are likely to have much company here all ye Summer as ye Parliament is not to be prorogued only adjourned, till things are more decided that is till our fleet has brought in some Spanish & French Ships—adieu my Dearest Duchess, I shall write to you very often whether you write to me or not. Ld Carlisle[33] has resign'd his Place which he says he always intended to do at ye End of ye Sessions as he did not think it a proper place for him. Parise has got a Swelled Face. Ld Sefton is going into ye Militia & she is sure she never shall be able to Live in Camp—I have Spoke but once to Roland since you went, he has look'd vastly Cross & goes on as usual. M^r. Lowther[34] has told me over & over again how miserable he is that his Father won't let him go abroad this Summer. I long to hear from you.

Lady Melbourne to Henry Fox (Melbourne 234/3/40)

London Decr. 28th
1781

Mr. Fox

    I beg you will hire me a Dairy Maid as soon as you can as I am obli^d. to part with Ruth, she has Eight p^ds a Y^r. & her Board Wages when we are away but If you can I had rather you would hire one for less than that with a promise of increasing her Wages if she behaves well, but not to more than Eight p^d p^r Year—I wish her to understand a Dairy, & not to be afraid of Work as she must also help ye Confectioner in the House, & when we are away help ye Housemaid who is left to take care of the House. I should like her ye better if she can Cook a few plain things as we want them to dress our Dinner sometimes when we go down for a day with-out any Family—all this Ruth did—as soon as you can get me one I wish you to send her to Brocket Hall as we shall be distress'd till we get one—

    I hope you continue to have y^r Health well and I am y^r Friend

Eliz. Melbourne

Lady Melbourne to Henry Fox (Melbourne 234/4/1)
[February 28, 1786]

M^r. Fox—

I inclose you a bill of M^r. Trafford's which I beg you will pay, & I beg that you will also pay M^r. Evans Marble Mason at Derby, 4:5 L s for some Egg Cups he sent us & 1:16 Ls or 1:18 Ls (I am not sure which) for a Vase he sent the Duke of Richmond & which he will pay me for, when I receive the account from you. I shall also be much obliged to you if you enquire of Mrs Phillips at ye Kings Head what I am indebted to her for some Beef she sent me, & pay her—& charge all this to Lord Melbournes Account.

Lord Melbourne desires me to tell you that he wishes to make a present to a Gentleman of a Hogshead of Burton Ale, and he begs you will buy one of ye Age that will come soonest into Drinking Order, after coming to London & y^t you will send it by ye safest & quickest conveyance to Melbourne House—he begs it may be the best that can be got—I hope you have finer Weather at Melbourne than we have here for the Snow is laying a very great thickness.

I am
Y^r. Obliged Serv't
EMelbourne

Brocket Hall
Feb^ry 28th 1786

Cap^n Milbanke has given L^d M[elbourne] the Money for his Bill so you will be so good to pay it with ours.

[Hatfield Feb Twenty Eighth 1786/Mr Fox/Melbourne/Derby Melbourne/stamped "free"]

Lady Melbourne to the duchess of Devonshire (Chatsworth 753)

July 24, 1786

My Dearest D^ss

There has been a report for this last Week about L^y D[uncannon]^35 which I would not write you word about as I was in hopes it would not have gain'd credit, but as I find it has in a most Surprizing manner I think I had better venture to make you a little uneasy, than run ye chance of y^r. not knowing it, & being by y^t. prevented from taking any method of checking it, especially as I think it probable you may know something about it. There have been some paragraphs in ye News papers^36 to say she was gone off but as there were as I thought no Name or Initials I was in hopes it would not be known who was meant, which indeed I did not know myself till March told me there was such a report, but I determined not to mention it to any Creature thinking y^t even saying how ill natur'd it was would only propagate it ye more.

Yesterday M^r. Grenville^37 came to me to ask me if I ^heard it &^ had mentioned it to you as he met L^y Beauchamp^38 coming to Town who ask'd him ye News in a very curious manner which he did not understand till Ld Wm Gordon told him y^t she actually believed it & did not enquire of them whether it was true but how it happened &c—we consulted whether we should write you word but decided not as we were in hopes this might only be known in y^t Set which were not undeceived, but last Night I received ye inclosed Note^39 (which you may be sure I answered immediately) & that has determined me to let you know it in case you might think it better for her to come & show herself.

There will be a good many people in Town & ^this Week^ I fancy he will be at Lewes Races^40 as they begin Thursday, but this I dont know. I am sure y^t nobody can have been in Town for these last Ten days without meeting him at every place & in every Street, which makes me so vastly Surprized at people believing it. Ld W. told Grenville y^t L^y B[eauchamp]^41 had seen some Newspaper in which his Name was mentioned. This I did not see. L^y Fairford is to be presented Thursday & all ye Talbots Essex & c. come which will fill ye Town. I am to have a party Thursday for him & shall ask every body I can pick up. [I]f you think she had best come she might be seen there & I will ask or not ask any Body you please—if you dont intend to do anything you had better not tell her as it will make her so unhappy. God bless you my Dr Duchess

Sunday Morning —

Lady Melbourne to Henry Fox (Melbourne 234/4/14)
[July 16, 1787]

Mr. Fox—

I beg you will get me Twelve papers of Powders for Cows that have the Red water of the Man who lives as you go upon the Common & makes Basketts. I don't know his name but I bought some of him last time I was at Melbourne—which have answer'd extremely well. I am

your Friend.

EMelbourne

if these Powders are too heavy to be sent in Letters, you may send them by ye man who will be sent from here with some Hounds in a Week or Ten days and will bring back those you have at Melbourne—Ld Melbourne will let you know in time to get the Puppies in four Weeks.

I beg you will bespeak me two Dozen pair of Cotton stockings of Mr. Trafford exactly the same Size as the last he sent me at four Shillings a pair[.] [Y]ou may send them at the same time—

July ye 16th
desire Mrs Guidon to make sweetmeats of the fruit in the Garden. I wish she would dry some Bunches of Currants
[Hatfield on July Seventeenth 1787/Mr. Fox/Melbourne near Derby/ Melbourne, stamped "free"]

Lord Melbourne to Henry Fox (Melbourne 234/4/33)

[February 21, 1790]

M^r. Fox

I am sorry to find by a Gentleman who call'd upon me in Town, that M^rs. Dale of Bakewell is much distress'd by the notice given her to leave her House—he says she has lived there Forty Y^rs & has no Subsistence but from the school she keeps. I think she might very well spare the Ground to M^r. Taylor, & be allowed to keep the House & Garden. I desire you would inquire about this without loss of time because tho' I wish to Serve Mr. Taylor I have no intention to use M^rs. Dale ill.

I am sorry to inform you M^r. Hill is dead therefore I can give no directions at present, but upon any thing that occurs you must send to me in London—

Melbourne[42]

Brocket Hall
      21st Feb^ry.
            1790

[Hatfield Feb Twenty One 1790/Mr Fox/Melbourne/Derby/<u>Melbourne</u>]

Lady Melbourne to Charles Burney (Yale, Osborn 50, f.93)

[post 1791]

Lady Melbournes compliments to Doctor Burney she sent a note to Chelsea this month—to inform him that the Prince of Wales has settled to dine at Whitehall on Tuesday next & that she & L^d. Melbourne hope for the honor of his company & Doctor Charles Burney's—his Servant was told he was gone to Hampstead for the whole day, & she therefore sends this note, as she supposes from the conversation she had last Night with Doct. Burney that he wish'd to know as soon as possible what was the Princes determination, & she also thinks he said he should see Doct[or] C[harle]^s Burney to day, to whom L^y Melbourne begs he will make her excuses for not sending him a particular invitation, which she should have done if Doct[or] Burney had not obligingly undertaken to mention the Party to him——— Saturday

[<2d Sept?>]

———————————

Lady Melbourne to Ralph Milbanke (Lovelace 11, f.88; Elwin, Wife *53-54)*
[March 20, 1791]

My Dr Brother

      I have not answered y^r last Letter sooner because I was in hopes that by giving you a little more time to consider you would find out that neither you or M^ss Milbanke can have ye least reason for being out of humour with me as differing in opinion only can not justify either side for being so—& I only write now that you may fully understand that I am determined not to dispute or quarrel with either of you about any thing that has past, as I should think myself extremely absurd if I did, & as I know that there has been no Coldness on my part or the most distant intention to show either of you any Slight. I feel that I am just as good friends with both of you as I ever have been & if you are not the same it is not my fault.

                  I am y^r most affec^te Sister
                  EMelbourne

Brocket Hall
March 20th

[Ralph Milbanke Esq./Wimpole Street/London]

Judith Milbanke to Lady Melbourne (Elwin, Wife 54-5)

[1791]

Milbanke introduced the Subject on which he wrote by saying he was sorry to have observed *a coolness* between You and me. As You might *imagine* I continued ignorant of the groundless suspicions which were entertained in regard to my conduct, and I readily allow nothing in your outward manner to me gave room for the Assertion. But your disapprobation of things you have *supposed* or been *informed* I was capable of has been too frequently expressed and too strongly marked for it not from *various quarters* to have come round to my knowledge . . . had You under these impressions taxed me openly and upbraided me ever so warmly, it could not have hurt me like the insinuations you have dropped to *others* . . . whilst to my face you observed the appearance of civility if not even friendship. To a mind of the least sensibility it became almost impossible to acquiesce in Silence to such conduct, I acknowledge my temper is too warm and my heart too sincere, to submit to it, being extremely hurt by it, being conscious I have never deserved to incur such suspicions or merit such treatment. In the common intercourse of the World it is idle and foolish to regard what is said by people indifferent to one, but with my Husband[']s family, especially with a Sister he loves, it becomes more interesting & I have longed for nothing more ardently than to come to an explanation with you regarding certain points in which I could have convinced you . . . You say You cannot even guess at any reasons I may have for coldness on my Side— do you think it *none* to be perpetually hinted at as wishing to deter Milbanke from doing what is right? *none* as being the Person who advises measures that You deem unjust? *none* as supposing it necessary to exclude me from every consultation to induce Milbanke to do what is kind by his family? Ask your own heart whether You should not be wounded by such insinuations in regard to yourself from any of Lord Melbournes family or friends . . . I have suppressed resentment on various occasions which would fully have justified me shewing it, but it has been the Interest of *some* to deceive you . . . ever since I married it has been my sincere wish to conciliate the good opinion of Mr. Milbanke's family & perhaps to that wish I have sacrificed too much. I have every reason to believe these endeavours have not met with the Success permit me say they meritted. Nothing however shall deter me from persevering in what I deem just & right and if I meet with no other return the consciousness of doing so must be my reward. No other return have I *yet* met with.

I must now request of You that if You either believe or have been informed of any thing that appears to you reprehensible in my Conduct in regard to any family transaction that You will fairly and openly avow it . . . After a forbearance of some years under Circumstances I cannot but think injurious you may wonder at my coming forwards in this open manner but there is a point in every thing which turns the Scale . . . I need hardly say it will give me the truest pleasure to find *myself mistaken* in regard to your Ideas about me, because it is very unpleasant to be thought so unjustly of.

Lady Melbourne to Lady Milbanke (Lovelace 11, f.101)

30th July [1805][43]

Dear L^y Milbanke -

I received this Mor^g a Letter from Mr. Russell enclosing the one I send you—which she had desired me to shew you—You will see it is not entirely Mr Nelson who objected to the House at Halnaby, but I wonder M^r. <Davison>[44] had not express'd himself to this purpose sooner, as it is now so near ye Assizes[.] how odd that he should say he had not heard from you when you have written repeatedly on the Subject. I am very sorry to trouble you about it, as I know how you must be plagued by them—& I see that your Servants like every other persons always add to it & that is the case with <Davison> who does not like to let these poor people make a House which he thinks he has a right to himself, & I have no doubt has been urging them to make objections, in hopes to throw the blame upon them whilst it has been all of his Suggesting—

I shall be happy to hear that you have not suffer'd from y^r Journey pray give my love to my Bro^r & <hence> & believe me

Very aff^ly y^rs

EM

News is anxiously expected from Ld Wellington—

Lady Melbourne to Henry Fox (Melbourne 234/4/34)

[February 15, 1793]

M^r. Fox—

Lord Melbourne desires me to tell you y^t as he has given up his seat in Parl^t. to M^r. Lamb,[45] & believes you had a News paper sent you directed to him at Melbourne—you will be pleased to order the person who sends it to you in future to direct it to M^r. Lamb—

L^d M[elbourne] desires that ye Letters you send him may in future be inclosed & directed to M^r. Lamb, Melbourne House, Whitehall London[.] [W]rite L^d. Melbourne word what days you send us up rents this Spring, & from what places & he will send you franks[46] for that purpose.

Y^r friend,
EMelbourne

Brocket Hall
Feb^ry. 15, 1793

[Hatfield Feby Fifteen 93/Mr Fox/Melbourne near Derby/Free <u>PLamb</u>; stamped "free"]

Viscountess Melbourne to the Prince of Wales (Aspinall, Correspondence 3:75)

Brocket Hall, 10 July 1795

Lord Melbourne not being able to write himself, hopes your Royal Highness will excuse his taking the liberty to employ me to address a few lines to your Royal Highness. He has seen with much concern the resolutions of Parlia^t. which have caused the necessity of the arrangements you have now made, and it is with the greatest regret he is obliged to relinquish a situation he has held for so many years with so much satisfaction, as it procured him constant opportunities of paying his respects to your Royal Highness & more frequent occasions of showing his sincere attachment to your personal service than can he presumes be now allow'd him when he is removed from it.[47]

He desires me with his duty to offer his attendance & services if at any time they can be agreable to your Royal Highness, without any other consideration than the pleasure he shall receive from being useful to your Royal Highness. He begs leave to add that he shall ever remember with extreme gratitude the unvaried friendship & kindness you have shown him ever since the time he first had the honor of belonging to your Royal Highness's family, & feels particularly obliged for the earnestness with which you endeavoured a few months ago to procure him an object for which he must ever be anxious, for the sake of his family, for whom he begs to claim your protection & hopes that by their conduct, at some future day they may merit your Royal Highnesses favour. Ld M. is sensible that by this he takes the liberty of ad[d]ressing your Royal Highness in the free & friendly way you have so long allow'd him, & he hopes he shall not be consider'd as presuming too much if he endeavours to pay his respects to you sometimes at Carlton House.

After all L^d. Melbourne's form is over I hope you will allow me to say simply how sorry I have been for all the arrangments made by Par^t as I always shall be for anything that diminishes your happiness & comfort.

Lady Melbourne to an Unknown Creditor (45548, f.100-1; Airlie, *Whig* 15)

[1799]

Sir

I have to apologize for the liberty I take in addressing you, but as the comfort of a near Relation of yours is so much concerned I hope I need make no further excuses, & should only observe that the bad state of my Brother John Milbanke's health[48] which renders him unable to attend to any business, is the reason of my interfering upon a Subject which would have come more properly from him—I am afraid my Nephew Cap^n. Milbanke has not been so explicit as he ought respecting his affairs to you Sir, & to M^{rs}. Milbankes other Relations; for if he had I feel convinced you would have seen the necessity of making some provision, for the pay^t of his debts, & would have advised him accordingly—or had his Relations known y^t his Marriage was to have taken place so soon some arrangement of that sort would have been proposed by them, for tho' they were unacquainted with ye extent of his debts, yet we knew it was impossible he should not have some, from the very small income his Father could give him, & from his situation in his profession which must lead him into great expenses; at the same time I must say that I can not accuse him of any great extravagance, but he seems to have fall'n into bad Hands, & of course to have obtained money on very exorbitant Terms, & I must own y^t considering all these circumstances I am surprised his debts do not amount to a larger Sum—his conduct in not explaining his Situation more fully can only be attributed to the embarassment a Young Man naturally feels in confessing his imprudences, as he might have settled his affairs with more facility previous to his Marriage than he can now.

I have no doubt in my own Mind that were he once clear of debt, his future conduct would be prudent, & that having suffered so much distress & difficulty, a lesson would be imprinted, which he could not easily forget—it is under this conviction that I venture to apply to you—as I think it may be in your power to assist him materially & I do not see how he can in any other way extricate himself even from his present difficultys which press upon him daily, & which distress him the more as they must involve M^{rs}. Milbankes happiness by wounding her feelings—& from her amiable Character, I feel highly interested in her Welfare & most sincerely hope they may be happy—from a variety of causes, relating to Family affairs which it would at present be unnecessary & tedious to enumerate, but which I have not ye least objection to relate to you, if I have the honor of seeing you, my B^r has it not in his power to assist him which he certainly would wish to do if he could—for if he has appear'd averse to his marriage it has not been from ye least want of affection or from any ^other^ reason, but from a consciousness of his inability to make his situation comfortable. I understand you are Trustee for M^{rs}.

84

Milbanke & that her fortune of 2,000 ^L^ is settled upon her—if you would consent to call in a Thousand p^d- of it, & it could be stated in what time it might be raised I should hope that sum might be borrowed on reasonable terms ^till the time of pay^t^—& as he has 500 p^d. at his Father's Death which is not settled, & secured to him by his Mothers will; & another 500 secured also—by his Father these two Sums might be settled upon Mrs Milbanke in lieu of 1000 of her fortune which would be paid to him—This would I think relieve him effectually, & you must be sensible that nothing except being clear of debt can enable M^rs. M[ilbanke] & him to live upon their present small income and that any calls for Money to pay off old Debts must, not only be of ye greatest present distress, but also of the Worst consequences ultimately.

My anxiety for my Nephew & my wish to explain his situation clearly & fully to you, are my reasons for having presumed to trouble you with so long a letter, which I trust you will have the goodness to forgive.

I am,

Sir,

your most obe^t.

& most Hum^ble Sert.

Eliz. Melbourne

Whitehall

Lady Melbourne to Henry Fox (Melbourne 234/4/38)

Whitehall

23^d Sep^r, 1801

M^r. Fox

Ld Melbourne has rec'd y^r Letter acquainting him with the death of M^rs. Guidon,[49] which in her melancholy Situation was to be expected & must be look'd upon as a happy release, altho' it is impossible not to feel great regret for the loss of so worthy a Woman. L^d M[elbourne] desires you will tell Mrs Howe that he shall be very glad to have her in M^rs. Guidons place, & will take her on the same Terms, &

we shall be perfectly satisfied if she keeps every thing exactly in the same way as M^rs. Guidon did, as she can do no better.

I am Y^r Friend
EMelbourne

[Mr Fox/Melbourne/Derby/23^d Septr 1801]

Lady Melbourne to Mr. Fox (Melbourne 234/4/90)

[October 11, 1801]

Mr Fox—

Lord Melbourne received your Letter, & desires one Hundred P^ds may be taken out of the Melbourne rents, & paid on Acc^t to the Workmen employed about Mr Briggs House, in such proportions as you may think proper—the remainder shall be paid out of some of the other rents, which he will let you know in time— Mr Banton's sallary for 1/2 a Year, due to Christmas rents, he would have you pay to what ever person of his family who may have the power to receive it, to the day of his death. L^d. Melboune is anxious to know in what Situation his Wife & family are left, as he shall interest himself very much to see them in a comfortable situation and he desires that you would take his Son with you to all the rent days this Autumn in the way he has been accustom'd to go with you when Burton was prevented by illness—Hassard[50] having occasion to Melbourne on his own business. L^d M had sent you this Message by him, & has desired him to remain there till the rents are received, to bring the portion of them with him, which you would otherwise have sent by the post—

I am y^r Friend
EMelbourne

11th Oc^r 1801
[M^r. Fox/Melbourne/near/Derby/stamped "Wobourn 42"]

Lady Melbourne to Henry Fox (Melbourne 234/4/47)

[January 21, 1802]

Mr. Fox—

You left Ld Melbourne a list of the rent days, as they have been sign'd late-ly—but he wishes you to send him a list of the manner in which you proposed they should be received at home allowing a fortnight to intervene as you men-tioned at Brocket Hall—Ld Melbourne desires you will send this list immediately as he wishes to have it to consider about.

Ld Melbourne encloses you a Letter he has received from Mr. Jackson—he desires you will make all the inquiry you can about the circumstances mention'd in it, & thinks you had better see Mr. Upton about it & consult with him whether some information might not be obtain'd from Page who Mr. Jackson says is in Derby gaol—Mr. Lamb thinks this is the Man who is a notorious Poacher & used to go out at Melbourne with his face black'd & once pointed his gun at Young Bowman. Ld M[elbourne] also desires yt Mr. Upton may be applied to whenever proper information can be laid before him to prosecute any Men who are known to be poachers, in the most effectual manner as it seems they are too powerfull & determined to be deterr'd in any other Manner.

I am yr Friend
EMelbourne

21st. Janry 1802

Lady Melbourne to Henry Fox (Melbourne 234/4/49)

[February 15, 1802]

Mr. Fox

as Ld Melbourne has given Ld & Ldy Tamworth leave to pass a Short time at Melbourne—I beg you will give Mrs Howe directions to get the rooms air'd below Stairs & the Bedchamber that she thinks will be the most comfortable for them, and tell her that I hope she will be attentive to them & do all she can for them. I dont know what Servants they will bring but I suppose not many—& I assume they will keep themselves—but I shall be obliged to you to give them every assistance as to the best method of procuring what they may want—

Your Friend
EMelbourne

They are now at Kedleston, & I have desired them to write to you or M^{ss} Howe when they mean to come, but I would have her get the House in readiness directly.

[Mr Fox/Melbourne/Derby/Fe^{ry} 15, 1802]

Lady Melbourne to Henry Fox (Melbourne 234/4/59)

Augst 13th 1802

M^r. Fox,

     Ld Melbourne desires me to tell you that something should be done to the House, before the Winter & therefore wishes you to go over to Derby to the person who you employ'd before & ask whether he does not think that by taking up some of the Stucco floors in the Garrets, the Timbers might be inspected & the place where the damage is ascertained—by which means he might be able to decide whether it would be necessary to take off the roof—if he agrees to this you might fin[d] a day for him to come over and have the Stucco broke up, ready for him to examine, & let us know the result, and what his opinion is. I shall write to L^{dy} Tamworth to acquaint them that we are now going to begin upon the House, & L^d M[elbourne] begs you will give this business as much despatch as you can.

Your Friend
EMelbourne

[Brighton Aug. Thirteen/1802/M^r. Fox/Melbourne/Mr. Lucan/Derby]

Lady Melbourne to Henry Fox (Melbourne 234/4/62)

[October 2, 1802]

M[r]. Fox

L[d] M received the second parcel of Bank notes safe, & desires me to say y[t] he has given directions to M[r]. Cookney to answer y[r] Letters respecting y[e] interest in y[e] Cromford Canal[51]—L[d] M[elbourne] is very glad y[e] Architect thinks the House at Melbourne can be repaired without y[e] trouble & expence of unroofing, & desires y[t] you will prepare the Materials so y[t] it may be set about early in the Spring if <foreign> should be thought necessary. L[d] M[elbourne] conceives it may easily be procured by Water carriage without much expence.—L[d] M[elbourne]- says you did very right to keep y[e] 50 L for the build[s] at Mr. Brigg's.—

L[d] M[elbourne] desires you will inform M[r]. Billiston, that he is satisfied with his opinion, so y[t] he has given you orders to consult with him, & make the necessary preparations, under his direction, for the repairs, & hope when once they are begun y[t] he will forward them as expeditiously as possible, & hopes they will be done with in the cheapest manner———

I am yr H[ble] Serv[t]
EMelbourne

Whitehall
2[d] Oc[t]. 1802

Lady Melbourne to Lady Holland (Airlie, Whig *71-72)*

October 15, 1802

William will be very much flatter'd by your remembrance, he is still in Scotland, & I hope at this time at L[d] Lauderdales on his way Home. His intention is to put himself immediately under a Special Pleader, & to study from morn[g] till night for a year—which is not a very agreeable prospect tho' it may turn out very useful. I am extremely obliged to you for thinking of my young men & for all y[r] kindness to them, & altho' I have ye highest opinion of y^r skill yet I believe even you would find bringing them to what is call'd polish a very arduous undertaking.

Lady Melbourne to Henry Fox (Melbourne 234/5/20)

Whitehall

Dec'r ye 5th 1804

M^r. Fox,

     Ld Melbourne has desired me to write to you about the plantations at Melbourne which have been represented to him in such a state as not only to destroy all cover but also to be very hurtfull to the Trees—& all for want of management & being properly thin'd—as this is the time of Year to mark the Trees he desires you will go thro them with Bowman & let them be thinn'd—& then the other Trees will Shine & those cut down will Shoot again—there should ^not^ be too many cut down at once, but they should be gone thro, regularly every two or three y^{rs} at farthest—& Ld Melbourne prefers this method very much to that of cutting down a portion of the Wood entirely for tho' that may improve the Cover yet it destroys the Timber Trees—& we know from the Woods in Hertfordshire that it is very possible to have both.—

     L^d M[elbourne] will be very glad when you come at Christmas to have some conversation with you respecting the woods in Notting^{he} which Mr Lamb says do not do at all where they have been new planted—Mr Lamb is much surprized to hear that the Plantation he order'd upon the Commons when last at Melbourne has not been completed & that one Side is not yet fenc'd, which must have been very hurtful to the Trees that were planted. I have the pleasure to inform you M^r. Lamb is much better and will I hope be out of his room in another fortnight. I am

Y^r H^{ble} Servt

EMelbourne

[London Dec. five 1804/Mr. Fox/Melbourne near/Derby/P. Lamb]

Notes: Part I

1. "You say You cannot even guess at any reasons I may have for coldness on my Side," Judith wrote back defensively. "Do you think it *none* to be perpetually hinted at as wishing to deter Milbanke from doing what is right?" (Elwin, *Wife* 54).

2. In 1789 Sir Richard Arkwright took a leading role in raising funds for the Cromford Canal, which cost about £79,000. Benjamin Outram was the engineer. The canal facilitated transportation to iron-works, collieries, and limestone quarries on the line, as well as to the textile mills at Cromford. It aided in carrying coal and other necessary commodities into a very rural area and, like the Oakham Canal into Rutland, could not expect a large trade (Hadfield, *Canal Age,* 78). The canal contributed to poaching from boats moored for the night.

3. I want to write to you my charming friend, to return the small note you sent me and to remind you of your promise to write to me right away.

4. Anne Seymour Damer's husband, John, shot himself on August 15, 1776, leaving her in debt. She became a sculptress and a close friend of Lady Melbourne's (*DNB* 5:450).

5. Park Place was the seat of General Conway, Mrs. Damer's father (Walpole 25:576, n.4).

6. Anne Damer's mother, Lady Caroline Campbell, married Charles Bruce, third earl of Ailesbury (also spelled Alisbury and Aylesbury) in 1739.

7. Joseph Damer, Lord Milton, afterwards earl of Dorchester, was the father of Mrs. Damer's husband.

8. Charles Lennox, third duke of Richmond and Lennox, was Anne Damer's brother-in-law. He married Lady Mary Bruce, daughter of Lady Ailesbury and half-sister of Mrs. Damer (Walpole 25:576, n.9).

9. Lord Edward, duke of Kent.

10. Lady Horatia Seymour, wife of Lord Hugh Seymour, whose daughter Minnie was adopted by Mrs. Fitzherbert in 1800.

11. That she is so heavy that it stops her from visiting as much as she would like.

12. Wife of James Harris, Lord Malmesbury (Priestley 31, 122).

13. The parents of Georgiana Spencer, duchess of Devonshire.

14. Another name for Brighton.

15. Admiral Mark Milbanke.

16. Write to me as soon as you can I pray you, goodbye my dear duchess.

17. Barbara St. John, the daughter of Colonel Bladen and the sister of the countess of Essex.

18. This letter shows that Lady Melbourne's close friendship with the Prince Regent, which ultimately resulted in the birth of George Lamb on July 11, 1784, began as early as 1780.

19. Written diagonally on a new sheet of paper.

20. Godfrey Meynell.

21. The debates in the House of Commons regarding the doubling of the militia took place on June 19 and 20, 1780 and were partially a result of the Gordon riots (Hansard 726).

22. Lord Clermont, William Henry Fortescue.

23. The previous year, on July 9, 1779, France and Spain planned to invade England. England had only forty-six ships as protection. On August 16, the enemy was off Plymouth while Sir Charles Hardy looked for them beyond the Scilly Islands. He anchored at Spithead on September 3. Only the disabled state of the French and Spanish ships kept off an invasion. In 1780 the French had assembled a force of fifty thousand men at Le Havre and St. Malo, collecting four hundred vessels for their transport. Their plan was to seize the Isle of Wight, using Spithead as an anchorage for the fleet and conducting their enterprise from this nearby base. Had the French general D'Orvilliers entered the Channel directly his invasion might have been successful. "Not their own preparations, but the ineffi-

ciency of their enemies, in counsel and in preparation, saved the British Islands from invasion," William Clowes has written (Clowes 445). As it happened, the French government changed its mind about the advisibility of the expedition and an east wind prevented the convoy from proceeding. The ineptitude of the British goverment was nevertheless exposed by the presence of a vastly superior hostile fleet in the Channel. "What a humiliating state is our country reduced to!" wrote John Jervis, earl of St. Vincent (1735-1823), to his sister, but he laughed at the idea of invasion (Clowes 445).

24. In 1779 Sir Charles Hardy the younger commanded the Channel fleet. He was to resume command when he died at Portsmouth on May 18, 1780 *(DNB)*.

25. Pierre De Vaux (1705-1788), the French general, and Charles-Juste de Beauvau (1720-1793), marechal of France, second prince de Beauvau-Craon.

26. The French writer Stanislas-Jean, chevalier de Boufflers (1738-1815), who received the attention of Voltaire.

27. If Monsieur de Veal [Vaux] was a little more handsome [Beau], and Monsieur de Beauvaux [beautiful veal] a little less, Monsieur de Vaux [Veal], would be a pretty veal, and Monsieur de Beauvaux, would be nothing but veal. The French language version makes use of the homonym "Vaux/veau" and might be rendered in English as "If Mr. de Veal had a bit more appeal, and Mr. de Veal-of-Appeal had a bit less appeal, Mr. de Veal would be a veal full of appeal, and Mr. de Veal-of-Appeal would be nothing but veal (second translation courtesy of Pascale-Anne Brault and her class at DePaul University, 1996).

28. The seat of Damer's father, Henry Seymour Conway (Walpole 29:72, n.6).

29. Lord Malden, son of Lord Essex (Masters 290).

30. In 1782 Lady Elizabeth Compton (1760-1835) married Lord George Augustus Henry Cavendish, earl of Burlington (1831). She was known by the name Lady Betty Compton (Walpole, index).

31. Charles Manners, fourth duke of Rutland.

32. Possibly Edward, twelfth earl of Derby.

33. Frederick Howard, fifth earl of Carlisle.

34. Possibly William Lowther, first earl of Lonsdale of the second creation.

35. Henrietta Spencer, sister of the duchess of Devonshire, was attached romantically to a number of men before and after her marriage (1780) to Viscount Duncannon, by whom she had four children. I have not been able to determine whom she may have been involved with on this occasion, or if the rumour was accurate. Her affair with Lord Granville Leveson-Gower, which produced two illegitimate children, began in 1793. Sheridan pursued her actively, especially in the late 1790s, though she continually discouraged his advances (Surtees 307).

36. The paragraph Lady Melbourne refers to may well be the following: "The temporary residence of two noble families at Southampton, gives a full contradiction to the recent reports respecting the female at the head of one of them, it being well known that she and her Lord live upon terms of the warmest affection" (*Times,* July 24,1786).

37. Possibly Thomas Grenville, who seems to have been a close friend of Lady Melbourne's.

38. A friend of Judith Milbanke's (Elwin, *Noels* 296). At Spa in 1786, Lady Milbanke wrote that "the Beauchamps & Colemores have been the greatest addition to the Society & we have lived entirely together" (298). Elsewhere she writes that "the Beauchamps are sociable & cheerful & always promoting some party or other; we have also some very charming French men, particularly the Marquis de Coigny" (297). Viscount Beachamp, afterwards the marquis of Hertford, married Lady Marchioness of Hertford. She was close friends with the Prince Regent and was described by Wraxall as a woman of extraordinary beauty (Wraxall 1:323-25).

39. *Lady Salisbury to Lady Melbourne (Chatsworth 751)*

[July 1786]

My dear Ly Melbourne

      I did not know till it was too late Thursday that you were in the Country as I should have call'd on you, but yesterday it was impossible. I shall be much obliged to you for a party Wednesday or Thursday evening as for dinners we have Talbot's & Fairford's to whom we are engaged. Ly Essex will be in town. I was assured yesterday that Ly Duncannon was gone off, surely it cannot be true, do write me word that I may contradict. Yrs ever my dear Ly Mel.

                                 E.M. Salisbury

[Viscountess Melbourne/Send an Answer to Arlington Hts]

40. Lewes Races took place in Sussex (Walpole 19:495).

41. Lady Beauchamp is referred to as "Lady B." in Elizabeth Foster's letters (December 21, 1799; Foster).

42. Though signed "Melbourne," this letter is written in Lady Melbourne's hand.

43. This letter is placed near a letter of November 12, 1816 in the Lovelace collection but appears to form a sequence with 11, f.97-102.

44. Thomas Davison. "Mr. Davison's House is a very comfortable one, but badly situated," Judith Milbanke observed in a letter to her aunt (September 10, 1777; Elwin *Noels* 71).

45. Lord Melbourne relinquished his seat in Parliament for his son Peniston.

46. By writing their names and titles on the corner of the letter, government officials and members of Parliament secured free delivery. After the Restoration, this practice was exploited by individuals signing for friends and associates, as Lord Melbourne does here. By an act of 1764, each member of both houses of Parliament was permitted to send ten free letters daily and to receive fifteen. Lord Melbourne, though no longer M.P., signs under his son's name to obtain free delivery, as the stamp on the envelope to this letter shows (*Brewer's Phrase and Fable* 409).

47. Parliament voted not to increase the Prince Regent's salary, and as a result the prince terminated Lord Melbourne's services as gentleman of the bedchamber.

48. Lady Melbourne's brother, John, died in 1800.

49. Mrs. Guidon was the housekeeper at Melbourne Hall.

50. Hassard was apparently an employee engaged at Melbourne Hall.

51. See note 2.

PART II

"A Keen Politician," 1805-1811

*I*n January 1805, Lady Melbourne's son Peniston was on his deathbed. "I am alarm'd & frightened more than I ever tell & every move & alteration of his countenance has an effect upon me that I cannot describe," Lady Melbourne wrote to her son Frederick (January 20-21, 1805). Two days after Peniston died, Lady Bessborough described the scene at Whitehall as "dreadful" (January 26, 1805; G. L. Gower 2:8). By May 27 of that year, Lady Melbourne could announce happier news. Her daughter Emily had married Lord Cowper, and her son William had married Caroline Ponsonby.

On November 6, 1805, Lady Melbourne informed her warden at Melbourne Hall of Nelson's victory over the combined "Fleets of France and Spain" (November 6, 1805). Four years later, Sir Arthur Wellesley triumphed over the incursions of Napoleon's forces in Spain. "The Battle lasted two days—& the loss is great on both Sides," Lady Melbourne wrote to Fox of the Battle of Talavera, which took place July 27 and 28, 1809. "Ours is 5376—killed wounded & missing" (August 14, 1809).

In 1811 Frederick Lamb was offered an opportunity to take a diplomatic position in the Two Sicilies.[1] There Lord William Bentinck was trying to unseat Napoleon's popular king of Naples, Joachim Murat,[2] but Lady Melbourne worried about the danger of the mission and was unwilling to have her son reside abroad. The Prince Regent to find him a position at home at the first opportunity, and with this promise in mind Frederick sailed for Sicily in October 1811. When the prince was unable to deliver on his promise the following year, he avoided mentioning Frederick's name to Lady Melbourne again.

Lady Melbourne was "a keen politician" who not only understood the meaning of events, but did her part to shape them. When her close friend Thomas Grenville became first lord of the Admiralty (1806-7), numerous people requested that she use her influence to obtain preferred assignments for their children. Further evidence of her political skill is provided in a letter she wrote to Daniel Giles, the member for St. Albans in the county of Hertford. Giles was a "pleasant bachelor of fifty" (Airlie, *Whig* 121) whom Lady Melbourne clearly viewed as a placeholder for her son William. When William indicated his intention to replace Giles, however, Giles denied that there had been any such understanding. In a masterful if prevaricating letter, Lady Melbourne cleared up the misunderstanding (September 1811).

She was less successful in controlling her daughters-in-law. Caroline Lamb had an affair with Sir Godfrey Webster in 1809, while Caroline George left her husband for several months to travel on the continent with Henry Brougham in 1816. "Two such curses were never inflicted upon a family which was so perfectly happy and united before they came into it," Frederick wrote to his mother ([January 28, 1817]; 45546, f.177). But William and George were neglectful husbands who too often regarded their wives as play-toys. Frederick, who did not marry until much later in life, never could find a woman to live up to his mother's example.

Lady Melbourne to Frederick Lamb (45546, f.24)

[January 20-21, 1805 or earlier][3]
Wednesday

Dst F.

I have just received y^r. Letter & am so persuaded of your kindness y^t I should not hesitate a moment in desiring ^you^ to come if I thought it necessary, which thank God it is not at present, & I hope & trust Pen's amendment will continue gradually & preclude any such necessity—I am alarm'd & frightened more than I ever tell & every move & alteration of his countenance has an effect upon me that I cannot describe. I am here alone with him & Emily & have been so since Sunday & I am sure I need not tell you the state of nervousness I have been in but I do not think I am apt to deceive myself[.] my thoughts are often too gloomy for this & I am convinced y^t he has no complaint that may not arise from debility. I do not say they do—I wish I could be certain of that fact—but they may—he has no burning heat at any time of the day—& I would fancy that his countenance looks better & more like himself today—I am now writing after he is gone to bed, & am more anxious for to morrow than I can describe & so I am every night two or three days more in the way he has pass'd the two last would be great comfort, for if I see amendment I don't care how gradual it is—Farquhar[4] did express his fears to Grant when he first perceiv'd his Health being derang'd but as ye Pistula was not cured could not insist but as soon as that was the case, he came forward openly—for they all agree that ye pistula is cured but that there is a little Wound at the bottom which only wants skinning over, which it can not do till his constitution regains more strength—he had got a Saddle made to enable him to ride which he talks of doing tomorrow if it should be fine—I will add more tomorrow at present I will only say a word on the Subject of y^r private note—

What ever dread you may have of my eagerness I do assure you y^t I have not given way to it on this occasion—& if she[5] has given you any hint that makes you think so it must have arisen entirely from commonsense for I declare to you there has not been ye least reason—ye Week he was here I certainly saw more attention from him than I liked, but I determined not to take one step to prevent it then, but when I return'd to London to ask him less often than I was used to do either to go to places with us or to come to ye House. We were to have gone from hence on the Thursday, and every body understood they were to go that day, we ^changed &^ staid till Friday & when I came down in ye Morning I saw y^t B Byng[6] & H[arbour].[7] had both a mind to stay but I determined not to perceive it. There was also Luttrell[8] & Macdonald[9] lamenting they were going, so that it all pass'd together—when they were gone she s^d. B[ob].B[yng] & H[arbour] had a mind to stay today if you had ask'd them—I said why didn't you tell me so before & I would have asked them, but why did you think so, for they had settled for a Week to go today & I dare say they had some engagement—she s^d No that North—had s^d that he dreaded the cold drive in his C[rg], & that B[ob] B[yng] did not know how to get to his Brothers. I s[d] if I had known it they might have staid & I had once thought of asking H[arbour]- but I thought I could not without asking B[ob] B[yng]—& William has taken such an aversion to him y[t] he would have been quite Savage—could any thing be more prudent or moderate. Since y[t] time I have seen very little of him & y[t] when ever I have mention'd him it has been in consequence of George[']s abusing him for a <Box>[10] in which I sometimes fuss & sometimes not—& often take his part—you do not seem to be so much surprized as I am at his confidence in Mad[emois][elle][11] & not only about H[arbour] but about many other people. I am not sorry for it as I hear it all (though in a tiresome manner)[.] she says she does not conceive herself how she can often feel so differently about y[e] same people sometimes liking them very much & y[e] next time she sees them, finding them very disagreeable—all this is so Natural that one can but laugh—certainly she has never had an idea of liking Harbour but as a friend, at least I believe so & there are several others she prefers to him, but y[t] is such a dangerous idea that it must be guarded ag[st]

She had a great flirtation at Brighton with L[d] Dunley[12] —& this Winter he came to our Box at y[e] Opera & Toby who was sitting by her kept his place & she never had an Opportunity of speaking to him—at Night she s[d] to me Mama how I hate Toby—& what is more provoking I must always be very civil to him as I know him so well but don't you think he's grown a great bore.

D[st] Fred I write all this in a terrible agitation which lasted thro' Wednesday Night & was much <assured> on Thursday Night by Pen sending me word his Night had been indifferent & he wish'd to come to Town

Yesterday was a nervous day but this Morn[g] I am in much better Spirits. Pearson,[13] Farquhar & Grant met here & he is gone back to B[rocket] H[all]. & George with him—

They think that he has no appearance of any other complaint except Frustrated Nerves—but this to a degree you can have no idea of—Pearson's opinion was very favorable & I think Pen is return'd much better satisfied—They gave him doses of Opium to calm his Nerves—he got on Horseback Yesterday before we set out & is now gone with y[e] idea of y[e] greatest delights in riding. I have been so

<fuss'd> to day & Yesterday y^t I could not put Pen to Paper

God bless you I'll write to morrow

Lady Melbourne to Henry Fox (Melbourne 234/5/23)

[May 27, 1805]

M^r. Fox—I find Hassard did not believe the paragraph he saw in the papers about Williams Marriage—but it is fact & I believe they will be married on Monday next. The Lady is Lady Caroline Ponsonby, daughter to Lord Bessborough. Emily is also going to be married to Lord Cowper, & we are extremely happy at both Matches

Y^rs EMelbourne

[1805/London May Twenty Seventh/Mr Fox/Melbourne/Derby/Egremont; stamped "free" May 27, 1805]

Lady Melbourne to Henry Fox (Melbourne 234/5/24)

[November 6, 1805]

M^r. Fox—

Ld Melbourne has received y^r Letters very safe & begs you will remit the others

EMelbourne

6th Nov^r

Whitehall

I send you a Gazette which will go free & I think you will like to see an Acc^t of this glorious Victory, which has caused great rejoicings here altho' a gloom is thrown over the whole by the loss of Lord Nelson, who must be sincerely and deservedly regretted by the whole nation[14]

Returned with this note:

My Lord

I beg leave to thank Lady Melbourne for sending the London Gazette Extraordinary announcing the very important intelligence of the glorious victory obtained by the British Fleet over the combined Fleets of France & Spain, which I conceive has occasioned as strong sensations of joy in the Country as in Town, tho' very much damped by the afflicting news of the death of the great Lord Nelson

I am y^{rs},
H.F.

Melbourne

11th Nov. 1805

Lady Melbourne to Henry Fox (Melbourne 234/5/31)

[October 11, 1806]

M^r. Fox—

Lord Melbourne desires me to tell you that as Hassard has been unwell, he does not allow him to go to receive the Rents this time & therefore thinks you had best endeavor to take some confidential person with you—to whom you may make some acknowledgement for his loss of time—as he thinks it so much better to have two people in that Sort of business. L^d M[elbourne] wishes you when you go to <Barthby>—to inquire about the Manor & in what state Genl Burke has left it, as M^r. la Tour writes us word he has left that Country in which case L^d M[elbourne] certainly would not allow him to have ye deputation[15] another Year—but he can hardly believe he would keep it—& therefore begs you to inquire particularly into the circumstances.

Mr Lamb & L^y Caroline are set out this Mor^g—& as they have taken a Kitchen Maid she will pay for every thing both for the kitchen & the House, & as she never was at Melbourne before I beg you will speak to her about keeping out all the Idle people with which the House will be fill'd if she is not caution'd against it.

Y^{rs} EMelbourne

Whitehall
11<u>th</u> Oc<u>r</u> 1806

[M^r. Fox/Melbourne/Derby]

Elizabeth Emily Milbanke-Huskisson[16] to Lady Melbourne (Huntington, Box 154:10)

Earlham, October 27, 1806

My dear L^y Melbourne

I am afraid you will think me a great plague for troubling you upon the present occasion, but you have so often assisted me in my *Distresses,* that I naturally apply to you this to[o]. Being at this moment from Home I do not know what are the proper steps for me to take in the service of a *Protege* of *mine,* to whom delay might be prejudicial. *He* is a young Relation of Mr. H[uskisson]'s who entered the navy at *my* recommendation & is now with Sir John Warren, who has made him a Lieutenant; Yesterday I received a Letter from him inclosing his *actin*g Commission (now Sir John), which must be sent through his agent to the Admiralty for *Confirmation Now, tho' no Politician,* I do not think myself authorized to trouble Mr. Grenville on the Subject but if you could mention it warmly to him, I am sure he would have the goodness to confirm the appointment. I am not now very conversant in these affairs, but I believe that the merely confirming a Lieutenant, particularly when the appointment is made, as is the case in the present instance, to a Vacancy in the Command in a Chief's Ship, is not a Point of great Difficuty & certainly not nearly so much so, as *Making a Lieutenant at once.* Sir John has written to the Admiralty to recommend this young Man, who is two & twenty and has really some little Claim from having seen a great deal of Service, & from having been in the *Battle of Trafalgar* where he was charged with the *signals,* on board his then ship the *Defence,* on that and the following day, I was so much approved of by Captain (George Hope) that upon each Captain being allowed to select a Youngster,

101

after the Engagement to be made a Lieutenant he would have named him Thomas Huskisson but unluckily He had not then quite completed his Time. This was really very hard upon him, & makes me the more anxious that he should succeed at present & will I hope form part of my excuse for troubling you with this long History—

I see by the Newspaper that you are come to Town, Lady Cobbett's that the Prince is to bring in William for a "favoured Borough,"[17] so I hope the bustle of these Elections will not prevent your intended Visit to Petworth, as I hope to meet you all there. Mr H. was *proposed* to stand for Dover that he was forced to go there to make his *Excuses* in Person, as he likes to be returned again for his late deal but as somewhat the troublesome Spirits raised by our Friend Tom are not yet allayed. He has no time to lose in getting from Dover to Liskeard so I don't know when he will leave home again—Pray write me word how you all do, not forgetting the Bambino &

Believe me dear L[ady] M[elbourne] to be always
Yours affectionately,
Emily Huskisson

Lady Melbourne to Thomas Grenville (Huntington Library, Box 155:41)[18]

[October 28, 1806]

Dear Mr. Grenville

I am again obliged to trouble you in consequence of a Letter I have received from M^rs. Huskisson which I enclose, & I hope her relation may be one of the Lieut^s whose prayers are heard favourably by you—at least I am sure it will be much more pleasing to you to assist a Young Man in his promotion than to stop it—unless there should be very strong reasons against y^r granting this favour I shall be delighted to see you when ever you have a little time to throw away upon me. We shall be in town I believe till the middle of the next Week—

believe me truly yours
Melbourne

Tuesday Eve—

Lady Melbourne to Thomas Grenville (Huntington Library, Box 155:42)
[February 9, 1807]

Dear M^r. Grenville—

Ld Melbourne desires me to send you the enclosed Letter, & to say that if it should be in your power at any time to comply with the request contained in it, he shall think himself very much obliged to you—he dislikes troubling you very much but he has so many reasons for wishing to serve M^r. Graham both personal to himself & also his having been of great use on many occasions to poor Pen that he trusts you will forgive it—thank you for your kind Note respecting Miss Tilghman[,][19] believe me

truly y^rs,

EM

9th Feb^y, 1807

10 February 1807

My dear Lady Melbourne,

I need not assure you that I will do all I can to assist any wish of yours or of Ld Melbourne's. It is not always practicable to change the station of any ship in service very immediately & we are obliged to make a rule of never promising to any Officer any particular service or destination, as great embarrasment would arise from any such engagements, but knowing Lord Melbourne's wishes upon this subject I will not fail to keep them in mind & to do every thing that may be practicable in the view that is described.

Y^rs.

TG.

Lady Melbourne to Henry Fox (Melbourne 234/5/40)

[September 13, 1808]

Mr. Fox

Ld Melbourne desires me to acquaint you that L^d and L^y Cowper, M^r. Lamb & M^r. George Lamb will be at Melbourne on Tuesday next, & as they will bring 5 or 6 horses Ld Melbourne begs you will lay in Hay & Corn for them & have the Stables ready as they will probably be there on Monday. I have written to Mrs Howe about getting some help into the House. I believe they will not stay longer than a Week.

Y^rs

EMelbourne

Brocket Hall
13th Sep^r
1808

Lady Melbourne to Henry Fox (Melbourne 234/5/42)

[London, March 7, 1809]

Mr. Fox

By your Letter of the 6th <instant> I received the Estimate for the Several Works at the Pool and Garden and approve of there being done as proposed and you may Appropriate the 10 Plant deposit on the proposed Sale of Timber for those purposes.

By your Letter of the 7th I find you have Sold the Timber very well. Oak is at about 4 pd foot here and in Hertfordshire, if you Have any on the Estates Walnut does very well at an enormous price. I am glad the Wood plants last year but one goes on well

Y^rs. Melbourne

Ld Melbourne desires me to add that M^r. Cookney has purchased some plants which will be sent to M^r. Bennett and L^d M[elbourne] has written to him to desire they may be put into some part of ye Land as in a <framing>, and afterwards planted out & he has also mentioned to M^r. Bennett that he will allow her to have five Guineas for him for his trouble, as he did not recollect if he had told it you decidedly

---

Lady Melbourne to Henry Fox (Melbourne x94 234/5/44)

[July 7, 1809]

M^r. Fox

Ld Melbourne desires me to say that he has received y^r Letter this Mor^g & that he does not like after M^r. Abney has been so good a Tenant to send him notice to quit but that he will write to him to morrow to desire to know what are his intentions——Lord Melbourne would prefer L^{dy} Charlotte Rawdon for a Tenant provided you could let the Farm equally well without the House but he is very doubtfull whether she has not been enquiring about it for Sr William Rumbold—— however as Lord Melbourne can give no answer till he hears from M^r. Abney, he thinks you may have an opportunity of making further enquiries, & he wishes you to tell M^r. Dawson[20] that he will let you know as soon as he receives an Answer & at the same time you may ask him whether L^y Charlotte Rawdon would wish to have the Land, & by those means you may discover whether she really wants it for herself—

The only reason why L^d. Melbourne would prefer her to S^r. Wm Rumbold is on Acc^t of the Shooting——Ld Melbourne says he has inquired respecting fruit trees & he finds that no Tenant has any right to take away *any thing* that has been put into the Soil as it then becomes the Landlord's. Therefore if M^r. Abney should be doing any thing of that Sort you had better object to it, as also about any other depredations he may be com[m]itting if it should be any thing reasonable Ld Melbourne would certainly not refuse him if he is applied to—but certainly he should remove nothing without his permission

Y^r. Friend

EMelbourne

7th July 1809

[Mr Fox/Melbourne/Derby]

Lady Melbourne to Henry Fox (Melbourne 234/5/50)

[August 14, 1809]

Mr. Fox

Ld Melbourne desires me to tell you that he has had an Application from Samuel Nin—Brother to Adam Nin one of his Tenants—who wishes to rent a farm at Westwood in ye Parish of Selston Vacant by the death of James Hinley who has left as he says no family—Ld Melbourne begs to know if this Land is disposed of— or if you think this Man a proper Tenant——

The Guns in the Park are now firing on Acc^t of a Victory obtained by Sr Arthur Wellesley over the French in Spain[21] commanded by Joseph Buonaparte[22] in person. The Battle lasted two days—& the loss is great on both Sides—ours is 5376—killed wounded & missing. The French are computed to have lost 11,000 Men.[23]

The News was brought this Mor^g by Lord Fitzroy Somerset Aide de Camp to Sr Arthur Wellesley—& the particulars are not yet known, further than what I have Stated——

I am y^r Friend

EMelbourne

14<u>th</u> Aug<u>st</u>
1809

Lady Melbourne to Caroline Lamb (45546, f.16; Airlie, Whig 118)
[April 13, 1810]

I only write you a few lines for the purpose of preventing y^r coming to me loaded with falsehood & flattery under the impression that it will have any effect—which I most solemnly assure you it will not—I see you have no shame nor compunction for y^r past conduct every action every impulse of your mind is directed by Sr Godfrey Webster[24]—I lament it, but as I can do no good I shall withdraw myself and suffer no more croaking upon your hurt—Y^r behavior last night was so disgraceful in its appearances and so disgusting from its motives that it is quite impossible it should ever be effaced from my mind

     when any one braves the opinion of the World, sooner or later they will feel the consequences of it and although at first people may have excused your forming friendships with all those who are censured for their conduct, from y^r youth and inexperience yet when they see you continue to single them out and to overlook all the decencys imposed by Society—they will look upon you as belonging to the same class—as you lose singularity it may be some Satisfaction to you to know that you are the only woman who has any pretension to Character who ever courted Lady Wellesley's[25] acquaintance, that I never before saw any person sup in her party, or brave ye World so much as to appear in it belonging to her Society— You not only did this but left every one of y^r connections for ye purpose of forming an intimate acquaintance with L^d and M^{rs}. Wellesley because they are friends of Sir Godfrey Webster—had you been sincere in your promises of amendment or wished to make any return to W^m for his kindness—you would have discarded & driven from yr presence any persons or things that would remind you of the unworthy Object for whose sake you had run such risks & exposed yourself so much—but on the contrary you seem to delight in every thing that recalls him to you—& to honour those disgraceful feelings which have caused so much unhappiness to those who ought to be dearest to you—a Married Woman should consider that by such levity she not only compromises her own honor and character but also that of her Husband—but you seek only to please yourself—You think you can blind your Husband and cajole your friends—

Only one word more *let me alone.* I *will have no* more conversations with you upon this hateful Subject—I repeat it let me alone, & do not drive me to explain the meaning of the cold civility that will from henceforward pass between us

13th April
1810

Lady Melbourne to the Prince Regent (HRO D/ELb, F8/2)

[Feb. 4] 1811

Sir

After having so long experienced your kindness, I can not but feel confident that your Royal Highness will not be offended at my taking up a few minutes of your time, as I have a particular reason for wishing to inform you, that Frederic has received an offer from Lᵈ Wellesley of a situation in the diplomatic line—

We are perfectly aware that it is entirely with a view of doing what may be agreable to your Royal Highness, and it is highly flattering to Frederic that Lᵈ Wellesley should consider you in any degree interested about him, but still it must be consider'd in the light of a personal obligation & Frederic is anxious to prove that he feels it as such, by doing what he knows will be most pleasing to Lᵈ Wellesley which is by naturally acquainting ~~your Royal Highness~~ yr R.H. with it, as Lᵈ Wellesley expressed his wish that he should do so, at the time he made him the offer, and I trust your Royal Highness will accept this as an excuse for the liberty I take in troubling you with this Letter.

Frederic has not yet decided whether or not he shall accept this offer, as Lᵈ Wellesley allow'd him some days to consider of it—it is to go Secretary of Legation to Sicily—I am I confess against his accepting it, as I think it so unpleasant to leave your Family & Friends & all your connections for a length of time, & in a situation that holds out no particular advantage, & knowing that Frederic's inclinations lead him to wish to be employ'd in some line of business at home, where I am confident he would be found very useful—I had therefore stated my wishes to Ld Grey[26] who had kindly promised to forward them & this will I believe explain what Ld Melbourne told your Royal Highness upon this Subject when he had the honor of being admitted into your presence.

Allow me Sir to add my Sincere Wishes along with those of Ld Melbourne for your Health & Happiness—& to assure you of the sincere attachment & Gratitude with which

I have the Honor to be

Sir

Your most obliged

& most sincere & Honorable Servt.

Eliz Melbourne

Whitehall

Thursday Mor^g, February 4th

The P[rince] R[egent] on ye receipt of the above came to Whitehall & strongly advised Fred to accept this offer, saying y^t at this time it was not in his power, to give him any Situation here—& that when ye restrictions were taken off he should find it much more easy to provide for him after he had been employed—& particularly from such an Employment enhanced Arbuthnot[27] & several others who had been in the foreign office here for such reasons, &c &c. I agreed to all he said, only adding y^t when people were out of the way they were often put by—& I s^d will your R.H. promise now that when you have ye power you *will* provide for him—he s^d most certainly & I answered upon that promise, I agree he should go—& it was settled—before they set out Fred had an Accident which disabled him from moving—& Ld Wm Bentinck[28] went without him—he was laid up several M^ths & in October (I think) L^d W^m returned to England upon particular business & wishing Fred to return with him. I wrote to ye P[rince]- to say he was unfit to undertake a long Voyage but if H[is] R[oyal] H[ighness] still advised his going—he certainly would run the risk of ye harm it might do his Leg—the P[rince]. saw him—stated to him clearly & decidedly y^t he wished him to go as he should find it so much more easy to provide for him for ye reasons he had before stated—and y^t he wished it the More, as it would be for a Short time, the Restrictions expiring in March 1812 & that he might depend upon his recalling him to fill some other Situation at that time—

I am writing this October 12, 1812. Fred is still in Sicily & the Prince never thinks about him[.] that is he thinks enough about him to cover mentioning his Name with the greatest care & when I say I have heard from him never says, even how is he, & often makes me no answer.

EM

Prince Regent to Lady Melbourne (HRO)

[February 14, 1811]

Many thanks dear Lady Melbourne for your kind note regarding Fred[.] If you have nothing particularly to do this evening, & will allow me to call upon You at eleven o'clock, I will then talk this whole matter over with You. This is, or rather will be the first moment, I have had it in my power to call upon you, & I think it an Age, since I have had the pleasure of seeing you. I remain dear Lady Melbourne ever your very sincere Friend & humble Servant.

George P.R.

Carlton House
February 14, 1811

Dear Mr. Giles

 ever since I have been informed of the discussion, for I will not call it dispute, going on between ~~W^m~~ you & W^m. respecting St. Albans, it has been my determination to keep myself entirely aloof & not to give any opinion on the Subject— but since you have chosen to bring me forward in y^r. last Letter to William I think it only fair to state to you, what I must say to any one who question'd me, respecting the compliments you say I paid you, upon y^r. great Strength & great popularity at St. Albans.

 I must in fairness answer that I have not the least recollection of having done so.—I don't[31] mean to say that it is not true, because I now think it very probable that you may recall it to my memory by some circumstances connected with it, but really at ye present I can not remember it or any thing like it ~~& I have been in the way of knowing so little about St. Albans except from you~~ that it appears odd to me how such a fact ~~circumstance the only thing~~. The last time I recollect having mentioned St. Albans to you was when I told you that I had heard you found fault with Jedmund having given ye Voters an Election Dinner, & y^r. answer to me was that it was a difficult thing to do as some of those who thought they had a right to partake of it, were not thought proper company for the others & I ~~then~~ s^d. then you ought to give two Dinners.—I mention this as y^e. only thing I can remember except that at the time of the Election you often Stated y^t. you had no intention of making an Interest for Yourself, & that what you were then doing William would profit by at some time, & you never have since y^t. hinted to me that you had changed your intentions in this respect. This last part I have mentioned to no-one ~~but yourself~~ but I thought it fair to tell you what I must say if I am in any way referr'd to.—I hate any dispute & hope you will both settle this amicably.

Notes: Part II

1. From the fifteenth to the nineteenth century, the name "Two Sicilies" was given to the state uniting the southern part of the Italian peninsula with the island of Sicily. Expelled from Naples by the French Revolutionary army in 1799, Ferdinand I established himself in Sicily from 1806 to 1811 under British protection. As ambassador in virtual control of the government, Lord William Bentinck tried to portray Ferdinand as an apostle of liberalism by forcing him to establish a constitution in 1812. Frederick Lamb accompanied Bentinck to the Two Sicilies in October 1811 and was present during this tumultuous period. The restoration of the Bourbons to Naples in 1815 put an end to the constitution, and a united kingdom of Sicily was proclaimed in 1816, with a centralized government operating from Naples under Ferdinand I.

2. When Joseph Bonaparte was transferred to Spain in 1808, Napoleon gave Naples to Joachim Murat, who had married Napoleon's sister Caroline.

3. This date, suggested by the British Library, seems to coincide with the last illness of Peniston Lamb, Lady Melbourne's first son, who died of tuberculosis on January 24, 1805. Lord Melbourne wrote to Fox: "Upon this melancholy occasion you will be so good as to put yourself and Mrs. Horre [the housekeeper] &c. in proper mourning at my expence" (Usher, *Owners* 5).

4. Sir Walter Farquhar, the well-known physician.

5. Emily, Frederick's sister. Frederick seems critical of his mother's efforts to ingratiate herself with the Prince Regent (Stokes 302). She seems to answer Frederick's concern about Emily's interest in a man named Harbour while muting her own role as matchmaker. From 1802 to 1805, Lady Melbourne kept up a close correspondence with Lord Cowper, who married Emily on June 3, 1805.

6. Robert Byng, son of George Byng, and brother of the first earl of Strafford (Gower 1:222).

7. The Harbour referred to in this letter may be Edward Harbour, brother of the Honorable William Assheton.

8. Henry Luttrell.

9. Possibly James MacDonald.

10. Perhaps a "box" at the theater. George Lamb worked at Drury Lane and was much involved in theatrical life.

11. Emily Lamb.

12. John William Ward, first earl of Dudley.

13. The physician and chemist George Pearson.

14. The victory of Trafalgar took place on October 21, 1805. Georgiana, duchess of Devonshire, wrote a poem titled "The Victory of Trafalgar and Death of Nelson," which includes the lines "Superior Force his ardent soul defied, / He conquer'd, knew it, 'blessed his God,' and died" (Foster 252). Her husband also wrote several lines to commemorate the occasion. Characteristically, his strike a more somber note: "Britons received from Heaven a mixed decree / To crown their virtues, but to check their pride / God gave them victory, but Nelson died" (November 1805; Foster 252).

15. Deputation: an appointment as gamekeeper on an English estate, often made as a way of giving hunting privileges.

16. Elizabeth Emily Milbanke-Huskisson was Lady Melbourne's cousin.

17. William Lamb was elected to Haddington Burghs (1806-7), his first position in Parliament, after replacing Kinnaird's father in the summer of 1805. Ziegler describes the 1806 election as the result of a deal between the duke of Bedford and Lord Lauderdale. Haddington Burghs, he writes, was Lauderdale's gift and required only a minimum amount of compliance with his wishes. Elizabeth Milbanke-Huskisson's letter emphasizes the role of the Prince Regent in facilitating Lamb's victory

(Ziegler 59).

18. This letter was sent with Elizabeth Emily Milbanke-Huskisson's letter of October 27, 1806. Lady Melbourne's letter to Thomas Grenville is dated "[October 28] 1806" by the museum, though the letter itself says October 20.

19. Harriet Tilghman, who was married to Mr. Tilghman of Philadelphia, was Elizabeth Emily Milbanke-Huskisson's sister.

20. Thomas Davison.

21. The battle of Talavera was fought on July 27 and 28, 1809.

22. Joseph Bonaparte (1768-1844), eldest brother of Napoleon.

23. On August 14, 1809, Elizabeth Foster wrote to Augustus Foster announcing the same news. "Twenty pieces of cannon, four eagles, and 10,000 slain of the French bear testimony to this. [Marshal] Sebastiani [1776-1851] wounded, two generals killed, and two others wounded; Joseph Bonaparte a witness to his defeat. The dear English alone were engaged, but it is said that the Spaniards are pursuing the defeated French army . . . Here were we with about 20,000 against fully forty thousand French. Perhaps you will hear fuller and better accounts, but good news bears a repetition. How it makes one regret that Sir John More did not trust more to English valour and hazard a battle sooner. The battle was, you see, at Talavera la Regina. Cuesta was said to be following them and Varegas to have advanced to Toledo and Aranjuez" (Foster 335).

24. Caroline Lamb's "affair" with Webster may have been nothing more than platonic and was done partly to gain the attention of her increasingly preoccupied husband, William. Webster was a notorious libertine, but the only tangible evidence of their fliration was his gift of a diamond collar for her dog. When the dog later went mad, Caroline thought she was being punished for her behavior and apologized profusely to her mother-in-law. Her letters upbraiding William for teaching her to disregard moral notions only angered Lady Melbourne more.

25. "Lady Wellesley was of French birth, and her morals, even judged by the permissive company in which she mixed, were held to be deplorable" (Blyth 76).

26. Three letters on this subject passed between Lord Grey and Lady Melbourne. They are included here in appendix D.

27. Charles Arbuthnot.

28. Lieutenant-General Lord William Henry Cavendish Bentinck.

29. Daniel Giles.

30. Dated 1911 in Airlie, *Whig* 121.

31. "do" is changed to "don't.

As Byron's affair with Caroline Lamb came to an end, Lady Melbourne found herself lured into a correspondence with the man who had cuckolded her son. Her ostensible aim was to induce Byron to end his affair with her daughter-in-law, yet she soon found his cynical wit irresistible. From 1812 to 1815, they engaged in a correspondence reminiscent of that of Madame de Merteuil and Valmont in *Les Liaisons Dangereuses*. William Lamb was as appalled at his mother's flirtation with a man almost forty years her junior as he was with his own wife's indiscretion. He might well have agreed with the Prince of Wales' contention that Byron had bewitched the entire family.

Byron had two reasons for writing to Lady Melbourne. The first was to have her advance a proposal of marriage to her niece, Annabella Milbanke.[1] When Annabella rejected his suit, Byron assured Lady Melbourne that he felt "no *pique* nor diminution of ... respect" for Annabella (February 1813; 3:18). The second reason was to end his relationship with Caroline Lamb. At times Byron disapproved of Lady Melbourne's cruel methods. She would sometimes leave portions of Byron's more biting letters on the floor of Melbourne House for Caroline to see.[2] Annoyed by her daughter-in-law's previous flirtation with Godfrey Webster, however, Lady Melbourne was determined to seek revenge.

To the surprise of William and Caroline, Lady Melbourne's "clandestine" correspondence with the poet continued, even after he had turned his attentions to Lady Oxford.[3] But Lady Melbourne was not blind to Byron's narcissism or to the manner in which he tried to manipulate the entire Melbourne family. On one ocasion, she chastised him for not complying with Lady Caroline Lamb's request for a lock of his hair. She reminded him that "it is not for a Gentleman to *faire le difficile*" (March 25, 1813). When Byron sent a "double lock" of his and Lady Oxford's hair instead, however, Lady Melbourne laughed at the ruse, while Caroline Lamb inserted the accompanying letter in her roman à clef, *Glenarvon*.

Many of Lady Melbourne's letters to Byron from April 1813 seem to be missing. He wrote frequently,[4] denying his resemblance to the Giaour. In one letter, written on April 7, 1813, he satirized the Prince Regent's presence during the opening of the tomb at Windsor, which contained the bodies of Charles I and Henry VIII.

> Famed for their civil & domestic quarrels
> See heartless Henry lies by headless Charles!
> Between them stands another sceptred *thing*
> It lives—it reigns "aye every inch a king!"
> Charles to his people—Henry to his wife
> The double tyrant starts at once to life,
> Justice & Death have mixed their dust in vain
> Each royal vampire quits his vault again!
> Curst be the tomb that could so soon disgorge
> Two such to make a Janus or a George. (*LJ* 3:38).

Byron wrote several versions of this poem, which may have been inspired by one of Lady Melbourne's letters that have not been preserved. He encouraged Lady Melbourne to circulate his squib to Lord Holland, even though he knew she was too "*tender* or *afraid*" to do so (April 7, 1813; *LJ* 3:38). Throughout his correspondence with Lady Melbourne, Byron displayed his jealousy over her close and continued association with the Prince Regent.

Shortly after penning this *jeu d'esprit*, Byron found that his affair with Lady Oxford was spinning out of control. Fearful first that Lady Oxford was pregnant, and then that a letter of his had been discovered by Lord Oxford (June 21, 1813; *LJ* 3:65), he boasted to Lady Melbourne that he would elope with his mistress. This crisis resolved itself, but when Lady Oxford departed for Europe with her husband, Byron asked his closest confidante to avoid bringing up his mistress' name. "To tell you the truth—I feel more *Carolinish* about her than I expected," he wrote (June 29, 1813; *LJ* 3:69).

Caroline Lamb continued to pursue Byron, cutting herself with a penknife at Lady Heathcote's ball on July 5, 1813, when he made a sarcastic remark about her waltzing. When Lady Melbourne heard the news of Caroline's self-mutilation, she believed Byron's side of the story.[5] She again defended him to Annabella Milbanke when he was accused of bilking Claughton out of his deposit on Newstead Abbey.[6] "Say what is most proper," Byron wrote. "I have not the skill—you are an adept" (July 18, 1813; *LJ* 3:78).

That summer, Lady Melbourne complained about Byron's epistolary silence. However, he knew that she disapproved of his relationship with his half-sister, Augusta, and kept silent about it until August 5, 1813, when he announced their intention to travel abroad. Two weeks later, Byron decided to travel with Lord Sligo instead, though a plague in that part of the world prevented their immediate departure (August 18, 1813; *LJ* 3:90). Further delays ensued when Sligo discovered that he had impregnated a ballerina, who became the subject of several coarse jokes by Byron. "If any Woman suffers him, he is a fortunate person," Lady Melbourne responded (August 23, 1813; *LJ* 3:97).[7]

On September 21, 1813, Byron retailed his comic efforts to seduce the wife of his friend James Wedderburn Webster.[8] The two swore their love to each other in a billiard room, but Byron boasted of not having the heart to compromise her virtue. He derived as much pleasure in narrating his adventures to Lady Melbourne as he did in acting them out, claiming that "anything that confirms or extends one's observations on life & character delights me even when I don't know people" (September–October 1813; *LJ* 3:129). Aware that his letters exceeded her responses, Byron confessed that he had "no other *confidential* correspondent on earth" (October 13, 1813; *LJ* 3:142). Presumably, Lady Melbourne again avoided writing because she thought her letters in peril at the Websters (October 14, 1813; *LJ* 3:144). The few that Byron did receive, which he dubbed the Aston letters, led him to meditate on the "intellectual pleasure" he had gained from the exchange (October 23, 1813; *LJ* 3:152). He described her epistles as "the most amusing—the most *developing*—and tactiques in the world" (October 23, 1813; *LJ* 3:153).

Though Byron worried that Lady Melbourne would consider him "hollow

& heartless" on account of his "epistolary levity" (October 25, 1813; *LJ* 3:153), Lady Melbourne retorted that she never doubted his capacity for true feeling. So implicitly did he trust her judgment that he showed her an early copy of *The Bride of Abydos* to see if his relationship with Augusta "showed through."[9] He now referred to her in his diary as "The best friend I ever had in my life, and the cleverest of women" (*LJ* 3:209). He borrowed Lord Salisbury's box at Covent Garden for the express purpose of being able to talk with Lady Melbourne "for an hour on Emergency" (November 23, 1813; *LJ* 3:171).

Distracted as she was by these events, Lady Melbourne had little time to devote to the maintenance of the Derbyshire estate. Her son Frederick wrote her a long letter rebuking her for maintaining Henry Fox as warden there.[10] "Fox if not a Cheat, is at least willing to underlet my father's whole estate in order to get his own miserable farm upon easy terms, and that Mr. Black has either been in league with or duped by him, probably a little of both. You have no way of getting out of this nest of roguery, but by employing an entirely new man and no man so good as Ivison. I see you have a whim against it, and why I can't conceive, unless from the same sort of feeling which prevents yr ever changing yr bridle let yr hourses mouths hang as they may. I always thought it was my father who could never be got to change Fox and that you was convinced that it would be a wise measure and now I see you afraid of hurting the feelings of Cookney. Get this out of your head pray and profit by the opportunity of getting my father to do what is so evidently wanted. And may be so very advantageous to him" (HRO).

Lady Melbourne to Lord Byron (45547, f.43-45; Airlie, Whig 143- 46; Elwin, Wife 150-51)[11]

29th Sept. 1812

Dear L B.

I am ashamed to think of the number of Letters I have plagued you with Lately, yet instead of reforming, I send you another, and an enclosure. You see how

I go on trusting you, & putting myself entirely in y^r. power[12] treat me generously, &, confess that I give you full proof, that I had no secret understanding with L^y B[essborough][13]—in my Letter I desired she would ^tell^ me her real opinion about C[aroline]—which she says she can not do,—I have no belief in the parts about W^m[14] unless it is, that she can manage him more easily than she can any other person, & she thinks it as well to give it y^e appearance of fondness, if she determines to remain—You are too suspicious, after all I have said, it makes me half angry—in one of your last Letters you hinted y^t perhaps I left your Letter in y$^{e.}$ way on purpose. These are your "wounding floats"[15] and shew what those persons are to expect "that lye within the mercy of your Wit"[.] I can not bear her having got that Letter whether she opened it, or found it, 'tis all one, it will be long before I forgive it, if it was either on my Table or in my Drawer, she has added falsehood to her other iniquities, for in that case she could not think it was for her,—I have not been in right good humour since I heard it.—what high flown compliments you have paid me, for Heavens sake lower me to my proper level, or I shall be quite alarm'd when I see you again, I shall neither dare Speak before you, nor to you, & as to talking my usual nonsense that must be quite out of the question, as I shall soon drop from this Pinnacle where you have placed me[.] do let me down easily, that I may not break my Bones by a sudden fall; what can you have in y^r. Head, "Men of distinguished abilities" ce sont des Hommes, comme les autres, &, I am a Woman, comme les autres, Superior in nothing[16]—I happen fortunately to be gifted with a fund of good Nature & chearfulness, & very great Spirits—& have a little more *tact* than my Neighbours, & people call me pleasant because I am always inclined in conversation to enter into ye Subjects that seem most adapted to the taste of those with whom I happen to be—when they are not too high for aspiration (as M^r. Ward[17] says) like some I have lately been with—You say, "I admire you certainly as much as ever you were admired," & a great deal more I assure you than ever I was admired, in y^e *same way,* I may have been beloved—but Love is not admiration. Lovers admire of course without knowing why—Yours therefore is much *more flattering* as I s^d the other day—but you quite astonished me when I found your usual playfulness chang'd into such a formal *tirade.* I have hardly yet recover'd my Surprise—now I have told you every thing & have shewn myself truly to you; I can not see why you should wish that you had not known me,—it can not lead to any regrets, unless circumstances should not stop it entirely, our Friendship will be very pleasant to both as any sentiment must be where all is sunshine—&, where love does not introduce itself, there can be no jealousys, torments, and quarrels;—& should this catastrophe take place, it will, at least to me, always be a pleasing recollection, that we should have been *good friends* (there is something in your expression I like very much) if imperious circumstances had not prevented it,—once you told me you did not understand friendship—I told you I would teach it you, & so I will, if you do not allow C- to take you quite away[.] do you remember some Verses of Voltaire's, ^where^ after lamenting that he was old—he says

> Du Ciel alors daignant descendre,
>
> d'amitié vint à mon secours
>
> Elle étoit peut-être aussi tendre—
>
> Mais moins vive que les amours—[18]

I admire you entirely for your resolutions respecting *her* but D^r. L^d B[yron] you deceive yourself you never will be able to keep them, what, pass your time in endeavouring to put her into good humour, & to satisfy her, & disguise from her that you are unhappy, fine Dreams indeed. This first is much beyond your power and finding how ill you succeed, must inevitably prevent you from perishing in ye last—do not however mistake me, I would not have you say a harsh sentence to her for the World, or any thing that could be deem'd insulting. I had not ye least intention of advising you to do it. There is no kindness that I would not have you shew her, but sacrificing yourself to her, would only be romantic, & not kind—for supposing y^r Sentiments you express to me, are real, it would be quite ye contrary for it must lead to unhappiness & misery, if a little trifling expression of coldness at present would prevent this *finale,* how much more kind, to give a little present pain, & avoid her total ruin; however I do not mean to give any advice, you probably know much better than I do, how to act; You may depend upon my giving you the earliest intelligence in my power of their return. I hear no mention of it yet—& if they come back thro' Scotland which was their intention, we shall hear of their leaving Ireland a long time before they arrive here[19]—I must however add that I think you attach too much blame to yourself—she was no Novice, & tho' I give her credit for being what one must believe, every Heroine of a Romance to be, (except Made Cottins)[20] yet she knew to be upon her guard, & can not be looked upon as the Victim of a designing Man—all the World are of a very different opinion. She always told me you continually sd—that she had exposed herself so much before she was acquainted with you, yt her character could not suffer, as it was already gone—I abused you at the time, for giving it this <color> tho' what you said was perfectly true, & in my opinion exculpates you entirely—Poor Annabella,[21] her innocent Eyes will have to contend with the Black and probably experienced ones of yr Innameratta[.][22] recollect in ye mean time how much they will improve *if* she should be in love with you; ye others are *acquernis*[23] & will be no better. Eyes require yt sort of inspiration. Many people have fine Eyes who do not know what to do with them, & many have nothing behind them, then it is hopeless—Mon cher Neveu, vous etes bien changeant, much like the Man in ye farce we saw together (the Weathercock)[24] do you recollect it. I thought then it was a character not to be found in nature—however, the wind that blows one way may blow from ye contrary point tomorrow—So penser—but where is all yr boasted power of forgetting those you have liked—a Sound brings those objects (I put them in ye plural) back, to yr recollection & displays all ye charms yt had captivated you—& you fall in love anew, but not with them—with *that* sound—something like <Vassir>[25] I think, & his Grandmother's picture—I can forgive any thing but the Custom. Post is very bad, & weather too, does she pick the Chicken Bones, like Catalini.[26] do you think you can manage both her and C.— impossible, as a friend I say flirt as much as you please, but do not get into a serious Scrape before you are safe from the *present* one—

I have been two days at Home Tete a Tete with Mon Mari. he has not been well, & I am in ye greatest alarm lest he should not think himself sufficiently recovered to go to M[elbourne]—if this should be ye case, I will let you know it—Tho' I conclude you will hither at all events if you can *tear yourself away*—I have no guess whether ye others have left London

yrs Dr Ld B truly EM

As I was folding up this Letter, a Servant arrived f^m town & brought me two Letters f^m C[aroline]-, if I know her, vous n'en etes pas quite, both ye Letters are written on the same day, one full of Spirits, gayete, Dinner Parties, & c. & c. ye other *false* written to deceive me, talking of her unhappiness & affecting to be perfectly quiet & resign'd—as this is not in her Nature, you will most likely, know the contrary by this time—she is trying to act upon my feelings, & to make me tell her something about you. *This I shall not do*—she says you are angry begs me to tell her why—entreats me to speak openly—& she will not betray me perhaps I have shewn you her last Letter—if so she will forgive me & so on

I am now inclined to think that if you could get her into a quiet state by any means, it would be ye best chance—you might agree to see her quietly when she returns, provided she makes none of ye scenes she is so fond of[.] it might *possibly* go off in that way, but it never can while she is in this consistent state of imbalance, and whilst she thinks all about her wish to put an end to it—if she thought her friends cared less she would be more likely to take some other Fancy— the result of all this seems to me that ye best thing you can do, is to marry & that in fact you can get out of this Scrape by no other means[27]—

Post Office: Cheltenham

At top of letter:
She desires me to tell her whether I have heard from you since I left Ch[eltenam][.] perhaps she may have ask'd you ye same question—let us be in ye same story, I shall give her no answer till I hear from you or see you, therefore decide what *we* shall say

Lady Melbourne to Annabella Milbanke (Lovelace 92, f.44; Elwin, Wife *155)*[28]

Whitehall

21st Ocr 1812

Dear Annabella———

I have this day received an Answer from Lord Byron, who is much disturb'd at not having received my Letter as soon as he ought to have done, owing to his Servant not having forwarded it to him immediately———he desires me to say, how much obli'd he is to you for the candour, & fairness, with which you have told him your Sentiments,——that altho unfavourable to his hopes, or more properly to his Wishes, for hopes he declares he had not, your conduct on this occasion has encreased the high opinion he had before entertain'd of your abilities, & excellent qualities, & encreases the regret he feels at your decision, as well as his admiration for your character,[29] that he shall in future endeavour, however painfull the effort may be, to limit his feelings to that Sentiment only, as his first object will be now as it would have been, in a different situation, to endeavour to act, as will be most agreable to you; he feels very sensibly the kindness of your conduct, in allowing him to decide whether your Acquaintnce shall continue, or the reverse, that he prizes it much too highly, not to give up every consideration personal to himself, for the chance of obtaining your Friendship—& therefore promises, that you shall never have any renewal of this Subject, which he perceives is so disagreable to you, & therefore if when you meet he should endeavour to improve by Acquaintance with you, he trusts you will not mistake his meaning,—as he now upon his Honor declares that with whatever Good nature you may receive him, it will not mislead him, for he sees by the openness and sincerity of your expressions that he can form no hope. he then appeals to me, whether I think he is likely to "form such hopes," in these Words, ["]God knows whether I am right or not, but I do think I am not very apt to think myself encouraged, what is your opinion"? I really agree with him, & have always seen him very slow in believing yt people even like his Society—he says to me, "I can not Sufficiently thank you for the trouble you have taken on my Account. The interest with which you honor me, is very flattering, & I feel it with the sincerest gratitude. You may rely upon me, that I would not desire you to give any Message, or make any promise for me to Miss Milbanke, that should not be Strictly true & fulfill'd with the utmost rigor, *I never will renew* a Subject which I am convinced would be *hateful* to *her*, & no *condescension* or *indulgence* from her will ever lead me to Suppose, that I can be more to her, than the most common Acquaintance to whom she shews civility when she meets them in Society"[30]——

    I place the greatest reliance upon what he says, & I am sure he will trouble you no more—I therefore hope you may now meet without any awkwardness, there can be no reason for it on either side, & as to you I agree perfectly with him, that it must have raised you very highly not only in his opinion, but also in that of any other person acquainted with the transaction—Believe me

> Dear Annabella
>
> Y^{rs} ever most aff^{ly}
>
> EMelbourne—

I forgot to mention that Ld Byron return'd me your Letter, & seem'd much touch'd by the confidence repos'd in him

---

Annabella Milbanke to Lady Melbourne (45547, f.82-83)

> [21-25 Oct. 1812]

Dear Aunt—On the opposite side you will find what I promised[31]— do not forget *your part*—

    It is so difficult to speak of oneself exactly as one means, that I think you might mistake the account I gave of my defects of temper—As I do not wish you to think *worse* of me than I deserve, I will try to explain myself more correctly—

    I am never irritated except when others are so, and then I am too apt to imitate them—This makes good temper in my companion very necessary for my peace, and if, I am not disturbed by others in this way I have not any disposition to disturb them—I am never sulky, but my spirits are easily depressed, particularly by seeing any body unhappy—

What I call *my Romance* is this—that if I had not acquired the habits of reflecting before I act, I should sometimes have sacrificed considerations of prudence to the impulse of my feelings —but I am not conscious of ever having *yielded* to the temptation which <assaulted> me—

I can assure you *from experience* that I am very thankfully submissive to correction, so tell me where I am wrong—

Yours aff^{ly}

A Mi

AIM's husband-

He must have consistent principles of Duty governing strong & *generous* feelings, and reducing them under the command of Reason—

Genius is not in my opinion *necessary,* though desirable, *if united* with what I have just mentioned—

I require a freedom from suspicion, & from *habitual* ill-humour—also an equal tenor of affection towards me, not that violent attachment which is susceptible of sudden encrease or diminution from trifles—

I wish to be considered by my husband as a *reasonable adviser,* not as a guide on whom he could *implicitly* depend—

So much for the chief requisites of *mind,* and for the sake of these I could overlook many imperfections in other respects—In regard to *external* qualifications I would have fortune enough to enable me to continue without embarassment in the kind of society to which I have been accustomed—I have no inclination to extravagance, and should be content to practise economy for the attainment of this object—

Rank is indifferent to me—*Good connections* I think an important advantage—

I do not regard *beauty,* but am influenced by the *manners of a gentleman,* without which I scarcely think that any one could attract me—

On the back of this sheet:

I would not enter into a family where there was a strong tendency to Insanity—

———————————

———————————

Lady Melbourne to Anne Isabella Milbanke (Lovelace 92, f.46)
[October 25, 1812]

Dear Annabella—

You will see by yᵉ enclosed that I have made free use of yᵉ permission you gave me to tell you, where I think you are wrong. I have stated my ideas very fully, they may be erroneous, but such as they are you have them, in the Account you gave me of yourself, I saw every sort of amiable quality, & feeling & that you may fix upon someone worthy of you, is my sincerest wish—but in your Letter you mention, what I think a quality that requires correction in the highest degree, & that is allowing Yourself to be irritated when others are so—it is the very time when you should be cool & composed, & not allow yʳ Temper to be ruffled— & you who require that the Man of yʳ choice should have a perfect command over his feelings, & who say yᵗ you from habit, have learnt to controul Yours—<u>own</u> yᵗ when others are irritated, you imitate them; how does *this* agree. I really look upon it as a most essential point & most necessary to yʳ happiness to learn to be cool & have entire possession of yourself, when you see others in a passion; otherwise you must be in the wrong, & Aggravate the feelings of those with whom you live;— with common Acquaintance it may be of no consequence,—but if your Husband, should be in ever so absurd a passion, you should not notice it at the time, no Man will bear it with patience; afterwards, if you have been good humour'd at the time he will listen to you with patience, & feel the obligations he has to you—till you can attain this power over Yourself never boast of your command over yʳ passions,—& till you can practise it—you have no right to require it in others—

I have stated this rather strongly, from my persuasion of its importance, & I am sure it is not difficult to acquire, I speak from experience—You say it proves yᵗ you require good Temper in a Husband, but the best Tempers are Subject to Passion, & if opposed at yᵉ time, Passion turns to Rage[.] besides it is mighty ridiculous that you are to be irritated because another person is so,—when coolness & Good humour on yʳ part might set it all right—do consider this point.—As to your Romance, I think in all cases of yᵉ Sort consideration, must be of the greatest advantage—but do not expect too much,—remember Perfection is not in human Nature,—& the *least imperfect person* is all you can hope to find—

believe me

Dear Annabella

Yʳˢ ever Most Aff^{ly}

E Melbourne

Whitehall

(Sunday) 25th Oc^r 1812—

[To/Miss Milbanke]

Enclosure in Lady Melbourne's Letter to Anne Isabella Milbanke, October 25, 1812 (Lovelace 92, f.102)[32]

He must have consistent
principles of duty, governing
strong & generous feelings,
and reducing them under
the commmands of ^Reason^ ~~feeling~~.

this is altogether too
generally express'd—&
consistent principles of duty
not strong enough—

　　as Man should have strong *fixed*
principles of duty—generous
feelings ^are^ absolutely requisite,
but once having strong fixed
principles, & generous feelings
it is unnecessary to say, that

they must be under ye command
of Reason, the having them
implies that—

Genius is not in my opinion
necessary though desirable
if united with what I have
just mentioned—

Genius certainly not necessary,
but very agreeable, as it serves
to lighten the Weight, and
sometimes *dullness,* that is
often attendant, upon good
sense & reason when not
join'd to chearfulness & other
pleasant qualities.———

I require a freedom f^m Suspicion
& from habitual ill humour
also an equal tenor of affection
towards me, not that violent
attachment which is susceptible
of sudden increase or diminution
from trifles.

whether y^r Husband is suspicious
of you or not, must in a
great degree depend upon
yourself—if your conduct
is fair & open, nobody can Suspect you,
unless he should
have a very bad temper
which of course you must
perceive before you marry
him—the same
will do for habitual ill humour, nobody

can deceive you on that

point if you should have even a Slight

acquaintance; an equal

tenor of affection without

any Variation, would be

very tiresome, & cannot

be expected, no person's

manner can be always exactly yᵉ same,

altho' their affection may remain

unalter'd that is yᵉ point to look to——

I wish to be consid—

er'd by my Husband as

a reasonable adviser,

not as a guide on whom

he would implicitly

depend————————

Whoever you may marry

will look upon ^you^ as yᵉ *first*

I have no doubt, as for

the second you need have

no fears————————

So much for yᵉ chief

requisites of mind, & for

yᵉ sake of these I could

overlook many imperfections.

In regard to external qualifca

tions I would have fortune

let us consider what these

chief requisites are when stated together—

consistent principles of

duty, governing generous, & strong

feelings. he must be unsuspicious &,

not habitually ill humour'd

enough to enable me to continue without embarassment in the kind of society to which I have been accustomed—I have no inclination to extravagance; and should be content to practise economy for yᵉ attainment of this object.

an even sort of liking for you. I wonder you leave out good nature & cheerfulness—for without yᵉ first every other quality *may* be disagreable let them be ever so worthy of admiration; & the second renders every thing pleasant.

A man in this case has your free leave to be obstinate perverse morose, sulky and ill natured— the great requisites to me would be good Sense, good Nature and chearfulness. The first aided by the second must combine every sort of good feeling—& the third added to them must produce amiability—& surely that is yᵉ sort of Man with whom you may hope to pass your life happily, & whom you must like, I had rather have a foundation such as I have mention'd, & depend upon its producing the others

than look for trifling perfections

while ye greater & more amiable

feelings are left unexplored

I mean particulary good nature

which I look upon to be

the most essential requisite for

for any person with whom you

are to pass your Life—The rest as to fortune

&c I approve

Rank is indifferent to me,
—good connections I think have
an important advantage.

The Rank of any person you

would marry would entitle

you to make good as well

as agreable connections,—

often when you are obliged to

live with the family, into

which you marry, it may be

very unpleasant

I do not regard beauty, but
am influenced by the manners
of a gentleman without which
I scarcely think that any

a good looking Man is often

preferable to a

beautiful one—I am

strongly of ye same opinion

one could attract me—	as to the manners of
	a Gentleman without
	which no person can
	be agreable or ought
	to be tolerated, with a
	view to making him y^r Husband.
I would not enter into a	This I think a very wise
family where there was a	determination, as it may
strong tendency to insanity	prevent a thousand disagreable occurrences
	you might be liable to[33]———

On ye whole it appears to me that it is almost impossible while you remain on ye Stilts on which you are mounted, y^t you should ever find a person worthy to be y^r Husband. As you are determin'd to look only for Sterling worth, & make it a point to yield to no Amiable qualities, you will never yield at all, for the first without ye assistance of the Second, are not captivating——^a Man possessed of^ Such a Character as you have drawn would marry you from reason, & not from Love— which *you* will not say is what you would wish or like

Marriage after all we can say, or do, must be a sort of Lottery, I ^do^ not mean by this to advise any one, to give way to an Attachment, hastily or *lightly,* As much care should be taken ^as possible^ & no pains spared to ascertain ye Character of ye person,—but yet deceit may be practised, & ye very qualities you describe, are ye easiest to be assumed—any one can pretend to have ye best principles They need only read the part of *Joseph Surface* they may also pretend to Strong feelings, & ill humour may be disguised, that however is ye most difficult, but good nature, openness, frankness, generosity; kindness of heart—these can not be mistaken if you have any opportunity of judging, such as you would have in those circumstances—

[after 25 Oct. 1812]

I thank you most warmly for the trouble you have taken which will be of great use to me—I wish to make some remarks on parts of your very kind letter & Counsell.—

I am so deeply sensible of the mischievous consequences that would ensue from want of temper were I married to a man of warm feelings, (and I could not love one who had them not) that I have thought it a sufficient reason for deferring matrimony. I should at present <recuse>[34] disappointment to a husband who expected to find me possessed of constant self-command & composure—I most fully agree with you in thinking a reciprocation of Passion highly culpable & absurd—it is therefore my constant endeavour to practice Self-government in my present slight trials in order to prepare my mind for enduring those I may hereafter encounter, in such a manner as will make myself & others happy—I have confessed that my good resolutions on this subject sometimes fail when their execution is most requisite, but as the failures become gradually *less frequent,* I hope I may without presumption look forward to the time when I shall *not* disappoint my husband—I do not exactly recollect in what way I *gave myself credit* for Controuling my feelings, but I think I must have applied it to those which border on Romance, not to my irritable disposition, as I reproach myself so painfully for not having completely subdued the latter.

With this consciousness of my own deficiencies in what is so essential to the conduct of a good wife, I am not in danger of being dissatisfied because I do not find perfection—Believe me I have never imagined myself deserving of attachments from the best kind of *imperfect* characters, and on that account I did not venture to include in my demands some qualities which you justly consider very great advantages, (as those of Talents & Chearfulness) because I would not be conceitedly unreasonable

To some particulars you have not exactly estimated my meaning, which I cannot be surprised at when I consider the obscurity & insufficiency of my statement owning to my wish for brevity—You are mistaken in thinking that I meant to dispense with the amiable feelings—I thought those of "good nature, openness, frankness, & kindness of heart" included under the term "generous" and if that expression was not correct I cannot explain my meaning better than by those particular qualities which you have enumerated as the foundation of Love—So far from supposing that I could be attached by a character of *dry* Reason, and *cold* Rectitude, I am always *repelled* by people of that description.—

With regard to the *Principles*,[35] I thought that if they are *consistent* they cannot be *unsettled*, therefore that it is needless to add that they should be *fixed*— However you are very right in reproving vague expression and I should have made the sense less equivocal—

You say that with all these requisites "man has my free leave to be obstinate, perverse, morose, sulky & ill-natured"—How can these dispositions exist with the well-regulated good feelings which I mention in the first place?—Besides I afterwards specify the absence of ill-humoured *habits*.—If I had not ^thought^ this sufficient to secure the exclusion of ~~all~~ such bad qualities as you describe I should have named them distinctly as objectionable—

After so full an explanation you will perhaps take off my *stilts,* and allow that I am only *on tiptoe.* I quite agree with what you say, and I am trying to shew you that it agrees more nearly with what *I* said than you seem to suppose.

Most aff^ly yours

AMil

Lady Melbourne to Lord Byron (45547, f.46-47)

<24th>[36] Feb^y

1813

Dear L^d B.

I had heard the parts concerning *them* from a person to whom *she* had told it, & am very sorry to have it confirm'd by you,[37] y^r determination[38] I must admire, however much, I may lament the consequences of it[39]—I am very glad y^t you are not implicated, for ye reason y^t probably you could have done them very little good & that you would have distressed yourself——Y^r Observation respecting money transactions is too true, nothing so rare as meeting with people who act handsomely on such occasions—in Love you have every claim to be better treated, but I think I know why you have not been so, & I judge by ye Character you have given me of yourself—You say you are Suspicious, & unreasonable when you are in Love;—when a Man is unreasonable, it is quite *impossible* not to deceive him, because no one will expose themselves to be quarrel'd with, & Scolded when they can avoid it, by some little Subterfuge; altho' what they may wish to hide is perfectly innocent, yet if they are to be found fault with, that is quite reason enough for concealment—& then when in addition a Man is suspicious, there is some little satisfaction in being too cunning for him.—I believe much ye best way is to confide, in the person you love, you have much ye best chance—if you meet with an honorable person she will love you ten times better, for ye confidence you repose in her—& if a bad one it dont much Signify, she will deceive you do what you will— there is my creed, & it is not entirely Theoretical. You know you may come to me whenever you please, & that I am always happy & delighted to see you & really I could never forgive you, if you left England without seeing me *more* than ye once or twice you mention——L^{dy} Bl[arney]. is gone to B[rocket].H[all]. when she returns I shall have some Acc't of C[aroline]-&, how she is going on. I really think you should give her Notice before you depart, in case she should wish for this interview as it would be hard upon her not to know of it—& she certainly would feel the more Sensibly from having to reproach herself with having behaved so very ill to you—but I conclude y^r departure is not so near at hand as to make any arrangement, of this last, necessary at present, & we can talk about it when I see you, which I hope will be soon

Y^{rs} ever Dr L^d B

EM

[The Lord Byron/Bennett Street]

Lady Melbourne to Lord Byron (Murray)

Monday, Mor^g [No Date]

Dr L^d B.

they dont come till Wed^y. or Thursday[.] I am going to Covent Garden to Miss O'Neill will you come? I shall be in Ld Egremonts⁴⁰ Box & Emily ye only Lady—if this *be* not agreeable perhaps you will call upon me to morrow, at any time after 1/2 past four

Y^rs ever,

EM

[The Lord Byron]

Lady Melbourne to Lord Byron (45547, f.49-50)

Bennett Street
15th March
1813

Dear L^d B.

I will neither burn, read, nor keep y^r Letter—but I have written to C[aroline]- to desire her to decide (as you will not) whether I shall send it to her, or return it to you—⁴¹

You are mistaken when you say "you believe I am not unacquainted with her abuse of L^y O[xford]"⁴² for I really do not know what she has said. The only time she has mentioned her ^character^ in her Letters to me, she certainly did not praise her, but that, I have never told any body, & no other person knows what it was, not even yourself—C[aroline]- writes me word that L^y O[xford] says in her Letters that all the Females of her family as well as herself have spoken of her in a "gross manner" it may be so—I answer for nobody—all I can say is that I have never heard any thing of the Sort from any of those I have met,—as to myself I have had no conversation about her with any person except with you—& I do not *think* you will say I ever abus'd her—Therefore on the whole I should rather guess that L^y O[xford], has taken up this idea on light grounds. Ladys sometimes hear some trifling thing that has been said & fancy ten times more was meant.[43]

I do not at all wonder that you should dislike seeing C- before a 3^d person, the only wonder is that you ever agreed to it, but still you did not act with y^r usual judgment in preferring L^y O[xford] to me—no tirade, declamation or mention of C-could have signify'd if s^d before me, and I know nothing of *Lovers* if *any thing* she had s^d before L^y O[xford][44]—would not have subjected you to some reproach at some time or other—besides you might have depended upon my leaving ye room if she had shewn a disposition to be quiet—& most assuredly in any case should not have been a listener—however I really am very glad that my attendance upon such an Occasion has been dispensed with & <am most> obliged to you for having got me off—indeed if *you* had not desired it, I should not have agreed to it from the first—If it should be possible for me at any future time to obtain y^r picture I certainly will do it[45]—but at present I see no hopes—& if any Letters ever should be in my possession, I will burn them instantly——

have you read the *Times* of to day[46]—there is an Acc^t. of L^d. Moira's having examined two Medical people,[47] which will not redound to his kind nor to that of his employer[48]—the remarks before the depositions, are very good.[49] I am told but *not* from good authority that they are written by M^r. Whitbread[50]—I hear it is the fashion amongst Ladies to burn their News papers—that the Servants may not read such improprieties. They had better burn them without reading, when they are first brought, that would really be acting with propriety—

If you leave Town as you intended, the time is very near—& I conclude I shall not see you, but if you wish to hear what is going on when you shall have retired, send me y^r. directions[.] Many Thanks for y^r good Wishes—if they are selfish,[51] they are the more flattering

Y^rs ever

EM

As you s^d I *must* get *well,* I have been out this Mor^g which I was told would do me good, & I have thoughts of going to L^{dy} Hollands this Eve & you see this is doing ye best I can in obedience to y^r orders but if I should catch cold in so doing, and be lay'd up in a Fever—I shall say *you* made me do this it is all y^r. fault[.] This is y^r. Lord's method of reasoning——

———————————

Lady Melbourne to Lord Byron (45547, f.51-52)

[March 15-18, 1813]

D^r L^d B—— C[aroline]- wrote to me Yesterday, to desire to have y^r Letter, which I sent last Night, & you will probably hear from her to morrow—& I hope she will send you the Picture——

I am sorry you did not come to Mrs Hopes[52] as it was a very good party—or I might perhaps think so from its being new to me as I had not been out for a fortnight—after all—Novelty has its charms,[53] & you would have thought it pleasant too—I wish'd for you at Supper—tho' we had neither Lobster Sallad nor Champaign[54]— Ministers & their Wives & their Supporters were very cross & peevish at the awkw from ye House of Com—s it was quite laughable to see them.

Y^{rs} D^r L^d B ever truly,

EM

———————————

Lady Melbourne to Lord Byron (Murray)

24th March

1813

Dear L^d B—

they are gone this Morning to Roehampton and return Satur day. If you like to call upon me to morrow, you will find me at home & I am the more anxious not to miss this opportunity of seeing you, as I hear nothing of their intention of returning even into Hertford^re— indeed if she continues to behave quietly, I think *he* will prefer remaining here—& I wish she may for her Sake, & for Yours—altho' the consequences of it promise to be so disagreeable to me——I call'd upon L^y H[ollan]^d. Yesterday Morn^g—who complain'd that *Your Guardian* would not bow to her, on Acc'^t of her *intimacy* with you—I said, he bow'd spoke and call'd upon me.—which proved y^t he must have some other reason for his behaviour to her. She s^d Oh No!—for he hardly touch'd his Hat to Ld Holland & she ask'd me if I had seen ye meeting between you ^& him^ at L^y L[ansdowne?]—I said I had seen you both in the Same room, & was close to you when he came in, & that I afterwards Spoke to him & y^t certainly if he quarrel'd with people for being intimate with you, I should be one of the first to suffer—she appear'd alltogether very much dissatisfied as this pass'd before a number of persons,—to whom I guess'd she had been representing herself as a Martyr in your cause before I appear'd—but this did not induce me to give up the argument

Y^rs ever

EM

I am busy reading D^r. Gall's[55] book, & find Miss Burney,[56] was quite wrong, it was she who told me ye Nonsense I was talking to you ye other Night, so you may come

Envelope of letter of March 24, 1813:
I see what I have written is so easily read y^t I must put this in another cover

On the other side of this envelope:
without fear of examination or Shears, or any thing even x x x will, not <see through it>[57]—I am going to a party at L^y Westmoreland to Night & should not be much surprised to see you there.

> L^y Heathcote had
> a Supper last Night
> but I did not stay

Lady Melbourne to Lord Byron (Murray)

25ᵗʰ March

1813

Dʳ Lᵈ B.

As you say, C[aroline] certainly prevents my dropping yʳ. Acquaintance, tho' I beg once for all to state yᵗ if there was no Caroline in yᵉ World—it is yᵉ very last Acquaintance I should wish to drop—& never will unless I am drop'd——⁵⁸

She writes to me more reasonably to day, reproaches me with wishing to "leave her in the lurch", as she can depend upon *no one* but me—this alludes to yᵉ Picture & the Letters which she now says she will give up to me provided I will pledge my Word to have a copy taken of the Miniature⁵⁹—I have ans'd this by yᵉ post to day, first stating that I never left any one in yᵉ lurch in my life—(I am very tenacious of my honor—you see) & that if she chuses to give me the Picture on these conditions, they shall be fullfill'd before I trust it out of my possession——I neither ask'd for it nor seem'd anxious to have it, as yᵗ would certainly have prevented her giving it me—she then bids me recollect the *Hair* & this is yᵉ purpose of my writing—do send me some for the little bits, I took by force will not Satisfy her—& really when a Lady condescends to make Such a fuss, for such a trifle⁶⁰—it is not for a Gentleman to *faire le difficile* & really by yʳ reluctance to have yʳ Hair touched, or to part with any of it,—I am tempted to think there is some particular charm attached to it⁶¹—& yᵗ some of yʳ powers will be lessen'd, I will not say lost, if you granted all yᵉ requests of *that sort* made to you—something like Sampson[.] She⁶² has sent me a copy of part of yᵉ Letter, you told me she⁶³ had sent you. What a wicked Man!!!!

13th of August—What is rather odd is, yᵗ from a particular circumstance not connected with you,⁶⁴ I know where *we* were on yᵗ day—it was yᵉ Night you had the Spasm at Mʳ. Dicks⁶⁵—& I now discover that was a punishment for yʳ perjuries—but whether sent from Allah, or another person,—I can not pretend to determine—You must so often have taken them separately as yʳ <philosophy>⁶⁶ on Similar Occasions, yᵗ you may know, which punishes most Severely—next time take <fever>[67] he'll do you no harm—what a fool I am, but let me have my laugh while I can—& all this nonsense will make me too late for Dinner

Y[rs] ever EM

Lady Melbourne to Lord Byron (45547, f.53-54)

[before May 21, 1813]

Dear L[d] B I found L[y] Bessb[orough] much better than I expected, she had found herself rather unwell, & expressed a wish to be Cupp'd[68] which alarmed them, but she was relieved by putting her feet in warm water and flour of Mustard Seed, & I left her in Bed & very comfortable—I told her how anxious you were about her,[69] & she desired me to say how very much obliged to you she was & wish'd you to be told that the only thing to quiet her mind was to be assured y[t] no more meetings will take place at present between you & C- for she is now convinced y[t] every one of these that she has Witness'd have done incalculable Mischief & that her mind is so Strongly impressed with this idea, that every time she closed her Eyes last Night & to day she fancied she saw you two running away together, & y[t] she awaked in the greatest alarm & horror—You will perceive that this has taken entire possession of her Nerves —& they must be quieter,.

Lady Melbourne to Lord Byron (45547, f.55)

21st May
1813

L[d] B

we dine at L[y]. Cowpers at 1/2 past five,[70] & she begs you will favour her with y[r] company—but if you should prefer fasting—& will come there at a quarter before Seven we can go all together, for as we are allow'd but one Ticket amongst us, you would be requir'd here to gain admission separately.—Your accusation ag[st] me of wishing to prevent your going to L[y] Spensers[71] was very unjust, for you are not bound to remain there the whole time, & if I find it dull I may perhaps go there myself[.] our party consists of Six. L[d] & L[y] Jersey[72] Emily & myself—You K[73] of — and Augustus Foster[74]—

yrs ever

EM

[The Lord Byron/Bennett Street]

Lady Melbourne to Lord Byron (45547, f.57-58; Airlie, Whig 155)

7th July 1813

D[r] L[d] B-

     She[75] is what she calls calm this Mor[g]- & I was in hopes I might have read some parts of y[r] Letter to her—& in that intention told her I had heard & that you wish'd to know how she was, but I soon found, that the less I s[d] the better—I ask'd her if she had any Message to send, she s[d] tell him I have been ill, that I am now calm, but not very well but dont tell him what pass'd y[e] other night. I then s[d] probably you have told him y[r] own story, have you written? after an untoward attempt at equivocation, she confess'd she had, but denied your having sent an answer—however, this I dont believe, as I do not see how you could avoid answering her—she then s[d]—she should not abuse you she should keep her thoughts to herself—& to y[e] World she should praise y[r]. behaviour—& upon my just hinting that she had s[d] shameful things y[e] other Night & that I was glad she had made this determination she went into a rage, saying y[t] she would expose you[76] and clear herself & so on—she is now like a Barrel of Gunpowder & takes fire with y[e] most trifling Spark,—she has been in a dreadfull—I was interrupted & obliged to put my paper into my drawer, & now I can not, for my life recollect what I was going to say—oh now I have it——I was stating y[t] she had been in a dreadful bad humour this last Week with her, when y[e] fermentation begins there is no Stopping it—till it boils forth, she must have gone to L^y H[eathcote's] determin'd to pique you by her Waltzing & when she found that fail'd, in her passion, she wish'd to expose you, not feeling how much worse it was for herself—now she seems ashamed for ye first time I ever saw ye least mark of that feeling—it might have been kept Secret—but for L^y Os^s[ulstone][77] & L^y H[eathcote]—the first from folly—the other from being entirely ignorant how to be good natur'd—& from a wish to display her fine feelings—That is ye reason why all these Women abuse you, how I hate that affectation of Sentiment—I know they would talk & thought if it reach'd you it must make you uncomfortable & therefore desired L^y O[xford] to say to you there had been a Scene—but y^t she was calm'd & I would write to you next Mor^g

at present I am trying to get her out of Town & hope I shall Succeed——I was able to send for Fre^d[erick Lamb] whom I knew could hold her & I could not by myself & indeed I must do L^y Bl[arney]- y^e *justice* to say that her representations of her Violence in these paroxysms was not at all exaggerated, I could not have believed it possible for any one to carry absurdity to such a pitch—I call it so, for I am convinced she knows perfectly what she is about all the time, but she has no idea of controuling her fury

She broke a Glass, & Scratched herself, as you call it, with the broken pieces—L^y O[ssulstone] and L^y H[eathcote][78]—discussed instead of taking it from her, & I had just left off, holding her for 2 Minutes—she had a pair of Scissors in her hand when I went up with which she was Wounding herself but not deeply— pray if you answer her Letters do not let her find out I have written you word of all this—I shall perhaps meet you Somewhere but if I do not, you shall know how we go on,—I can not describe how fatigued I was Yesterday—I must finish

Y^rs ever,

EM

Augst 8th

1813

D^r L^d B.

very mysterious without doubt, but quite right in looking upon me as a true friend

If you have any Secret you wish to confide to me you may do it Safely, but I shall not plague you to tell me—do what is most pleasant to yourself——I am not given to make professions but so far I will say that you will never find me either deceive or betray you,—come & see me if you can Monday about 1/2 past Three I mention y^t time, as I must go out late, or if that should not suit you come Tuesday at any time you please. I think I shall be gone towards ye end of ye Week which makes me anxious to see you as soon as I can, but to day both Emily and Frederick leave London so my time must be given up to them—I am very sorry for Mad^e de Stael tho' I think her so disagreeable, you judge her quite truly, about her wish to shew off[.]⁷⁹ The D^{ss} of D[evonshire] came to Town to see her Yesterday, & Ward has been with her every day—Nugent was ill & put off his Supper, Ward took it, & Nugent got well & was one of Wards guests.—who was very Cross, thought he had been playd upon & receiv'd us all a contre Coeur⁸⁰ & gave himself all sorts of Airs⁸¹ & showed us all plainly he would have preferr'd our absence to our presence—& in this humour he chose to sit by me at Supper, which did not answer, for we began a dispute upon Politiks, & he heard several truths, that did not add to the sweetness of his Temper,.—Yesterday I was all day in a Water party, & feel quite weary to day at ye recollection of ye length of time we were confined to a Boat only *Nine H^{rs},* as we *continued* to have ye tide agst us both going & coming—not a [fragment; letter ends here]

Cheltenham

23[d] Aug[st] 1813

D[r] L[d] B—

My Stupidity was not at all exaggerated Yesterday, as you well know for on reading y[r] Letter once again, I find I had mistaken several things in it, & as there were people in the room whom I did not wish should partake of y[e] amusement I always receive from y[r]. Letters I put it in my pocket in a hurry. You forget y[t] mine upon which you comment was in answer to a very deplorable one I had from you, that I had received two or three in y[e] same Stile & that your merry one, had not reach'd me, and pleas'd me, as it has Since.

You can not expect me with my head full of these Waters,[83] (which make even Nugent[84] twirl about, strange as it appears)—to understand & unravel y[e] confusion y[t] exists amongst all y[e] different Ladies you allude to[85]—You are accustom'd to it, therefore to you I have no doubt it is clear—my Magical influence, you make me Laugh—I won't say, as the Marechalle D'anise[86] (I think it was) when she was going to be executed ^for witchcraft^, & was ask'd by what means she obtain'd her power over some person, whom I have forgot—par le pouvoir qu'ont les Esprits forts sur les ames faibles[87]—for I have no pretensions to strength of Mind, & I always think that when people talk of my power they are laughing at me and you more than any one I have ever met with,—& I have no objection to it, for I like a Joke even when against myself & it always appears to me that when you are describing my influence over you, you mean yours over me.

I am entertained at y[r] taking up the Cudgels in defence of L[d]. S[ligo's]. beauty.[88] 'tis a bad cause, depend upon it.—after all I don't know him & have never seen him nearer than across y[e] Opera House—were we to come closer to one another, perhaps I might *alter* my Opinion but at y[t] distance he is hideous, it may not be positive ugliness but it is something indescribably disagreable—& according to my opinion if any Woman Suffers him, he is a fortunate person, you think I mean only his Size, which after all is no advantage either to a Marquis or a Prince altho' their rank may be with some description of persons, as to y[e] P[rince]. I don't believe any Man in that Situation ever met with so little Success; & as to being really liked (for himself) I believe he is to this day ignorant of yᵉ delight and Witching of such a feeling—this may astonish you from me, if you meant *as I thought,* ~~the~~ ^a^ Sarcastic reflection upon me.—however, when ever you may think it worth Your while to gain any information on that Subject, I will Satisfy you fully—⁸⁹ recollect in yᵉ mean time yᵗ the Picture was not a likeness of his RH—But I am glad you deny both yᵉ Malady and yᵉ Melancholy,⁹⁰ & I hope you will convince me of it and of yᵉ truth of what you say, yᵗ you wish to see me by calling upon me on Friday in Town, You see I don't intend to be Satisfy'd by mere words— about four is yᵉ best time but you will find me at any other Hour, if that should not be convenient to you.

                                        Ever yʳˢ Dʳ Lᵈ B
                                        EM

an invitation to B[rocket].⁹¹ why—I invited you last Year—oh but, I forgot, you were then obeying my Commands in *this place*[.]⁹² however there are few things I should like so well as to have you Visit me there—but two yʳˢ hence!—I shall be in my dotage—& yet *perhaps* it may still be prevented by C[aroline]—how provoking that is to me is impossible to be confess'd

[The Lord Byron/Bennet St. St. James's/London; to be kept/My Mother/to Lᵈ Byron⁹³]

Lady Melbourne to Lord Byron (45547, f.65-67)

                                        13ᵗʰ Ocʳ
                                        1813

Dear L B

        Lʸ Holland call'd upon me this Morᵍ to ask me if I knew the name of a Physician, whom you had engaged to go abroad with you, & on my saying I was quite ignorant about it, she beg'd me to write, or *communicate* with you by *any means* I might *have,* that if you had given up all thoughts of leaving England,[94] she wish'd to know something about this person, & where he could be found, as some friends of hers were in distress[95]—I suspect it was for the D[uch]ᵉ[ss] & D[u]ᵏ[e] of Bedford,[96] but she would not tell—pray either let me know what to say, or write to her yourself

I was happy to find you seated over a Table &c. with him, for when I saw the date of your Letter, I began to fear some *catastrophe,* as I did not expect you would have left A[ugusta]- just at that time, however it was perfectly right,—I have no doubt what he says about *Ph*[ryne][97]- is quite true, but what of that it only tells against himself—& yᵉ probability is, that Sʳ *Brilliant*[98] may have the power to say to him *some* day,—Mon Ami—tout cela est changè,[99]—for in so many words it is only saying, she does not like me.—Poor Soul, she seems very interesting ^with^ great Susceptibilities and quietness of feeling—I am very sorry for her, she must be so unhappy,[100] yet still, I believe that that state when the mind is fully engross'd is preferable to the one of distaste and Nausea in which she has hitherto existed.— she must enjoy those *petit soirs,* which you will not detail[101] & which I should say were indescribable if I did not recollect some lines I think so beautiful, perhaps *you never* read them

Pass too the glance none Saw beside
The smile none else could understand;[102]

The exchange of papers seems to me what *You would* call the best Sign were it not for that circumstance I should think, she was what I *once* sᵈ C[aroline]- was *not*—I ought to be able to form some judgment, for I was once in yᵉ same Situation—the same things said. The same resolutions taken,—You are inclined to Laugh, & I dont wonder at it, but were I to tell you how long it lasted, your Laughter would change into Sorrow—but no writing pass'd & it was a person not "fram'd to make Woman false"[103]—like the present *pretendant*—that's for your comfort,—

What a Strange thing altogether, as you sᵈ of A[nnabella]-, these things happen when people think themselves *infallible,*[104] where is it that someone says—

"*Villainous thoughts* when these *Mutualities* marshall the way"[105] I could laugh—but I do not, it is too serious to indulge in that,—& I will just make one observation which prudence Suggests—it appears to me that the turn this must take *is Serious,* is Sir Brilliant prepared to go all lengths, if necessary? is he sure it is what he should like entirely? then proceed.—you can not mis understand me—I *think,;* I do not allude to the sort of thing that might have arisen from a conversation you related to me,—it is always necessary to be prepared for what may happen——

I have turned your Likeness into ye Garden[106] till I have finish'd my Letter, & he disturbs me every few Minutes to know if it is done so y^t I hardly know what I write, & it will Shorten my Letter, so much the better for you. C[aroline]- told me you had written very crossly, & wishing her much domestic happiness—I answer'd I supposed she had mention'd her feelings about her Husband[.] She s^d Oh no, not a Word I thought you had!—no indeed I answer'd, *if I write* I say as little as possible about you, & in fact I had not told you then,—she then s^d no Matter, once I should have been in fits, but now I shall take no Notice of it—/ I did not reply, & she really seems so much more at her ease, that I hope there is no danger of any of ye Epistles you apprehended—though there is no answering for her,—if she *hears* any thing, which I hope she will not—

I went last Night to Drury Lane to see a New Operatic Drama, very Stupid—by a M^r. <Thompson>, they say, I see it is given out for to Night but so much dissatisfaction was shewn I think it will not be allowed to go on—the Jokes in ye comic part worse than Lewis's the Ale Boy's[.][107] patience is quite exhausted and y^rs pretty well tried—So adieu

Ever y^rs
EM

At top of first page:
Mad^e de Stael says she has work'd two Miracles upon M^r. Ward—She has taught him to be civil to Women & to be devout.[108]

[45547, f.67, October 30, 1813; The/Lord Byron/Aston Hall/Rotherton/Yorkshire; Marked "Free"; To be kept, my Mother to L[or]d Byron][109]
Lady Melbourne to Lord Byron (45547, f.68)

Canning is not pleasant in my Eyes—his countenance is false & he always looks Suspicious, & a sort of imitation of Sheridan,¹¹² but so inferior, that with me it loses all its effect—I long to see yʳ Tale,¹¹³ I make no doubt it is beautiful not from yᵉ Opinion Lᵈ & Lʸ H[ollan]ᵈ have given for I think neither of them have any taste in Poetry¹¹⁴—she never judges for herself—but is guided by the opinions of some one whom she thinks good authority—Canning & Frere's¹¹⁵ judgment is not to be disputed—& tho' they write themselves they will not abuse what is really good—I hope you'll come very soon, do you hear? or rather do you heed?

Yʳˢ Ever

EM

[The/Lord Byron/Bennett Street]

Notes: Part III

1. Byron might have known better than to ask Lady Melbourne, for she had already facilitated the disastrous marriage between his half-sister Augusta and the gambling rake George Leigh. "I think her thanking you for your abetment of her abominable marriage (7 *years* after the event!!) is the only instance of similar gratitude upon record," he wrote of Augusta (July 1, 1813; *LJ* 3:70).
2. "I found a half sheet full of ridicule of me . . . in a hand I knew," Caroline explained when Lady Melbourne accused her of going through her desk drawers (1812; 45546, f.54).
3. Byron and Lady Melbourne discussed his negotiations concerning the sale of Newstead Abbey, as well as the depositions of Lady Douglas claiming that Queen Caroline had an illegitimate daughter (March 13, 1813; *LJ* 3:25). Byron planned to travel abroad, perhaps visiting Lady Melbourne's son, Frederick, who was stationed in Sicily (February 28, 1813; *LJ* 3:23).
4. Byron wrote to Lady Melbourne on April 5, 7, and 19, 1813, with no extant response from her.
5. Lady Melbourne had been having breakfast with the Prince Regent when she heard the news. Byron argued that "real feeling does not disclose its intention and always shuns display" (July 6, 1813; *LJ* 3:72). He was careful to keep on good terms with Lady Melbourne during this period, if for no other reason than to tell his side of the story (July 9, 1813; *LJ* 3:74).
6. Thomas Claughton, a Lancashire lawyer, offered £140,000 to purchase Newstead Abbey, but became reluctant to follow through and delayed even paying his £25,000 deposit (Marchand, *Portrait* 131-32). On August 20, 1814, Byron signed papers that terminated Claughton's contract and freed Newstead Abbey for subsequent sale. Claughton lost £5,000 he had left as a deposit when he failed to pay the balance (174). Newspapers falsely reported that Claughton was a young man who had been "ill treated" in the transaction and accused Byron of taking "an unfair advantage of the *law* to enforce the

contract" (July 18, 1813; *LJ* 3:77).

7. Fifteen other letters to Lady Melbourne went unanswered, or the responses have not survived. Byron was attempting to overcome his passion for Augusta Leigh at this time (September 8, 1813; *LJ* 3:112), which may account for the silence.

8. His letters on this subject are dated October 1, 5, 8, 10, 11, and 13. During this period, he also received Lady Melbourne's flattering remarks on additions to *The Giaour* (September 28, 1813; *LJ* 3:123), attended the Aston races with Augusta (September 29, 1813; *LJ* 3:126), and dined at Holland House (September-October 1813; *LJ* 3:127-29).

9. Byron had already altered the relationship between Selim and Zuleikha from brother and sister to cousins to avoid speculation about autobiographical intent.

10. See Lady Melbourne's letter of December 5, 1804, which alludes to Fox's mismanagement of the Derbyshire estate.

11. Airlie's version omits the first six lines and the postscript to the letter. Elwin includes a line from Lady Melbourne's letter (*Wife* 150-51).

12. Byron wrote, "I have trusted you with my heart & am entirely in your power" (September 13, 1812; 45549, f.40). Lady Melbourne transcribed this letter in her own hand (45547, f.40-42).

13. Byron feared that Lady Melbourne and Lady Bessborough were working together to end his affair with Caroline Lamb. Lady Bessborough was Caroline's mother.

14. William Lamb, whose marriage to Caroline Lamb had failed even before her notorious affair with Byron began in 1812.

15. *floats:* insults, jeers. "Flouts" (Airlie, *Whig* 143).

16. Byron had written: "When I do see a woman superior not only to all her own [sex] but to most of ours, I worship her . . . And when I know that men of the first judgement and the most distinguished abilities have entertained . . . an opinion which my own humble observation, without any great effort of discernment, has enabled me to confirm . . . you will not blame me for following the example of my elders and betters, and admiring you certainly as much as you were ever admired" (September 25, 1812; *LJ* 2:208).

17. John William Ward.

18. Descending from the sky, / out of friendship she comes to my relief,/she would be perhaps as tender, / but less lively than love.

19. In September 1812 Caroline Lamb left for her family's estate in Kilkenny, Ireland with her husband and mother. Her affair with Byron was so widely discussed that a separation was proposed to end any further embarrassment. This letter sets the ground rules for Lady Melbourne's correspondence with Byron and explains, through her attack on her daughter-in-law, her motive in corresponding with Caroline's lover.

20. The novelist Madame Cottins (1770-1807).

21. In a letter of September 18, 1812, Byron had indicated that he was now attached to Annabella Milbanke (*LJ* 2:199).

22. See Byron's letters of September 25 and 27, 1812, in which he refers to an Italian woman with whom he had become infatuated. Her large appetite led Byron to comment, ironically, "a woman should never be seen eating or drinking, unless it be *lobster sallad & Champagne,* the only truly feminine & becoming viands" (September 25, 1812; *LJ* 2:208). Two days later he wrote again of being "rather captivated with a woman not very beautiful, but very much in the style I like, dark & lively" (September 27, 1812; *LJ* 2:217).

23. *acquernis:* acquired, bought.

24. A play by John Till Allingham, which Byron performed at Southwell and apparently saw with Lady Melbourne (Boyes 125). *The Weathercock* was published in 1806.

25. Airlie transcribes this as "Vapid" (*Whig* 146).

26. Madame Angelica Catalani, the popular Italian opera singer, came to London in 1806 and was singing at Covent Garden. "Altamont is a good deal with me," Byron wrote to John Cam Hobhouse. "Last night at the Opera Masquerade, we supped with seven whores, a *Bawd* and a *Ballet-master*, in Madame Catalani's apartment behind the Scenes, (of course Catalani was *not* there)" (February 27, 1808; *LJ* 1:159).

27. Byron relied on Lady Melbourne to disentangle him from Caroline Lamb. "I see nothing but marriage & a *speedy one* can save me," he wrote to Lady Melbourne. "If your Niece is attainable I should prefer her—if not—the very first woman who does not look as if she would spit in my face" (September 28, 1812; *LJ* 2:218).

28. Sometime before October 8, 1812, Lady Melbourne forwarded Byron's proposal of marriage to her niece Annabella Milbanke. This letter is no longer extant. Annabella rejected the proposal. Lady Melbourne forwarded the rejection to Byron, together with a copy of the "Character" of him which Annabella had confided to her (Elwin, *Wife* 153). Elwin mistakenly dates the letter reproduced here as October 25, when it is in fact October 21.

29. Elwin indicates no omission in his transcription of this text. However, his version ends here and continues many lines later, with "He says to me . . ." (*Wife* 155).

30. We have no record of the paragraph from which this quotation comes. It is interesting, nevertheless, to compare Lady Melbourne's quotations from Byron's letters with his sentiments as expressed in letters written on October 17 and 18, 1812 (*LJ* 2:226-27, 229).

31. Elwin notes that on receiving Lady Melbourne's letter of October 21, "Annabella apparently went up to London to see her aunt, who asked to be informed what qualities she required in a husband" (*Wife* 156). She returned to Richmond and composed this reply.

32. Lady Melbourne copied out Annabella's list and added her responses in the right-hand column.

33. "prevent . . . liable to" appears on the left-hand column of a new page in the letter.

34. *recuse:* refuse, reject.

35. Annabella's footnote reads: "which I would have founded on a sense of Religion—".

36. Possibly "27th".

37. This may be a reference to Byron's letter of February 12, 1813, in which he writes: "I trust that Mrs. C. & the C. of Cs. will not break—it would be an infinite loss to both—on *my* account they certainly shall not" (February 12, 1813; *LJ* 3:19). "Mrs. C. & the C. of Cs" is one of the few phrases marked unidentified in Marchand's edition of Byron's letters. It may refer to Caroline & the Countess of Cowper.

38. To go abroad with Lady Oxford. "*We* have great ideas of going abroad—in which you will heartily concur" (February 12, 1813; *LJ* 3:19).

39. "The idea of meeting you was a great *temptation* to L[ad]y Cowpers the other night but—I resist temptation better than I used to which you will be glad to hear" (February 25 [1813]; *LJ* 3:22).

40. Lady Melbourne's lover, Sir George O'Brien Wyndham, third earl of Egremont.

41. Lady Caroline Lamb wrote a letter to Lady Oxford requesting an interview. Byron instructed Lady Melbourne to "read [this letter] & put in the fire or keep as you please" (March 14, 1813; *LJ* 3:26).

42. Byron was arranging an interview with Caroline Lamb, and he wanted Lady Oxford rather than Lady Melbourne as a witness. Lady Melbourne may have felt that she was in danger of surrendering the role of confidante to Lady Oxford. Though critical of her daughter-in-law, Caroline Lamb, Lady Melbourne protected the honor of her family and tried to keep negative gossip within the family circle. Byron explained his decision to consult Lady Oxford: "My wish that Ly. O[xford] should be the third person was to save you a scene—& I confess also—odd as it may seem—that it would have been less awkward for me—you will wonder why—& I can't tell you more than that she might make some

brilliant harangue to which—[Lady Oxford] would be a less embarrassed listener than you could possibly be" (March 14, 1813; *LJ* 3:26).

43. Byron's explanation was as follows: "If L[ad]y O[xford] entertained or expressed such opinions of you or yours—we should quickly quarrel—I w[oul]d not hear those who have treated me with forbearance & kindness traduced even by her—& I certainly like her better than any thing on earth" (March 15, 1813; *LJ* 3:27).

44. Byron had implied that he had relieved Lady Melbourne of a chore. He added, by way of explanation, that Caroline Lamb "wrote to Lady Oxford desiring to see *her*—& I thought it as well to *lump* the interviews into one—& cut you out as the third—for reasons below mentioned" (March 14, 1813; *LJ* 3:26).

45. Caroline Lamb had stolen Byron's picture from John Murray, his publisher, and Byron requested Lady Melbourne's assistance in retrieving it. "Will you have ye goodness to forward the enclosed?" he asked her. "It contains a request for the picture—& a *hint* at ye letters.—I wish to make this one more effort—which may succeed" (March 13, 1813; *LJ* 3:25).

46. Two days earlier, Byron had written: "I shall make you blush by asking you if you have read the *perjuries* in the Morning Post—with the immaculate deposition of the Lady Douglas" (March 13, 1813; *LJ* 3:25). In 1806 Sir John and Lady Douglas had testified that the Princess of Wales had borne a child by Sir Sydney Smith in 1802 (March 15, 1813; *Times*). The Tory *Morning Post* revived the discredited story to aid the Prince Regent in his efforts to divorce his wife.

47. During a parliamentary investigation, Lord Moira had examined two surgeons, Samuel Gillam Mills of Croome-Hill, Greenwich, and Thomas Edmeades, of Greenwich, Kent. These surgeons testified that the princess was not pregnant in 1806.

48. The Prince Regent.

49. Lady Melbourne refers to the editorial position taken by the *Times,* which defended Queen Caroline against charges that she had given birth to an illegitimate child. "The great and guiltless woman who is the subject of these nauseous attacks is now indeed triumphant," the *Times* declared on March 15, 1813.

50. Lady Melbourne's suggestion that the lines were written by Samuel Whitbread is in keeping with his political orientation, for he was a consistent critic of Pitt's wartime policies and of the Prince Regent, who had raised the charges against his wife to discredit her and obtain a divorce.

51. Byron had indicated his "selfish" concern for Lady Melbourne's health. "So—you won't get well-you must—or what is to become of me? I am very selfish about you" (March 14, 1813; *LJ* 3:26).

52. Byron responded on March 18, 1813: "If I had gone to Mrs. Hope's I should have found the only *'novelty'* that would give me any pleasure in yourself" (*LJ* 3:27).

53. "'After all there is charm in Novelty' is there indeed? it is very wicked of you to say so to a person who is so bigoted to the opposite system," Byron responded (March 18, 1813; *LJ* 3:27). Marchand states that the party was held by the wife of Thomas Hope. Hope was the author of *Anastasius* (1819), a novel set in Greece and admired by Byron.

54. On an earlier occasion, Byron had written that *"lobster sallad & Champagne"* were the "only truly feminine & becoming viands" (September 25, 1812; *LJ* 2:208). See Lady Melbourne's letter of September 29, 1812.

55. Francis Joseph Gall (1758-1828), the Austrian anatomist and founder of phrenology.

56. Fanny Burney.

57. be thought of?

58. Byron wrote: "I certainly am indebted to C[aroline] for the continuance of your *countenance*—& this cancels all her libels & larcenies" (March 26, 1813; *LJ* 3:31). This letter is either misdated, since it responds to Byron's of March 26, 1813, or there is a missing letter in which Byron expressed the same

sentiments.

59. Lady Melbourne obtained the miniature on April 7, 1813 (*LJ* 3:36).

60. Byron responded to this letter directly the following day: "It becomes you wonderfully to reproach me for *fussing* about *trifles*—after the lectures of last summer about things of no great importance—I send you nevertheless the precious addition—though I already gave you enough to make a peruque—and now pray let me lay hands upon the picture immediately" (March 26, 1813; *LJ* 3:31).

61. Caroline had asked Byron for an ornament combining their hair. The ornament was destroyed and instead Byron sent a lock of Lady Oxford's hair with his own (Villiers 273). "The *double* hair amuses you—she will never discover the difference . . . it was a lucky coincidence of colour & shape for my purpose—& may never happen again—& surely it is a very innocent revenge for some very scurvy behaviour" (April 7, 1813; *LJ* 3:37).

62. Caroline Lamb.

63. Lady Oxford.

64. On August 12, 1812, Caroline Lamb had run away from home and threatened to travel abroad. The following day Byron had restored her to her family. He may have met Lady Melbourne that night at a party of Quentin Dick's (August 12, 1812; *LJ* 2:188). Lady Melbourne reminds him of his chivalrous behavior in 1812 in order to gain a repeat performance in 1813. Lady Melbourne thought that a few strands of Byron's hair was a small price to pay if it would make her daughter-in-law, Caroline Lamb, more manageable.

65. Richard Sheridan is referred to as Dick in Villiers' *The Grand Whiggery* (41), but the reference is more likely to Quentin Dick.

66. catastrophe?

67. fire, five?

68. In the late eighteenth and early nineteenth centuries, "cupping" was used to improve circulation. It drew blood to the surface of the body "for producing counterirritation or for bloodletting by application of a glass vessel from which air had been evacuated by heat, forming a partial vacuum" (*Webster's Third International*).

69. "How is the L[ad]y. Blarney—if that sagacious person knew how matters stand just at present I think her alarms wd be at rest forever—if ever I were again smitten in that family it wd be with herself & not C[aroline]- but hatred is a much more delightful passion" (April 19, 1813; *LJ* 3:41). Lady Blarney was Byron's nickname for Lady Bessborough, the mother of Caroline Lamb.

70. Byron indicated that he would attend "before 7:00 p.m." (May 21, 1813; *LJ* 3:50).

71. The mother of Georgiana, duchess of Devonshire, and the maternal grandmother of Caroline Lamb. Byron indicated that he was invited to Lady Spenser's on May 7, 1813 and would go there "first if possible—solely and entirely to see you—& *not* to hear about C—" (May 7, 1813). Byron worried that Caroline Lamb would be going as well, but she was ill (May 7, 1813; 3:47). He also had a citizen's ball he planned to attend, hence Lady Melbourne's comment that "if I find [Lady Spenser's] dull I may perhaps go there myself."

72. George Villiers, fifth earl of Jersey, and his wife, Lady Sarah Sophia Fane.

73. Prince Kozlovksy, a Russian diplomat who was visiting England. Since he bore the title "prince," he may have been a grandson or some other descendent of Prince Feodor Alexeivitch Koslofski (d. 1770), a Russian literary man and general who knew Voltaire (March 15, 1813; *LJ* 3:45, 3:48).

74. Sir Augustus John Foster.

75. Caroline Lamb. This letter refers to Lady Heathcote's ball, held on July 5, 1813. Byron had written to Lady Melbourne the following day: "Since I wrote ye. enclosed I have heard a strange story of C[aroline]'s scratching herself with glass—& I know not what besides—of all this I was ignorant till this Evening.—What I did or said to provoke her—I know not—I told her it was better to *waltze*—

'because she danced well—& it would be imputed to *me*—if she did not'—but I see nothing in this to produce cutting & maiming" (July 6, 1813; *LJ* 3:72). Airlie (*Whig* 155) and Villiers (275) differ in their accounts of this event. According to Villiers, Lady Rancliffe was on Byron's arm when he passed Caroline; Airlie makes no mention of another woman being present.

76. Caroline did "expose" Byron during the separation from his wife, by alluding to his incestuous affair with Augusta.

77. The "Oss" is difficult to decipher. Airlie assumes that this is Lady Oxford, but Marchand and Villiers do not indicate that she was even there.

78. Possibly "Ly R." Villiers lists this person as Lady Rancliffe (275).

79. Lady Melbourne felt "very sorry" for Madame de Staël because her son, Albert de Staël, had been killed in a gambling duel at Doberan, on the coast of the Baltic Sea (*LJ* 3:86). She responds to Byron's letter, posted the same day, in which he writes: "Corinne [Madame de Staël] is doubtless very much affected—yet methinks—I should conjecture—she will want some spectators to testify how graceful her grief will be—& to relate what fine things she can say on a subject where commonplace mourners would be silent.—Do I err in my judgment of the woman think you?" (August 8, 1813; *LJ* 3:87).

80. *a contre Coeur:* unwillingly, reluctantly.

81. Lady Melbourne seems to have been jealous of Madame de Staël, who may have preferred Ward's company to her own. In a description of a party on October 9, Miss Berry wrote that "Madame de Staël and Ward talked a great deal and very well" (2: 543). Staël describes how she exhausted Lord Melbourne.

82. Airlie omits the first paragraph of this letter.

83. See letter of August 8, 1813 for reference to a "Water party" that Lady Melbourne attended.

84. Richard Temple-Nugent-Brydges-Chandos-Grenville.

85. Byron wrote to tell Lady Melbourne that "I should have been glad of your advice how to untie two or three 'Gordian knots' tied round me—I shall cut them without consulting anyone though some are closely tied round my *heart* (if you will allow me to *wear* one)" (August 11, 1813; *LJ* 3:87).

86. Possibly D'Ancre *(Grand Larousse)*.

87. by the power strong spirits have over weak souls.

88. Byron had defended Lord Sligo's beauty in his letter of August 21, 1813, provoking Lady Melbourne's response. The poet planned to leave England for "Cadiz . . . & thence wherever the Gods permit" (August 20, 1813; *LJ* 3:92). Either Lord Sligo or Augusta was to be his traveling companion. The relevant passages from Byron's letters are included below:

"Ld. S[ligo] is in town & we are much embarrassed with ye. plague which is it seems all over ye. Levant—but having been both at a prodigious expenditure in large trunks—small clothes—& small arms for ourselves—snuff boxes & Telescopes for the Mussulman gentry—& gewgaws for such of the Pagan women as may be inclined to give us Trinkets in exchange—why—lest so much good preparation should be thrown away—we are determined to go—God knows where-for he is bewildered & so am I.—His Balarina has presented him with a babe—& Malice says that he divides the honours of paternity with the Editor of the courier—who—I suppppose—published his trial & tried his fortune with the Lady . . . he is going to part with her—& is right—those Opera house connections are not very creditable—besides the eternal chaldron of boiling *suspicion* into which a man must be plunged if he likes one of those women must be insufferable—at least for a permanency" (August 18, 1813; *LJ* 3:90).

Sligo "wants to go to Russia—only to see a *worse* London at St. Petersburg—he prefers—(as anyone in their senses would) the Mediterranean but is staggered by the pestilence.—he is not I believe the least jealous of his precious appendage but *tired* of her—& I don't much wonder—poor fellow—why should his *"figure"* prevent him from jealousy—I think it would be a very good cause—

though he is less than the Prince—who I fancy did not find his *figure* in his way—Heaven knows what is to become of any or at least most of our Sex—if our masculine ugliness is to be an obstacle — it is fortunate that the caprice of your gender generally gets the better of their taste" (August 21, 1813; *LJ* 3:93).

89. Byron alluded to the Prince Regent not finding "his *figure*" (face) an obstacle to his affair with Lady Melbourne. He seems to also allude to Reynolds' flattering portrait of the Prince Regent that hung at Brocket Hall. Lady Melbourne countered this insolent remark by observing that the picture was "not a likeness." Lady Melbourne did what she could to lessen Byron's jealousy of her former relationship with the Prince Regent. That jealousy was in fact misplaced, for Lady Melbourne's opinion of the prince declined after he neglected her son Frederick's diplomatic career and mistreated Queen Caroline and Princess Charlotte.

90. At the beginning of this letter, Lady Melbourne refers to a "deplorable" letter received from Byron. "I am 'sick & serious' am I?" he responded. "Then you must cure the one & laugh away the other—but I equally deny the malady & the melancholy" (August 21, 1813; *LJ* 3:93).

91. Byron had requested the invitation. "You don't know how much good your conversation does me—you must promise me—if I stay away two years—to send me an invitation to Brocket on my return" (August 21, 1813; *LJ* 3:93).

92. Lady Melbourne's advice about ending the affair with Caroline. A sarcastic reference to Byron's insistence that he obeys Lady Melbourne's commands.

93. Lady Cowper wrote this on the envelope in pencil.

94. Byron wrote frequently of his plans to leave England (August 18, 1813; *LJ* 3:90).

95. Byron responded on October 17, 1813: "Tell Ly. H[olland] that Clarke is the name—& Craven Street (No. forgotten) the residence—may be heard of at Tri. Coll.—excellent man—able physician—shot a friend in a duel (about his sister) & I believe killed him professionally afterwards—Ly. Holland may have him for self or friends" (October 17, 1813; *LJ* 3:147).

96. John Russell, sixth duke of Bedford, and his second wife, Georgiana.

97. Lady Frances Webster. She was married to James Webster, whose brother had indicated to Byron that the marriage was one of convenience. Phryne was the name of a famous Roman courtesan of the fourth century B.C. (*Brewer's Myth and Legend* 788).

98. James Webster.

99. My friend, all that has changed.

100. Byron wrote of Frances Webster as a victim of an unhappy marriage: "Her health is so very delicate—she is so thin and pale that I doubt her being much longer" (October 17, 1813; *LJ* 3:147).

101. Lady Melbourne may not yet have received Byron's letters, which provide full and comic accounts of Byron's evenings with Frances Webster and her husband.

102. "Ours too the glance none saw beside; / the smile none else might understand" is from Byron's poem "To Thyrza," written on October 11, 1811—the day he reported John Edleston's death. Lady Melbourne uses Byron's own poetry to describe his furtive communications with Lady Frances Webster.

103. "He hath a person and a smooth dispose / To be suspected, framed to make woman false" (*Othello* 1:3:404). Lady Melbourne may refer to Lord Egremont, with whom she was in love for a number of years and who was not as deceptive as Byron.

104. See Byron's letter of 1813, in which he refers to Annabella as "Clarissa Harlowed into an awkward kind of correctness" (September 5, 1813; *LJ* 3:108).

105. "Villainous thoughts, Roderigo! when these mutualities so marshal the way" (*Othello* 2:1:267).

106. Byron's picture, retrieved from Caroline Lamb by Lady Melbourne.

107. The London *Times* concurs with Lady Melbourne in calling *Godolphin, the Lion of the North* "one

of those pieces of pompous name, at this theatre [Drury-Lane], called an operatic drama . . . whether the dialogue of *Godolphin* was meant to convey the songs, or the songs the dialogue, we must, however painful it may be, say that the carriage and its contents were equally wretched, and well worthy of each other" (October 13, 1813).

108. In a letter to Lady Georgiana Morpeth of November 25, 1813, Miss Berry seems to have been the first to use this expression: "I tell her [Madame de Staël] she has undertaken two miracles, to make him [Ward] *poli envers les femmes, et pieux envers Dieu* [courteous to women and pious to God]. And there is no saying, if they go on, what her success may be. *En attendant*, they make very good company for other people" (Berry 2:546).

109. The note on this envelope is from Emily Cowper, who was entrusted with Lady Melbourne's correspondence after her death.

110. This date is given by the curator of the British Library.

111. The manuscript is torn.

112. George Canning was an eloquent speaker, hence the comparison to Sheridan, whose play *The Rivals* (1775) was a particular favorite of Byron's. Canning had received a copy of Byron's tale *The Bride of Abydos* and wrote to Murray: "It is very, very beautiful" (November 25, 1813; *LJ* 3:173). In November 1813, Byron wrote to Lady Melbourne to tell her that "My new Turkish tale will be out directly—I shall of course send you a copy. Frere & Canning & the Hollands have seen it & like it—the public is another question" (November 25, 1813; *LJ* 3:175).

113. *The Bride of Abydos*. On November 4, 1813, Byron wrote to say that he was "in the very heat of another Eastern tale—something of the *Giaour cast*—but not so *sombre* though rather more villainous" (November 4, 1813; *LJ* 3:157). More than three weeks later, he added that "You know me better than most people—and are the only person who can trace & I want to see whether you think my *writings* are me or not" (November 27, 1813; *LJ* 3:175).

114. Lord and Lady Holland's literary tastes tended toward Pope and the Augustans (Mitchell 167).

115. George Canning and John Hookham Frere (1769-1846) were among the founders of and contributors to *The Anti-Jacobin*. Byron sent the earliest copies of his poem to Frere, Canning, Lord Holland, and Lady Melbourne, among others. Surprisingly, he also sent a copy to Caroline Lamb (November 22, 1813; *LJ* 3:170)

PART IV

Byron's "Zia," 1814

In 1814, Lady Melbourne apparently wrote Byron a number of letters concerning the publication of "Lines from a Lady Weeping." This controversial poem had been published anonymously two years earlier. It first gained notice, however, when Byron's authorship was acknowledged by his decision to include it with *The Corsair,* which sold ten thousand copies in a single day. At a dinner party in 1812, Princess Charlotte had burst into tears when her father announced he would abandon his former Whig friends—Lords Grey and Grenville—for refusing to join Lord Liverpool's administration (Elwin, *Wife* 184). Byron's poem exploited Princess Charlotte's reaction in order to portray the prince as a turncoat. Byron ignored Lady Melbourne's advice to prosecute one or more of the editors of the *Morning Post* and *Morning Courier,* who were abusing him for the antiroyal poem. They wrote at cross purposes about this event, however, for he was as flattered by the press attacks as she was concerned about public appearances.

Lady Melbourne continued to conceal her meetings with Byron from her son and daughter-in-law (February 20, 1814). They usually met at "some third place" (February 20, 1814), comparing mutual dinner invitations (February 25, 1814; April 1, 1814). If Byron married Annabella, Lady Melbourne could justify her frequent contact with the poet more easily. Then too, she was anxious to thwart his relationship with Augusta (May 25, 1814), for the letters Byron had shown Lady Melbourne made her "melancholy" (April 30, 1814; *LJ* 4:110; June 10, 1814 [Murray]; June 28, 1814; *LJ* 4:134). A final benefit of Byron's marriage, of course, would be ending her daughter-in-law's public infatuation with him. Upon hearing the news of his imminent marriage, Caroline demanded the return of her letters, pictures, and gifts. She made a scene at the duke of Wellington's ball held at Burlington House (July 1, 1814) and even contradicted the published announcement of his engagement in an anonymous letter sent to the *Morning Chronicle* (October 5, 1814; *LJ* 4:194).[1]

Lady Melbourne was now to be Byron's "Zia" (September 26, 1814; *LJ* 4:180).[2] In a letter to her cousin, Emily Huskisson, she compared Byron and Annabella to "Pyramus, & Thisbe of old" (September-October 1814). But Lady Melbourne was not content with mere wordplay. She urged Byron to visit Annabella's family and consolidate their union.[3] "Surely you cannot wonder that I should wish to arrange my property first," he replied, "& not proceed hurriedly in a business which is to decide her fate & mine forever" (October 4, 1814; *LJ* 4:192).

Shortly before Byron's engagement, Augusta tried to encourage his interest in her close friend Charlotte Leveson-Gower (October 1, 1814; *LJ* 4:187; October 19, 1814; *LJ* 4:217). This must have unnerved Lady Melbourne, who informed Byron that Charlotte was unavailable.[4] When Byron finally arrived at Seaham, he found that he preferred Annabella's father to her mother, a prejudice that accorded well with Lady Melbourne's own.

That December, Lady Melbourne gave an account of Lord Roseberry's trial as a final warning to Byron about the danger of eloping with Augusta. Archibald John Primose, fourth Earl of Roseberry accused Sir Henry Mildmay of criminal conversation with his wife. In his closing argument, which was quoted in the newspaper, Sir William Garrow accused Mildmay of multiple incest for eloping with Lord Roseberry's wife, who was the sister of Mildmay's wife. Reading Lord Brougham's speech in defense of Mildmay brought the pathos of Annabella's situation back to Lady Melbourne with all its force. "I pity her very much," she wrote of her niece. "It is in some play I think—that they say 'the best Men are moulded out of faults'[5]—I am sure yt ought to be impressed upon the minds of all unmarried Ladies—the Married ones know it" (December 15, 1814).

16th Jan^{y6}

1814

Dear L^d B-

    "This oath though sworn by one has bound us both"[7]—rather wild even in theory!—but must be s^d by a person quite ignorant of the practise in such cases— how you might be bound without even knowing it—& to what—really to be *constant*—does not this frighten you—the word itself must be discordant to your Ears—dont you blush at the question that follows *"are you my <L[over]>?"*[8] ~~how~~ ^in^ what manner could you answer this Letter?[9] I wish I had seen it—You could not even make use of your favorite basis—truth—not even swear to it in "motley guise." You must have given it up entirely, or talk'd entirely of the past—perhaps that may have satisfied this poor little ignorant Girl,[10]—There is much simplicity in many parts of her Letter—& I am very sorry for her, as I believe she is very sincere—& you must believe that she loves you dearly,—tho' you will hardly own it to yourself, you have imbibed such ideas of the deceit practiced by all Women,— that you would never confess y^t you, had any dependance upon their constancy— & yet such things have come to pass—& from all I have heard & known of her character & her actions, I am impress'd with a belief that all she says is true, & that she is not at all as you express'd yourself ^to me^ in one of your[11] former Letters "embarassed with her constancy"[12]—&[13] my opinion is that you never were *so* loved before as you would know better how to appreciate her feelings——after all this I think her a little Childish, & now & then tiresome, that may proceed from being restless & dissatisfied with herself————how curious the account you give me of y^r being seen at N[ottingham]- but do you believe that I think you have no feeling—because if so, you wrong me very much—I never was acquainted with any person who had so much—I have s^d. it over & over again, when ever I have conversed Seriously about you—& must I think have told it you.

    I am curious to know, why *she*[14] conceal'd what she had seen from Ph-[15] she seems to me an unamiable person—I have never heard a hint about Ph except from C[aroline] who would have s^d. it about any body——You ask me how she goes on?

in better humour, & I hope will be quiet at least for a little while,—she ask'd me the other Night whether you had written another poem—as Me de Stael in a Letter had ask'd her if she had seen it—This I know was not true but merely to bring up y^r Name—I s^d dryly enough that I had not heard any thing one way or the other— she then s^d she believed she had been very much misrepresented to you, for she had reasons to think you were angry with her—but she shd let it rest as it was, without enquiring further.—I said I thought her very right, as it was the purpose of the Message I had deliver'd by y^r desire, & which put her into such a passion— she s^d. it was Mad^e. de Stael that had driven her into a frenzy[.] I s^d that would not do for me, as I knew the humor she was in before M de Stael came here[16]—but y^t I declined any further conversations upon the Subject—& never would talk to her about you,—she s^d she own'd she behaved very ill but she hop'd I forgave her—I s^d I believed I never Should, that there *were* things never cd be forgiven. She s^d she had written a detail of ye reports that had been made to her, which would be given me if she died, & that I should see how she had been work'd upon.

The idea of *her* leaving a paper for *me* to see,[17] made me laugh & some one coming into ye room, ended our conversation which she has not resumed, but is chearful enough to be very tiresome with her theory's and her discussions which she ^is^ eternally beginning & always turn upon some supposed ill usage, which Women receive from Men, evidently alluding to you

Certainly her ~~other~~ Theorys & your Ethics as you say, are extraordinary[18] but whether I draw the conclusion from them which you Suppose is what I can not tell, as it is not decided in my own Mind—I am very glad I have knowledge enough to understand y^{rs}—so far I know,—You may envy the R^h[19] the Visit he is going to make, as it might be rather pleasant than otherwise to you to see me—but you are mistaken if you think any part of his former Life ever was enviable—unless rank & power is look'd up to—he never was liked which may seem strange to you, who have such Numbers who doat upon you—but it is nevertheless true—& if ever we Should have an opportunity of conversing together upon indifferent Subjects I will convince you of it not only in *one* instance, but in Several—I believe I shall have L^y <u>B</u>^{l}[arney][20] here to meet him—I think a f[rien]^d & this cold weather together a great deal too much to bear—for I can do nothing but Sit in the Fire, &

even then I am frozen however I wish it may last during y^r Journey as it will be much better travelling than if it was to thaw——What odd things happen, Lewis,[21] & M^{rs}. Fitzherbert[22] have both proposed themselves to me, not knowing *he*[23] was coming. The first of ye two tells me he quarelled at Oatlands[24] with Me de Stael— she was in a passion, he laugh'd, she s^d his "rire" showed her he was "inferieur" mais "tres inferieur"—she talk'd loud, so did he, & the Singers at the other end of the room could not hear one another & were obliged to Stop—I wish I had seen it—there never was such a person for tracasseries as she is—There are two in love now with C[aroline]- which I could explain, but shall not, as it would produce ten more so I remain Silent—which I may as well practice at this moment towards you—as I run on Strangely whenever I write to you

Ever y^{rs}

EM

Lady Melbourne to Lord Byron (Murray)

Jany 19th 1814[25]

Dear L^d B.

I think you would proceed so far on y^r Journey on Monday—that even this very deep snow, would not prevent your reaching N[ottingham]—& shall therefore send you a few Lines in answer to y^r. last Letter. I am certain you have no such trick as M de S[tael]. described unless you have acquired it since we last parted.[26] probably it was the brilliancy of her Eyes, that had the same effect upon yrs that the Sun has upon an Owls—or still more probably she stared at you with such determined *effronterie,* that the *Family Shyness* induced you to shun her observation. Seriously tho'—I would tell you if I had observed any peculiarity of the Sort, but I have always seen your Eyes so open, that[27] I can not assert that you have the power of Shutting them, & have never even seen your Eyes look Sleepy, or heavy— ^or^ half closed, or ^you^ Wink or blink in any manner—it is only when Eyes are not sufficiently expressive to convey their meaning, that such aid is requisite——I

take some credit to myself for discovering that it would be difficult for you—
Yourself—to answer Ph's[28] Letter; those who believe in C[aroline]—think falsehood
is so easy to you that you prefer it to truth[29]—you see I judged otherwise—what
another? a Young one coming up in Succession not contented with five or Six I
know of—& twenty I don't—You are looking after another?—^well^ be it so—& I
only pray that this one may go on—as it will settle all the others in the best manner possible—what is she 14 or 15? & you say a fool—how should you know?
believe me tho' so Young, she is old enough to conceal a great deal of her
Character[.] [T]here is so much Shyness at that Age, in general, that it obscures all
their Ideas, & hardly knowing them, they can speak clearly on no Subject,—If she
has no prevalent unamiable qualities it is most likely she will turn out well, when
these appear it is hopeless for living in ye World generally increases them & only
Softens them in appearance, Witness C[aroline]-

  I see the Night is so very severe that I shall not send this Letter the Man
may lose the Bag in a Snow drift, & I shall have the Letters found & brought back
to the House & examin'd a Week hence—so I will ^not^ run the risk but finish to
morrow————

25th Jany

  by this date you will perceive how long this letter has lain in my drawer,
but the Post has been so irregular, from the roads being Stop'd in various places,
that I have had no opportunity of sending it; every Evening there have been questions about sending ye Letters & often examinations, to see, whether it was necessary they should go that day, which has prevented my finishing my Letter————in
the mean time, where are you? I am quite anxious to know, but still hope you have
perform'd your Journey before the Weather was so very bad—& that you have
been sitting over a warm fire, & have only seen the Snow at a distance, I envy you
the good Nott[inghamshi]re[30] Coals—which I think the best in the World, & which I
always regret do not come up by the Canal as well as the Staffordshire[31] which are
much inferior—it is rather extraordinary having hit upon such a Subject in a Letter
to you but if ever one is to think of Coals or fire or Warmth, it seems justifiable at
this moment for really I have been frozen all this last Week—& this is the first day
the weather seems at all settled—but to return to our usual topics, I have at last

wrung from you a confession that you believe Ph Sincere. I have no doubt of the fact, but I think your reason a bad one. You Estimate the force & truth of a person's liking by the imprudences they commit (C[aroline]- always told me so)—now I think it a false way of judging—& that a persons conduct in such Situations depends upon their character—a Woman who respects *les bienseances*[32]—& is driven from them, by a Strong passion, gives you the greatest proof of attachment— but she still adheres to propriety & decorum in trifles, when she has given *it up* in reality; & is much more to be relied upon & believed than one of those light whimsical Ladies who defy the World & run headlong into every sort of imprudence—& then call it Violent Love which cannot be controul'd—I think Ph's deserves that name—You differ from me I know, because you have as yet only seen one Sort of Woman—or to express myself more clearly Women of one turn of mind—I think you may understand what I mean & your *Anger* with Ph convinces me I am right— —I long to hear something upon which I can found some opinion of M—& as probably you are at present engross'd entirely by y^t friendship—I shall say no more of the others——*les Autres* (dans le *grand pluriel*) how odd that Sounds. & yet you have some pretensions to *Sentiment*!!—according to your own Acceptation of ye Word—

If you should not be detain'd in Notti[ngham]- I shall see you sooner than I expected for we are not to remain much longer here— I shall therefore only say one word on ye Subject of the person you say *you envy*—would you envy any one who liked another, who never had the least liking, I could almost say toleration for them?—If you have any reliance upon my Veracity—You must believe that,— why should I deny it? I have never denied other things, & why should I that? I certainly from some strange circumstances—got myself into a disagreeable embarrassment, but from which I extricated myself as Speedily as it was possible; & which alltogether makes an odd history—& which it is no wonder should be misrepresented in ye World, as I assure ^you^ that I never told half so much to any one person as I have to you, but have always allow'd every body to make their own comments, without ever trying to set them right——the Post is just going—believe me

Y^{rs} ever,

EM

I think if you had return'd to Town I should have *heard* it either from you or from others, so I shall direct to N[ottingham]- you accuse me wrongfully when you think y^t what I s^d about Selfishness was ironical

[The Lord Byron/Newstead Abbey/Nottingham]

Lady Melbourne to Lord Byron (Murray)

12th Feb^{ry}
1814

Dear L^d B—

many thanks for your Letter, hearing from you is the pleasantest thing in ye World next to seeing you—but that will come soon I hope,—call upon me to morrow or Monday about the usual time—C[aroline] has thoughts of coming to Town for 2 or three days—& talk'd of Wednesday—but as her Letter stated that she should *not* come if you were here, & desired me to tell her, perhaps she may give it up, as I wrote her word I knew you were here, but I had not seen you. I do not feel so confident of her making no more Scenes (~~as you represented her~~)[33] —she is never quiet, & makes disturbances continually, tho not about you, & she still persists in it, that if you were to repeat the same mal Words to her, that she should behave exactly as she did at L^y H[eathcote's]—& maintains y^t she should be perfect-ly justified in so doing,—& her remaining in ye country is entirely because she will not promise to behave reasonably,—she says it is not in her power. Therefore you are not so Safe as you suppose———The best thing is to be *as you are,* perfectly quiet, & to answer no Letters, for altho' she says she shall write no more I never feel secure———I agree with you perfectly in every thing you say & in all your resolutions respecting this strange fuss,—& am glad you do not intend to answer &c. &c. at the same time I must say that when I wrote to you there had not been half so much in the News papers, as has since appeared, & it has always been my opinion, that though I would never enter into controversy with the Editor of a

News paper, Yet if they ever published any thing Actionable, I certainly *would prosecute,*[34] & they seem inclined to be so personal to you, that I should think you might find it worth your while to do so—it puts a Stop to all their invective at once, but should not be done unless you are upon undoubted good safe ground— You know probably that notice was given in the Courier last Night of a paper about you to Night, now should you think it worth your while to attend to what I have said, you ought to send some person to buy one of the Couriers *at the Office,* who could swear that they bought *it there* as you can not prosecute upon one that is bought from a News man or from any of the Booksellers—I mention this as it is as well to have the power in your hands ^even^ if you should not wish to make use of it—saving one I have seen that has mention'd the paragraph in yᵉ Mornᵍ post, thought it nonsense, but I see it as you do— & believe that there are personages in that House foolish & shabby enough to do any thing to Court the — —[35] however for his own sake I should think he would be unwilling to have a discussion upon the part of his having given up his friends & abandoned his principles—tho' he is so blinded by flatterers, that nothing he can do will Surprise me——Lᵈ Carlisle[36] they assert never had read the lines about himself till they appear'd in the Courier,—his friends say he had heard of them but never had seen the Book. I can not believe it——I read you a Letter I have received to day fᵐ An[nabella]- with her opinion of the Corsair.—You say you thought it would be too Larmoyant for me[.][37] I shall answer it by two of yʳ own Lines

   And many a withering thought he's had—not lost—

   In Smiles that least befit who means them most—[38]

I have been interrupted & must finish[.] let me see you as soon as you can make it convenient to yourself to spare so much time

                              Yʳˢ Ever

                              EM

Lady Melbourne to Lord Byron (Murray)

18th Febry

1814

I am quite out of patience Dear L^d B—why wont you call upon me—have you promised not *to do so,* I believe it, & it makes me very angry—M^r. Rogers[39] says you are very much out of Spirits,[40] & this makes me the more anxious to see you,—we dined together at Ld Stairs, & he asked me before every body, if I had seen you since y^r return. I said *gayly* No; he has neglected me very much——There was ye Smile & the "Withering thought"[41]—not because you had not been near me, but because I knew why you had not[42]——pray come to me to morrow, You will find me at home after 1/2 past three

I want to talk to you about these odious News Papers——There was *Something* which to every body but myself must appear unintentional but really I dont know—its had an unpleasant effect upon my feelings—& I wish it could be Stop'd which I know it Ought.[43] The other day Ward wrote to Perry[44] which put an end to the Epigrams appearing <dayly> don't mistake, I would not for [y^e] World have you write about this—but I want to talk to you & quote a *great example* of what ought to be done in certain cases— do come

Y^rs
ever
EM

———

Lady Melbourne to Lord Byron (Murray)

20th Febry

1814

Dear L^d B

I think R[ogers]. was perfectly right in ye advise he gave you[45] & I wish I had met you at both the places you mention. Your either going *into* or *out of* the Country, would only confirm and Strengthen ye idea of y^r being much annoy'd at what has taken place, if such an opinion exists—which I rather believe, tho' I do not know it; I guess it is so, from the number of questions I am ask'd about you, & particularly if I have ever seen you——I long to add, to my No,—it is his fault, not mine, I should so much dislike any one should think I am the least inclined to pay Court— —or that I care for any thing that has, or *may be*—put into the News papers——by the bye how ill naturedly that part was turn'd in the Courier,[46] to make every one who did not recollect the original, think it alluded to W^m & not to George. I should not scruple taking any revenge in my power upon the Man, whoever he may be that wrote those papers—They are so rancorous and illiberal——I am grieved that you are forbidden[47] to come to me, (tho' in fact it is a great compliment to me) but as I know you move only by the String held by those *in power* I shall plague you no more on that Subject except to say that whenever you do come I shall be exceedingly happy & rejoiced to See you[48]

in the mean time I hope we may meet at some third place, tho' at present I see no probability even of that—but as I often observe the most improbable things happen I lives in hopes——

C[aroline] does not leave ye Country at present, but is trying hard—two days ago she sent to *the* illustrious,[49] who is also in ye Country, to beg to see her— & when she went, said it was to ask her advice, whether she did not think "her Character would be the worse" if she did not go to London—as people made reports & said she was parted from *him*—the answer was, y^t such reports could no[t] Signify—as so many people know ye contrary and that any thing was better than fresh Scenes——she is trying ^every sort of^ pretence to get here without making a promise to behave well—& which does not Signify for she'll certainly not ~~behave well~~^keep to it^; & most probably will be in her "accustomed haunts" soon after her arrival,——[50]

I was pleased with M^r. Dallas's Letter[51] it is so unlike ye generality of persons to put themselves forward on such occasions that I have the greatest respect and admiration for those who do, I hope it is of no consequence to him, what the most illustrious thinks for his delicacy will not be understood in that quarter and I dont agree with him as to ye magnanimity attached to cant

when I say I was so glad to see the Letter, dont think that I had the least doubt before, I was as sure of it as that I am now writing to you—but I was glad to see it so fully & satisfactorily explained to yᵉ World—What faces you are making, & how you despise me at this Moment for casting away a thought upon yᵉ World⁵²—but you are wrong—I care very little about it, but it is pleasant to be on high ground, & that those for whom you feel great interest are so too

Yʳˢ Dˢᵗ Lᵈ B ever,

EM

[The Lord Byron/Bennet St]⁵³

Lady Melbourne to Lord Byron (Murray)

25ᵗʰ Febʸ 1814

Dear Lᵈ B—

They do not come to Town at present, so I hope you will call upon me Soon,—*she* says that some time next Month she will come for a few days to see Mʳ. Kean⁵⁴ & make up quarrels—but with whom she dont tell me, probably Madᵉ de Stael, who is more inclined to meddle & to make Tracasseries than any person I ever met with.

The illustrious⁵⁵ writes me word, that *she*⁵⁶ told her she would only come to Town when she heard you were away[.] This is a proof—of what her intentions are should you be here——

Wᵐ has decided according to your *opinion*—I know it is very unlikely any one should mention this subject to you but if by accident you Should hear it talk'd of at Lʸ H[ollan]ᵈˢ—do not say a word; for I am so strongly enjoined to Secrecy that I ought not to have told it—& I have, only, *to you*—You said in one of yʳ Letters yᵗ I would not trust you which is not true for I should have no hesitation about trusting you on yᵉ Subjects *that* you alluded to—& my not having done so, has been from the fear of being a great bore—as what pass'd several yʳˢ ago must be so very uninteresting to a person unacquainted with the parties—

I am not sure however that my confidence is not a little Shaken by these Letters fᵐ N[ottingham]—come here to keep me company! & to see this old Gothic

Mansion! & so on, a good deal of treachery in that I think, not to me; for it could not deceive me, but it could & did the person to whom it was Shown—for I think y^t part must have been written for other Eyes than mine; & that it amused you at the time I don't doubt

I am so anxious to hear your Stories about Frederic that I hope you will not keep me long in Suspense

Yours ever

EM

I suppose you are much pleased with the figure your Hero[57] *makes!*—I hear Ministers are very much out of Spirits & Ld Liverpool[58] particularly so—of *the most Illustrious*[59] as Mrs D-[60] calls him I have heard nothing

[The Lord Byron/Bennett Street]

Lady Melbourne to Lord Byron (Murray)

1st April

1814

Dear Ld B. I send you two more Vol^s & you shall have the fifth to morrow[.] [T]hey are *heavy* & thick or I should have read them quicker, especially as I was not well Yesterday & staid at home; to night I am going to Carlton House to a party for the grand Du^{ss}[61] who seems by what I hear to expect the Strictest Etiquette here, tho' in Russia she was reckoned very Affable, & very clever so says Ld Granville Leveson.[62]

I was in hopes I might have seen you to day as they[63] went to Roehampton Yesterday—but I dare not propose to you to come when they order their Horses to go there as they so often ride here, unexpectedly but I hope I shall find an opportunity soon & that *no arrival* will have taken place to prevent your coming—for this last wish—you do not feel much obliged to me though it is a very friendly one——So you are settled in Albany,[64] where most of my happiest days were pass'd,—whilst I lived in that House, no Misfortune reach'd me, & I should not have disliked to be an appendage to yᵉ Lease to live in it again.—every despairing and distressing event of my Life has happened since I lived at Whitehall.

I never was much in the Apartments you have taken, but the furniture which used to be in your Sitting room would have now been pleasant & useful to you, opposite to the fire hung the view of Constantinople which you see here, & over the Chimney a painting of Joseph turning in disgust from Potiphar's Wife[65]— Thus on one side you would have been delighted with the resemblance to ce *beau Ciel* you love so much, & on the other you would have seen a moral precept—of which I do not mean to say you stand in need—but there there[66] can be no disadvantage in having a good example always before your Eyes.

I am rejoiced for another reason that I did not ask you to come & see me to day—as so many people have appeared during the whole Mornᵍ that I am quite bored, & should not have been able to say five Words to you—amongst them Lᵈ Holland, who is very Gouty & says Lʸ H[olland]- has not been well. They are settled at Holland house—[67]

yʳˢ ever, EM

[The Lord Byron, Albany]

Lady Melbourne to Lord Byron (Murray)

25th April
1814

Dear Lᵈ B—

I have had some serious conversation with her, & certainly as far as one can *judge* of *her* she seems determined to act like a reasonable person,—& I think it is not in the least necessary that you should keep away from any place on Accᵗ of her,—she is very undecided about going out,—but for the first time has own'd that she *is* aware of yᵉ consequences that must attend on any more Scenes,—therefore I think she will avoid making any—I told her she ought to determine to behave to you as to any other person—which she said she could do—provided you *spoke to her,* & said only common things, nothing too kind—nothing reproachful,—I said I was sure you would behave *properly* but I did not acknowledge having had yᵉ least communication with you on the Subject—so if you should see her mind & dont betray me⁶⁸—I told her I had seen you at Lʸ Lans[dow]ⁿᵉ's which was fortunate, as she had heard it & put the question, to try my *truth,* which you know ought never to be *Suspected,* for when it is—*it Vanishes,* & so it did here, for upon her asking me if you had mention'd her—I sᵈ No—we had no opportunity—does he ever? followed,—I sᵈ yes sometimes & always expresses himself much obliged, & pleased with your Behavior lately—in having been so quiet——to sum up the whole—it seems as if she would not go out at present, & that when she does, she will make up her mind to meet you as she would any other person.

If as you say I compliment you & not her, I think it only common justice. You, have acted fairly ^by^ me—which she never has—& tho I may not have much dependance upon either—it is for very different reasons—upon her I can have none—when you fail me, it is from Weakness—in her it is treachery, & never having had any ~~attention~~ intention of keeping any promise——["]mutual decorum"!⁶⁹ how could those two words come into your head as Applicable to you two— "Villanous mutualities" it should be read—she has no decorum even in outward & Visible Signs. You have the greatest certainly in manner & behavior; but what do you say to yᵉ inward & Spiritual grace; so yᵗ in the part where yᵉ one is wanting the other is ready to supply it—so what becomes of discretion & propriety? it must sink and be ingulph'd—& yet I am supposed to be *wrong in doubting?*—thats a very good Joke indeed—almost as good as yʳ doing what I like on *"other points"*—Vastly obedient?! You are fair, & do not try to deceive me & in that you have great merit, I confess,—but on *"other points"*—XXX I wish I could flatter myself I had the least influence, (You say I put too many of these hieroglyphics in but as your *one* puzzles me I think it a proper return to puzzle you three times as much) for I could talk & reason with you for two Hours, so many objections have I to urge,⁷⁰ & after all, for what—~~for the sake of Augusta⁷¹~~—is it worth while!⁷² and to involve— —indeed indeed, if I had powers of persuasion on this Subject, &

could use them with effect you should fall down & adore me. When you return fm A. I shall not dare to make use of Such a term you will deem it, irreligious[.] by ye bye did you promise to deceive me—I hope so—What a Medley it all is[.] You talk of Laughing—is it possible to think of it all & not laugh—supposing they were all brought together as people are at ye end of the fifth act in a play[.] What a confusion it would make—& what explanations would come, & how you would be put to shame—write one—You have the Materials quite ready it can give you no trouble——

What became of me ye other Night?[73] I remained 1/2 an Hour after yr departure talking Nonsense to one of ye Foreigners who are here with whom I am intimate. I like Foreigners in public, they are gay & understand what you call *Buffoonery* but they are very tiresome dans l'interieur. I shall probably see you at Ly Hard[wic]kes[74] & perhaps first at Ly Jerseys Wedy—I do not know whether C[aroline]- is invited to this last, & do not dare ask her, as any of these questions put her out of humour

C[aroline]- is gone to dine at H[ollan]d H[ouse].—I have just received an invitation for ye 4th of May—If they should send you one pray accept—I do not think it unlikely, as she is *just now* inclined to pay me great court—because I believe it is above a Month since I have call'd upon her.

                                        Yrs ever
                                        EM

[The Lord Byron/Albany][75]

Lady Melbourne to Lord Byron (Murray)

                                        Morg[76]
                                        [March-April?]

Dear Ld B

I have just heard from C[aroline]- who says they come to town Thursday Therefore pray call upon me to day or to morrow as I may not see you again for a long time

I came home Yesterday just after you had been here & was very much provoked with myself for having staid so long with your likeness[77] whom I had been
to see

Y^rs Ever

EM

[The Lord Byron][78]

Lady Melbourne to Lord Byron (Murray)

30th April

1814

Dear L^d B———

I return this note to you & also the Letter I received—in which you will
see the grossest *deceit* attempted, & very awkwardly executed[79]—however in my
answer I shall act the part of a complete dupe—when people try to impose upon
me, I have great pleasure in imposing upon them it always produces some fun—as
to her, I do not feel myself the least bound to give her any advice. When I did so
she would not take it, & since that time she has endeavour'd to conceal all her feelings about[80] ^upon^ y^t Subject from me———I do not by this *mean,* that I should
give her now any contrary advice; *you know* there is but one point which makes me
hesitate, on all others my former opinions are Strengthened, by mere knowledge—
& if this one ceases, I should only look upon it as a bad Dream from which the persons concerned are awaken'd,[81] & now I fear I shall make you angry—but as
A[nnabella] says I make "Truth ye first principle of conduct"[.][82] I must act up to
the Character so very discerning a person has given me—to say you are not to
blame would be absurd, but for my Life I cannot blame you half so much as any
other person would, & this is not from partiality but from a knowledge of y^r circumstances, & of y^r Character———You have been led into it, & never allowed to

173

escape from the Nets that first entangled you——I have seen you try, I have heard you confess the truth of yᵉ Sentˢ I have express'd, & you have allow'd me to say things for which any person of less good nature, & less real feeling would have quarrell'd with me.—is it possible then, that I should not excuse you, whatever I may do about—— ——[83] which I own I view in a very different light—is it not sᵈ in one of the Books upon which you are going to convene with *her (the northern light)*[84] that you are only required to act according to yʳ Strength—& if it is inadequate to the task you must *pray* for more—that is certainly yʳ Situation & is not the tempter most to be blamed?—& have I not seen in black & white—"I was so provoked because I could not make you love me" or something like that, though it might not be exactly in those Words————for all these reasons you have my free permission[85]————& indeed I think that as I not only accepted but invited yʳ confidence I ought not (if I were inclined which *mind* I am not) to act in consequence of that with which I have been trusted[86]——

Now as to your going there[87] I think yᵉ objections you make nonsense, for no one will suppose you go, without being invited; & in that case it is much more likely the truth should suggest itself & yᵗ the world will say she has repented, & wished to draw *him* on Again but he would not be caught—& in fact there is no reason why you should—You go there in perfect liberty either to behave like a friend—or declare yourself a Lover. I dont think *you will* fall in love with her;[88]— that you may think her a proper person to marry is just possible, & she will understandably make a friend (a female one) of any person you may point out—& *all friends* is very much to be wished,—You know you had leave to marry—but leave is freely given on all occasions which imposes a Sort of restraint upon You—who are unlike any other person breathing—& when I knew that to be yᵉ reason—with me, the effect would cease—You say if yʳ wishes when you are there should tend to yᵉ point I have named it would put you ^out^ of humour if you fail'd—I can not believe you would, but still she is so odd a person—but surely you could easily discover that, tho' I know you are more likely to err—to yʳ own disadvantage—in short I have written so much that I will write no more except to say—that no one ever went to a place so perfectly at liberty to act in any way that may please themselves.[89]

If you dont like her you may talk only on the prayer Book & if you should like her that subject will cease to make way for another, without any effort. I am afraid it will be treated like the Hazards at Billiards⁹⁰ on another occasion—and admittedly if she persists in conversing on yᵉ two Subjects you mention, Religion & Rhyme⁹¹ you will not remain there long—there never yet was such extraordinary behaviour as her's & after all I gave her credit for being perfectly undesigning, she has been Spoiled & allowed to do exactly what she liked from her Childhood—& like most persons, who reason much, she bewilders and deceives herself

There can be no doubt yᵗ she likes you, altho' I should not be Surprized if she was not aware of the extent of that liking; & yet saying how much she wishes to see you, & telling me yᵗ yʳ society will make her amends for that which she loses by not coming to Town, when in all former Letters she has stated how much she regretted the society she should have had in Town is *altogether* unaccountable & therefore I shall leave it.

should you have any thing to say in answer to this tiresome Scrawl, which deserves none—do not send your Letter to Night as I think C[aroline]- may probably see it, in the Morᵍ—it will be Safe—but she came into the room & I fancied by her manner she Suspected I was writing to you—& therefore will be on the Watch all the Eveᵍ

Yʳˢ Ever most truly

EM

I see Lʸ Heathcotes party Monday is put off to that day[.] terrifying at all events it would be a bad place for C-[aroline] to go to at first—I have tried to persuade her to go with Lʸ C[owper] & me to yᵉ Opera—every Night there has been one Since she came to Town, & she will not—& of course there is no persuading her—

[The/Lord Byron/Albany]

*On the envelope:*⁹²

If you write pray don't *hint* at any of the things I have sᵈ in this Letter—for as I think I have a chance at yᵉ picture I should be sorry if you were to make her angry at this time.

[The/Lord Byron/Bennett Street]
Lady Melbourne to Lord Byron (Murray)

23ᵈ May

1814

My Dear Lᵈ B -

    I have had a conversation with C[aroline]- & as I think there is one part of it, which if in the least mistated, may seem extraordinary to you, I shall write it word for word as I spoke it.

    There is no use in repeating what pass'd, of course a great deal of conversation that led to nothing, & only proved a determination to pay you another Visit, having something particular she wish'd to say—& on my remonstrating & stating it never had led to any good—she reminded me of yᵉ *calme* that Succeeded to yᵉ *meeting* last Summer just before she Left Town—this will make you Smile——but to return to yᵉ purport of my Letter, she was talking of yʳ marrying & how much she should dislike it⁹³—I said, now listen to me quietly, I will state one thing to you, but I shall answer no questions that you may ask in consequence, you say you should dislike Lᵈ B[yron].'s marrying—very much—then it is my opinion that if you persist in yʳ present behaviour—that you will drive him to marry. I know nothing about it I only judge from my knowledge of his character—I dont even know whom he told you, he thought of marrying, but I think he wishes much to be quiet & that any plague may determine him—by way of getting rid of it——

    this made her look very grave—and she left me. I hope the word marrying may turn her thoughts from what you mention'd⁹⁴ last Night⁹⁵——but if she Succeeds in seeing you & had left out that word in relating what I sᵈ—Your response might have shewn her, there was some mystery——

    don't send any answer to Night—the morning is yᵉ safest time, tho' this requires none, unless you have any thing to say—or any questions to ask——I see Lᵈʸ Heathcote has a party Wedʸ——I don't know whether she is invited—if I can find out I will send you word—as it would be foolish to meet there

Yʳˢ ever

EM

I said you had not told me any thing, don't betray me. she *don't know* I saw you *yesterday.*

[The Lord Byron/Albany]

Lady Melbourne to Anne Isabella Milbanke (Lovelace 92 f.48-50]

[Wednesday May 25, 1814]

My dear Annabella

I had a frank given me this Mor^g for the purpose of writing to you, but have had so many plagues, that it has been impossible for me to get rid of them in time for the post—you understand that I call plagues those persons with very few exceptions, who loiter away their mornings in going from one House to the other, to hear the News of the day—Your last Letter rejoiced me very much, as it brought me so favourable an account of your Health—& I have heard a confirmation of what you say of your looks from several of your northern friends whom I have met—& with whom I mutually condole on your non-appearance amongst us this Year at the same time we always agree that if your good health is re-established by your absence, it is fully worth the Sacrifice—I was very much pleased with your friend Miss Doyle,[96] the morning I met her at L^y Milbankes & as far as it is possible to judge in so short a time, she seems to be all you represent, & I shall be happy to improve my acquaintance, if any opportunity should occur—

I was very glad to hear of my B^{rs} invitation to L^d B[yron's]—& should he accept it, I am sure you will be highly delighted with his Society, & I have no doubt, you will all think me justified in the Character I have always given you of him[97]—I have just been interrupted by Mrs Lamb, who is looking remarkably well, & desires her Love to you—You must not expect any amusement or News from me, as all expectation of the last, has vanished since the late wonderful events, & all the former is suspended till ye arrival of the great Potentates—by ye bye a gentleman just arrived from Paris told me last Night that we should be woefully disappointed, in the appearance of these same Sovereigns, that the Emperor Alexander,[98] is certainly a handsome man but does not look like a Gentleman, that his manner is very theatrical & what he says accompanied by a great deal of Action—if so, it is to be hoped ye D^e of Cambridge & he will not meet or one of them must be knock'd down but to return to ye acc^t given—The Emperor of Austria,[99] this person says looks quite like an idiot shifting his feet, & twitching his Arms, as if he did not know what to do with them, & as to ye King of Prussia[100] he was all high top'd Boots & black Stock—a sensible Man without ye least firmness—

This is not very attractive—& I begin to think of the Mountain[101] & ye Mouse—in ye mean time we pass our time at Assemblys in pushing about & begging pardon of two Princes—one the Prince Paul of Wirtemberg the other, The Prince of Orange, whom people say is a *jilted Prince,*[102]—this I do not believe & am inclined to think she (the P^{ss} C[harlotte]) likes him, but not enough to risk being obliged to pass her life with him *in Holland*—If they would but secure her against going there when she may not be inclined to do so, all would be quickly settled— she does not say she will not go; but she wants to have it so secured, that she shall have ye power of following her inclination, he has no objection, as I am told—but her friends have such an exalted idea of conjugal duty—that they think a Wife bound to obey her Husband implicitly & to have no will of her own—which party will give way first I dont guess.—but this is ye present Situation of the parties—

great preparations are making for a Fete at Carlton House & for illuminations & Fireworks in the Park, on ye arrival of the Treaty of Peace,—I will write you word what happens; at present I do not feel much rejoiced at the prospect & think there is generally more trouble than amusement at any of these great Balls— They are commonly so very ill managed,—but as I have promised you an acc^t of such trifles, I must add a dash of Science to make this Letter more palatable—have you ever heard of Gall's System of Craneology[103]—we have one of his *Confrere's* here a Doc^r Spurtzheim, whom Frederic recommended to me,[104] they have discovered Muscles in ye Head for every sort of propensity, & if it is not so in fact, it is very amusing, & the Docteur very agreable—the Muscle for Bonté[105]—is in ye middle of the top of the Forehead—which ought to be much elevated as I think yours is—& the Muscle *for calcul* is just above each Eyebrow at the end nearest the

Temple where the Bone should be prominent—which yours must be of course or the whole System must fall———many objections are made to this, some say they are charlatans—& it is all nonsense, others more serious—think it favours Materialism—& consequently Atheistical—& in yᵉ mean time all professional people allow that Gall's manner of disecting a Head is much preferable to yᵉ old way, & that in consequence of it, he has made discoveries that are very curious as to yᵉ Structure of yᵉ Brain—& of the Muscles of the Head—whether Useful or not time must shew—

I must now finish, as Fordwich[106] is at my Elbow of which you may see proofs in yᵉ foregoing page

make my best Love to my Bʳ[other] & Lʸ M[ilbanke] & believe me

Ever most affᶦʸ yʳˢ

E M

Whitehall
25ᵗʰ May (Wednesday)
1814

Lady Melbourne to Lord Byron (Murray)

10ᵗʰ June
1814

Dearᵗ B-

She has just been with me, & after asking me twenty times if I had any thing to say to her & receiving as many *No's* she ask'd me if I had seen you last Night, I said Yes—did he ask you any thing about me—I'll answer no Questions of any Sort—that's very ill natur'd I only want to know if he told you that I had written to him *once* & desired him to answer some questions I ask'd him, to you, if he would not write to me.———if you desired him to give me any message to you he has not done it—did he say nothing about me—Nothing—oh I dont want to ask for any thing else I dont want to <bitch> any of y^r Secrets or to hear any confidences he may make you————very well, I s^d—she then added it was strange treatment for she wanted only to know one or two things, & you would not give her an answer—

She then began upon other Subjects & left the room. I am curious to know if this is true, & whether she desired you to give me your answer for I doubt it very much;[107] & think it was a story made at the moment, to excuse her writing, which she supposed I should hear from you—she dines out to day, & will very probably endeavour to receive *this* answer in person to Night—if so dont leave this note about the room, nor tell her y^t she has talk'd to me, pray mind this.

I am shock'd[108] at some of the things you s^d to me last Night, & think the *easy* manner in which two people have accustom'd themselves to consider, their Situation quite *terrible*[109]—but I shall not say more at present, as I see it is so useless. I can not reproach myself with having omitted any thing in my power to prevent the mischief and calamitys, that must happen, I fear—but I will not croak or prophecy misfortunes—tho' I am very melancholy[110]

Y^{rs} Ever
EM

[The/Lord Byron/Albany]

Lady Melbourne to George Lamb (45547, f.7)

13th July
[1814]

Dear George   so much to say, so little time to write. What can I do? write away you'll say, & so I will—on Tuesday y^e P[rince]. R[egent]. went to y^e P$^{ss.}$ Charlotte & told her, all her attendants were dismiss'd, y^t L^y Roslyn, L^y Flahurter, Miss Campbell,[111] were to replace them & in y^e next room—that she was to go into Carlton House, to receive no Letters write none but what were seen[,][112] receive no Visits, &c &c, every loss of Security threat'ned—I must explain y^t four days before ye D^ss of Salisbury had written her a Letter, advising her to write to ye P[rince]. expressing her willingness to renew with the P[rince]. of O[range].- & stating that if she did not, she must expect very severe measures would be adopted—so y^t she was prepared—after hearing this lecture ye D^ss of S[alisbury], being there with ye P[rince]. he desired to speak to Miss Knight.[113] She went out to her & s^d every thing I had so much reason to dread is come to pass, but the P[rince]. wants you. Miss Knight went to him & the P^ss walk'd down stairs found nobody opened the Door, went out call'd a Hackney coach, & drove to her Mothers who was at Blackheath—she was sent for & on her way call'd at ye H of Commons[,] ask'd for Whitbread then Tierney then Ponsonby, then Ld Grey[114] none of them to be found—she then either sent or went to Michael Angelo's where she got Brougham—in the mean time the D^ss of Salisbury & Miss Mercer[115] who was in some part of Warwick House, drove to find a night place[.] the P^ss. was denied, so they went away, but still having some idea she was there, they went back & gain'd admittance, & were there when ye P^ss & Brougham arrived, they all joined in entreating her to go back so that at first having shun'd the party she at length gave way it is s^d. by having receiv'd assurance that she should not experience the Severity with which she had been threaten'd—others say without conditions—it seems evident they want to force her to marry the P[rince] of O[range]- & I own I wonder y^t people instead of abusing her for going into a Hackney Coach which they do should not blame those who want her to marry ag^st her inclination——but she did like him s^d a Lady to me. Well if she did, I answer'd she has found cause to change her opinion & besides marrying him is being taken out of this Country.

I have just had a dispute with L^d Et.[116] who maintain'd that she mention'd her wish to marry him before it was mention'd to her; I s^d that was impossible for when he was just sent to Cambridge it was s^d every where to be with that view—& at last I silenced him—there seems to have been fine confusion created by this step of hers—The Queen had a party—neither she nor the Princess appear'd at last L^d St Helens was sent for by P^ss Eli^th[117] & desired to make the company sit down to Cards.——They persisted in Waiting—another Message obliged them to do so, & poor affremeuse was play'd, then they applied to L^d St. Helens to know what was to be done next—he s^d stand not on the order of y^r going but go—& away they went—some of them could not help blabbing this very extraordinary occurrence at Mss Byng's[118] Assembly & at Ldy Carrington's[119] Ball—This spread like Wildfire I know a person told Ly Carrington She ran about like Mad to find out & they say the confusion was extreme—the D[uk]e of York had company at Dinner, was called out, & three Cabinet Ministers with him—nine of them Whitbread Ld Ellenborough[120] was summoned, a writ of Habeas Corpus made out—Some say the Judges were sent for some say that would have [been] unconstitutional—Therefore others say it was no such thing but yt Sr V Gibbs[121] was there how happened that—without [his presence] they say it will be mentioned in Post to day—the Prince told Miss Knight she was dismiss'd he was now determined to take the Charge of his Daughter himself—; after this when Miss Knight left him she went to Speak to the Pss Charlotte, & could not find her, after ye closest search she returned to tell him this he stormed & swore yt it was all settled amongst them & with her Mother, Miss Knight sd she had often heard the Pss C[harlotte]. say yt if they resorted to extremities she would take measures, but never had heard her say yt she would go away—& pray sd he what did she mean by measures[.] I always heard her declare these measures should be an Applin to Parliament—he turn'd pale & quite scared she thought—

by ye bye I must tell you what Ld Wellington[122] sd when he was ask'd about ye reception that P[rince]- met with when he took her in the State Coach with him to Guild hall,[123] he sd to be sure there was much discontent shewn to ye Prince personally—but then they made very kind enquiries about his Family

We went to Brocket Sunday & returned last Night, I did not go out, but this Morg. those whom I had seen with ye exception of Ld Cow— & Giles have put me in a passion as they all seem to be inclined to abuse Pss C[harlotte]- for tho' I don't say she was right yet merely those who drive her to it by severity & cruelty are much more to be found fault with. Ld C[owper]. was by way of being candid— he sd these Women would worry him to Death I sd he was much more likely to kill his Daughter who was in a bad state of Health, & who was ordered to ye Sea— where he would not let her go—so we went on till he sd he had heard enough of the Story——which I think was a Surrender. God bless you Dst George—I have not seen Dst Caroline[124] but she dines here

EMelbourne

Lady Melbourne to Mrs. Huskisson (45547, f.104)

[Sept-Oct. 1814]

Dear M^rs. Huskisson,

as I heard y^t L^y M[ilbanke] had announced the Marriage formally to M^rs. Gage I conclude she must to you—Pyramus, & Thisbe of old were nothing to these Lovers. They only talk'd thro' Stone Walls & were within a few Inches of one Another, but these have made love at 250 Miles distance,——Annabella wrote me word of it first, two days after Ld Byron did ye Same,[125] & he is now settling the business with his Lawyers, after which he repairs to Seaham,—but when they are to be married I don't know nor any further particulars; I have received a Letter from L^y M[ilbanke]. stating her approbation & my Brothers,—& I sincerely wish they may be happy.—Emily is going on quite well; but has not yet got down Stairs except for an Hour in ye Evening, Ld Cowper in hearing of her accident[126] determined to return along with George, & most probably they are in England now, as they were to be at Calais Yesterday.—Mrs Lamb does not come back till the end of the Month—as George is now only on his way to Sessions, & must be at Liverpool next Sunday, pray tell M^r. Huskissons if he has any private communication to send to his New friends—George will be happy to be employ'd—

Ld Cowper says all Supplys are cut off from ye American Minister at Paris, & that he has petition'd Government to give him degrever se nombre,[127] or he must Starve[.] he can not speak a Word of French & at all the diplomatic dinners is set next to y^e. Parl't—Talleyrand[128] s^d to Ld Wellington—Voyez comme il est malin, il ne veut pas parler[129]——I am sorry you are at such a distance or I should have propos'd to you & M^r. H[uskisson] to meet a great personage here,—L^d M[elbourne] is in Town & writes me word the Regent will be here to morrow or next day[130]—so I'm in a great fuss; I hope it will not be for nothing—suppose I tell him that were I Judge I should convict <Quarters>[131] upon the Duc de Guiche refusing to come,—for could he have s^d any thing in his favour, he could not have been so savage as to refrain from giving his testimony—he would not be pleased & yet it is obvious I think a paragraph in y^e. Mor^g. herald about three weeks ago prepar'd one to expect this, it s^d that ye Duc de Guiche was now an English Captain but could not Stir unless by express permission from yᵉ King who probably would not allow him to be called in as Evidence in an English Court of Justice—132

Lady Melbourne to Lord Byron (45547, f.70-73)

B[rocket].H[all]
19th Ocr— 1814

Dʳ Lᵈ B.

You will see by yᵉ enclosure I sent you last Night, that *the secret* had been kept like most others,—your account133 however surprised me, what can Lʸ S[tafford]- mean, has she lost all sense or propriety! What,—enter into an arrangement with a Young Man, to marry her Daughter unknown to his Father?134

I have no idea of his consenting & I can not think him in yᵉ wrong if he does not, he is a Strict roman Catholic, & a very obstinate Man,—You will wonder at my knowing so much about them all, but Lʸ Charlotte Belasyse & Lʸ Lucan (Mʳ Howard's Mother) are Neices to Lord Melbourne—my correspondent Mʳ Belasyse is a very foolish pompous person who has made himself mightily busy about this Mʳ Howard ^because he is his wife's Nephew^ & accosted Lᵈ M[elbourne] last Year with—My Lord won't yʳ. Lordship be very proud of having a fine Young Man for yʳ Nephew when he is Earl of Surry?—Lᵈ M[elbourne] stared at him with wonder not grasping what he meant,—which confused Belasyse who repeated Earl of Surry—great Nephew hardly knowing what he sᵈ; at last Lᵈ M[elbourne] understood him, &, answered— If he's a fine Young *fellow* I shall be very glad to see him, but as to his being Earl of Surry, I don't care, one D— I was standing bye them and laughed heartily— ——

So at last yʳ Agent condescends to find some time when he will meet my Bʳˢ people—I knew yᵗ all those sort of ~~people~~ ^personages^, who have the *Management* of an Estate & of course of the ward of it, are displeased, when they think it likely they may lose a portion of their power, by its being transferr'd to a Wife—I mean power over their employer, & mostly dupe—they are enemies to matrimony, as much as you or I am to them, in truth, I never knew a Man who had not the *cleverest* & *honestest* agent in yᵉ World—& if ever I have become acquainted with them or their Actions, I have seldom found them honest—sometimes sinning from Stupidity, but invariably turning every thing to their own advantage & selfish to the highest degree, and always enriching themselves[135]—Mr. Hanson may be an exception to this rule I certainly have no acquaintance with him, & never heard his Name but from You—so I do not say this from any knowledge I have either of him or his Character—but were I to Judge from appearances I should say he has been unpardonably dilatory in this business ^from yᵉ beginning^—& were I Annabella & were I Annabella I should *never forget* him—& indeed it may be well for your Lordship that I am not, for you should come in for your share ^of blame^ too,[136]— but we'll say no more about it,———George often makes use of an expression when he means to say a *Cause* is weak—"it would be pooh pooh'd out of Court"—now thats my opinion of all your reasons, however ingenious & clever they may be,[137]— which, I allow but still I should say Pooh *Pooh*. dont mistake me, this is all putting myself in A's situation—& I never breathe a Word of my thoughts to any person except Yourself—so don't scold me—when I am ask'd any questions I pretend yᵉ. greatest ignorance except as to the fact[138]—by which means people tell me their opinion & very comical they are—I'll tell you some without the Names—one person says she is a[139] [text missing]

I have not yet heard what it was, & afterwards gave the Boys a ball and some Supper. She had written me word in one of her violent Letters yᵗ she was going to burn a greater Traitor than Guy down,[140] & that his odious Book yᵗ first made her like him should be burnt at yᵉ same time—but I did not believe she could mean to do it—I should not wonder if there was an Accᵗ of it in the News papers— for I hear yᵉ Servants talk of it with astonishment, as well they may———she has written Volumes to Em[ily][141] & yᵉ other day her little Girl[142] seeing her open one of these paquets sᵈ—"Mama don't read that Newspaper"—very comical for a Child just two yʳˢ old—I may mention a Child to you *now* without yʳ. making a face at me, which is a great improvement amongst many others—talking of children makes me think of Marriage, & that leads me to A[nnabella]—& I recollect that I never told you she denies *the Poohs* most Stoutly—I first ask'd her whether she was acquainted with them without saying why——she answered me she was not,——but that yᵉ Dow[age]ʳ Lʸ Gosford was a Miss Pooh, I was satisfied yᵗ *our favourite* Miss Montgomery[143] was yᵉ culprit, & I think so now, tho' I have had Letters both from Lʸ M[ilbanke?][144] & A[nnabella], swearing they had never told it to any person whatever

      I must add a *trait* of yʳ friend Banks[.][145] the day before you had a certain conversation with him he had seen Lʸ M[ilbanke], & talk'd a good deal about you, & told her he had some Verses written by you, When you were very Young, which had never been publish'd——& would prove yᵗ you had the best heart——& every Virtue I believe excepting none,——& promised to take them when he went to Richmond, but this being yᵉ day after you had made him yʳ confidant; he forgot them in Town.——by asking what day she had seen him & what day he went there I made this out quite correctly——pray remember & do not frank yʳ Letters——direct them to Whitehall——<&c. &c.>——Dr Lᵈ By very truly yours, EM

[45547, f.73; The/Lord Byron/Albany/London]

Lady Melbourne to Lord Byron (Murray; Murray 1:285)

B[rocket].H[all].

28ᵗʰ Ocʳ 1814

Dear Lᵈ B-

      I find that we shall certainly be in Town on Monday[.] if you should not have left it[146] pray let me see you on Tuesday Morᵍ at any time most agreeable to yourself——but if it should so happen that you are Setting out on Tuesday, you might call upon me Monday Evening——les entrèes sont libres pour un Neveu a toute heure[147]——as much as I have been wishing you to go, I can not help acknowledging that I am selfish enough to feel that I shall rejoice, to find you in London

yʳˢ ever,

EM

[The Lord Byron/Albany/<u>London</u>]

18ᵗʰ Novʳ

1814

Dear Lᵈ B——

What? a chance still of my not being a Zia[.]¹⁴⁸ I can not bear it, You can not think how much I have been annoy'd by what you tell me—I once saw something of the Sort, which ended in a Head ache for two days, & which I never could quite understand, but created surprises & this was in fact the reason why I thought it best to be cautious about my Letters——

You have always accused me of being Suspicious, but really without it one is not on a par with yᵉ rest of the world—I hope things are better arranged by this time, do you recollect the Speech of some body in yᵉ Rivals recommending Julia to marry Falkland, by way of a cure for all his absurdities¹⁴⁹—this may now be applied to you—she always sᵈ that all her folly's should be over before she married, as she never would commit any after, & I hope she'll keep her promise.

Seriously, it is very impolitic,¹⁵⁰ & she is sure to suffer for it after—as it must give you a bad impression of her temper, tho' I think, you see it in a proper light, for I do not believe it to be bad,—she is always so ready to make atonement, if she thinks she has been wrong—& after all if *coaxing* will set all right—every thing is in your own power—for tho' you are dextrous in most things, that is your *forte*¹⁵¹—— I met with a person who had seen A- answer to + [Augusta] & your Letter with an Account of your arrival &c &c—You will believe this rather Surprised me as I am sure there must have been some little that was not perceivable to common Eyes—if I understand your meaning when you say, "I can only interpret these things one way"¹⁵²—I think you are wrong; if you think they proceed fᵐ disinclination to you—quite the contrary. They are very tormenting but they prove a strong partiality—like you I detest agitations, & am fond of good quiet common sense—but at the same time, one must be *just*—& few people have felt strong liking without being a little unreasonable at times——wont you acknowledge this? I am you know, a pattern for composure on all occasions—so you will not retort yᵉ question upon me—if you did, perhaps I might be puzzled—but you are not my

Father confesser——I am writing away to you & shall be too late for Isabella——I am going to see Miss O'Neil[153] to Night—for ye first time I hope you are all indignant at ye proceedings upon ye Officer[154] of ye 10th—there never was so much despotism exercised before except perhaps in Turkey upon ye Corps of Janikaries—a person told me this Mor^g that *another person* who out of prudence I shall not name, never is actuated by any motives but partiality & resentment[155]—justice is quite out of ye case——but I must have done

Y^rs Ever

EM

I am anxious to hear from you again

Lady Melbourne to Lord Byron (45547, f.77); only a part of this letter survives

[after November 18, 1814][156]

to Many families—on this Occasion I should *wish* ye whole to be conducted Speedily, & as I am well acquainted with ye dilatoriness puzzle headedness &c. &c. of my Brothers Agents—if I were you I would try & be married upon Articles—if you laugh at this at least acknowledge y^t I am engag'd to Sign myself y^r aff^be. Aunt. I have enter'd on this dry Subject in a Letter knowing y^t I never should have got you to listen even to Twenty words of it in a conversation[157]

Yrs Ever

EM

I hope there are no Omissions in my Letter that you can not supply as I have no time to look it over

[The Lord Byron/the Albany/London]
[45547, f.76; The Lord Byron/Seaham Stockton/Upon Tees]

Lady Melbourne to Lord Byron (Murray)

Wed^y 30th Nov.¹⁵⁸ [1814]

D^r L^d B

They do not come for 2 or 3 days & promise to give me notice of their intention so that till I send you word to ye contrary this House is open to you at all times, & I hope you will dine here to morrow; L^d M[elbourne] was going to call upon you to invite you in person—but I suggested that I might as well write—as I thought it as well not to *risk* what, he might have found, tho' *he* would have forgiven you.

don't you think this is being very considerate & like a kind affectionate Aunt?

Y^{rs} ever

EM

[The Lord Byron]

Lady Melbourne to Anne Isabella Milbanke (Lovelace 92, f.52, 54; Elwin, Wife 239)

1st Dec^r

1814

My dear Annabella

I received y^r Letter in the Country, & intended to thank you for it much sooner, but the old story of not having time prevented me, indeed I know that you must have so many Letters that mine can not be much look'd upon, & must be lost among so many interesting ones,—I have seen Ld Byron who is grumbling at having so much business upon his Hands which will probably prevent his returning so soon as he wishes—I told him I supposed his leaving you, was unavoidable, otherwise I should have scolded you for allowing him to come away, as I am far from agreeing with you—when you say "I dont think that a short separation will be disadvantageous." to you two personally it certainly will not—but there are disadvantages attending it to yᵉ World, & it puts me out of humour to be ask'd by every person I meet, what is the reason of this delay? Why he is come to Town? as it is a proof that all sorts of reports are current & you see also things have occur'd to delay his return which was to be expected at such a distance, for three Hᵈ Miles is a serious Journey he now finds that he cannot take the House in Hampshire¹⁵⁹ & must look out for another—but of this he will have informed you himself—he seems averse to coming to Town & it must be difficult to find a place immediately—why should you not remain longer at Halnaby? it seems to me as if that would be no inconvenience as he would have time to look out, for some residence.—I am talking to you about these things, as I hope you intend to descend to yᵉ common details,—Tho' that expression of yours strikes me as if you were still a little in yᵉ Clouds of Romance—& above the feelings of common hum drum beings, who would not have affected to be indifferent to a separation just at this time—which he laments, & says he wishes most sincerely he had not been forced to leave you— he tells me you have parted with your Maid, this has somehow or other got about—& Mʳˢ Lamb was Yesterday applied to by her Servant to recommend his Sister. She did not at yᵉ time believe it but when I told her it was true she said she would enquire into particulars & where she had liv'd & let you know, as he is an excellent Servᵗ it is possible it may run in the Family, & it is as well to know something about her.

2d Decʳ I was interrupted Yesterday & could not finish my Letter—at Night Mʳˢ Lamb told me this Maid has lived two Yʳˢ with a Lady Williams who will give her an excellent Character & that she is now working at one of the fashionable Milliners to make herself perfect in Mantua making & Millinery—& if you wish her to make any further enquiries, she will with great pleasure——

I was very happy to find by yʳ Letter that yʳ Sentiments concerning Lᵈ Byron were exactly the same as what he had express'd to me in a Letter from Seaham about You.—

You say he has every thing that can make me the happiest Woman in yᵉ World——& he says I am convinced that your Neice can make me extremely happy & has the power of keeping me so,——nothing surely can be better, & must be so pleasing & comfortable to your Mutual Friends—amongst whom I trust & hope you assign me a distinguish'd place

believe me, with kindest love to my B[r] & L[y] M[ilbanke]—

Yours my dear Annabella

Most aff[ly]

E Melbourne

[London Dec[r]: Second, 1814/ Miss Milbanke/Seaham/Stockton upon/Tees/Egremont]

Lady Melbourne to Lord Byron (Murray)

Sunday Eve

4th Dec[r]

1814

Dear L[d] B-

William is detained in the Country by illness & C[aroline]. by nursing him, which is always the business of a good Wife. I think he will not be able to come to London for some days—If you should have nothing better to do, perhaps you will call upon me to morrow or Tuesday—if the first come earlier as I am going to the Play, if on Tuesday come about the usual time[160] have you seen the Lines in yester-days paper (Morn[ing] Herald) upon Anna[a] & you?[161] the two first must mean C[aro-line]—They might have been better applied, & heavier loaded. The 2 Next have no fault except not being matter of fact which I wish they were. The last remain to be proved—at present no one can tell, it is only devoutly to be wish'd; & I have only to add my prayers y[t] it may soon come within y[e] Scope of possibility

Yrs ever,

EM

15th Dec[r]

1814

D[r]. L[d] B.

I suppose by this time, you have settled your departure,[162] & I want to remind you of your promise of leaving me a successor in yr Box at Drury Lane, for I find we are likely to remain here longer than I expected, or look forward to, with any pleasure & I shall like to go to y[e] play now & then. I saw you there last Saturday, y[r]. Eyes were up rais'd to the higher Spheres; even +[163] must have been absent from y[r] thoughts they were so strongly invested on present Objects.—I think I pass'd unobserved,—in y[e] crowd

You, like every other person in this Town, must have been employ'd in reading Ld R[y]'s[164] trial—some words of Broughams struck me very forcibly, did you take notice of y[e] following sentence "happy had it been for them if any strong necessity any over ruling power had stepped in, to check their mad, their infatuated career" was there ever any thing more true or more applicable.[165] This strong necessity exists—dont cast it away, rather cherish it, as a most fortunate circumstance[166]

What an admirable Speech B[ms] was, & how skillfully he turn'd all Garrows violence & unfairness, to the advantage of his client, no one could have made more of so desperate a cause[167]—he told a person I know, y[t] he thought it so hopeless, he would at any time in the day have compromised for 25000[168]——I am not quite satisfy'd with C[aroline]- I think her good resolutions seem to be ebbing—last Night she injured herself upon A's name being mentioned, luckily no strangers were bye— this morning she enquired if you were in Town. I s[d] I did not know, which is fact, for I should not be surprised if you were gone to X[169]—how can she[170] allow you to put An[a][bella] into such an unpleasant Situation, she ought to feel for her. I was told to day by a person who heard it out of the North, that the Clergyman was there & every preparation made, I could not Joke, on what I think so serious, or I might have repeated An[as] words, the Spouse absent &c &c—but I am in a sad Stupid way—& have not laugh'd for a Week, it is I think about y[t] time since I saw you[171]—

My thoughts on reading the Trial[172] all turn'd on what I have so often observ'd, the abominable selfishness of Men, they never can be satisfied till they have exposed a Woman past redemption & sacrificed her to their Vanity——S[r] H[enry] M[ildmay] tho' so well assured of her love could not rest till her ruin was complete, & she taken from her friends, relations, & her Children, & devoted to a life of misery——& perhaps after all this he will desert her as being entirely in his power will treat her with indifference & cruelty——is not this true? You must know it is ~~true~~ ^so^ tho' I don't expect you to own it[173]——tell me when you go to N[ottingham]? My B[r][other] has I hear completed the Sale of the Farm I mentioned to you, therefore you will receive a large portion of An[a]'s fortune very soon, this you don't care about, but it may be convenient—C[aroline]- questioned me this Morning about the delay, I laid it all upon H[anson] with whom she said you had made her acquainted. I hope she won't think of inquiring about it from him—

Poor An[a][bella] I pity her very much—it is in some play I think—that they say "the best Men are moulded out of faults"[174]— I am sure yt ought to be impressed upon the minds of all unmarried Ladies—the Married ones know it—

The Countess *par excellence*[175] is at Middleton, & says they are very gay altho' the L[d] of Gloucester is one of the party[.] I expect her in Town in a day or two—I think I have now bored you till you must be out of patience, even if you had a greater share of it than I think you possess

Y[rs] ever, EM

Viscountess Melbourne to Annabella Milbanke (Lovelace 92, f.56)
Whitehall

20th Dec[r]

1814

My dear Annabella

I am very glad the Boxes were what you wanted & that you liked them— The other part of your Letter did not please me so well, & was News to me, as I have not seen L[d] Byron for a Week, on account of impediments, which he told you—when you are married there must be an end to all that nonsense, but at present I submit to it, as I hate Scenes—tho' in justice I must say, that I believe my fears are groundless, as she[176] seems so much changed & so much quieter than I have ever seen her, she also talks very kindly of you, so that altogether we should I am persuaded do very well if that odious M^r H[anson], would but exert himself a little more dont tell L^d B[yron] I call'd him so, for that is a tender Subject.— —I suppose You know that y^r Friend Harriet Pearce is married to day to Mr Germaine, Brother to Lord Sackville, I knew him formerly when he was a Jockey, but for some y^{rs} he has become a Farmer & lives at Ld Sackvilles at Drayton constantly—I hope she will be happy, as she is a charming person, but his temper is not very good, it is said; & he has nothing very attractive to make her overlook that fault. I believe however he is a good sort of Man, & her home is very uncomfortable.—

we are now going into ye Country for Christmas, & shall remain there I hope all January—of course you will not be in the South till after that period, but I hope at some other time, to receive you & Ld Byron there, which I trust I need not add will be great pleasure to me, pray let me hear from you, as soon as things are Settled which I hope will be very speedily believe me

Ever most aff^{ly} yrs

EMelbourne

as I was folding my Letter Ld Melbourne came in, & told [me] he had just call'd upon Ld Byron who admitted him, & told him he was in hopes of being able to set out for the North Friday or Saturday next

make my kindest Love to my B^r & L^y Milbanke

[92, f.58; London December twentieth, 1814/Miss Milbanke/Seaham/Stockton upon Tees, Cowper]

Notes: Part IV

1. Lady Melbourne responded to Byron's concern about Caroline Lamb in a letter that is missing. On September 18, 1814, he replied to thank her. "May I hope for your consent too?" he asked Lady Melbourne (September 18, 1814; *LJ* 4:175). "It is a match of *your* making, and better had it been had *your* proposal been accepted at the time."

2. This is the same word that Byron had used to describe her two years earlier (September 28, 1812; *LJ* 2:218), when Annabella had rejected his first proposal of marriage.

3. This letter appears to be missing.

4. She was marrying a cousin of Lord Melbourne's (October 19, 1814).

5. "They say, best men are moulded out of faults: / And, for the most become much more the better, / For being a little bad" (*Measure for Measure* 5:1:444).

6. Lady Melbourne is responding to Byron's letters of January 8 and 11, 1814 (*LJ* 4:20; 4:23). Byron was staying at the house of his friend James Wedderburn Webster. Annoyed by his host's boasts about his wife's virtue, which Webster compared to that of Christ (September 21, 1813; *LJ* 3:115), Byron set out to seduce Frances Webster. The two exchanged letters privately. Lord Byron kept Lady Melbourne informed of all the proceedings, even sending her copies of Frances Webster's letters. The clandestine couple declared their love in a billiard room, but Byron decided to "spare" Webster and avoid the duel with her husband that he foresaw as inevitable if they eloped.

7. In a letter to Byron, Lady Frances Webster quoted this line from Byron's *The Bride of Abydos* (1:350). In Byron's poem, Selim interprets Zuleikha's statement of affection for the young boy as an "oath" that has bound them both.

8. Paston and Quennell read this as "Are you my Selim?" but leave out other parts of the letter (including "swear to it in 'motley guise'"). Their transcription is not entirely reliable (104).

9. Byron wrote as follows the same day: "To tell you the *truth* (where I could not tell her) I have not answered it at all" (January 16, 1814; *LJ* 4:35).

10. Frances Webster.

11. Written over an illegible word.

12. January 8, 1814; *LJ* 4:20.

13. Brief cross out precedes "my".

14. Webster's sister, who saw Byron through a keyhole (January 15, 1814; *LJ* 4:32).

15. Lady Frances Webster, whom Byron and Lady Melbourne referred to as "Phryne." See Lady Melbourne's letter of October 13, 1813.

16. Madame de Staël arrived in England in June 1813 and had dinner with Caroline Lamb as early as September and probably in October when de Staël was in London. Byron dined with de Staël on October 2, along with Davys, Ward, Malthus, and Curran, the famous Irish advocate (Berry 2:543). On September 23, 1813 de Staël wrote to Miss Berry to say "Il y a ici Lady Cowper, Lady Caroline, les maris de ces dames, Mr. Nugent, Mr. Ward. Lady Bessborough est partie ce matin, et Lord Melbourne nous a quittée, quoiqu'il fut assez bien apprivoise avec moi" [Lady Cowper, Lady Caroline, and the husbands of these women, Mr. Nugent, Mr. Ward. Lady Bessborough is leaving this morning, and Lord Melbourne left, having being tamed by me] (Berry 2:542). Lord Melbourne may have been somewhat tamed by de Staël, but Lady Melbourne and Byron were not. Miss Berry, de Staël's close friend, described her visit to England in the following terms: "The said Staël is still at Richmond till the end of the month, when her torrent of words and ideas will no longer flow into the Thames, but turn its course towards London, and then to Lord Lansdowne's and then into Staffordshire, and then—'To Nova Zembla and the Lord knows where;' but still she sticks to being at Wimpole the middle of November" (Berry 2:541).

17. This suggests that Lady Melbourne did leave a letter for Caroline to see, despite having denied this to Byron on September 29, 1812.

18. Byron alluded to this topic the day before Lady Melbourne composed her letter: "I do think between her theory and my system of Ethics you will begin to think our first parents had better have paused before they plucked the tree of knowledge" (January 15, 1814; *LJ* 4:32).

19. "So you have his R[oyal] H[ighness] on Tuesday," Byron had written. "Well—I envy him his visit"

(January 15, 1814; *LJ* 4:32).

20. Byron's malicious nickname for Lady Bessborough, the mother of Caroline Lamb, was borrowed from Goldsmith's *Vicar of Wakefield*.

21. "Monk" Lewis, author of *The Monk* (1796), was a friend to William Lamb during his visit to Scotland.

22. Maria Anne Fitzherbert.

23. The Prince Regent.

24. Oatlands Park, Weybridge Surrey, seat of Lord Lincoln (late duke of Newcastle) and of Frederick, duke of York: "The conduct of the Duchess of York is exemplary; she resides wholly at Oatlands, in retirement; and domestic virtue predominates in all her actions. Economy is her first principle, a plan worthy of imitation in these days of public expense" (Walpole 12:98).

25. Misdated "Jany 19th 1812" in Lady Melbourne's hand.

26. Madame de Staël accused Byron of shutting his eyes during dinner (January 16, 1814; *LJ* 4:33).

27. Possibly "thus."

28. Frances Webster's. See note 15.

29. William Lamb's opinion.

30. Nottingham was Byron's parliamentary district and the site of Newstead Abbey.

31. The northern Staffordshire coalfield region was known as The Potteries. Coal and iron had been mined on the Upper Trent and around Cannock Chase since the thirteenth century. During the eighteenth century, the pottery industry of northern Staffordshire gained fame through the work of Josiah Wedgwood.

32. *bienseances:* decorum.

33. "as you represented her" is crossed out with Xs.

34. Byron responded: *"Prosecute"*—Oh No—I am a great friend to liberty of the press—even at the expense of myself" (March 1814?; *LJ* 4:75).

35. "Mob"? This space is left blank in the manuscript.

36. On February 14, 1814, Byron wrote that "the Hollands &c. have been worrying me to say & do I know not what about Lord Carlisle and I will neither do that nor anything else but be silent which has put them in no very good humour" (February 18, 1814; *LJ* 4:65). Presumably the Hollands were trying to persuade Byron to apologize for his attack on Lord Carlisle in *English Bards* (line 726). Byron still harbored bitterness over his relative's refusal to introduce him to the House of Lords in 1809 (Marchand, *Portrait* 56).

37. "I am glad you like the Corsair," Byron had written to Lady Melbourne, "—& was afraid he might be too larmoyant a gentleman for your favour" (February 11, 1814; *LJ* 4:54).

38. "Full many a stoic eye and aspect stern / Mask hearts where grief hath little left to learn; / And many a withering thought lies hid, not lost, / In smiles that least befit who wear them most" (21.638).

39. "R[ogers] I should conceive not [to] be a very exact thermometer as to 'spirits,'" Byron responded (February 18, 1814; *LJ* 4:64). Samuel Rogers, the poet and banker, lived on Bennet Street, the same street on which Byron lived at this time.

40. Byron's apparent dejection had less to do with the newspaper articles than with his obsession with Augusta (February 18, 1814; *LJ* 4:64).

41. See Lady Melbourne's letter of February 12, 1814, in which she quotes from Byron's *Corsair* (21.638) using this phrase.

42. Byron had not been near Lady Melbourne because he was with Augusta Leigh at Newstead Abbey (Marchand, *Portrait* 161).

43. Byron was less concerned than his correspondent. "I do not know to what you allude—nor does it matter—whatever they *can* they will say—but if stepping across the room would stop them I would

not cross it" (February 18, 1814; *LJ* 4:65).

44. James Perry, editor of the *Morning Chronicle* (August 3, 1814; *LJ* 4:152).

45. Byron had written to say: "I was near meeting you at Lady Lansdowne's & Miss Berrys' but did not go—Rogers says I should—as it looks as if I was disturbed—but you know I did not go out much last year—& have still less inclination this—but if I felt all this so deeply—what should prevent my leaving town or the country?" (February 18, 1814; *LJ* 4:65).

46. See Byron's letters of February 18, 1814; *LJ* 4:64; and February 21, 1814; *LJ* 4:69.

47. "I am not 'forbidden' by —— [Augusta]," Byron responded, "though it is very odd that like *every one*—she seemed more assured (and not very well pleased) of your influence than of any other" (February 21, 1814; *LJ* 4:69).

48. See Byron's letter of February 21, 1814; *LJ* 4:69.

49. Byron uses this phrase to describe Emily Cowper in a letter of October 25, 1813(?) (*LJ* 3:154).

50. Byron had written: "I don't think that I shall be able to call upon you before C[aroline]'s arrival—& that will stop my visits for a still longer period" (February 18, 1814; *LJ* 4:65).

51. On February 18 Dallas wrote a long letter saying that Byron did not receive a shilling from any of his works and acknowledging Byron's gifts of the copyrights of *Childe Harold* and *The Corsair*. The letter was published in the *Morning Post* on February 21. Byron wrote that "I am glad that you think poor Dallas acted rightly—I told him that I saw no reason why he should interpose—& Hobhouse said it was better not" (February 21, 1814; *LJ* 4:69).

52. This comment provoked Byron's ire, as Lady Melbourne predicted it would. "As for the *world*—I neither know nor enquire into it's notions—you can bear me witness that few ever courted it—or flattered it's opinions less—if it turns or has turned against me I cannot blame it—my heart is not in it—& my head better without it" (February 21, 1814; *LJ* 4:70).

53. This envelope is separated and may not belong to this letter.

54. The actor Edmund Kean.

55. Emily Cowper.

56. Caroline Lamb.

57. Napoleon. On February 5 the Allies were successful enough for Caulaincourt to accept the "ancient frontiers" in order to save Paris and prevent a battle. The French victories at Montmirail and Montmoreau a few days later changed this, altering the Allied counsels at Troyes and leading Napoleon to disown Caulaincourt's conduct on February 17 (Thompson 354).

58. Robert Banks Jenkinson, earl of Liverpool.

59. Possibly the Prince Regent.

60. Possibly Mrs. Damer.

61. There are several possible identifications, including Princess Lieven, who arrived in London in 1813, and Princess Esterhazy, a grandniece of the queen of England. The most likely candidate, however, is Madame Narischkine, who was also in England at the time.

62. Lord Granville Leveson-Gower.

63. Caroline and William Lamb. According to Torrens, his biographer, William preferred the Bessboroughs' house at Roehampton to Brocket and Melbourne Hall.

64. Byron moved into Albany House in Piccadilly. The Melbournes lived in this residence until 1792 (not 1789 as Marchand states [*LJ* 4:87 n.2]), having exchanged houses with the duke of York at his request. Melbourne House, Piccadilly, as it was known when Lady Melbourne lived there (1770–92), was designed by Sir William Chambers and was converted into bachelor apartments by Henry Holland in 1802, after which it became known as the Albany. Other residents of the Albany include Monk Lewis, George Canning, and Jane Austen's brother. "I am in *my* & *your* Albany rooms," Byron wrote on March 30, 1814. "I think you should have been included in the lease.—I am sadly bewildered with hammering—and

teaching people the left hand from the right—and very much out of humour with a friend—who tells me of a serious report that I am turning Methodist!" (*LJ* 4:87).

65. *Genesis* 39:7-20. Potiphar, captain of the pharaoh's guard, bought Joseph from the Ishmaelites and made him steward of his household. When Potiphar's wife clutched his robes, pleading with him to make love to her, Joseph fled, leaving his cloak in her hands. She avenged her humiliation by accusing Joseph of trying to violate her, using the cloak as evidence. Joseph was imprisoned but later released after interpreting the dreams of the pharaoh. Byron referred to Lord Oxford as Potiphar (October 17, 1813; *LJ* 3:147).

66. Begins a new page, hence the repetition of the word.

67. See Byron's reply of April 8, 1814 (*LJ* 4:90).

68. Byron thanked Lady Melbourne for her discretion. "Thanks as to C[aroline]—though the task will be difficult—if she is to determine as to kindness & unkindness—the best way will be to avoid each other *without appearing* to do so—or if we jostle—at any rate *not to bite*" (April 25, 1814; *LJ* 4:104).

69. She responds to Byron's letter of April 24: "I really think you pay me too great great a compliment—& her none—to imagine any doubts of our mutual decorum & discretion & all that" (April 24, 1814; *LJ* 4:103).

70. Since Byron and Augusta's "child" was already born on April 15, 1814, it seems that Lady Melbourne is objecting here to Byron's plan of running away with Augusta. Marchand (*Portrait* 166; *LJ* 4:104) accepts Moore's view that Medora was not Byron's daughter by Augusta (301-2). Lady Melbourne's letter, transcribed here for the first time, supports Moore's argument, since Lady Melbourne adopts a decidedly playful tone about what would have been a much more serious subject (i.e. Byron's paternal responsibility for Medora).

71. The words "sake of Augusta" are crossed out heavily.

72. "It is worth while," Byron wrote in response (April 25, 1804; *LJ* 4:104).

73. "What became of you last night?" Byron asked her in a letter the day before. "I don't know but I got into a roundabout conversation with Miss M—& was obliged to call carriages a service in which I got wet through & consequently took refuge in my own & came away" (April 24, 1814; *LJ* 4:103).

74. Byron had written: "I wish to know whether *I* may go to Ly. Hard[wick]e's on Thursday or not—because you may be sure I will do what *you* like on that point—as on *all* others—saving one— though methinks I am vastly obedient there too.+" (April 24, 1814; *LJ* 4:103). See earlier in this letter for Lady Melbourne's use of the phrase "other points."

75. This envelope is separated from the text and may not belong to it.

76. The year and month of this letter are conjectured from its placement in the John Murray archive folder, where it follows March 24, 1814.

77. Augusta.

78. The address is on the same page as this letter.

79. This letter may refer to Annabella, whose "deceit" consisted in pretending that she was engaged to George Eden. Lady Melbourne may also be referring to some more specific deceit. Byron wrote: "Did you observe that she [Annabella] says '*if* la tante approved she should' she is little aware how much 'la tante' has to *dis*approve—but you perceive that without intending it she pays me a compliment by supposing you to be my friend and a sincere one—where *approval* could alter even *her* opinions" (April-May 1, 1814; *LJ* 4:11).

80. "upon" is written over the word "about."

81. Lady Melbourne refers to Byron's affair with Augusta.

82. I have been unable to find the source of this quotation, but Annabella did not believe in Lady Melbourne's truthfulness, as the introduction to this volume shows. "When I *know* Truth I follow it," Annabella wrote about herself on one occasion, "or return to it, come what may" (February 15-19, 1814;

Mayne, *Life* 88).

83. Augusta Leigh.

84. Annabella Milbanke. Lady Melbourne plays on an expression Byron used in a letter of April 18, 1814: "I have as yet no intention of serving my sovereign 'in the *North*' and I wish to know whether (if I did incline that way) you would not put Richard's question to me?—Though I think *that chance* off the cards—& have no paramount inclination to try a fresh deal" (*LJ* 4:99). After seducing Anne over the corpse of Henry VI, whom Richard has killed, Richard asks himself, "Was ever woman in this humour woo'd? / Was ever woman in this humour won?" (1:2:ln.228-9). Byron alludes playfully to his own libertine conduct between Annabella's first rejection of him and her acceptance of his second offer (April 18, 1814; *LJ* 4:99).

85. Free permission to pursue Annabella. "I should be not only unwilling but unable to make the experiment without your acquiescence," Byron had written (April 18, 1814; *LJ* 4:99).

86. This letter states explicitly what many biographers have conjectured. Lady Melbourne did not prevent Byron's marriage to Annabella because she felt she "ought not" to "act in consequence" of the knowledge with which she had "been trusted" (that is, Byron's incestuous affair with Augusta). To read this letter in its full context, however, is to become aware that Lady Melbourne went from "acquiescence" to actively encouraging the marriage.

87. Seaham, home of the Milbankes.

88. The day before, Byron had written to Lady Melbourne, that "I am not now in love with her" (April 29, 1814; *LJ* 4:109).

89. Lady Melbourne was responding to Byron's indecision: "I am quite irresolute—and undecided—if I were sure of *myself* (not of her) I would go—but I am not—& never can be—and what is still worse I have no judgement—& less common sense than an infant—this is *not affected humility*—with *you* I have no affectation—with the world I have a part to play—to be diffident there is to wear a drag-chain—and luckily I do so thoroughly despise half the people in it—that my insolence is almost natural" (April 29, 1814; *LJ* 4:109).

90. Byron once described how he declared his love for Lady Frances Webster in a "billiard room" (October 8, 1813; *LJ* 3:134).

91. Lady Melbourne again alludes to Byron's previous letter: "I don't suspect myself of talking often about poets or clergymen—of rhyme or the rubrick—but very likely I am wrong—for assuredly no one knows *itself*—and for aught I know—I may for these last 2 years have inflicted upon you a world of theology—and the greater part of Walker's rhyming dictionary" (April 29, 1814; 4:109).

92. This envelope has no date and is separated from the text above. It refers to a time when Byron was living on Bennett Street and trying to get a portrait of himself back from Caroline Lamb.

93. When Lady Caroline Lamb heard a rumor that Byron was marrying Lady Adelaide Forbes, she demanded her letters and trinkets returned. Byron wrote that "*I* have not proposed to anybody" (May 28, 1814; *LJ* 4:119).

94. Written over another word, which is illegible.

95. Augusta.

96. Colonel Francis Hastings Doyle later advised the Noels during Byron and Annabella's separation negotiations. His sister, Selina Doyle, was a confidante of Annabella's during this period (April 6, 1816; *LJ* 6:62).

97. The first sentence of this paragraph is quoted in Elwin, *Wife* 196.

98. Alexander I, emperor of Russia.

99. Francis II.

100. Frederick-William III.

101. The "advanced section of the Whig party" was referred to as the "Mountain" (Aspinall, *Lord*

Brougham 24).

102. In June 1814, after a six-month engagement, Princess Charlotte rejected the Prince of Orange, the person selected to be her husband by the Regent and his ministers.

103. Franz Joseph Gall founded the discipline of phrenology, which posits a relationship between skull shape and intellectual and social attributes.

104. Frederick Lamb may have heard of John Caspar Spurzheim, the German phrenologist and follower of Gall, during his tenure as a diplomat in Frankfurt. Spurzheim visited England in 1813 and lectured on the new "science" for four years.

105. *Bonté:* goodness, kindness.

106. Emily Cowper's firstborn son, George Augustus Frederick, later Lord Fordwich, was born June 26, 1806.

107. Byron responded directly to this portion of Lady Melbourne's letter: "I don't remember one syllable of such a request—but the truth is that I do not always read ye. letters through—she has no more variety than my Maccaw—& her note is not much more musical" (June 10, 1814; *LJ* 4:123).

108. Byron responded to Lady Melbourne's letter that same day: "All you say is exceeding true—but who ever said or supposed that you were not shocked and all that?—you *have* done every thing in your power—& more to make me act rationally" (June 10, 1814; *LJ* 4:123).

109. Lady Melbourne refers to Byron's affair with Augusta.

110. Byron responded to the last line of Lady Melbourne's letter in a reply written the same day: "I am sorry to hear of your tristesse" (June 10, 1814; *LJ* 4:124).

111. Lady Rosslyn, Lady Flahurter, and Miss Campbell were among Princess Charlotte's attendants at Cranbourne Lodge and afterwards at Weymouth (Stuart, *Daughter* 207).

112. On the very day of Princess Charlotte's death, the duke of York implored Lady Flahurter to surrender the letters to him "out of respect to her memory." She refused. Nor did Lord Lauderdale, acting on behalf of Prince Leopold, succeed. The "sour and determined" lady, as Leopold called her to Queen Victoria, was adamant. The Prince of Orange returned to Charlotte the letters touching on their engagement for which she had applied to him in vain at the time of their engagement (Stuart, *Daughter* 291).

113. Ellis Cornelia Knight, one of Princess Charlotte's attendants, was among those dismissed by the Prince Regent.

114. Samuel Whitbread, George Tierney, George Ponsonby, and Charles Grey.

115. Margaret Mercer Elphinstone.

116. Lord Egremont.

117. Princess Elizabeth, the daughter of George III.

118. The Honorable Lucy Elizabeth Byng, daughter and coheir of George Byng, the fourth Viscount Torrington, married Orlando, the first earl of Bradford (1762-1825) (G. L. Gower 1:371).

119. Lady Carrington, the wife of Robert Percy Smith.

120. Edward Law, first Baron Ellenborough.

121. Sir Vicary Gibbs.

122. Arthur Wellesley, first duke of Wellington.

123. Guild Hall, the largest hall in England after Westminster, served as the center of civic government. Lord mayors and sheriffs were elected and meetings of the Court of Common Council held there. The hall now houses monuments to men of national importance, including Nelson (1810), Wellington (1857), and Winston Churchill (1958).

124. Caroline, George Lamb's wife.

125. Byron was accepted by Annabella Milbanke on September 14, 1814 (Marchand, *Portrait* 176). He wrote to Lady Melbourne four days later to ask for her consent (September 18, 1814; *LJ* 4:175).

126. Lady Cowper had injured her leg in a riding accident.

127. *degrever se nombre:* to disencumber, free him from this responsibility.

128. Charles Maurice de Talleyrand-Perigord.

129. See how shrewd he is, he does not want to speak.

130. Though this letter is undated, the Prince Regent is listed as having visited Lady Melbourne on October 18, 1814 (*Morning Herald,* October 19, 1814).

131. Possibly "Quentin." Lady Melbourne refers to the court-martial of Colonel Dick Quentin (spelled "Quintin" in the London *Times* on October 18, 1814), who "happened to be a favourite" of the Prince Regent, according to George Tierney (*Morning Herald,* November 18, 1814). Captain Count De Grammont, duke of Guiche by the time of the trial, wrote several letters accusing Quentin of various infringements but was in France until November 20, during the duration of the trial. Lady Melbourne goes on to imply that the Regent made the duc de Guiche an English captain to prevent him from testifying against Quentin. Elizabeth Huskisson had a particular interest in military discipline because of "a young Relation of Mr. H[uskisson]'s who entered the navy at *my* recommendation" (see letter of October 27, 1806).

132. Colonel Quentin belonged to the 10th Hussars, a regiment that it was particularly desirable to join because it was under the direct command of the Prince of Wales. However, in 1814 the prince was also Regent, and Tierney accused him of acting "alternately in the chair of Regent and Colonel of the Regiment" during these proceedings. By doing so, the prince was protecting Quentin and punishing the officers who brought charges against him (*Morning Herald,* November 18, 1814). When Quentin was acquitted, Colonel Palmer asked and obtained permission for the proceedings to be laid before the House of Commons. Lord Egremont, perhaps at Lady Melbourne's instigation, agreed with Colonel Palmer that the matter should be discussed before the House of Commons. On April 20, 1815 he spoke at length on the subject in a "Motion relative to the Courts Martial upon Captain Philip Browne of the Hermes, Colonel Quentin, &c."

133. Byron had written to Lady Melbourne on October 7, 1814: "The new plan is this—(a secret of course & do *you* keep it better than *I* have in this instance) young *Howard the Norfolk* & a Mr. Bellasyse his uncle or cousin are invited—& he is to take his choice of the family—so that *both* are in requisition for the present" (*LJ* 4:198).

134. Lady Charlotte Leveson-Gower was engaged to marry Howard, earl of Surrey, the only son of the duke of Norfolk (October 7, 1814; *LJ* 4:198, 4:214). Howard's father was apparently a strict Roman Catholic and would have objected to the match.

135. Ironically, this is precisely how Lady Melbourne's father-in-law, Matthew Lamb, made his fortune. He "did the Salisburys out of some land," according to the second Lord Melbourne. The widow of the first marquess of Salisbury used to declare that the rise of the Lamb family was from the plunder of the earls of Salisbury (Sedgwick 2:196).

136. During the month of October 1814, Hanson was dilatory in preparing Byron's marriage license. Byron's "share of the blame" was that he did not visit Lady Melbourne until October 30, more than a month after his proposal was accepted on September 18. Lady Melbourne may have been responding to the *Morning Chronicle,* which had already taken note of his delay: "Lord B—, it seems, though so great a traveller, cannot get to *Milbanke*" (October 15, 1814).

137. Byron defended his conduct in letters of October 4 and 17. "Surely you cannot wonder that I should wish to arrange my property first—& not proceed hurriedly in a business which is to decide her fate & mine forever.—" (October 4, 1814; *LJ* 4:192). "I shall not set off till a day or two after Hanson—and then I must take Newstead in my way but shall not remain there above 48 hours.—there have been several intimations to me from all quarters to proceed—which I am very willing to do—but as Lawyers are as essential in this buisness as clergymen & post-horses—I must wait for the former before I harness either of the latter" (October 17, 1814; *LJ* 4:212).

138. Lady Melbourne's letter to Mrs. Huskisson confirms that she pretended the "greatest ignorance except as to the fact," for she fails to mention the important role she played in arranging Byron's marriage.

139. It is more than likely that the remainder of this letter was removed because it contained disparaging remarks about Annabella.

140. Guy Fawkes (1570-1606), a convert to Roman Catholicism, was a participant in the Gunpowder Plot, for which he was arrested on November 4, 1605. Recruited by Robert Catesby and others, he planned to blow up the Parliament building while James I and his ministers were inside. The plot was conceived as a reprisal for England's oppressive laws against Roman Catholics.

141. Emily Cowper.

142. Minnie, Emily Cowper's daughter, was born in 1808.

143. Annabella had pretended to be engaged to George Eden and used Miss Mary Milicent Montgomery, an invalid, to corroborate the information (Mayne, *Life* 14).

144. This could possibly be Lady Montgomery, who was Annabella's close friend. I have indicated Milbanke because I have no evidence that Lady Melbourne corresponded or was friendly with Lady Montgomery.

145. William Bankes and Lord Byron had both proposed to Annabella without each other's knowledge. A Cambridge friend of Byron's who later traveled in the Near East (*LJ* 3:15n), Bankes surprised Byron by confessing that he too had proposed and been rejected (August 31, 1813; 3:103). In June 1833 Bankes was almost prosecuted for sodomy (Crompton 358).

146. Byron's letter arrived too late: "Your letter was delivered just as I was leaving town—or I do believe a day sooner would have stopped me—since I had much rather not have set out on my present expedition at this moment" (October 31, 1814; *LJ* 4:227).

147. The doors are open for a nephew at all hours.

148. Lady Melbourne worried that Byron's visit to Annabella's had not been a success. According to Byron, Annabella was "overrun with fine feelings—scruples about herself and *her* disposition (I suppose in fact she means mine)" (November 13, 1814; *LJ* 4:23). Byron first referred to Lady Melbourne as "Aunt" on September 26, 1814: "Excuse this scrawl—it is the 100th of today—& believe me ever my dear *Zia*" (*LJ* 4:180).

149. Sir Anthony Absolute, in Sheridan's *The Rivals* 5.3: "All the faults I have ever seen in my friend Faulkland, seemed to proceed from what he calls the *delicacy* and *warmth* of his affection for you—there; marry him directly, Julia, you'll find he'll mend surprisingly!" In Sheridan's play, Absolute playfully considers marrying the aunt rather than the niece, a topic alluded to by Byron on several occasions.

150. Byron had written to Lady Melbourne on November 13, 1814: "A few days ago she [Annabella] made one *scene*—not altogether out of C[aroline]'s style" (*LJ* 4:231).

151. Lady Melbourne's shrewd flattery of Byron's "forte" is a response to Byron's letter of November 13, 1814: "I have lately had recourse to the eloquence of *action* (which Demosthenes calls the first part of oratory) & find it succeeds very well & makes her very quiet which gives me some hopes of the efficacy of the 'calming process' so renowned in '*our* philosophy'" (*LJ* 4:231). Lady Melbourne's letter also indicates her emotional investment in Byron's marriage.

152. Byron had written that Annabella "is taken ill once every 3 days with I know not what . . . I can only interpret these things one way—" (November 13, 1814; *LJ* 4:231).

153. As late as November 7, 1814, Eliza O'Neill was still playing Juliet at Covent Garden Theatre, "to an overflowing house" (*Morning Herald,* November 8, 1814).

154. Lady Melbourne defended the officers who testified against Colonel Quentin and whom the Prince Regent seemed disposed to punish for giving testimony.

155. The Prince Regent's "partiality & resentment" were shown by his decision to disperse into various regiments the officers who had complained about the conduct of Quentin.

156. The date of this letter is based on its placement in the Lamb collection by the curator in the British Library.

157. Lady Melbourne advised Byron to be married upon Articles in order to circumvent lawyers' delays. This letter also shows the active role she played in encouraging, rather than merely permitting, the marriage.

158. "I am asked to dine at Whitehall today," Byron wrote on "Novr.-Decr. 1st, 1814" (*LJ* 4:238).

159. Hanson's country house in Hampshire (November 6, 1814; *LJ* 4:230).

160. This letter shows that Byron often visited Lady Melbourne when William and Caroline were away. "I am cut off from Melbourne House for the present—because that family firebrand—Ly. C[aroline]—has this day returned to Whitehall—and now I shan't see Ly. M[elbourne] again for some time which I regret," Byron wrote to Annabella on December 3, 1814 (*LJ* 4:239).

161.   By Miss M—LB—K.

—"Pray! let a jealous rivalle strive in vaine
"To drawe him, sated, back to lawlesse joyes,
"For firmlie are our youthful heartes betrothed,
"And our congenial soules fast bound in one!
"Now since a sparke of his poetic fire
"Hath caught my glowing soule, I will become
"Love's proxie for his Ninth prolifick Muse,
"And yield him ever ninth revolvinge Moone
"A sweete *Childe Harold* to delight his Sire!"
        (To be continued) (*Morning Herald,* December 3, 1814)

162. Byron's letter to Lady Melbourne on this subject appears to be missing. On December 5, 1814, he wrote to Annabella to say, "I will write & fix the day of my arrival" (*LJ* 4:239).

163. Augusta.

164. Archibald John Primrose, fourth earl of Roseberry (1783-1868), was the plaintiff in an action against Sir Henry St. John Mildmay, who was accused of criminal conversation with the plaintiff's wife. Sir William Garrow was the prosecuting attorney and Henry Brougham was the attorney for the defense. The damages were laid at £30,000 and a verdict was returned for £15,000, "the highest given in any *crim. conv.* cause upon record" (*Morning Herald,* December 12, 1814). Mildmay's effort to elope with Roseberry's wife was soundly condemned by Garrow. Lady Melbourne may have hoped the court proceedings, which dominated the first two pages of the newspaper for that day (December 12, 1814), would serve as a cautionary tale for Byron to avoid the obloquy he would face if he eloped with Augusta.

165. Brougham's speech, as quoted in the *Morning Chronicle,* reads as follows: "Thus those two young persons in the height of blood, had by degrees their feelings so excited, their fancies, so exalted, that their judgment was laid asleep, and they knew not the awful precipice upon which they stood. He had a right to say their judgment was lulled asleep, for it was even so with Lord Roseberry himself, who was free from that greatest of all deluders, self-delusion, and confided in that relationship which had betrayed the Defendant, and the unhappy Lady his partner, in the offence. They awoke at last from their trance, and if he were permitted, he could produce numberless letters and numerous witnesses which would prove the agony, the sorrow, the wretchedness which the conviction of their transgression had excited in their minds. He should be asked, perhaps, why when they discovered their error, they didnt at once come to the resolution of abandoning it; but that very remedy pre-supposed the offence. Happy had it been for them if any strong necessity, any over-ruling power had stepped in to check their mad, their infatuated career" (December 12, 1814).

166. Lady Melbourne appears to be warning Byron about the danger of running away with Augusta, which he seems to have contemplated as late as December 15.

167. Brougham accused Garrow of exaggerating the enormity of the crime. "Such overcharged comments weakened more than they benefited a cause," he stated, "though nothing was more common than for an advocate to fall into the error of pourtraying a present case, merely because it was a present one, as the most atrocious, the most dreadful, the most horrible, the most abominable that he had ever before been known" (*Morning Chronicle,* December 12, 1814).

168. The damages against Roseberry were assessed at £15,000.

169. Augusta Leigh.

170. Augusta Leigh.

171. Lady Melbourne may refer to the first time Byron informed her of his affair with Augusta.

172. The trial of Queen Caroline.

173. Lady Melbourne places the blame on Sir Henry Mildmay for encouraging the earl of Roseberry's wife to elope with him and thus compromise her reputation.

174. "They say, best men are moulded out of faults: / And, for the most, become much more the better, / For being a little bad" (Mariana, *Measure for Measure* 5:1:444).

175. Emily Cowper.

176. Lady Caroline Lamb

ILLUSTRATIONS

The Milbanke and the Melbourne Families, by George Stubbs
(courtesy National Gallery)

Gates of Melbourne House, Piccadilly, designed by Sir William Chambers
(courtesy Victoria and Albert Museum)

Melbourne House, Piccadilly in 1960
(courtesy Athlone Press)

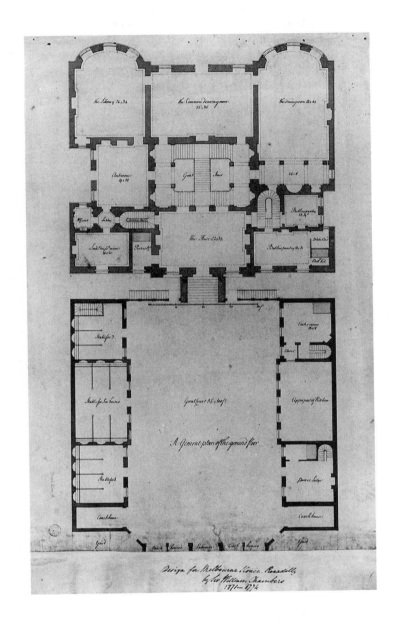

Plan for the Ground Floor of Melbourne House, Piccadilly
(courtesy John Soane Museum)

Statues in Staircase at Melbourne House, Piccadilly
(courtesy Athlone Press)

6

Ceiling of Melbourne House, Piccadilly
(courtesy Athlone Press)

Melbourne Hall, Derbyshire
(photo by Thomas Tivey)

Brocket Hall, Hertford
(photo by Claire Lunnes)

Brocket Hall *in Hertfordshire, the* Seat *of* Lord Melbourne.

Published as the Act directs, Feb 1, 1787, by W. Angus, N.4, Gwynne's Buildings, Islington.

9

Sketch of Brocket Hall in the Nineteenth Century
(courtesy Victoria and Albert Museum)

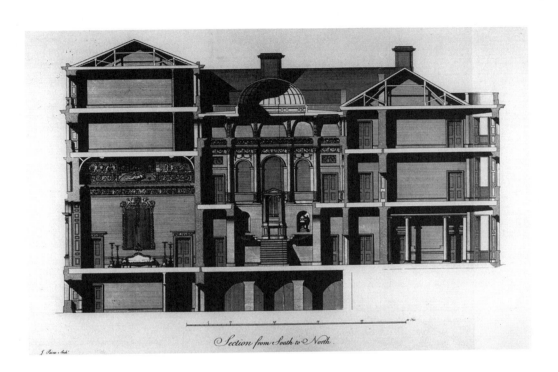

Section from South to North.

Brocket Hall Sectional, by James Paine
(courtesy Gregg Press)

11

Brocket Hall, Interior
(courtesy Melbourne Hall, Derbyshire)

Sir Joshua Reynolds pinxit.

E. Welsh fecit.

Mrs. BADDELY

Publish'd Aug.st 10th 1772 : as the Act directs.

12

Mrs. Sophia Baddeley, engraving after Sir Joshua Reynolds

(courtesy British Museum)

13

The Melbourne Service
(courtesy Mrs. Quentin Gage, Firle Place, Sussex)

J. Reynolds Eques pinx.ᵗ   THE RIGHT HON.ᴮᴸᴱ ELIZ.ᵀᴴ LADY MELBOURNE,   J. Finlayson sculp.ᵗ

Humbly inscribed to the Right Hon.ᵇˡᵉ Lord Melbourne.

Published Aug.ᵗ 16.ᵗʰ 1773 sold by J. Finlayson, Orange Street, Leicester Fields.

14

Elizabeth, Viscountess Melbourne, engraving by J. Finlayson after Sir Joshua Reynolds
(courtesy British Museum)

15

Maternal Affection, engraving after Sir Joshua Reynolds
(courtesy British Museum)

Georgiana, Duchess of Devonshire and Child, engraving by George Keating after
Sir Joshua Reynolds (courtesy British Museum)

Painted by Sir Joshua Reynolds.   Engraved by J. R. Smith.

The Honble. Mrs. Damer.

Publishd March 1st 1774, by J. R. Smith, No 4, Exeter Court, Strand.

Honble. Mrs. Damer, engraving by S.W. Reynolds after Sir Joshua Reynolds
(courtesy British Museum)

Witches 'Round the Cauldron (Lady Melbourne, the Duchess of Devonshire, and Anne
Damer [from left to right] as the three Witches from *Macbeth*) by Daniel Gardner
(courtesy Mr. and Mrs. Julian Salmond)

Witches 'Round the Cauldron (the Duchess of Devonshire, Lady Melbourne, and Mrs. Dawson Damer [from left to right] as the three witches from *Macbeth*) by Daniel Gardner (courtesy Christie's Images).

Tales of Old Witches are no longer heard,
    Fictitious legends once receiv'd for truth.
And wisely here the Artist has transferr'd
    the pow'rs of sorcery from age to youth.

Beware, ye Mortals, who those comforts prize,
    which flow from peace from liberty, and ease,
Th'Enchanter's wand, and magick spells despise,
    But shun the witchraft of such eyes as these.

                                    (Williamson 44)

Poem in Daniel Gardner's notebook written to accompany "Witches 'Round the Cauldron" (Williamson 44).

20

Georgiana, Duchess of Devonshire, by Sir Joshua Reynolds
(courtesy Huntington Library)

Scale of Bon Ton.

	Beauty	Figure	Elegance	Wit	Sense	Grace	Expression	Sensibility	Principles
Duchess of Devonshire	15	17	13	11	10	5	3	9	16
Duchess of Gordon	12	5	0	14	13	5	15	13	3
Countess of Derby	4	11	5	2	3	7	4	9	11
Countess of Jersey	11	6	1	2	0	11	12	5	0 .
Countess of Barrymore	19	18	18	19	18	19	17	19	18
Countess of Sefton	14	16	13	3	4	6	9	12	13
Lady Harriot Foley	9	17	14	13	7	12	11	13	16
Lady Anna Mar. Stanhope	7	17	13	15	12	11	2	18	17
Lady Melbourne	9	0	11	3	5	14	6	8	15
Mrs. Damer	7	16	15	13	14	12	14	5	2
Mrs. Crewe	15	7	4	6	8	0	15	14	12
Mrs. Bouverie	12	16	14	7	9	10	8	19	12

Scale of Bon Ton, in *Morning Post*

Sir George O'Brien Wyndham, Third Earl of Egremont, engraving by T. Lupton after G. Clint
(courtesy British Museum)

A Perspective View of Tunbridge Wells Walks.

T. Roberts del.   Walker f.

Tunbridge Wells
(courtesy Tunbridge Wells Museum and Art Gallery)

24

The Ladies Waldegrave, by Sir Joshua Reynolds
(courtesy National Portrait Gallery, Scotland)

25

Monuments Lately Discover'd on Salisbury Plain
(courtesy British Museum)

26

The Political Churchyard
(courtesy British Museum)

The Ladies Church Yard
(courtesy British Museum)

28

Lady Melbourne, by Richard Cosway
(courtesy The Royal Collection, Her Majesty Queen Elizabeth II)

Lot 275.

George IV, when Prince of Wales, Standing by His Charger, by Sir Joshua Reynolds
(courtesy Hertford County Record Office)

Sr Joshua Reynolds Pinxᵗ   Peniston Wᵐ & Fraˢ Lambe   S W Reynolds Sculpᵗ

THE AFFECTIONATE BROTHERS.

The Affectionate Brothers, engraving by F. Bartolozzi after Sir Joshua Reynolds
(courtesy British Museum)

PROCESSION TO THE HUSTINGS AFTER A SUCCESSFUL CANVASS.

31

Campaigning on the Hustings, by Thomas Rowlandson
(courtesy British Museum)

Georgiana Duchess of Devonshire and Elizabeth Foster
(courtesy Wallace Museum)

Lady Betty Foster, Later Duchess of Devonshire, by Sir Joshua Reynolds
(courtesy Chatsworth Estate)

34

William, Fifth Duke of Devonshire, by Pompeo Batoni
(courtesy Chatsworth Estate)

35

Charles Grey, Later Second Earl Grey, by John Hoppner
(courtesy National Portrait Gallery)

36

Henrietta Frances, Viscountess Duncannon, Later Countess Bessborough, engraving by J. Grozer, after Sir Joshua Reynolds (courtesy Courtauld Institute)

Duke of York's House, Whitehall, in 1789

(courtesy Athlone Press)

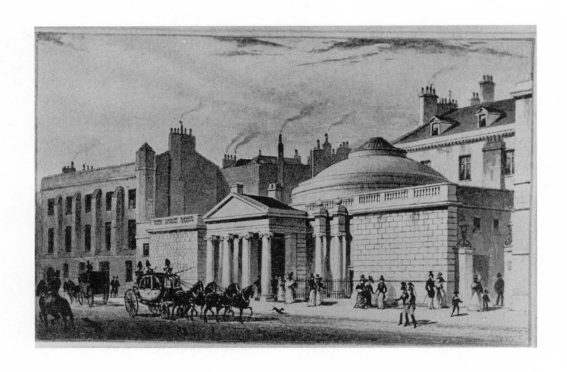

Melbourne House, Whitehall and Part of the Old Treasury

(courtesy Athlone Press)

Melbourne House, Whitehall
(photo by David Lloyd Roberts, courtesy Arcaid)

40

Francis, Fifth Duke of Bedford, engraving by P. W. Tomkins after J. Hoppner
(courtesy British Museum)

41

Lady Melbourne, by Sir Thomas Lawrence
(courtesy British Museum)

Emily and Harriet Lamb, by Sir Thomas Lawrence
(courtesy Royal Pavilion Gallery and Museums, Brighton)

43

Peniston Lamb with his horse, Assassin, and his dog, Tanner, by Ben Marshall
(courtesy Courtauld Institute)

44

William Lamb, by Sir Thomas Lawrence
(courtesy National Portrait Gallery)

Caroline Lamb, engraving by F. Bartolozzi after J. Hoppner
(courtesy British Museum)

46

Emily Cowper, by Sir Thomas Lawrence
(courtesy *Country Life Publications*)

47

Peter Leopold, Fifth Earl of Cowper, by Sir Thomas Lawrence
(courtesy Courtauld Institute)

48

Lord Palmerston, by J. Partridge
(courtesy National Portrait Gallery)

49

Lord Granville Leveson-Gower, by Sir Thomas Lawrence
(courtesy Yale Center for British Art)

The HON^{BLE} GEO^{GE} LAMB.

George Lamb, engraving by R. Dighton after painting by R. Dighton
(courtesy British Museum)

51

Caroline St. Jules, later Mrs. George Lamb
(courtesy Tresham Lever, *The Letters of Lady Palmerston*)

Augusta Leigh (from a miniature, courtesy Ethel Mayne, *The Life of Lady Byron*)

53

Lord Byron, by R. Westall
(courtesy National Portrait Gallery)

54

Anne Isabella Milbanke
(courtesy Newstead Abbey)

55

Ralph Milbanke, by John Downman
(courtesy Lord Lytton)

56

Judith Milbanke, by John Downman
(courtesy Lord Lytton)

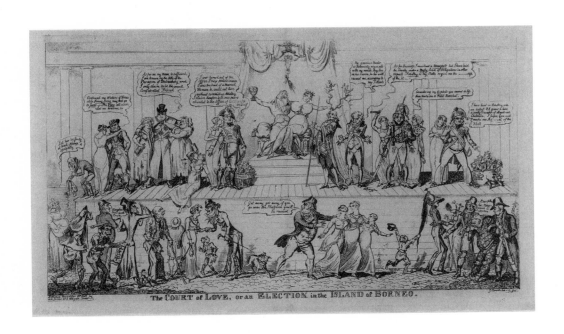

The Court of Love, or an Election in the Island of Borneo
(courtesy British Museum)

58

Lord Henry Brougham, by James Lonsdale
(courtesy National Portrait Gallery)

Frederick Lamb, by J. Partridge
(courtesy National Portrait Gallery)

Princess Charlotte and Prince Leopold at the Opera, by G. Dawe
(courtesy National Portrait Gallery)

61

Viscountess Melbourne, by unknown artist
(courtesy Earl of Arran)

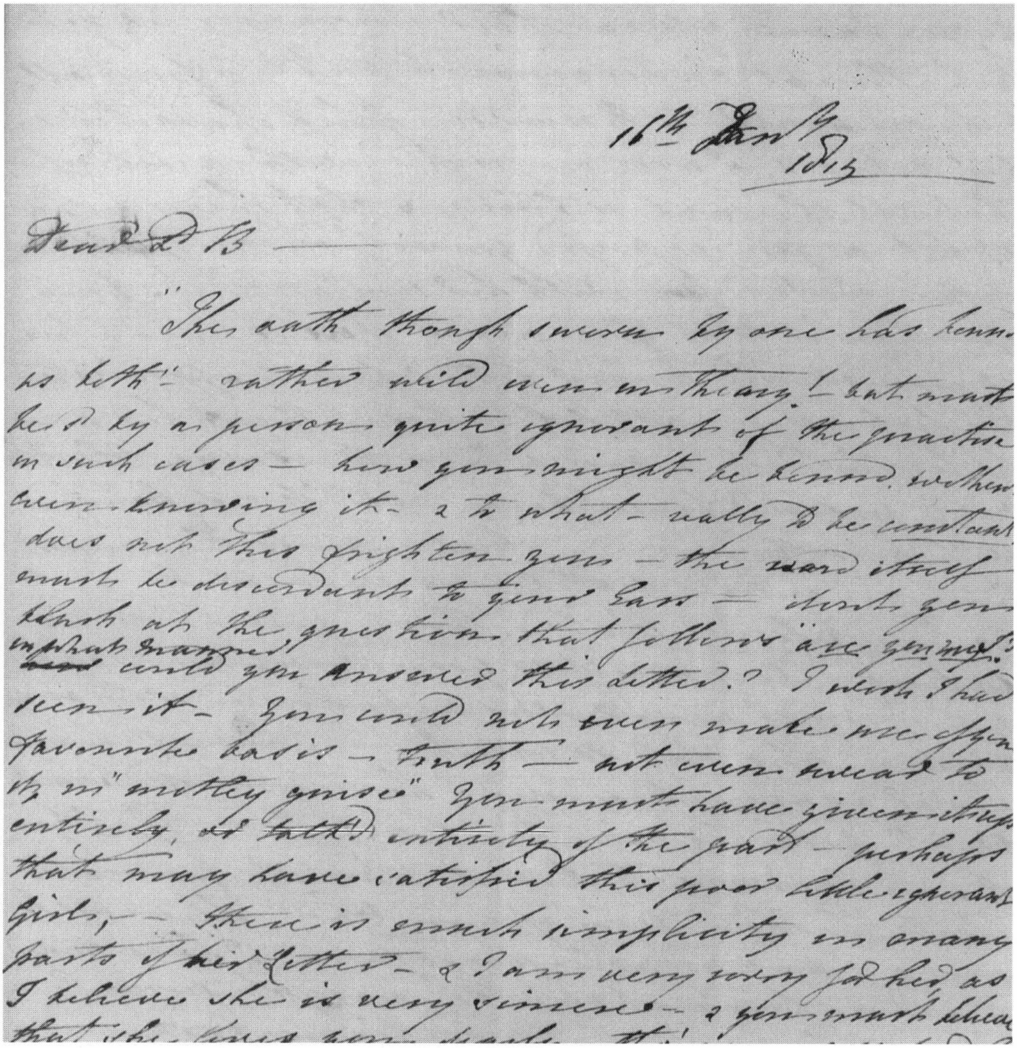

16th Jany
1814

Dear Ld B —

"This oath though sworn by one has bound us both"— rather wild even in theory!— but must be s.d by a person quite ignorant of the practise in such cases — how you might be bound without ever knowing it — & to what — really to be constant! does not this frighten you — the word itself must be discordant to your Ears — don't you shrink at the question that follows "are you not?" in what manner could you answer this letter? I wish I had seen it — You could not even make use of your favourite basis — truth — not even dressed up in "motley guise" You must have given it up entirely, or ~~told~~ entirety of the part — perhaps that may have satisfied this poor little ignorant Girl, — there is much simplicity in many parts of her Letter — & I am very sorry for her as I believe she is very sincere — & you must believe that she loves you dearly —

Handwriting of Lady Melbourne

(courtesy John Murray, Ltd.)

Envelope to Lord Byron
(courtesy John Murray, Ltd.)

64

Lady Melbourne, miniature by Richard Cosway
(courtesy Newberry Library)

65

Lady Melbourne, by George Romney
(courtesy H. Belsey)

A "New Code of Confidence," 1815

*R*efusing a large ceremony and any reception at all, Byron finally married Annabella in the drawing room of her home in Seaham on January 2, 1816. John Cam Hobhouse, the best man, was present, along with Annabella's former governess, Mrs. Clermont, and Annabella's immediate family. With a constantly fluctuating date and a sister-in-law who was hostile to her, Lady Melbourne knew her attendance would be more of a disturbance than a blessing. Nevertheless, Byron assured Lady Melbourne that her "benediction" was "very essential to all our undertakings" (January 3, 1815; *LJ* 4:249).

Lady Melbourne knew that she could not maintain the same intimacy with the poet as she had before. She wrote to Annabella first, declaring her intention to be on "ye most cordial & affectionate terms with you & your caro Sposo." This letter disturbed Byron who could not help but note the "new code of confidence" his aunt seemed determined to maintain. When he complained she reminded him that only three weeks had passed since his marriage, and if "that is not the time to be cautious I don't know what is" (January 31,1815). She closed by faulting him for his lack of discretion in sharing a letter about Lady Bessborough with others.

After only a month, Annabella was unhappy enough in her own marriage to be impatient with Harriet Pearce's boasts of marital bliss.[1] Byron must have had some second thoughts of his own, for he was unusually curious about a rumor that William and Caroline Lamb were about to separate (February 5, 1815; *LJ* 4:266). Lady Melbourne assured him that the "wicked scandal" was untrue (February 8, 1815). The following day he almost succumbed to suffocation because of a badly ventilated fire. He would have died without his wife's assistance (February 6, 1815;

LJ 4:267-68), as he later wrote of the incident, but the marriage proved more suffocating than asphyxiation. Desperate to renew their confidential correspondence, Byron wrote three letters to Lady Melbourne's one during this period (February 6, 1815; *LJ* 4:268). She denied that she was a negligent correspondent and she did what she could for the young couple, renting the duchess of Devonshire's house for one year amidst riots. Annabella was pregnant by mid-April, and Byron hoped the spacious house would render her more comfortable in her precarious condition (April 22, 1815; *LJ* 4:289).[2]

A gap of seven months exists in the correspondence between the Byrons and Lady Melbourne (June-December 1815). These were the crucial months of the marriage, when the couple was harassed by debt.[3] During this period, Annabella confided in Augusta Leigh, and even the indiscreet Byron would not confess his marital infidelities to his *aunt*. A daughter, Ada, was born on December 10, and Lady Melbourne sent a stream of advice to 13 Piccadilly Terrace. "You will allow me the use of my eyes by this time without a lecture, to tell you that I and the child are perfectly well," an exasperated Annabella finally wrote on January 4, 1816. Less than two weeks later, she left her husband for good. Byron received a letter from Annabella's father on February 2, requesting an amicable separation.

The events leading to this separation remain shrouded in mystery. Despite her increasing friendship with Augusta Leigh, Lady Byron was as ignorant of her husband's sexual imagination as ever. She even copied out "The Siege of Corinth" and "Parasina" that winter, without perceiving (or at least acknowledging) the latter's autobiographical references to incest. Clearly, Lady Melbourne was uninformed about the deteriorating marriage, for a letter describing how well Lady Byron was looking was written on January 19, 1816, four days after Annabella had left her husband. The appearance of domestic felicity continued until February 1816, when "at length the smothered fire broke out / And put the business past all kind of doubt," as Byron later put it in *Don Juan* (1:26).

Lady Melbourne to Lady Byron (Lovelace 92, f.61; Elwin, Wife 259)

Panshanger—

8th Jany.

1815[4]

My dear L^y. Byron—

I was very much delighted on receiving L^d. B[yron]'s Letter Yesterday & felt much annoy'd, at being obliged to defer my congratulations till this day on Acc'^t of the post not going from hence sooner.

I hope you will accept them now, & believe y^t. no one can be more truly interested in what ever promotes your happiness than I am; & that you may long enjoy it is my most sincere wish.

I know y^t. in proper form I ought to answer L^d. B[yron]'s Letter, but he must expect to see you have the preference on most occasions—& therefore it is best to accustom him early, to what he must learn to bear patiently in future, so pray tell him I will write soon & in the mean time, that I wish him joy with all my heart & soul—& if you are not too modest, or too Shy you may add, that he has drawn a prize—& that I believe you have too, only I make that reservation, as I never speak so confidently of a Man as I do of a Woman—but even as it is, I feel the greatest obligation to you for having given me a Nephew whom I like so much—Emily desires me to say every thing most kind to you both—& says she should have written to you, but has a scruple about giving you the trouble of answering her Letter; therefore begs me to assure you that she participates most truly in y^r happiness on this joyfull event—I have received a Letter from my Brother, who says L^y. Milbanke was much recovered from the agitation she suffered in parting with you—he says you are to return there soon—& conclude after that you will come Southward where we shall be most happy to see you, Ld Melbourne desires to offer his congratulations & best wishes to you & L^d. B[yron]. & believe me

Y^rs. most truly & affec^ly.

EMelbourne.

None of y^e. other parts of ye Family are with us[.] George is at Kendal & M^rs. L[amb] in town—Caroline & W^m at Brocket.

[The/Lady Byron]

Lady Melbourne to Lord Byron (45547, f.78-80; Airlie, Whig 169[5])

B[rocket].H[all]. 11th Jan^y, 1815[6]

My D^r L^d B.

    I forgot Yesterday to thank you for the order you sent me for y^r Box & to ask you whether you or L^y B[yron], would wish me to send it to any of your Friends for the next week, if I should not be in Town, which I think it most proba-ble I shall not,—your next tuesday I shall be there, and very glad to have it.—

    I have a Letter to day from L^y Bl[arney][7]—they are at Marseilles & living with Massena[8]—who when he saw ye the D of Wellin^n. at Paris s^d to him, vous m'avez tant fait jeuner Milord que vous voudrez bien me donner un bon diner—D^e Wellington answered—si je vous ai fait Milord que vous voudrez bien rendu, en m'empêchant de dormir—et je crois que pour avoir le droit de nous dire ces bons Mots nous nous sommes assez tormentès.[9]——

    Massena expresses great admiration of him & when he is mentioned always says—c'est un grand capitaine——L^y Bl[arney]- says if it were possible to forgive his rapacity—he might be thought very agreable—Your Friend & L^y By[ron's]-friend Mr. Douglas[10] has been to Visit Buonaparte at Elba—who told him he was afraid he had not had Wine enough at Paris,—but he would find plenty at Elba—it is Supposed he judged from ye appearance of his Face——M^r. Vernon[11] has also been to see him, & was much question'd by him about English Politicks, & on find-ing y^t he belonged to ye Oppo^n he said that is a party that is now very low. Yes s^d. M^r. Vernon, & that is because we maintained y^t you would conquer Spain; & you were right, he answered for I ought to have done so, & it is ye fault of my Generals that I did not—I believe by this time you wish my long Stories at an end—but dont be angry you have ye power of burning them—if they do not entertain you in a long Evening—which will be strange—& upon that reflexion I must tell you another. The P^ss of Wales is playing all sorts of tricks all over Italy & they say of her Mon dieu est ce là la Vertu opprimée dont nous avons tant entendu parler?[12] Now I shall wish you good Night. When I began I only intended to write three lines about the Box, but if one settled beforehand every thing one would do—as well might one be clock work always wound up for a particular purpose only—& would entirely destroy ye pleasure of intending one thing and doing another— don't you think so?

Ever y^rs most affectionate Aunt

EM

Em[ily Cowper]- has had a Letter f^m L^y Holland from Rome, she complains of her Health & says that she has had a Bilious attack which has reduced her to *a Skeleton* & that she is as much annoy'd now at being too thin, as she was before at being too fat—she says the roads between Rome & Naples are so much infested by Bandits y^t all people not extremely adventurous are detain'd in ye Papal territories—This reminds me of L^y H Stanhope[13] who they say[14] is travelling with a Horde of Arabs as their Queen & M^r. Bruce[15] dismiss'd 2 at Paris with a petite Sortè[16] & very affect- ed—the D^ss of Devonshire inquired of him where L^y Hester was he s^d he believed at ye foot of Mount Caucasus—

I was determin'd not to begin upon a fresh Sheet of paper for fear of conse- quences—as I am in such a humour for writing

[The/Lord Byron/Halnaby/Darlington]

Lady Melbourne to Lady Byron (Lovelace 92, f.59; Elwin, Wife 259-60)

11th Jan^y

1815

Dear Annabella—

You see how soon I profit by y^r permission & pray believe y^t my addressing you by y^r present name was no proof of want of affection as I have it much at heart to be on ye most cordial & affectionate terms with you and your caro Sposo & I hope to see you as much as possible—& far from being plagued by y^r Letters I shall be happy to receive them as often as you can possibly write—we have left Panshanger & are now at Brocket for a Week, before we go to London—I am Sorry I have not a chance of seeing you there as soon as I had hoped, but your reasons are very good,[17] & I hope a little patience will conquer all difficulties. I am more & more convinced every day, of ye efficacy of that receipt, & at Home I have so much occasion for it myself & so many occasions for preaching it that I go about repeating it habitually.

Mrs Lamb is just arrived, which puts me in mind of Harriet Pearce & her Marriage,[18] have you heard from her? to M^rs L[amb] she writes much of her happiness, & says Mr Germaine is the most indulgent of Husbands,—I hope it is so, but it is not his general Character, a Gentleman who knows him well, wrote to George just after the Marriage, desiring him to make M^rs L[amb] write & advise her, to subdue him at first for if she gave way to him she would find it impossible to live with him—he was of such a Sulky bad Temper—I hope this is not true for her Sake tho' I think she will make ye best of it she gives me the idea of a person who altho' very amiable, is not so very tame—& her Spirits seem likely to carry her thro' what L^y Asgill[19] says is ye real test of a Womans cleverness—that is managing her Husband—she says it is what every Woman ought to Study for her own happiness & her Husbands too—& she never can think any one can have any pretensions to cleverness who does not do so, by some means or other—dont let Ld Byron see this, for he'll abuse L^y Asgill who has always had ye greatest wish to know him— & he'll say I am preaching up rebellion—which by ye bye I'm always accused of in every sense of ye word—

but really & truly that would be a very unjust construction to put upon what I have said for I do not believe there will be any necessity for such advice, I have a totally different opinion of him & am convinced y^t I shall have an opportunity of retorting an expression of his, upon himself, & shall call him the Conjugal Baron—as he used to call Emily the Conjugal Countess

of one thing I am persuaded y^t nothing ever will have any effect upon him but ye greatest kindness & affection & that in no one thing does he resemble Mr Germaine, or indeed any other Man— —this is what you call a Galloping Letter. I have staid out very late & am in a hurry to dress—perhaps you have not found out how much longer the Days are become already & I hardly ever come in till it is quite dark—I hate short days so much y^t I watch for ye increase of day light when I am in ye Country

believe me Y^rs most aff^ly

EMelbourne

Lady Melbourne to Lord Byron (Lovelace 377; copy in Murray 1:296)

Whitehall

[Tuesday] 31st Jany. 1815

My dear L^d B

I have been longing to write to you these 3 or 4 days but have been incapable—a complaint which I used to be subject to, laid me upon my Couch in a state of stupefaction. I have not had it, for these last Eight Years & had hoped it was one of ye advantages of age, to be free from irritation of Nerves—you are all this time saying what is this? patience, & I'll tell as shortly as I can,—it is a sort of Nervous Head ache which affects y^r. sight & sometimes you see half a Face, & sometimes two Faces—I see you laugh!—& I know it is both laughable & lamentable! The first to whoever hears the description, the last, to those who feel it—for when it goes off it terminates in a Violent Head ache, & leaves you quite unhinged, & unfit for y^e. Slightest exertion but its gone now—& I have s^d. enough about it, in all conscience

what a suspicious person you are, on some points you guess right, on others wrong. You say I write cautiously, & you mention having been married 3 Weeks—if that is not ye time to be cautious, I don't know what is. You were wrong about y^e. Letter in which I mention'd L^y Blar[ney]—I had nothing particular to say & wrote about her, as the News of ye day, but I certainly did not write it to be seen, I never wish people to get into bad habits, I know once begun, they are not easily broken.

I must thank you for saying you forgive (what you are pleased to call) my doubts, & for not allowing my sincerity to prevent yr. still having confidence ^in^ me; I willingly accept the office, in which you have install'd me & hope always to be your Corbeau blanc.[20] (You remember Voltaire's tale)[21] I wish you may hit as justly upon the Corbeau Noir[22] & avoid her———So Ld Stafford[23] is gone over to Ministers for a Dukedom, & Erskine[24] for a Green Ribbon,[25] when a fool shews such a want of Steadiness & principle I only laugh at ~~them~~ him, but when a Clever Man like Erskine contradicts all his professions of so many Yrs standing for the sake of a few dinners, & a "painted String" I own yt it puts me out of Temper & out of patience & inclines me to indulge a bad opinion of all Men———he is named the Green Man which was told Sr S Romilly,[26] who said; and now in the House of Lords he'll be ye Green Man & still.[27] I hope you have not heard this before. I have had a copy of Moore's[28] lines sent me today, with which I am delighted (Complaint of a Mistress to her Lover) They have acquired great celebrity, by its being known, that You Wept when they were Sung to you[.] do you acknowledge the truth of this?——

Moore has had the greatest success at Chatsworth—all the Ladies quite enthusiastic about his agreableness. Emily writes me word, we have lost some of our company—but still are gay. Alas! Moore left us Yesterday,—Your former favourite Ly. Susan Ryder[29] has been there displaying all her Graces to the Master of the Mansion[30] who does not seem inclined to Grace her in return— —seriously they say the attack is quite a la Worcester[31] but will not succeed———a few days past I received a Letter ~~I received a letter~~ from a Lady with the following, "wish me joy of Ld B[yron']s being really married as I am saved a wonderful number of questions, seriously I am very glad of it for his sake as Matrimony appears to me ye. best chance of Steadying his Mind without weakening his Genius," I thought this opinion singular enough to be worth copying—I can only say Amen—ainsi soit il—& it seems to be going on prosperously & wisely whilst you proceed on ye. plan of allowing yourself to be directed by yr. Wife—that is the way to be a good & a contented Husband.—You know I agree with you when you say you are a very good natur'd person——every body will find you so if they abstain from plaguing you when you are not in *good Spirits,* (we'll *give it that name*) & if they do they deserve to meet with rebuffs—write to me Mon cher Neveu et Choisisez mieux votre temps—I am inclined to think that gave some *Ombrage* but keep faith with me, & say nothing, remember that altho' you have no Corbeau Noir, actually *Noir*— You may have one flying about, with *many* black Feathers in her plumage— —[32]

I am sorry to find people have a bad opinion of Ld Port^{th's}[33] case, Leach told George [Lamb] y^e. other day y^t. he thought the Chancellor[34] must grant an injunction—& S^r S Romilly soon after s^d. he could see no reason why he should—I certainly had rather depend upon the latter than upon y^e. former—but there is an idea that y^e. case is a very strong one ag^{st} him—

they tell me there is a very amusing Book just publish'd—memoires sur la Guerre des Francais en Espagne par M Roccard,[35] I am going to buy it shall I send it you? I believe it is the Man who was *le bien Aimè* de Mad^e de Stael (poor Man) & to whom it was reported she was married—but I do not believe that was true[36]—L^y Ossulston writes word ^from Paris^, "it is quite over with Mad^e. de Stael, since her Letter to Murat,[37] nobody can bear her. She thinks only of courting Ministers, but they will have nothing to say to her"

They are wiser than ours, did I ever tell you that most of them went to ye Regent to desire him to go & pay her a Visit, & gave for a reason, that she had such a *powerful Pen*—that it was of great consequence to make her speak well of this Country—what a mean Set they are—You will think there is no end to my Pen God bless you

Most aff^y. yr^s.

EM

Whitehall

8th Feb[ry] 1815

My dear Annabella—

by your little note, it seems that you are comfortably settled en famille at
Seaham, & altho' I am sorry that we are not likely to meet soon—yet I can not
regret your passing your time so much to Your own & L[d] Byrons Satisfaction, by
the way you are wrong when You Suppose that he has given me any information
respecting y[r] future intentions, or about Newstead—I am in a total state of ignorance, & dont guess who you are in treaty with, or with whom the contract is to be
signed of which you talk—I hope it is such, however, as to give you all
Satisfaction—

his Letters to me are extremely merry & gay, but as to business, I dont
think it is a Subject he is ever inclined to enter Upon—I think you are a little hard
upon M[rs] Germaine, if she feels happy why should she not say so[39]—because it may
not last in its full brightness—I think that, "sufficient for y[e] day is the evil there-
of" & it is quite time enough to think of any calamity when it happens instead of
foreseeing it—besides you are more interested than you are aware of, in this discussion—for I presume you will not condemn L[d] B[yron]—when he expresses his happiness in his Letters to his Friends, which I have heard from Chatsworth,[40] where
M[r] Moore was who had received them[41]—therefore do have more toleration for M[rs]
Germaine, she certainly must feel great contentment at not being tormented by her
Mother who used her very ill—I have just been interrupted by a Bride who is
something in y[e] same Situation as M[rs] Germaine, & shews it in her Looks & appearance—This is L[y] Charlotte Howard[42]—it is y[e] common opinon that her Mother was
severe & unkind to her—& certainly does not appear Shy & alarm'd ^as she did^
when following her into an Assembly but seems very pleasant & conversible—

I see my Brother has been making *un discours* at Durham—Ag[st] y[e] renewal
of the property Tax,[43] that comes so home to every ones feelings that I have no idea
of Ministers carrying it, which it is said they intend to try, & if they can not
Succeed, to Treble the assessed Taxes[.] You must now begin to think of these

things—no Young Lady before marriage knows what a World of trouble she entails upon herself by accepting a Husband—& y^r determination to be the best of Wives will make you feel it in all its force.

I am now in ye agony of chusing a new Cook which makes me talk of it very feelingly at this time—our present Cook chose to quarrel with a *Carter* two people whom one should ^think^ could not have much to do with one Another,—but so it was, & the Man threaten'd to *double him* & tho he does not to this moment know exactly the meaning of the phrase he has so horrid an idea of what may happen to him y^t he will no longer live in the Same County———London has been uncommonly dull hitherto, but it seems to be filling—& many people come to Town every day—I like it best when it is more quiet, if there happens to be some Society that is agreable—You probably expect to hear a little Gossip—& you shall be Satisfied—they say Sr Watkin Williams is to marry a Miss Crosby—15 & very pretty whom he has met at Paris, where she was with her Mother—on the other hand—Sr Wm Stewart^{44} & his Wife (Mr Douglas's^{45} Daughter) are parted from incompatability of temper—& Sr Gilbert & L^y Heathcote ^also^ from what cause I dont know—but he allows her 4000 a y^r & gives her the House & furniture in Grosvenor Square———there is I dare say a great deal more, but it has not come to my Ears———

God bless you Dear Annabella[.] give my love to my B^r & L^y M[ilbanke] & my Nephew—& believe me

Most affec^{ly} & truly y^{rs}

EMelbourne

pray write me word if you remain any time at Seaham—excuse all the blots, for I have been so often interrupted that I hardly know what I have written———

[The Lady Byron]

Lady Melbourne to Lord Byron (Lovelace 377; Murray 1:302-4)

[Ash Wednesday, February 8, 1815]

Dᵣ. Lᵈ B.

it may or it may not be "wicked scandal," but as far as I am inform'd, it is not true.[46] They are in yᵉ Country to all appearance like two turtle Doves—there may now & then be a little sharpness introduced but who knows that some part of yᵉ cooing of these same Birds may not be scolding[47]—really she seems inclined to behave better than she has done—& is now only troublesome, in private & a great bore in Society—this I know you never would believe—but I hope some day to see you undergo a Dinner, when she wishes to shew off is this confiding enough—You have no reason to complain of me either for yᵉ past or present—the future depends upon Yourself.[48]

I Yesterday enclosed you a Letter to Lʸ B[yron]. I could not answer yʳˢ while I was in her debt—but I really do not reckon how many I write to yᵉ one or to yᵉ other, of which you accused me—when I write to you it is as I talk to you *a Coeur ouvert* when you are sitting on yᵉ Couch opposite to me—& we soon laugh away an Hour. I am laughing now at your "Essentially"[49]—was that word ever made use of before in such a Sense? I was so much amused at it that I look'd for it in a little odd dictionary that was lying on the Table, & I found to my great astonishment & yʳˢ too I believe—the following—Essentially—Essentiellement—par nature—par Essence. I had never heard of it before, but as essentially worse or better—or serving any one Essentially, &c., &c. to me it was quite a new reading. I am going on changing Pens & each of them worse than the last——never mind, you must have time enough upon yʳ hands to Decypher what ever is written to you——

I did not mean yᵗ any favourite[50] of yours, was Synonymous to yᵗ term when you talk of the Grand Signiors, but I have heard you say she was agreable, & you thought her a Nice Girl—I have no objection to her or any other person entrapping his Grace, but like a good politician I had rather he would form an Alliance with some person hostile to yᵉ present System. You wrong me about X on one Subject. They are as black, & as hideous as any Phantasm of a distempered brain can imagine.—but, that ^Essential^[51] x out of the way, I dont know any one more fitted for y^r Corbeau blanc, from cleverness, Good-humour & a thousand agreeable qualitys—not forgetting the interest they take in You & the knowledge they have of You, which renders them more able to manage and advise——does this Satisfy you? does ye end make up for ye beginning? You know you gave me libertè entiere, & what is more I make full use of the permission.——I have written in a great hurry, & must finish. You will hear stories enough of all sorts—in Gossipping Letters from[52] Gossiping Correspondents—who are the Visitors?[53] how they must dislike You! don't start; that must follow of course, if you are not *prevenant*[54] for them—for you have ye power of being much otherwise when you please.—I may as well ask if this Letter pleases you better <than> my others[55]

Y^{rs} aff^{ly} E.M.

I am glad to hear so good an Acc^t of Anna—in short, you seem all together mighty comfortable which delights me.

do pray tell me if you stay on some time as I want to know not mere curiosity but I want to send her a Letter y^t will go direct to ye place where she is[56]——

[The/Lord Byron/Seaham Stockton/upon Tees; stamped "Free Feb. 1815"]

Lady Melbourne to Lord Byron (Murray; Murray 1:304-5)[57]

Whitehall

11th February

1815

Dear L^d B,

I hope you & Annabella soon recover'd from ye affects of your Accident,[58] it might have been very serious, & I was not surprised she was ill from the alarm she must have felt at ye Situation, & that in consequence of it you were not quite recover'd when you wrote; If the Coals have y^t Sulphurous tendency pray open y^r Window when you leave y^r dressing room to go to bed—there are many persons who are affected by it—Foreigners particularly who are acccustomed to Wood fires

& Sea coal is much more impregnated with that sort of Vapour than other coal.

   Therefore pray do not neglect to take measure by way of avoiding any recurrence, of so very unpleasant an event, & as much for yᵉ sake of yʳ friends as for yourself—& for my sake especially[.] I am heartily glad you were married & hope you find reasons to rejoice at it more & more every day. This has been a trial of *Bell's* presence of Mind, & adroitness which I am delighted to hear she possesses, as well as that the result was so favourable——You have no right to complain of me as a Correspondant. I always like writing to you, & often when I have not, it has been from the fear of yʳ thinking me a bore—that has not been yᵉ reason why you sometimes have been so long silent yourself—perhaps yᵉ following Character of you which is now given upon the continent may account for it better.

   in a Letter to me it is sᵈ "There is a Lady here, a great friend of yᵉ *Giaours* who says he is a mighty uncertain Gentleman in his Temper" who is this you'll say?⁵⁹—I guess—& I'll tell you, I think it is a Lady who might add "when people standing upon the Stairs shew a disposition to caress *people* standing by them, & that from decorum those people go away—but soon return (in the hopes probably of a *renouvellement*) but find the former disposition alter'd *essentially* in thought, not, & deed, have they not a right to say that Gentleman is uncertain—not to be depended upon &c &c &c.—Should you not recollect to what I allude, or shall yᵉ number of similar occurences puzzle you.—think of the Stair case at Mr. Pegou's— & I am very much mistaken if that ^is^ ~~was~~ not yᵉ Lady——I have a Letter from Mr. Hobhouse about yʳ Box—I have written to say he is welcome to yʳ Box at any time—if he will give me a day's notice, & added an invitation to him to come to it when ever I am there—I must now finish tho' it is a much Shorter Letter than I commonly write to you—but I have been pester'd with Lady Visitors all the Morᵍ who have prevented my writing—I think London so much pleasanter when it is not full—that every New face I see makes me cross—That is, those I do not love— & for that reason I shall rejoice very much when I see yours and Bell's—I hope you mean to try me Soon

         Ever affˡʸ yʳˢ,

         EM

Lady Melbourne to Frederick Lamb (45546, f.134; Airlie, Whig 173)
Whitehall
27th Febry
1815

Dearest Frederick,

I received y^r Letter f^m. Vienna of the 12th, & according to my calculation
you will probably be at Paris about the time this Letter reaches it,—I read with
pleasure y^r. favorable prognostics respecting finance, & I am sure if my easy sailing
could accomplish it, there would be no fear but where all the Crew are not agreed
& counteract one another, the Sails are often tightened even to breaking but we
will talk over these matters & it is a great comfort to have any one to whom one can
talk to without reserve—for tho' you are interested in the subject—you are not
selfish & that makes the great difference—but I won't bore about it now——

We are in the midst of violence & dissensions respecting this Corn Bill[60]
which to me, from the first, has appeared the simplest question that could be agitated—& all their reasons & calculations on both sides seem to puzzle the question.
I look upon experience as the surest guide on all such questions, where at the first
setting out much must depend on Theory——Now for a Number of ye most flourishing y^rs. we lived under the operation of a Corn Bill & everything respecting
importation & exportation went on to ye advantage of both growers & consumers—
two successive y^rs. of bad Harvests all over Europe raised the price to such a Sum,
y^t the Corn Bill remain'd on ye Shelf, & could nt be brought into action. The War &
depreciation of ye currency kept up the prices—when the first ceased, & there was
also a large produce the prices fell—does it not seem wise whilst the depreciation
of the currency continues to raise the price at which Corn may be imported—so as
to bring that trade again under the action of that same Corn Bill, which had succeeded so well—by raising the price according to ye circumstances of the times—
—I have gone more at length into this than I had any idea of doing & it may perhaps bore you but I must mention one circumstance more—the ports are now shut
from the average of the Corn having sunk below this original Corn Bill I mention—
which some of our great Political Economists asserted could never happen, but then

this is only for <those>[61] M^{ths}—& a very small rise, will, at the expiration of that time, open them again——The cry raised agst. high rents has very little to do with it, so you need not think that I am influenced.

[Tuesday] 7th March 1815

Dst Annabella

I have just taken the D^{ss} of Devonshire's House[63] from next Sunday the 12th for one Year at 700£[64]—as L^d B[yron] wants Space I hope it will suit him[65]—but after that, I am rather in a fright at what I have done—but all I can say, is, that I have not done it hastily—for at first I would not take it—& have this morning been with all ye great House brokers—& on seeing what they ask for very indifferent Houses & how few are to be let furnish'd I went back to this, & concluded the bargain—The great dispute between the Man who has the letting of it & myself was y^t he would only let it till Christmas & I would have the Year—

Now for an Acc^t of the House first perhaps you are not aware[66] that the entrance is down Some Steps, which makes what is commonly call'd the Ground floor, Up stairs, but the rooms are extremely pleasant, the D^{ss} lived entirely on this floor, she had a Dining room[,] Sitting room, & Bedchamber & a fourth room of a good Size but which she made her Maids Room—these are well furnish'd not Splendidly but comfortably with Good Couches & large Chairs & Drugget[67] over all the rooms in the House—Over these rooms there are the same Number but these are only furnish'd with common furniture, as Mr Foster lived in them,—if you should take these for Yourself you will be obliged to move the D^{ss's} furniture up Stairs—& I think you must have Some additions—which you may hire at some Upholsterers

The Atticks & Garrets are perfectly well furnish'd—in all there are Sixteen Beds in the House extremely good & Clean but no one very large—I think You might continue for 3 or 4 days to live in the D^{ss's} rooms as she inhabited them, as the rooms have all Separate communications—, & as there are two bedchambers close together You could do very well for that time & then Settle how the rooms Upstairs Should be arranged—

I found a House in Hertford S^t not so good as Mr Huskissons which ^being^ furnish'd they ask'd 800£ for—& M^rs H[uskisso]^n told me they let theirs unfurnish'd for 600 when they were in Downing S^t—I went to see a house to be let furnish'd in Curzon S^t looking up half Moon S^t—all the lower part of ye House cut off by a Gateway & all the back rooms looking into a Stable Y^d & for this they ask'd 600 Gui[nea]^s—I have been in 3 or 4 more & finding nothing You could go into with the least comfort I determined to run ye risk of taking ye D^ss's where ye furniture is all clean & ye Beds quite good & the Situation delightfull—she pays 800 p^r An^m & the Taxes but she wishes to have a House to go into if she should return to England next Y^r. & therefore decided to let it for less & be at some loss—rather than have to look for a House—You may come to this next Week if You please— There is a Housemaid there who has a room where all the D^ss's things which she left are put up—Of course whether you keep her on or not she may I have no doubt keep the Key of this room—as there are plenty &, it will be no inconvenience to you to have it lock'd up—The Offices are very good—& all sorts of useful things will be found in the House in plenty—The Bell is going—& I am in ye greatest hurry—we are in ye midst of riots—& I just Saw a Charge of Cavalry from my Windows[68] but I have no time to tell you any more

Aff^ly Y^rs
EM

[The Lady Byron]

11th March

1815

Dr Annabella—

      not having any idea of yr leaving Seaham so soon, there are some Letters upon ye road, but they are of no Signification

      I have just been at the House, to tell ye Servants that your Housemaid was on her way—& to prevent her being refused admission—

      I have also been at the House Brokers, & as Ld B[yron] will be in Town so Soon he thinks some sort of Agreement may then be drawn up, for ye time he has taken it/ so there is no necessity for your sending such a direction to any Upholsterer, as the maid you send will probably be competent to look over ye Inventory & take charge of ye things—there is no Linnen to go with the House, nor Glasses nor Knives & forks, Spoons &c—The only things left, are the Kitchen Utensils of all Sorts—Pewter for ye Servants—& some White Wedgwood plates & Dishes & crockery ware for all ye rooms

      You will therefore most probably give yr Servt directions about any things you may want and if I can be of any use, employ me *sans ceremonie* tell Ld B[yron]. I wrote him a Letter Yesterday being in a gracious humour—otherwise I should have taken no more notice of him than he has of me lately—but I wanted to send him This extraordinary News & also an Acct of Kean in Rd ye 2d—
Nothing further is Known about Napoleon to day

Affly yrs

EMelbourne.

[The/Lady Byron]

Lady Melbourne to Lady Byron (Lovelace 92, f.73–75)

[Sunday, March 12, 1815.]

Dear Annabella—

I am afraid you would hardly be able to make out the Letter I wrote
Yesterday—for I had been House hunting all ye Mor^g & could only just get home in
time to send ye post, & a Mob having assembled upon the Parade, to rescue a Man
who had been taken up by the constables, it was necessary to have ye assistance of
the Military & about a dozen of the Horse Guards, galloped *at* the people & dispersed them two Men were rode over but not hurt—& this passing close to my
Windows made it impossible not to leave off writing, & it was with great difficulty
I could finish my Letter, in which there may have been several blunders for I could
not read it over—last Night the Mob made many attempts upon different Houses,
but found them all guarded, & no mischief was *I believe* done[70]

to day it rains hard, which will probably prevent their assembling in great
Numbers—& the Town is full of Military, so I conclude the Ministers think themselves tolerably Safe—they were very much frightened, & not without reason, for
this Mob seems to be extremely savage & much more in earnest, than any I ever
remember—They tear up the Iron rails & force open the door of the House & if
they get in as they did at Mr Robinson's[71] they throw all the furniture out of the
Windows into ye Street where it is broken to pieces or carried away—Mr Yorks[72]
House & Ld Darnleys[73] have suffered considerably—Ld Eldon[74]—for ye honour of
the North—shew'd great courage—there is a private communication from his
House to ye Museum Garden thro' which he went, to get some Soldiers who were
on guard there, & return'd with them; & took two of the rioters himself——a Loaf
of Bread, Steeped in Blood & tied up in black Crape was thrown into Carlton House
Garden—this has caused some mirth, as it must have been done by some person as
a Joke—but which I have no doubt would be taken very Seriously.

I enclose you a very rough Sketch of the rooms on ye ground floor in y^r
House merely to shew you how ye rooms are disposed, as you may then consider in
what way it will be most convenient for you to live in them—I have mark'd them as
they are at present, & there is a very good Bed in No. 3 & also in No. 4—& you see

they all communicate upon the Stair case—if you can understand the marks I have made for doors—the rooms Up stairs are the same with the exception of a little variation in ye Size—as I think 2 & 3 are a little larger & the others rather less— but the stairs up to them altho *good* are many in Number therefore you may per- haps decide to have y^r Bedroom & dressing rooms there—both the large rooms have Bookcases in them; which are empty except one in which there are Some Folios— —the Duchess's Sitting room is furnish'd with low Bookcases Tables Couches & Great Chairs—in profusion but certainly the Rooms up stairs, have only common useful furniture in them—The offices excepting the Kitchen are small—but will do very well & are very comfortable—for all ye Servants belonging to Dev^re House, are <used> to take care of themselves—

I suppose you or L^d B[yron] employ some Upholsterer & in that case—he had better look over the things left in ye House & see they are all there according to ye Inventory which the Auctioneer will give him (Mr Denon)[75] & if you will either give me his direction or send him to me, I will give him directions about it— —If you know of no particular person I will employ ours so let me know—

I find y^t I was mistaken when I s^d no mischief took place last Night—Ld Bathursts House,[76] Ld Kings,[77] Ld Mansfields[78] & S^r Wm Rowleys[79] were attacked & much damaged before ye Military arrived—

I am very glad to hear y^t M^y B^r & L^y M[ilbanke]—are coming to London— pray make my love to them & to L^d B[yron]—

Most aff^ly y^rs
EMelbourne

I forgot to mention y^t all ye rooms are very light & pleasant excepting N° 4 which being <cornered> so far back is darken'd by some buildings——

This rough sketch of the rooms on the ground floor of the duchess of Devonshire's house at 13 Piccadilly Terrace was enclosed in Viscountess Melbourne's Letter to Lady Byron (Lovelace 92, f.77; March 12, 1815)

Front to the Street

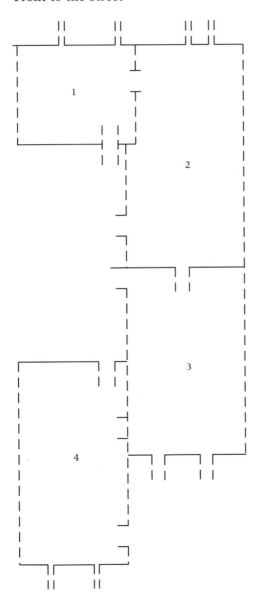

1. Dining Room
2. Sitting Room
3. Bed Chamber
4. Ditto

Lady Melbourne to Henry Fox (Melbourne 234/6/10)

[May 22, 1815]

M[r]. Fox

a brother of the M[r]. Woollatt who is Tenant of L[d] Melbourne in Nottinghamshire has applied to M[r]. Brand[80] to take a farm and has referred to you for his Character—M[r]. Brand has therefore desired me to write to you and begs you will let me know if his Character is good for honesty and integrity, and whether you believe him to be a good farmer and possessed of Capital Enough to undertake an arable farm of Two Hundred Acres. I shall be obliged to you, to let me have as early an Answer as [soon as] possible —

Y[rs]. EMelbourne

22 May
1815.

Lady Melbourne to Lady Bessborough (Yale, Osborne)

[28th July 1815]

Dearest Lady Bessborough,

If I have not written to you before, you will know y[t] it has not been for want of feeling the most anxious interest concerning you & Frederic[81]—but I thought it was only plaguing you on y[r] First arrival at Brussels when your attention must have been so much engaged—I was delighted to hear such good accounts & I trust & hope that in time his recovery will be perfect—but how much you must have suffered on y[r] journey D[r] L[y] B[essborough] I pitied you from the bottom of my heart—you should not however have avowed feeling some gratification if you had known how many people were in y[e] same Situation for you have no idea of y[e] general feeling either on this same account, he is so genuinely beloved—I really never saw any thing like it & I am a good Judge from y[e] numbers of questions I had to answer—& I hope it will not be very long before I shall see you all here, which will be great happiness—L^y Duncannon dined here Yesterday[;] she looks in very good health but rather thin in the face—the savage humour in which people are here would rather astonish you, who I know think, that as y^r guests, you should be merciful—here no such generosity is in fashion—& to give you an idea of the Language—I had a little *dispute* in ye mildest tone possible with two Gentlemen, who were for levelling the Calmness at Paris—& for what reason do you think? that there should be no trace remaining of Buo[napart]^e[.] [I]t was ye only thing I venture[d] to contradict & that only with an *oh fie* but for that was called a Jacobin—it really is so absurd it is almost impossible to help laughing—I think you will understand this—Blucher[82] is ye Hero— This last opinion is quite general & every fool you meet says oh Blucher's the Man, I wish he had got to Paris first—God bless you dear L^y B[essborough]—I long to see you & I hope I shall meet ye same two Gentlemen & you in addition & of *nobody's Age*. We'll give it them but with a Gallery you know it is impossible

Eliz. Melbourne

28th July
1815

Lady Melbourne to Lord Byron (Murray)

Whitehall

Dec. 17, 1815

      Lord Melbourne presents His compliments to Lord Byron, and informs Him that He had signed all the Deeds brought to Him more than ten days back.[83] M Cookney L^d M[elbourne's] man of Busyness, at that time complained of the delay, not in his Power to prevent, and L^d M[elbourne] signed a Draft on his Banker to pay the money to L^d B He was to receive, as soon as it was proper to do, and did not know but it was done '

      L^d M begs to assure L^d B, that if the delay, has been unusual, and uncanny? it is not been from any neglect of His

      L^d M is Happy to Hear L^y B & the young Lady are going on so well.

Notes: Part V

1. Harriet Pearce married the Honorable George Germain, younger brother of the fifth duke of Dorset and second son of the soldier and statesman, Lord Sackville of Drayton (Elwin, *Wife* 260). Her husband is not to be confused with Lord George [Sackville] Germaine d.1785 (*DNB* 7:1110-14). Harriet's Germain may have carried Sackville as an honorary title. My special thanks to Professor Carl Woodring for bringing this to my attention.

2. Lady Melbourne discusses the riots relating to the corn law legislation on March 7 and 12, 1815.

3. Byron drank brandy heavily during his wife's confinement. He was also involved in an affair with Miss Susan Boyce in November 1815, during his tenure as a member of the management subcommittee of Drury Lane Theater, which began in May 1815 (Marchand, *Portrait* 201).

4. Byron wrote to Lady Melbourne on January 3 (the day after the wedding) and again on January 7, with no response. Lady Melbourne acknowledged his first letter by writing to Annabella on January 8 and 16 without answering Byron directly (Elwin, *Wife* 259).

5. Airlie omits the first paragraph of the letter.

6. This letter is significant for being the first letter Lady Melbourne wrote to Byron after his marriage to Annabella. Written this late, she should have intended to write much more than "three lines," as she says later in the letter. Lady Melbourne seems to have been teasing Byron by showing him the new terms upon which their correspondence would exist.

7. Lady Bessborough. See part 4, note 20.

8. André Masséna (1758-1817), the celebrated French general whom Napoleon called "Enfant de la Victoire" (Foster 177, n.3).

9. "You have given me so little to eat My Lord that you must be sure to give me a good dinner." The duke answered, "If I gave you so little to eat you have returned the favor in preventing me from sleeping and I believe that having exchanged these witty remarks we gave ourselves torment enough."

10. The son of Lord Glenbervie (Airlie, *Whig* 169).

11. George Granville Venables Vernon interviewed the exiled Bonaparte, who extolled the solidity of the English aristocracy (R. G. Thorne 5:450).

12. My God, is this the oppressed Virtue about which we've heard so much?

13. Lady Hester Stanhope, who had left England for the Levant.

14. The remainder of this letter is written at the top of the first page.

15. In an undated letter to Granville Leveson-Gower, Lady Bessborough writes: "Think of poor L*ʸ* Hester Stanhope, Mr. Bruce, and Henry Pierce being taken by the Arabs! If they treat them well she will rather like an adventure, and perhaps end with becoming wife to an Arab Chief. I should not wonder" (G. L. Gower 2:435). This "undated" letter appears to be misplaced in the Gower correspondence, since it is between letters of April and May 1812.

16. *a petite Sorté*: an odd remark.

17. Lady Byron had been married just two weeks earlier and was finishing her honeymoon at Halnaby with her husband. She stayed until January 21 and celebrated Byron's birthday on January 22 at Seaham with her parents (Marchand, *Portrait* 194).

18. See footnote 1.

19. Jemima Sophia Asgill (Elwin, *Wife* 260).

20. Lady Melbourne used this expression again in a letter to Byron of February 8, 1815: "I dont know anyone more fitted for your Corbeau blanc, from cleverness, Good-humour, and a thousand agreeable qualitys."

21. *corbeau blanc*: white crow or raven. "Corbeau blanc" may derive from Voltaire's story "Le Taureau Blanc," a parody of the Old Testament that is based in part on Calmet's *Dictionnaire Historique*. In this story, a "corbeau" acts as a friendly guide to the white bull who is the hero. Voltaire alludes to *Genesis* 8:6,7, in which a raven is sent from Noah's ark but does not find land, and to Elijah's retirement near the brook Cherith, when the Lord fed him by means of ravens, who brought bread and flesh each morning and evening (1 *Kings* 17:5). The raven, as described in *Levitticus* 11:15, is "unclean by the law" (Voltaire 64; Calmet 1:462). According to Roman legend, ravens were once as white and large as swans. One day a raven informed Apollo that Coronis, a Thessalian nymph, had been unfaithful. Apollo shot the nymph and punished the messenger: "He blacked the raven o'er, / And bid him prate in his white plumes no more" (Addison, translation of *Ovid*, book 2; quoted in Brewer's *Phrase and Fable* 851). In French, corbeau has a cluster of interesting associations. It can be refer, pejoratively, to a priest or clergy-man; to an anonymous author of poison pen letters (Harrap's 66), or to a marriage that is not sexual. A "mariage blanc" would be a marriage in name only; one, for example, that conceals the sexual preferences of the participants. Though she may have had these other meanings in mind, Lady Melbourne seems most interested in contrasting herself as a "corbeau blanc" with Augusta Leigh, Byron's "corbeau noir," in the terms suggested by Voltaire's story.

22. Byron responded: "I suppose your "C-noir" is + [Augusta] but if + were a Raven or a Griffin I must still take my omens from her flight—I can't help *loving* her tho—I have

quite enough at home to prevent me from loving any one essentially for some time to come.—" (February 2, 1815; *LJ* 4:262).

23. Lord Granville Leveson-Gower, first marquis of Stafford.

24. Lord Thomas Erskine (1750-1823).

25. A green ribbon or sash was a sign of nobility (Stokes).

26. Sir Samuel Romilly.

27. Lady Melbourne argues that Erskine's political views will agree with those of George III and the Tories, now that he has been given a green ribbon by the government. Erskine was invested with the Order of the Thistle in 1815 on the death of Lord Lothian (Murray 1:297). Lady Melbourne may also be referring to the green man, representing the spirit of vegetation, who appears in festivals dressed from head to foot in green boughs or leaves. The public-house sign The Green Man and Still is "probably a modification of the arms of the Distiller's Company, the supporters of which were two Indians, for which the sign painters usually substituted foresters or green men drinking out of a glass barrel" (Brewer's *Myth and Legend* 115).

28. The poet Thomas Moore (1779-1852).

29. "Why did you call Lady S[usan] R[yder] *my* 'favorite,'" Byron responded. "I never exchanged a word with her in my life after she came out—nor before—except at her mother's & then because people seemed to treat her as a child & not talk to her at all" (February 5, 1815; *LJ* 4:267).

30. William, sixth duke of Devonshire (1790-1858).

31. Henry Somerset, marquis of Worcester (1792-1853) and seventh Duke of Beaufort (R. G. Thorne 4:225). Harriette Wilson remembered Lord Worcester as a romantic figure fond of quoting Byron's poetry (Wilson 1:310). He was a friend of Alvanley, a man with "mature worldly manners" (1:312), whose infatuation for Wilson led him to be ridiculed by his friends. He competed with the duke of Leinster for Wilson's attention (1:313) and was indefatigable (1:328) in his pursuit of her, if her memoirs are to be trusted.

32. Byron had objected to Lady Melbourne's negative assessment of Augusta Leigh's influence, and so Lady Melbourne suggested that Augusta was not "actually *Noir*."

33. On March 7, 1814, Lord Portsmouth married Mary Anne, eldest daughter of John Hanson, Byron's solicitor. Byron was present at the ceremony and at Hanson's request gave away the bride. Portsmouth's brother, the next heir, tried to annul the marriage, arguing that Lord Portsmouth was insane. In retrospect, Byron wrote facetiously that the groom "did not seem to me more insane than any other person going to be married" (Marchand, *Biography* 1:441).

34. Lord Chancellor Eldon ruled that Lord Portsmouth was capable of entering into a marriage contract and managing his own affairs (Marchand, *Biography* 1:441).

35. Albert J. Michael Rocca, a young French officer whom Madame de Staël had secretly married in 1811, was the author of *Memoirs sur la guerre des Francaise en Espagne* (London: 1814). The work was translated from the French by Maria Graham and published again in 1815 and 1817.

36. Madame de Staël did marry Rocca in 1811, but she kept the marriage, and their retarded child, a secret.

37. In her letters to Joachim Murat, Madame de Staël intrigued to keep Murat on the throne as a favor to her friend Madame de Récamier. "I worship you," she wrote, "because you are a true friend of liberty" (Herold 453). The British government did not recognize Murat as a legitimate sovereign, however, and was committed to maintaining Louis XVIII on the throne. Louis XVIII informed de Staël that "We attach so little importance to anything you do say, or write that the government wants to know nothing about it; nor does it wish to give you any fear on this account, or even allow anyone to hinder you in any way in your projects and mysteries" (450).

38. One paragraph of this letter is quoted by Elwin (*Wife* 277).

39. See Lady Melbourne's letter of January 11, 1815, which refers to Harriet Pearce's marriage.

40. Chatsworth is the seat of the duke of Devonshire.

41. See Byron's letter of January 19, 1815. Lady Melbourne exaggerates his expressions of "happiness" (*LJ* 4:255).

42. Lady Charlotte Howard, née Charlotte Leveson-Gower, was Byron's choice for a wife before his engagement to Annabella (Elwin, *Wife* 277).

43. Whig families objected to the use of property taxes to pay the debts of the war incurred by Tory ministers.

44. Sir Charles William Stewart.

45. The son of Lord Glenbervie.

46. Byron had referred to the rumor that William and Caroline Lamb were about to separate: "Pray is there any foundation for a rumour which has reached me—that les agneaux (W[illiam] & C[aroline]) are about to separate? . . . pray tell me as much as your new code of confidence will permit—or what is still better—that this report (which came in a letter) is—as the person says it may be a "wicked scandal" (February 5, 1815; *LJ* 4:266).

47. Lady Melbourne tolerated William's marriage to Caroline, but her facetious tone here

indicates her displeasure with her daughter-in-law.

48. See Byron's letter of January 22, 1815, in which he complains she does not confide. "I cannot sufficiently admire your cautious style since I became chicken-pecked" (*LJ* 4:258).

49. Byron had written of Augusta: "I have quite enough at home to prevent me from loving any one essentially for some time to come" (February 2, 1815; *LJ* 4:262).

50. Lady Melbourne is referring to Lady Susan Ryder. See her letter to Byron of January 31, 1815 and Byron's response, quoted in note 29.

51. Lady Melbourne plays on Byron's reference to loving Augusta "essentially" on February 2, 1815.

52. The remainder of this letter is written at the top of the first page.

53. Byron had referred to guests who were visiting him and Annabella. "We have 3 or 4 visitors here—whom I wish gone again though very good people in their way—but alas in my way too—I did not know of their approach till their arrival" (February 5, 1815; *LJ* 4:267).

54. *prevenant*: agreeable.

55. Lady Melbourne refers to Byron's complaint that her most recent letters were not intimate enough. "Pray tell me as much as your new code of confidence will permit," he wrote (February 5, 1815; *LJ* 4:266). Byron only hoped she would give him something worth betraying.

56. The postscript to this letter appears on a separate, smaller sheet of paper, which has been torn.

57. The version in the Murray archives is missing the paragraph about Hobhouse.

58. On February 6 Annabella had rescued her husband from smoke inhalation caused by a poorly ventilated fire. In a letter to Lady Melbourne, Byron wrote that he would have suffocated "if Bell had not in the nick of time . . . sluiced me with Eau de Cologne" (February 6, 1815; *LJ* 4:267).

59. The reference is to Augusta, who was indeed "a great friend of *ye Giaour's* (Byron's)," but who felt somewhat estranged from him after his marriage to Annabella. Lady Melbourne, who distrusted Augusta for her influence over Byron, delighted in circulating this gossip. The phrase "*essentially* in thought" is a playful reference to Byron's earlier suggestion that he loved Augusta "essentially" (February 2, 1815; *LJ* 4:262) or incestuously—by essence, by nature—which Lady Melbourne responded to in her letter of February 8, 1815.

60. The Corn Bill was particularly divisive because it pitted agriculturalists against manufacturers and directly affected the price of bread. The disparity between popular protests

against the bill and the near unanamity of landholders who supported it brought to the fore the question of parliamentary reform. The agriculturalists hoped to raise the price of corn from 63 to 80 shillings per quarter. A pamphlet by a Mr. Jacobs estimated that the bill would increase the price of wheat (and hence bread) by approximately one fourth (*Times,* February 16, 1815).

Lord Egremont and Sir Timothy Shelley voted against changing the corn laws, but they were in a minority. Sir Francis Burdett, who submitted a petition of more than forty thousand signatures objecting to the new laws, was criticized for using the debate to voice his sentiments in favor of parliamentary reform. The three readings of the bill occurred on March 9, 16, and 21, 1815. Most of the debates that occurred before the bill was finally passed concerned its effects on the manufacturing and agricultural sections of the economy.

61. "three"?

62. The first two sentences of this letter are quoted by Elwin (*Wife* 289).

63. The house belonged to the widowed duchess of Devonshire, who was in France at the time.

64. This letter contradicts Ethel Mayne's account, which states that "Hobhouse had taken [the house] for them at a rental of 700" (*Life* 180). It also contradicts Stokes (325), as well as Marchand (*Portrait* 196), who repeats this information: "Hobhouse had leased Lady Elizabeth Hervey (1759-1824), Duchess of Devonshire's house in Piccadilly for Byron in March, 1815" (November 3, 1817; *LJ* 5:270). Hobhouse did say "If I can however be of any service employ me" (March 8 [1815]; Graham, *Byron's Bulldog* 179).

Elwin offers the following explanation for Lady Melbourne's role in choosing the Byrons' first residence: "Apparently Annabella concluded that the tart tone of admonition [in Lady Melbourne's letter of February 8, 1815] was inspired by her aunt's pique at being left in a total state of ignorance about their plans, so she invited her assistance in finding them a suitable home in London" (*Wife* 278). Annabella later complained that the rent was too high.

65. Byron and Annabella lived in this house until their separation in January 1816. The house proved to be too costly, though well located at 13 Piccadilly Terrace (Mayne, *Life* 180).

66. Lady Melbourne would have been familiar with the house because of her friendship with the duchess of Devonshire. After Georgiana's death in 1806, Lady Melbourne maintained a close relationship with Elizabeth Foster, the sixth duchess of Devonshire, with whom she had been friendly her whole life.

67. Drugget: a coarse durable cloth, usually of wool mixed with linen, sometimes used to protect furniture.

68. See letter of March 12, 1815, in which Lady Melbourne reports that the riot was caused by a mob that assembled "to rescue a man who had been taken up by constables." Lady Melbourne's house at Whitehall was directly opposite the horse guards who were busy quelling riots at the houses of supporters of the Corn Bill. The London *Times* reported disturbances at the Burlington Street house of Frederick Robinson as early as 1:00 p.m. on Tuesday, March 7: "in fact, London is now environed with troops on all sides." Edward Vyse, a midshipman, was shot on Old Burlington Street on the Tuesday night and an inquest was held regarding the conduct of the cavalry. Other houses affected were those of Mr. Ponsonby (19 Curzon Street, Mayfair); Mr. Quintin Dick (next door); John Morris, one of the directors of the East India Company (21 Baker Street); Joseph Banks (Soho Square); Mr. Tomkins (Serle-street, Lincoln's Inn-fields); Serjeant Best (Lincoln's Inn-fields); and Mr. Peacock.

69. The first and third paragraphs of this letter are quoted by Elwin (*Wife* 291).

70. See Lady Melbourne's letter of March 7, 1815. The London *Times* reported that a few windows were broken at Lord Castlereagh's house in St. James's square. At Mr. Ponsonby's house, the mob "demolished the windows, and broke the iron palisades in front"; at the earl of Derby's house, they "tore down the whole of the iron railing which incloses that side of the square"; at John Morris' house, the mob "had completely demolished his windows"; and at Joseph Banks' residence the "parlour door was demolished, and boxes of valuable papers scattered in the street and area: the whole angle of the railing of the square was also levelled with the ground before a detachment of the military arrived" ("Continuation of the Tumults," March 8, 1815).

71. Frederick John Robinson was a vocal advocate of the corn laws, which would raise, by means of tariff, the price of corn. On March 7, when his house was targeted by rioters, Robinson called the army. At 9:00 p.m. officers fired on the crowd, killing a young woman and injuring a young man, Edward Vyse. Edward Davis testified that the soldiers had fired blank cartridges and exchanged those for live ammunition (swan shot), which he considered most "wanton." Robinson defended his actions in the House of Commons and was opposed by Francis Burdett (*Times*, March 10, 1815). A three-day "inquest" was held at the Red Lion in Portland Street (*Times*, March 11, 1815) and Robinson was acquitted.

72. On February 17, 1815, Charles Philip Yorke spoke in the House of Commons. He defended the landed interest and supported the corn laws, arguing that "the present

question was not whether any restriction at all should be imposed, for it appeared . . . that some provision of this kind was necessary" (Hansard 29:1060).

73. John Bligh, fourth earl of Darnley, believed that "were the price at 80s. the quartern loaf, would not exceed a shilling" (Hansard 30:4). He "warmly supported the Bill, and contended, that the measure would not be more beneficial to the agriculturist than to the manufacturer. It was not to be wondered at that the table was loaded with petitions from the manufacturers, who were crowded in great towns, while the feeling of six millions of people in Ireland, and many in this country, employed in agricultural occupations, could not be collected, though decidedly in favour of the Bill" (Hansard 30:704).

74. John Scott, first earl of Eldon.

75. Mr. Denen was the duchess of Devonshire's agent. Byron was unable to pay the rent in 1815. In 1817 he wrote to Elizabeth, duchess of Devonshire: "I shall write to the person who has the management of my affairs in England, and, although I have but little control over either at present, I will do the best I can to have the remaining balance liquidated" (November 3, 1817; *LJ* 5:271). The debt was never paid.

76. On February 20, 1815, Charles Bragge Bathurst spoke in the House of Commons in favor of the Corn Bill and protested against the "useless procrastination" (Hansard 39:842) produced by the petitions raised against it.

77. Possibly George King (1771-1839), third earl of Kingston (1799). Lord King argued that "the information at present before them was altogether insufficient; they had none as to the expense of growing wheat in Ireland, or as to what would be a fair protecting price for the Irish farmer." He nevertheless favored the passage of the corn law.

78. Sir James Mansfield, lord chief justice of the Court of Common Pleas.

79. Sir William Rowley sat on the corn trade committee "and his house in Welbeck Street was attacked by the London mob because of his support of the Corn Bill in 1815" (R. G. Thorne 5:59). Opponents of the bill included Sir Francis Burdett (who, however, claimed neutrality), Sir Gilbert Heathcote, and an enormous number of people who signed petitions.

80. Thomas Brand, who was a favorite guest of the Melbournes at Brocket.

81. Frederick was Lady Bessborough's husband. They were in Brussels visiting their son, Frederick Ponsonby (1783-1837), who had been wounded seven times in the Battle of Waterloo during the charge of the 23rd brigade. Palmerston wrote to Lady Melbourne to tell "Lady Caroline that the charge of the 23rd was one of the most gallant things that ever was done" (Ponsonby 116).

82. Gebhard Lebrecht Blücher, commander-in-chief of the Prussian army.

83. Lord Ralph Milbanke owed Byron £20,000 on account of the marriage settlement. The losses incurred from bankruptcies by Durham and Sunderland banks left Annabella's

family short of ready cash. A complicated arrangement was made by which Sir James Bland Burges and Lord Henley, as Noel trustees, would borrow on mortgage from Lord Melbourne and advance it to Byron. There was difficulty, however, in raising a mortgage on an entailed estate (Elwin, *Wife* 321). Byron had still not received the £6,000 he expected from Sir Ralph by the end of 1815. This added significantly to his financial anxieties and to his unpredictable temper at the time of his separation from Annabella (Elwin, *Wife* 327).

PART VI

As Much Fortitude as You Can Muster," 1816

News of Byron's separation from Annabella reached Lady Melbourne like a thunder-bolt on February 5, 1816. She wrote a series of letters to Judith Milbanke (February 10, 12, and 14), trying frantically to regain the good graces of her brother's family. Throughout the crisis, Lady Melbourne focused on dissuading Annabella from seeking a separation. She warned her about the prospect of a trial, of "public expo-sure," and of the unpleasant need "to give evidence" (February 17, 1816). To the Milbankes, these arguments were unpersuasive, especially coming from a woman who consistently defended Byron's conduct. Parting with Annabella after her mar-riage to Byron had been difficult enough. Now she welcomed her daughter back to Seaham as the victim of a deranged husband inflicted on her by her aunt.

There was much talk of Byron's madness at the time, but the truth is that Byron's debts and heavy drinking were primarily responsible for his ungovernable conduct. Annabella's priggishness only inflamed Byron's Calvinist sense of his own damnation. Caroline Lamb summed up the couple's prospects well when she wrote that Byron would "never be able to pull with a woman who went to church punc-tually, understood statistics and had a bad figure" (Marchand, *Portrait* 180). During the month that their daughter was with them in Seaham, the Milbankes thought Lady Melbourne was meeting with Byron privately. Lady Melbourne denied this and, after several skeptical letters, Annabella finally accepted her aunt's explana-tion (March 20, 1816).

When *Glenarvon* appeared two months later, Lady Melbourne wrote to Annabella that she could not read more than twenty pages before closing the book in disgust (May 29, 1816). She found a surprising ally in her old nemesis, Madame de Staël, who also expressed herself "shock'd at the famous publication" (October 18, 1816). De Staël had offered to assist Byron in a reconciliation with his wife, having become his virtual neighbor in Coppet, Switzerland during July and August. At this time he was living at the Villa Diodati, near the Shelleys.

Back in England, Lady Melbourne pitied Annabella, who had endured so much in the past few months, but their correspondence was relegated to a discussion of public matters. "The Antiquary I have not seen," Lady Melbourne wrote, "& only a quotation from Christabel in ye Newspapers, which did not tempt me to send for ye Poem." She liked Walter Scott's novel "prodigiously" (October 25, 1816) when she finally read it, as well as Benjamin Constant's *Adolphe,* a shorter work by the former lover of Madame de Staël (June 29 1816).

In 1816 Emily Cowper traveled to Italy with her husband. There they met Mrs. George Lamb, the Cliffords, and Lady Jersey. Emily wrote to her mother from Milan on October 10, after passing the Alps by the Simplon pass. Miss Berry, who was also there at the time, refused to give credit to Napoleon for building new roads. Emily was more cosmopolitan; she noted that Napoleon had actually "made" the Simplon, "& for that reason all ye Bourbon-nites tell you it is not passable" (October 25, 1816).

Lady Byron's health had been precarious in March, and Lady Melbourne conveyed news to Byron through John Cam Hobhouse. "Anxious tiresome friends are continually recurring to past events," she wrote (October 18, 1816). Annabella was staying at her father's house, where Lady Melbourne imagined that both parents were "tormenting her" (October 18, 1816), since visits to a physician uncovered nothing. In this same letter, Lady Melbourne noted that the economic troubles of the country were increased by "the very late & bad Harvest," and she faulted members of Parliament for proroguing until February at a time when the price of bread was rising uncomfortably high.

That fall, the Princess Narischkine visited London and Oxford, accompanied by Alexander I. Narischkine became the acknowledged mistress of the emperor, who found consolation in her companionship during his unhappy marriage. "Her manners & appearance are very pleasing but she is not so beautiful as she has been represented," Lady Melbourne wrote (October 18, 1816).

Having taken the duke of Devonshire's box at Drury Lane, Lady Melbourne could indulge her taste for theatrical entertainment. Kean "acts still better than he did the preceding y^{rs} & the applause he meets with seems to justify my opinion he is going to act Timon of Athens" (October 25, 1816), she wrote. But 1816 was one of Kean's worst seasons and the play closed after only seven performances.

Lady Byron to Lady Melbourne (Lovelace 376)

Piccadilly Terrace
[Thursday] Jan 4 [1816]

My dear Aunt,

You will allow me the use of my eyes by this time without a lecture, to tell you that I and the child[1] are perfectly well. We took even a drive in the Park today. My confinement has been rendered so comfortable by M^{rs}. Leigh's kindness and attention, which I never can forget, that I feel no inclination to break loose.—You will be glad to hear that my niece is now almost well, and also that I have had a better account of my Mother since she left Town. She regretted much not being able to make you a visit.

Not having seen any company, I have scarcely heard any news, and cannot give you any information except of a domestic nature. Of this kind I may (or perhaps may *not,* for I have not asked leave) mention two new poems, which the Newspapers have metamorphosed into one Epic—Likewise giving me the credit of "*tasteful* criticism," which I have hitherto exercised only in the most literal way over roast and boiled—The subjects are founded on historical facts—"The Siege of Corinth" and "Parisina." there is more description in the former and more passion in the latter—which will be preferred on the whole I know not—they are now in Murray's hands.

I hope Lord Melbourne has quite recovered from his rheumatism, for that grievance in addition to his absence from Town would be too much for human endurance. I shall not be sorry if he grows impatient and hastens your return—

Believe me

Dear Aunt

Yours most affe^{ly}

A.I.B.

Lady Melbourne to Lady Byron (Lovelace 92, f.79-80)

BH—

19th Jan^y

1816

Dear Annabella

You must give me credit for ye entire absence of Selfishness, if you Suppose I should scold you for making use of your Eyes in writing to me. I am afraid when good advice is brought to act against Yourself—that ye temptation to relax in some degree will often be found too strong to resist, as I confess it would have been in this case, when the accounts I had to receive both of You & Your little Girl, were so very agreable & so very Satisfactory—& I also had a few days ago, a confirmation of them as far as appearances can be relied on, for a Gentleman who saw you in your Carriage, was so Struck with your appearance, y^t he repeated to me three or four different times, how well you were looking.

You would now like to hear who this was,—but my regard & friendship for Lord Byron are much too powerfull to allow me to indulge You so far. I will say y^t it was a Young Man & what is more, a fashionable Young Man, The dinner Bell is now ringing, but as I have been so long in answering y^r Letter I will not put it off— now, but tell you that I hope to see you all very soon, as we shall be in Town next Week—L^d M[elbourne] is completely tired of ye Country, & tho' I am not I shall not be insensible to the pleasure of seeing those whom I love because it will be in London. The Weather has been delightfull & to day very fine, which I have no doubt will Surprise you as I know You must have been nearly Suffocated by a thick fog, for we had a little here but it clear'd up——thank you very much for ye intelligence you gave me[.] I am very impatient for the fulfillment of it, as I know I shall like it so much——

I conclude You hear nothing talk'd of in Town but Sʳ R Wilson[2] & Mʳ. Bruce, we are extremely anxious for a more particular account, some say it is horrible others think it very fine & so we are disputing which is a great amusement in a Country House; we have been told yᵗ the whole was discovered by a Letter of Mr Bruces which he sent by yᵉ post—I can hardly think, that even he could be foolish enough to have done so absurd a thing—I must finish

Yrs. ever Affly
EMelbourne

I see by Lᵈ Byron's Subscription yᵗ he has *again* changed his Opinion about Kean—
—I never have for one instant—tell him that now he is right I advise him to remain so[3]—

[The/Lady Byron]

Lady Melbourne to Lady Byron (Lovelace 92, f.82)

26th Jany
1816

Dear Annabella

I had written to you before I received your Second Letter, & as it was enclosed to Lᵈ Byron, I conclude he forwarded it to you—we arrived here Yesterday & to day is so fine that I regret the Country very much—I hope you have received every advantage both to Yourself & to the Child which You expected from it, I know that after a *confinement,* it is always of essential service, & formerly I never expected to feel strong & well till I had been in the Country, & particularly if you continue to be a Nurse,—I trust & hope it does not disagree with You, but if it Should I earnestly advise you to discontinue it, not so much for your own Sake as for that of the Child, because it is necessary you should be well, that she may be so too——I am going to Night to see this famous part of Keans. I hear such commendations of him that I do not doubt I shall be highly gratified, they say every Box in the House is taken till March for the Nights on which this play[4] is acted.—I have seen so few people since I came to Town that I can tell you no News, Opinions I hear are much divided respecting Sr Robert Wilson, & those who blame him most think y^t if he did not deceive Ld Stewart,[5] he may be excused, but y^t it would be unpardonable if he had obtained a Passport for La Valette[6] under a feign'd name,— this his friends say is certainly not true, & that he only got one for himself from our Ambassador—I was very happy to find by y^r Letter that my B^r & L^y Noel were well, as that makes me hope she is quite recover'd from her late illness—pray give my love to them & believe me

Y^rs very aff.^ly
EMelbourne

I am obliged to finish
in a hurry, as it is time
to dress for an early dinner on Acc^t of ye play

[Lady Melbourne to Lord Byron] [Lovelace 11, f.93-4; first paragraph omitted in Elwin, 402]

Feby 5th, 1816

D^r. L^d. B[yron]—

there is a report about you so much believed in Town, that I think you should be informed of it. They say you & Annabella are parted & even state y^e. authority upon which this is founded—

in general when reports are as false as I know this to be, I think the best way is to despise them & to take no measures to contradict them—but really this is so much talk'd about & believed, notwithstanding my contradictions, y^t. I think you ought to desire her to come to Town or go ^to^ her Yourself.———

I am still confined but y^e. first time I go out I will call upon M^rs. L— I

should like to see you then, & tell you several things which I do not like to write &
I can not see you at Home

Yrs. Ever

E.M.

I wish you would write me a Line—

Lady Melbourne to Lady Noel[7] (Lovelace 11, f.95-96)

10th Feby, 1816.[8]

My dear Ly. Noel—

    I cannot refrain any longer from enquiring into the truth about ye. reports
that have been so prevalent about Ld. & Ly. Byron for this last week—& as I would
by no means apply to either of them,[9] I beg you will have the kindness to give me
some information upon a Subject which interests me so much—at first I received
every report with the most decided disbelief—but Yesterday I was Staggered by
being assured that some friends of yours had stated that they had it from you, &
particularly that some Lady in yr. House but whose name I was not told, declared
that they were actually Separated, & that you said you hoped they never would
come together again—never having the most distant idea of any disagreement you
may judge, how astonish'd & grieved I felt at this statement—whatever may be the
cause I must lament such an event having taken place, & also the unhappiness in
which you must be involved in common with them,—

    Sometimes I still indulge in the hope that all this may be exaggerated, pray
relieve me from this anxiety & believe

Most affly. yrs.

EMelbourne[10]

10th Febry.

1816

Lady Melbourne to Sir Ralph Noel Baronet (Lovelace 11, f.90-91)

Feby. 12th

1816

My dear Brother

having been confined by a violent Cold, I have seen very few people, & have only heard this Morn^g that you were in Town—I have been very much vexed at the reports that have been circulated respecting Annabella & I therefore wish very much to see you for 1/2 an Hour—that you may set me right as to what I am, & am not, to believe, for nothing can be more unpleasant than to hear any one for whom you have as sincere an Affection as I have for Annabella sometimes praised, sometimes censured & constantly the subject of conversation for every Gossipping Man & Woman in Town without knowing what to contradict or assert—and now that I have been assured that two Ladies friends of L^y Noels & Y^{rs}. say they are desired to give this event every possible publicity, I may presume that you will have no Objection to give me some information upon a Subject which must give me great anxiety on Y^{rs}. & L^y Noels' account ^as well as^ as on Annabella's—for you must both have participated, in her Sufferings.

As it may be troublesome to you to come to this part of the Town, I beg you will tell me at what Hour I shall find you at Home, either Early or late to-morrow I can call, & I want to see you of all things—

very aff^{ly}. y^{rs},

EMelbourne.

I wrote to L^y. Noel last Week but think it likely she may be too much Agitated to give me an Answer—in short nothing can be so disagreeable as remaining so long in ignorance about you all—

Lady Melbourne to Lord Byron (Lovelace 376)[11]

14th Febry.

1816.

Dear Ld. B -

I omitted ye. other Morg. saying to you that if you wish to *see* me, or I can be of any use—I will go to you at any time—I hve received a Letter fm Ly. N[oel]—saying yt. it is not honourable to give any information to any persons except those whom it is necessary to trust—If you have any thing more favourable to tell me, perhaps You will write me a Line, or at all events I will call upon Mrs Leigh tomor-row or next day —

Yrs. most truly

EM

I have seen my Br.[12] who sd. he was then waiting for an answer from You which Mr Hanson was to bring him—

Lady Melbourne to the Hon. Lady Noel (Lovelace 11, f.92-94; Airlie, Whig 166-67[13])

15th Febry,

1816

Dear Lady Noel:

many thanks for Your Letter, you must have misunderstood me if you thought I wish'd ^you^ to tell me any Secrets,—You have told me all I ask'd, & what I regret very deeply,—that ye existing circumstances were as I had heard them represented—for when I wrote to you I was in perfect ignorance & ye only information I had, was from Baron D'~~arnheim~~ ^Arnim[14]^ whom you probably do not know—saying one Eveg at Ly Harringtons[15] that a person with whom he was acquainted had heard ^this event^ from a friend of yours, who had it from you & that you added she was at liberty to give it every possible publicity

I certainly gave this no credit at the time, nor do I believe it now, as far as regards you; but the fact is so, & I dare say I could bring forward Ten people who heard him say it.

I assure you I enter into all your feelings, on this distressing occasion, & am miserable when I think what Annabella must have suffer'd before she could resolve to bring such an Appeal before ye World.[16]

You say justly ~~that~~ you have every consolation from from [sic] her known character. it is not possible that any one can stand higher in public opinion than she does, or be more believed by her private friends—& I must add that it appea^d to me that Ld Byron knew how to appreciate her character most justly, for he came to see me the day before this report had made its way into ye World, & for an Hour talk'd only of her amiable qualities & how much he lov'd her. This you may believe rendered me perfectly incredulous at first, & made it difficult if not impossible for me to believe any thing I heard, till I enquired from you—& what ever may be ye cause of these unhappy differences[17] having arisen I must feel extremely sorry for them ^both^, at ye same time that I respect y^r motives for concealment—as I am sure your conduct can only arise out of affection & love for her—I do not write this with any wish you should answer it—Therefore pray do not think of taking the trouble to do so.

Aff^ly y^rs,

EM

[London, February Sixteen, 1816/The Hon Lady Noel/Kirkby Mallory/Melbourne/Hinkley]

Lady Melbourne to Lady Byron (Lovelace 92, f.84-86)
[Feb. 17, 1816]

My dear Annabella

Your very kind Letter has given me ye greatest pleasure, & proves to me that I judged rightly, in believing you would appreciate my motives for not intruding upon you at this time, to ye real cause, the fear of being troublesome—& that when you did think of me it would be as of a most affectionate & sincere friend full of grief for y^r present Situation, & wishing it were in her power to bring any alleviation to Your present Sufferings in which it is impossible to participate more Sincerely.

My Brother was all kindness, & proved it by coming to me at a moment when he was oppressed & unhappy under these lamentable circumstances;[18] I told him that knowing as little as I did, the only wish I could form, was, that it had been settled amicably & without public exposure, instead of being brought before a tribunal like ye World, where every thing is discussed & represented, with levity, indifference, & derision & without ye least regard to ye pain, such representations may give—what ever passes between Husband & Wife ought to be sacred, the Strongest reasons can hardly justify a departure from this rule; that you have them I do not doubt & without waiting for the explanation you promise I have no hesitation in saying that I am convinced your motives are perfectly good, & I have the fullest reliance both upon y^r conduct, & your Judgment—but even if I were sure that ye decision of a Court of Justice would be exactly what you had tried for—I should still say—I wish it had been settled without your going into it——This always has been my opinion, but if it had not, this event would have convinced me, for ye numbers of reports that have been spread, are really so disgusting, that altho justice is done to your Character, yet they are painful in ye extreme to those who love you —

The relative Situation of Husband & Wife, is so delicate so united & so blended together that ye World think it hardly possible that there should not be errors on both sides—pray observe that I do not Speak for myself, but when I hear what is s^d, I grieve more & more every day that this Separation, had not been settled Amicably for while some people talk of Cruelty & ill Usage, others mention, a bad Temper aggravated by pecuniary distress[19]—of course I take no part in all these differences & only wish as I told my Brother, & he agreed with me that some agreement could be entered into—satisfactory to both parties, to avoid public exposure.—it must be dreadful to you to have to give evidence, which must if establish'd disgrace the person against whom it is given—forgive me dear Annabella for having said so much upon a case on which I am so ill-inform'd—but which must affect y^r future peace & happiness so essentially—I hope you will do justice to my motives & believe y^t in what I have s^d I have been guided Solely, by love & affection for you —

Most aff^{ly} Y^{rs}

EM —

17th Feb^y
1816[20]

Annabella Milbanke to Lady Melbourne (Lovelace 92, f.88)

Feb^{ry} 20, 1816

My Dear Aunt

I am very glad that you so fully enter into my opinion ~~respecting~~ in deprecating legal measures *if possible*—and you must be informed that L^d B- has so little consideration for his own Character as not to have acceded before this time to the proposal of my Friends for a *private* ^& amicable^ arrangement—repeated applications have been made to him for that purpose—you seem to me ignorant of this circumstance which I therefore wished to tell you—I have so much writing that you must excuse this short answer to your kind letter—& believe me very aff^{ly} y^{rs}[21]

Lady Melbourne to Lord Byron (Murray)

[1816][22]
Wednesday

Dear L^d B -

I have received M^{ss} Leigh's note, telling me I may call upon you any Morn^g

about Three o'Clock—to morrow I have an engagement but will call on Friday

Y^{rs} ever

EM

if any other day should be more agreeable to you let me know—if I hear nothing I shall conclude you will be glad to see me

[The Lord Byron]

Annabella Milbanke to Judith Milbanke (Elwin, Wife 442)

[Sunday, March 17, 1816]

I have just signed my name after Lord Byron's to an article of Separation . . . I am so glad the whole has been managed without Lady M's interference. She is frightened out of her senses on finding from M^{rs}. G. Lamb that I knew her misdeeds towards me. On this point I want to have your opinion. I have now the fairest reasons for cutting her altogether, and I don't know what good she can ever do me. What do you think of it? I have just read "Les liaisons dangereux," which don't incline me more to cultivate her acquaintance.

Now pray "be aisy"—for I really think it is all finished in the best manner.

Judith Milbanke to Annabella Milbanke (Elwin, Wife 443)

[Tuesday, March 19, 1816]

I think it *incumbent* on You to *break* with her, that is *cut her intirely*—not from *resentment* so much, as to enable You and Your Friends to *contradict* the *Lies* and aspersions She has held out *lately*—because if You knowing *them,* continue on terms with *her,* it is a *tacit* confession that they are not *unfounded.* Now I think it *best* You should openly alledge *this part of her conduct,* as a reason why *You* and

Your Parents cannot notice her, hinting at the same time on *past* conduct. In this *Cut,* I include Lady C[aroline] and G[eorge] L[amb].

Lady Melbourne to Lady Byron (Lovelace 92, f.89-90)[23]*; Elwin,* Wife *443-45, partial quotation)*

[Wednesday] 20th March
1816

My dear Annabella

it is with yᵉ greatest reluctance yᵗ I intrude upon you under yᵉ present circumstances, &, I have forborne to do so, till really I have no longer yᵉ patience to endure, what I am told I am accused of by Yourself, & your friends, without contradicting it. I am inform'd that I blame you, & take Lᵈ B[yron']ˢ part most violently; I deny both most positively, & am totally at a loss to guess from what cause such a report can have arisen:—& indeed I should have expected more liberality from you, than to have given credit to such an assertion without hearing what I had to say, & which must have been told you by some person who wish'd to make a quarrel between us; a very simple Statement of facts must convince you how grossly you have been deceived, & how little foundation there is for such an Accusation,—I have seen Lᵈ B[yron], *once* & that quite at first, & before I saw my Brother—I could then have form'd no opinion for I had heard nothing—& he told me nothing saying only that the whole was a Surprise upon him & that he did not even know what charges were to be brought against him—Mʳˢ Leigh took an oppoʸ at the same time to tell me, that you had just cause of complaint & that you had borne more than any other person could, with yᵉ most exemplary patience, & she has since when ever I have seen her, held the same language.—This account shock'd me very much—& having then heard that my Bʳ was in Town, I wrote to him on my return Home, having before written to Lʸ Noel. The next day I saw my Bʳ, & after that you were kind enough to write to me, & I am not aware that there was any hostility in my answer for on the contrary I can truly say my heart bled

320

for you—after receiving y^r second Letter in which you yourself noticed my ignorance of what was going on; I told M^{rs}. Leigh when she call'd upon me, y^t I beg'd
her to tell L^d B[yron] y^t it was my decided opinion y^t ye best thing for both would
be to agree to an amicable Separation—to this I have had no answer & have had no
communciation of any sort with him either written or Verbal.—I beg at ye same
time to have it understood y^t if L^d B[yron] had express'd a wish to see me, I should
not have refused, as I am far from thinking that seeing him, necessarily implies that
I blame you, or think him in ye right.—I believe You had been in Town ten days
before I heard it, & then it was told me with ye greatest injunctions of Secresy as
you wish'd to remain quite private & to see none but persons on business—I confess I thought it rather strange that after ye Letters y^t had pass'd between us, &
after my Brothers promise to let me hear anything y^t might occur; I should not have
a line from either of you, but as I never force myself upon those who either do not
wish, or have an objection to see me, I waited patiently.—I was however extremely
anxious to hear how you were, & at one time had determined to write & enquire,
but still I refrain'd from ye fear of being thought troublesome or actuated by curiosity, but it never enter'd my head to suppose that there were people wicked enough
to make such false reports, or that if they had you would have listen'd to them,
knowing as I had hoped, my affection for you & how much concern'd I must be
when I heard of y^r affliction

       with these sentiments you may conceive my astonishment when I was told
that you s^d I blamed you—& this not from one person but from three or four
indeed this number was necessary to convince me—& also that I had been with L^d
B[yron] last Week—this as I have s^d before seems to me of so little consequence y^t I
should hardly take ye trouble to contradict it—if it were not to detect falsehood &
that it shows a decided mischievous intention of mis-representing all I do.—this
must have been fabricated, the last time I saw Mrs Leigh & y^e *second* time y^t I have
been in ye House, since you left it, & I most certainly did not see L^d B[yron] nor
did he know I was there.—I can hardly think a person whom I met on ye Stairs
could have stated that I had been with him, unless he had known it positively, as it
would have been so ungentlemanly, but if he did say it, I should advise him another time to remain in ye room, to ascertain ye fact before he ventures to assert it. It

never would have come into my head to accuse him if he had not told a friend of mine Yesterday that I took L^d B[yron']s part. I have I am afraid tired y^r patience but I assure you it is not at all an indifferent thing to me to have you suppose me capable of feeling any unkindness towards you, when it ^is^ so foreign to my real Sentiments.—& you will only do me Justice in believing me

most truly & most aff^ly y^rs
EMelbourne

Lady Byron to Judith Milbanke (Elwin, Wife *446-47)*

[March 20, 1816]

I have been so hurried that I have not been able to tell you of a long letter of exculpation from Lady Melbourne, not occasioned by any communication from me. She *positively denies* having ever thought or expressed blame of my conduct, and certainly makes out a very fair statement . . .

This letter of Lady Melbourne's would put me very much in the wrong if I were to cut her without further information—and I must appear to act still more unfairly by circulating such an opinion of her when she has authorized me & others in the most decided manner to contradict it. This matter is therefore still *suspended* . . .

Annabella Milbanke to Lady Melbourne (Lovelace 92, f.91)

March 21, 1816

My dear Aunt—

The painful impression which you assure me is unfounded was created in my mind by ~~the~~ a concurrence of ~~three~~ circumstances. First—It had been much asserted, and confirmed to me by particular testimonies, that you, expressed, or strongly implied, disapprobation of my conduct. Secondly—after the kindness of our ~~communications~~ ^correspondence^ when I was at Kirkby, you neither offered to visit me when I came here, nor explained the reasons of ~~that strange~~ ^an^ appearance ^which I could not but think strange^, and I was positively assured th[a]t you were then visiting Lord Byron, by a person who had one day been refused admission ^to him^ on that account. The mere fact of your calling at the house *in that peculiar situation of affairs,* might give a sanction to the opinion ^which^ you ~~claim to be false~~ disclaim—

    I think you will admit the propriety of my not naming those individuals ^by^ whom ~~in ang~~ I have been ~~concerned~~ ^informed^; But as I am far from having shown any uncandid or unfavorable dispositions towards you in regard to other circumstances, I can assure you that in this instance my belief was not hastily & lightly adopted—and I did not question the report till I found it so generally credited, that only your own authority could contradict it—I conceive that I shall act ~~in~~ conformably with your wishes by stating that authority to any one who may believe the contrary—^I hope by this means to recover^ all misrepresentations, which I

    ~~My mind is in a dispair which by the product prospect of a quiet~~[24] regret on the present subject as much, and as sincerely as on any—
Believe me—My dear Aunt— Yours most aff^ly AM.

Lady Melbourne to Lady Byron (Lovelace 92, f.92)[25]

[Sunday] 24th March
1816

Dear Annabella

    I am much oblig^d to you for your Letter, & can certainly have no objection to your telling any of the persons who talk upon ye Subject to you, the explanation I have made; neither can I object to ye names of your informers remaining secret they must be very Silly or very mischievous people, & in either case the less I know of them the better, one thing I can not help saying y^t whoever ye person was y^t told you he was refused at ye door because I was with L^d B must have told a positive untruth, for ye only day I saw him Mr Hobhouse was let in, so there could be no exclusion because I was there, & I have not seen him since——

but surely dear Annabella it is ye first time y^t any one was ever reckon'd unkind for not calling under such circumstances upon a friend of theirs, who had not inform'd them of their being in Town, in my humble opinion the unkindness was all on your Side, & your reporters must have made an impression on y^r mind at that time or I am sure you would have written me a line, & I cannot agree with you, when you say y^r opinion was not hastily or lightly adopted.

When you had persuaded Yourself that I blamed you, it was no wonder you should name it to others though I confess I think you ought to have told it me first & not have condemn'd me unheard; I may perhaps have been Spoiled by ye confidence those who are intimate with me have generally reposed in me, I do not mean confidence in ye light of telling me Secrets but ye sort of confidence You feel about a person whom you know will act fairly, openly, & honourably towards You; & altho' there is no analogy between this case & Ld Lucans,[26] yet at that time I saw *both,* I was trusted by both, & never suspected by either of not acting fairly though he knew perfectly that I must feel great interest for her——As to ye assertion y^t I implied blame of y^r conduct in my conversations, I deny it in ye Strongest manner, unless expressing for Several days my disbelief of ye reports can be so construed; & I think at that time I had good reasons for being so incredulous first from not hearing a word from Your family——Secondly from having seen L^d B[yron] when I first came to Town & from his having pass'd the greatest part of his Visit in talking of you, of your amiability, of his own happiness, & of his sincere attachment to you—& of his intention to go to Kirkby—it is not then Surprizing that four days after this Visit, when told of the report I should have s^d, it can not be, it is impossible, it is an illnatur'd Story, & I remain'd under this conviction for Several days, till George [Lamb] told me Mr Kinnaird had heard the fact from Mr Hobhouse & had told it him, for I must add that I never conversed on the Subject with any but my own family, & some particular friends, which with me are few in Number, & I am certain would give no Such account of what I s^d to them, as you have heard; none of my Acquaintance ever mention'd the Subject to me & if you had made use of your own Judgment you would have known it was impossible they should from our near relationship—which ought to have made you doubt the testimonies of those who reported to you—I have gone into these circumstances fully & explicitly, in hopes of removing all doubts from your mind, & of clearing my own from all disagreeable feelings—neither of which I hope & trust will ever return. I will call upon you to morrow or next day, & I hope you will have no objection to admit me—& that you will believe me

Y^{rs} most truly & affec^{ly}
EMelbourne

Lady Byron to Lady Melbourne (Elwin, Wife *447)*
[March 24, 1816]

The painful impression which you assure me is unfounded, was created in my mind by a concurrence of circumstances.

First,—It had been much asserted, and confirmed to me by particular testimonies, that you expressed, or strongly implied, disapprobation of my conduct.

Secondly—after the kindness of our correspondence when I was at Kirkby, you neither offered to visit me when I came here, nor explained the reasons of an appearance which I could not but think strange—and I was positively assured that you were then visiting Lord Byron, by a person who had one day been refused admission to him on that account. The mere fact of your calling at the house *in that peculiar situation of affairs,* might give a sanction to the opinions you disclaim.

. . . I did not mention the report till I found it so generally credited, that only your own authority could contradict it. I conceive that I shall act comfortably with your wishes by stating that authority to any one who may believe the contrary . . .

Lady Byron to Lady Melbourne (Lovelace 92, f.94; Elwin, Wife 467)

Copy—

April 17, 1816

My dear Aunt—

The circumstances of my present Situation having, to my great regret, become the subject of the *most* public discussion, I must authorize my friends to contradict the gross falsehoods thus circulated[27]——In regard to that of my having acted under any influence whatever, I declare that I did not admit from any person the slightest interference in regard to my Separation, until my own determination was irrevocably formed from my *personal experience* & *positive knowledge* of the facts that necessitated ^that^ ~~such a~~ measure.

~~I feel confident that it is~~ ^It cannot be^ necessary ~~for you~~ to make such a declaration to *you,* but you will have the satisfaction in being enabled to give so positive a refutation of this falsehood to others. ~~I will call upon you tomorrow, unless particulary detained~~ —

Yours most aff^ly

AByron

———

Lady Melbourne to Lady Byron (Lovelace 92, f.95)

[May 29, 1816]

My dear Annabella

I was in hopes of hearing from you before this time, but as I have not, I now write to remind you of your promise, as I am extremely anxious to hear how you found Your little Girl, & also some Account of your own Health—I am afraid I must not be Sanguine on this last Subject, as it must be longer before you recover from all you have Suffered but it would give me great satisfaction to know that you are tolerably composed, & that your Strength is returning—

I have been lately in a terrible state of plague & vexation, as you will easily believe—I have no doubt you know to what I allude, as Acc^{ts} must have reached you in ye Country of a most extraordinary publication[28] having appeared in ye World. I wish I could believe they might be exaggerated but that is impossible however I am not quite competent to talk on ye Subject, having been so indignant at ye first 20 Pages, that I read no more, however of course I have been told many circumstances by other people,—but on ye whole am in a state of ignorance about ye contents—Though I think I must soon break thro' my resolution

I heard a good report of L^y Noels Health from L^y Liddell which I should be happy to have confirm'd

believe me

Dear Annabella

Y^{rs} most Aff^{ly}

EMelbourne

29th May

1816

Lady Melbourne to Lady Byron (Lovelace 92, f.97-99)

29th June 1816

My dear Annabella

I am sure you will rejoice to hear that Emily & her little Boy are as well as possible, she rather wish'd for a Girl but is now quite reconciled to this Boy he is such a pretty little fellow, & has every appearance of being very healthy. I am much pleased with the account you give of my Neice, & hope she will continue to improve & that the Sea Air will agree with her, & be of great Service to you, I have considerable faith in its efficacy, & think the effect of it upon Children quite won-derful. I am very far behind you in reading. I had very little time before, but now my being constantly with Emily prevents my having leisure to read a line. The Antiquary[29] I have not seen, & only a quotation from Christabel[30] in ye Newspapers, which did not tempt me to send for ye Poem—I intend soon to begin my Studies, as you have made me eager to read the first—of Glenarvon[31] I have only read yͤ first Vol. & it is so disagreable to me that I do not feel as if I had courage to proceed, I never can excuse yͤ falshoods she tells about Willm[32] & yͤ acc^t she gives of a Society in which she had lived from her Childhood. She knew them perfectly, unfortunately they did not know her, & W^m yͤ least of all,[33] & to this Hour she has the art of deceiving him as to her real character & many other persons besides himself are dupes to her; I am sorry I can not agree with you as to yͤ interest it has excited being transient, on yͤ contrary it is as much talk'd about, as it was at yͤ first—the mixture of Characters[34] upon which you justly observe has had a great tendency to keep curiosity alive, as most people believe there are no fictitious Characters & this is a powerful motive to induce them to read this sort of publication, but it is time to turn to a more agreable Subject & that is Adolphe written by Benjamin Constant[35] of whom you must have heard as his reputation for talent is very high in France—unfortunately he listen'd to Buonaparte at an unfortunate moment just when he return'd from Elba, & his flattery prevail'd, united to his wishing Mon Constant to form a Constitution for France—the bait was swallowed & he & his constitution suffer'd the same fate as Buo^e himself & I believe he can not return to France at least it would be unsafe,[36] Adolphe is hard[l]y to be call'd a Novel as there is no Story and very little incident but it is beautifully written, & a description of a very weak Man, & if you read it you will hardly wonder at his having given way to Napoleon if you believe as people say y^t it is a description of his own Character—I have not heard whether yͤ translation is good or bad, but I am sure it must lose so much that I advise you to read it in French as the language is yͤ great charm—it is only one Short Vol-

I am not so good a person as you seem to think to tell you yͤ News of yͤ day, but I will endeavour to do my best[.] The Duel between Ld Buckingham & Sr Thos Hardy[37] has been the topic for yͤ last Ten days—it arose f^m an idea of L^d B[uckingham] being yͤ Author of several Anonymous Letters concerning L^y Hardy—& what is strange, it has fail'd to clear up yͤ doubts on that Subject—L^d B[uckingham] Still asserting his entire ignorance of these Letters, & Sr Thos continues to think the reasons he had for accusing him, very good, these are yͤ Water mark, & size of yͤ paper, & a resemblance in yͤ hand writing altho disguised

it seems to me quite impossible to form a judgment on ye Subject, every thing one hears being contradictory to what You had heard heard before, the best therefore is to wait patiently till something brings out a disclosure——of course you know that Mrs Lamb is at Paris—she seems to have arrived there at a lucky time to see all ye Fetes, upon ye Duc de Berri's[38] Marriage—they were at it; & she says ye Duc de Berri & several of ye Court being in Henri quatre dresses, gave it ye appearance of a Masquerade—She says it was curious to hear the Ladies among whom she Sat saying to one Another, Mon Dieu comme ceci rapelle—& stopping not daring to go on further or mention Names—& then adding—mais c'est bien en miniature—They went ye next day to see them at dinner & afterwards to ye Ball— where the Duchesse de Berri danc'd quadrilles Waltzes & Country danzes—not beautifuly never having danced them before[.] She seems eager to please very fair & almost pretty, but unluckily she Squints

pray give my Love to my Bro^r & L^y Noel, & believe me
Dear Annabella
Y^rs most Aff^ly
EMelbourne

Lady Melbourne to Lady Byron (Lovelace 92, f.100)

Whitehall
14th Aug^st
1816—

Dear Annabella

not having received any answer to a Letter I wrote you & sent directed to Kirkby some time ago, I begin to think that your departure for the Sea side may have prevented your receiving it, & I am the more anxious to hear from you as I have been told you have been unwell; & I should like to be assured by yourself that you have received ye benefit you expected from the Air of ye Sea, & that it agrees with your little Girl; whilst Children are about their Teeth, I am afraid of Sea bathing for them, as they often have sudden attacks of heat & Fever at those times—but as there are so many new fashions in medecine as well as in dress, I should probably be told by the Profession that I am wrong, & I never dispute with them—I think there is an end to the London amusements at last, the close was brilliant, a party at Carlton House & a party at the Queens House Sunday & Monday last, both very Splendid & very dull—Your Friend the Duke of Gloucester[39] looks fat & happy & comparatively, very lively, & it is but justice to add that she looks well & seems in good Spirits, as it was said that she was unhappy—but I really believe she suffer'd much at leaving the P^ss Sophia,[40] who is in a melancholy State of Health, & to whom she devoted herself entirely—otherwise she seems to appreciate the charms of liberty & appears to enjoy, even, walking about the Streets which she does with the Duke—I am told, they pass'd their time in such confinement that they were allow'd no wills of their own—& it reminds me of a Story told of one of ye late D^ss of Marlboroughs daughters who in describing the delight of being her own Mistress said she could open the Window & hear the Ducks quack—& if the croaking of ye Frogs should be added to it, I suppose the D^ss of G[loucester]—would think it delightful Musick——we have as yet no thought of leaving London at *least* till Emily & Ld Cowper set out for Italy where they mean to pass the Winter

This is a sad grievance to me, so much so that I can hardly bear to think of it & it is a hard task to keep up to my constant maxim—that you must in this life allow Yourself to be as little depress'd as possible & support every thing with as much fortitude as you can muster—they take the two Eldest Children with them, & leave the two Youngest with me, & if when we are in the Country You would be persuaded to come & make me a comfortable Visit & bring Your little one, You would make me very happy & I think there would be a merry little party which would delight us both[.] Pray dont refuse me hastily but keep it in your mind—& we will talk more about it when the time comes——

God bless you Dear Annabella

& believe me

most aff^ly y^rs

EMelbourne

I have a Letter of the 29th July from Mrs G[eorge] Lamb[.] She was on her way to the Dss of D[evonshi]re at Florence—who had promised to meet her & the Cliffords[41] at Geneva but was not well enough to take so long a Journey——

Lady Melbourne to John Cam Hobhouse (Lovelace 377)

18th Ocr 1816

Dear Sir

  I had written to you to Geneva *poste restante,* & I think you should have received it about the time you sent me yrs of ye 11th Sepr or perhaps it may have been lost—which is not of much signification, only, that I should like you to know that I had fulfill'd my promise of giving you an Acct of ye State of Health of a *Lady,* (I never mention names)[42] as soon as I could ascertain it, this I did, & sent you a favourable report written to me, by herself from ye Sea Coast—& which was afterwards confirm'd by her appearance when she return'd to London—where she remain'd nearly three Weeks, which *he* must have heard from his Sister.

  She was looking well in the face & much fatter than when I had last seen her, but her Spirits seem'd very indifferent, & altho' she tried to talk only on common Subjects, & evidently avoided any topics that might lead to others, yet it was easy to perceive that it was an effort, which made it painful to those who were with her, as any restraint that is not entirely concealed always must be—she afterwards went to her Father[']s, and writes me word she has had a return of her complaint which I have no doubt has been occasion'd by their tormenting her, for she says she went to some distance to consult a Physician, who told her that he thought her constitution much weaken'd but that it would recover by avoiding any exertion, it is most probably some of her anxious tiresome friends are continually recurring to past events, which must be heart breaking to her, & produce an irritation very hurtful to her nerves which appear to be much Shattered & harrass'd—in a few days I shall answer her Letter & advise a little more Sea air as a civil way of hinting that ye place where she now is must be consider'd unwholesome—The

Young one she says is without a complaint, really her situation must be consider'd as a very unhappy one & altho she might have conducted herself better, yet she is much to be pitied, as her sufferings must be great; I have just discovered that she refused to see Cᵃ[roline] who offer'd to pay her a Visit when she was in town—Apropos—I hear Madᵉ de Stael is shock'd at the famous publication—& says she will never see Cᵃ[.] I am entertain'd at the intimacy which I hear subsists—& I hope *he* does not give that worthy Man Monsr. Rocca cause for uneasiness,⁴³ for I rather like him, though I believe it arose from pity—I have received the same contradictions from others that you give me, respecting yᵉ reports, & I am inclined to believe they are not credited here & indeed there are so many things that weigh upon yᵉ minds of yᵉ people that I wonder they can think on any other Subject; I mean the general distress, which is so much encreas'd by the very late & bad Harvest that I see nothing but ruin to be expected from it, the necessaries of life rising in price, & yᵉ poorer classes starving forms no pleasing picture & in yᵉ midst of all this Par[liamen]ᵗ is prorogued, & does not meet till Febʸ—ill humour & discontent they tell us prevails all over yᵉ Country & the Ministers are yᵉ only persons who seem not even aware of our Situation—the idea of dissolving Parᵗ is quite given up as I wrote you word in my last Letter,—I have been in yᵉ Country & am just returned to London which I find quite empty,—I hear Mʳ. Wilmot is return'd from abroad & is boasting of having travel'd with Mʳ. Ward & quitted him on yᵉ best of terms—which he says never happen'd to any one before—how pleasant to have yʳ friend give such an Accᵗ of you—

We have had the Princess <Marriskin>⁴⁴ here whom you have of course heard of, her manners & appearance are very pleasing but she is not so beautiful as she has been represented. the route she followed in this Country was very sentimental, as it was yᵉ same yᵉ Emperor took but not yᵉ best for seeing England to advantage being from Oxford to Portsmouth, but it was impossible to prevail upon her to take any other—I suppose she obey'd Orders & she sᵈ to me very naturally, mais qu'est ce qu'on va voir a Oxford⁴⁵—this was a puzzling question from a fine Lady You'll allow—& I could only think of the Velvet Chairs in which the Emperor & Platoff⁴⁶ received yᵉ degree of Doctors, she sd she had heard of them & his being joined with Platoff seem'd to amuse her very much—as she treated the latter with great contempt it seems very hard to have given her such decided orders which she dared not disobey, instead of allowing her to chuse for herself—perhaps as ye Emperor when he was here said *he would have* such an Establishment as Oxford in Russia he might wish for her approbation—If you are with L^d B[yron]—say every thing most kind to him from me

Y^rs very truly

E.M.

[Lady Melbourne to John Cam Hobhouse/A Monsieur/Monsr. Hobhouse/aux soins de/Monsr d'Hentsch et Comie/Banquiers./a Geneve]

Lady Melbourne to Lady Byron (Lovelace 377)

25th Oc^r

1816

Dear Annabella

I wish you could have added to ye agreable intelligence you gave me of my B^r & L^y Noel being quite well; that, of your being so yourself, & as you ask me in my professional character, I shall say y^t I think it a pity you did not remain longer at the Sea side, as that bracing Air seems to agree so much with you that I wish you had given a longer time to fix ye amendment, which was so apparent when I last saw you,—I think this System agrees with Sr H.H.^s[47] opinion for at those places you are quiet, & amused, & you keep early Hours, which I know suit you, & which are probably ye order of the day at Kirkby but then ye Weather has been so damp, & so relaxing that it is no wonder it destroys the good effects of ye Sea air.

I was in ye country last week but we are again return'd to London where we shall remain some days—I intend writing to Mrs Lamb next post & will deliver your Message[48]—

The D^ss of Devonshire weary of ye delays they were obliged to make in their journey on Acc^t of Mrs Cliffords Situation set out to meet them on ye road, which she did at Milan & they returned with her to Florence & I had a Letter to announce their Safe arrival of ye 21st Sep^r———I thought it possible that Emily might overtake them, but she only arrived at Milan on ye 10th Oc^r after having pass'd ye Alps in a Most prosperous manner[;] they went by the Simplon, in perfect admiration (she says) of ye road ye whole way which is quite wonderful & very safe as there is a parapet almost every where & ye ascent & descent are so gradually managed, that they are hardly to be perceived, & no sharp turns any where——— Miss Berry's who are gone to Turin give much ye same Acc^t of the facility with which they crossed Mont Cenis; & owns with some regret as she detests him—that Buonaparte did understand how to make roads—he improved Mont Cenis consider- ably—but ye Simplon he actually made; & for that reason all ye Bourbon-nites tell you it is not passable, Emily heard so from all ye Courtiers at Paris, & they hurried on to Geneva very doubtfull whether they might not be obliged to take ye other road into Italy.

it is wonderful what prejudice will do.—Miss Berry has changed her route, for Mad^e de Coigny[49] wrote from Paris J'ai vu Miss Berry et son vieux pere, qui va a Marseilles, ou peut etre dans l'autre Monde[50]—I understand her object was to see the Staremberg's[51] with whom she was very intimate, when they were in England & he is now Ambassador to ye King of Sardinia—perhaps she did not decide till she was acquainted with the state of ye road—on Acc^t of son Vieux pere, who by ye bye seems to me just as able to undertake such a Journey as either of his Daughters, & enjoys it just as much—

London is quite deserted & except the two play houses there is no Amusement going on. I have been often to Drury Lane as the D[uk]^e of Devonshire lent me his Box, I think Kean seems fat & in good health & acts still better than he did the preceding y^rs & the applause he meets with seems to justify my Opinion, he is going to act Timon of Athens, there are beautiful things in ye play but I should be very doubtfull of its Success, however I understand he thinks otherwise[52]—

The only piece of News I have heard & which You will have seen in the Papers, is M^r. Lambtons Marriage to L^y Louisa Grey which is true[53]

I have at last read the Antiquary & like it prodigiously—I dont even agree with you about ye Antiquary himself for he amuses me very much, as ye Character is so well kept up—pray in y^r next letter send me a good Acc^t of Yourself & let it be soon. I hope ye little Girl continues as well as when you wrote—my two Boys are in perfect health & W^m very entertaining[.]

give my Love to my B^r & L^y Noel & believe me

Ever most aff^ly y^rs

EMelbourne

[London Oc^r Twenty five 1816/The Lady Byron/Kirkby Mallory/Melbourne/Hinkley]

Lady Melbourne to Ralph Milbanke (Lovelace 11, f.97)

[November 12, 1816]

Dear Brother

I received the Letters enclosed this Morning, & also the one directed to you,—Mrs Russells letter requires some explanation which is as follows, the Ten pounds she procured for him was by an application at the meeting for ye Sons of ye Clergy, when she got some person to relate his case—but they would not make an allowance only gave this Sum, which is now exhausted, but without which I really believe this poor Man would have been Starved—for I never heard of a more deplorable case.

in one place she talks of the *Idea I suggested*. This was offering to make him a trifling Allowance Weekly if Russell would do the Same; & and [sic] adding that I would apply to you to ask you to join with us—but you see by her Letter that she has not dared to mention this to him—& he remains in this dreadfull Situation—

I hope you are all well, remember me to L^y Noel & L^y Byron whom I believe is with you—

very aff^ly y^rs,

EMelbourne

Whitehall

12th Nov

1816

Lady Melbourne to Lady Byron (Lovelace 92, f.104-5)

[No date]

Saturday

Dear Annabella

I am very sorry I was not at home when you had the trouble of calling Yesterday.—I think you must be nearly on your return to Kirkby. I should like to see you, therefore perhaps you will either tell me some time at which I can find You at Home, or that you will come & dine with me some day—we have at present no engagement so that you may Suit your own convenience & fix the time, I could give you a Bed, now that George is not in yᵉ House, & a room for your Maid & you might have our Carriage to return to Hampstead—pray think of this, as it will make Lᵈ M[elbourne] & Myself very happy to have yᵉ pleasure of your company

believe me

Yʳˢ most affˡʸ

EMelbourne

If you should not be at home when the Servᵗ takes this Note—send me an answer by yᵉ two penny post

[The/Lady Byron]

Lady Melbourne to Rachel Cowper[54] (Lovelace 11, f.99)

[No Date]

Rachel Cowʳ—

I am very sorry that I can not yet settle any thing with you, as there is Still a Law Suit going on which prevents any of my Brothers affairs from being settled, but as soon as any thing is decided you may depend upon hearing from me & I desire you will let me have your direction that I may know where to send to you—

As you say you are in want of a Situation perhaps you would like to come to me as I have now the place of Still Room Maid Vacant.—

if you think this will suit you let me know directly—as I shall not fill it up till I hear from you—

I give Eight p^{ds} a Year & you have Tea & Sugar—it is a place of trust but not a hard place as you have only the Stewards Room & Housekeepers rooms to Scower—I will pay y^r Journey Up.

EMelbourne

Henry is very well & desires to be remember'd to you—

Notes: Part VI

1. Annabella's daughter, Ada, was born on December 10, 1815 (*LJ* 4:8).
2. Lady Melbourne refers to an incident in which Sir Robert Thomas Wilson, Michael Bruce, and Captain John Hely-Hutchinson assisted in the escape of Count Lavalette, who was held prisoner by the French Bourbons. On January 10, 1816, Lavalette passed the barriers in a cabriolet disguised as a British officer. A narrative of his adventures, which he sent to Earl Grey, was published in *Gentleman's Magazine*. Captured on January 13, the three Englishmen were tried in Paris in April and imprisoned for three months. The Prince Regent expressed his dissatisfaction with the behavior of Wilson and Hutchinson. Opinion started to change on the matter by April 24, when the *Morning Chronicle* objected to the manner in which Wilson and Bruce were being interrogated.
3. Byron admired Kean's acting. In a journal entry of February 19, 1814, he contrasted Kean with John Philip Kemble: "Just returned from seeing Kean in Richard. By Jove, he is a soul! Life—nature—truth—without exaggeration or diminution. Kemble's Hamlet is perfect;—but Hamlet is not Nature. Richard is a man; and Kean is Richard" (*LJ* 3:244). Byron held the same views as late as February 20, 1814. His opinion may have changed when he served on the Drury Lane Committee, along with Mr. Lamb, Mr. Dibdin, and Alexander Rae. In a letter to Alexander Rae, Byron apologized for attacking Kean "because I was heated with wine" (November 19, 1815; 4:333). Kean's biographer argues that their friendship dissolved when Kean, who felt uncomfortable around persons of title, failed to attend Byron's dinner party in favor of the Wolves Club (Hillebrand 154). No such dinner is recorded by Marchand.
   Kean played the part of Sir Giles Overreach in Philip Massinger's *New Way to Pay Old Debts,* which opened on January 12, 1816—just one week before this letter was written (Hillebrand 157). Byron was so affected by Kean's performance as the rapacious extortioner that he was "seized with a sort of convulsive fit" (Marchand, *Portrait* 1:452). At the time, Byron was in debt and bailiffs had appeared in the house that Lady Melbourne had obtained for him.
4. *New Way to Pay Old Debts*. See note 3.
5. Robert Stewart.
6. Count Lavalette, for whom Wilson had in fact obtained a false passport. See note 2.
7. Ralph Milbanke assumed the surname of Noel in 1815.
8. Lady Melbourne wrote to Byron (February 5) and to Judith Milbanke (February 10) about rumors of Byron and Annabella's separation. She also wrote to Sir Ralph (February 12), whom she saw the next day, though he had been in town for twelve days (February 1-12). Her delay in writing to Sir

Ralph was exploited by Judith Milbanke as evidence that Lady Melbourne was taking Byron's side and could not be trusted (Elwin, *Wife* 449).

9. But see her letter to Byron of February 5, 1816 in which she does ask Byron how matters stand with his wife.

10. The signature is cut out.

11. Elwin quotes one edited sentence from this letter (*Wife* 444).

12. Elwin notes that Lady Melbourne saw Sir Ralph on February 13. He had been in London for twelve days (*Wife* 444).

13. Airlie's transcription is missing the first eighteen lines and blends letters addressed to two different audiences. He does not indicate that the second addressee after his ellipses was not Lady Noel but Annabella (*Whig* 166-67).

14. "Arnim" is written in a different pen color. Lady Melbourne may be referring to Louis-Joachim D'Arnheim (1781-1834), a German poet who married the sister of his friend Clement Brentano (1811). D'Arnheim's principal works include popular songs that he edited with Brentano under the title *Des Knaben Wunderhorn* (Heidelberg 1806-8) (*Grande Larousse* 1:34).

15. Countess Harrington.

16. An earlier draft of this section of the letter, beginning with "on this distressing occasion" and proceeding to the end, is in the British Library (45547, f.106): "~~on this distressing occasion——& agree with you,~~ & am miserable ~~at thinking~~ to think what A— must have Suffer'd before she ~~must have~~ resolved to bring such an appeal before the World—as you say justly [in a different ink, as if she went back to add it] you have every consolation from her known Character, as it is not possible that any one can stand higher in publick opinion than she does, or be more beloved by her private friends——& I must add that Ld Byron appeared to me to appreciate her Value most justly for he came to me the day before this report had made its way into ye World & for an Hour talk'd only of her many amiable qualities ~~& stated~~ how much he lov'd her—this you may believe rendered me perfectly incredulous at first, & made it difficult if not impossible for me to believe any thing I heard till I ~~wrote~~ enquired from you—& from whatever cause these unhappy differences may have arisen I must feel extremely sorry for both—at the same time yt I respect ~~his~~ your motives for concealment."

17. The final draft ("what ever may be ye cause of these unhappy differences having arisen") is less provocative to Judith than the earlier draft ("& from whatever cause these unhappy differences may have arisen"). The final draft suggests ignorance of the cause, while the earlier draft faults Annabella and her mother for making more of the "cause" than was warranted (see note 10 for a comparison).

18. Lady Melbourne refers to Sir Ralph's visit on February 13.

19. Malcolm Elwin argues persuasively that Thomas Moore and others have not given adequate attention to the role Byron's financial difficulties played in the failure of his marriage. He had hoped to delay the wedding, knowing that Newstead Abbey and his Rochdale estates could not be sold and that Annabella's father was also in difficult financial straits. Lady Melbourne urged him to proceed with the marriage and did not help matters by renting the overpriced mansion at 13 Piccadilly, which attracted creditors who thought Byron was now in a position to pay his former debts (Elwin, *Wife* 243-46, 304, 327).

20. A letter that appears to be a rough draft of this one is in the British Library (45547, f.99): "You speak of ye necessity of ye measures you have taken, & I have a full reliance upon your Judgment—but knowing as little as I do I confess I wish it would have been settled amicably—& not brought before a tribunal like ye World where every thing of ye sort is discussed & represented with Levity indifference & derision ~~what you~~ & without regard to ye pain it may give[.] every thing that passes between Husband & Wife & ought to be sacred—ye strongest reasons can hardly justify a departure from this rule-that you have them[.] The relative Situation of Husband & Wife is so delicate[,] so unit-

ed[,] & so blended together that both must be affected in some degree by publicity"

Note the broken-off sentence that begins "that you have them" and the effort to repeat this sentiment in the final version of the same sentence. This fragment may belong with 45547, f.106.

21. There is no signature to this letter.

22. A date of 1816 has been indicated in pencil by the curator. This letter does not necessarily form part of the sequence of letters sent in February 1816 and could be any Wednesday of that year.

23. A portion of this letter is also quoted by Elwin (*Wife* 443-45).

24. Two lines have been scratched out and are illegible.

25. This letter is partially quoted by Elwin (*Wife* 447).

26. In 1804 Lady Melbourne had served as an arbitress when Richard, second earl of Lucan, separated from his wife, Elizabeth.

27. Lady Byron refers to the *Morning Chronicle,* which on April 17 published a defense of Byron at the instigation of Hobhouse. The paper spoke of the "atrocious conspiracy against his Lordship's domestic peace." Sir Ralph contradicted the report the following day, writing that "*he knew* of no conspiracy" (Elwin, *Wife* 466-67).

28. Caroline Lamb's *Glenarvon* was published on May 9, 1816.

29. Walter Scott's *The Antiquary* (1816) was the third of the "Waverly" novels (after *Waverly* in 1814 and *Guy Mannering* in 1815) to treat Scottish history from the 1740s to the early 1800s.

30. Coleridge's poem was included in a volume titled *Christabel, Kubla Khan: A Vision, The Pains of Sleep* (1816).

31. Caroline Lamb's roman à clef included satires of almost every member of Lady Melbourne's immediate circle at Holland and Devonshire House. The novel included, in altered form, Byron's farewell letter to Caroline, which had been dictated by Lady Oxford.

32. Caroline's account of William in *Glenarvon* was actually quite favorable. This was one reason why Lady Melbourne could not persuade her son to have his wife declared mentally unfit. The portrait of Lady Melbourne, in the guise of Lady Margaret Buchanan, was far more negative.

33. Despite Emily Cowper and Frederick Lamb's best efforts, William would not agree to a separation from his wife. Lady Melbourne seems to have been against a separation because of the publicity it would cause and the damage it would do to William's political career. She tried to have Caroline Lamb proved insane (G. L. Gower 2:541-43).

34. Perhaps to avoid speculation that she had been faithfully rendered as Lady Margaret Buchanan, Lady Melbourne encourages Annabella to believe that Caroline Lamb blended the characteristics of the society women she represented. Scholars have tended to read *Glenarvon* as a straightforward roman à clef.

35. Benjamin Constant's *Adolphe* (1816), reputed to treat his break with Madame de Staël in 1806, also captures the flavor of his early romance with Madame de Charriere (who was twenty-seven years his senior). At first a harsh critic of Bonaparte, Constant was expelled from the tribunate in 1802. Disappointed when the Bourbon monarchy was restored, he reconciled himself to the Napoleonic Empire of the Hundred Days under the influence of Madame Récamier.

36. In fact, Constant returned to Paris after a short exile and was elected a deputy in 1819 and president of the council of state after the revolution of July 1830.

37. On June 16, 1816, a duel was fought between George Villiers, duke of Buckingham, and Sir Thomas Masterman Hardy. The *Morning Herald* reported that "An hostile meeting took place between the Marquis of Buckingham and Sir Thomas Hardy, at Kilburn Wells. After discharging a brace of pistols each, without effect, the seconds interfered, and an amicable adjustment of differences took place. The quarrel, we understand, originated from some misinformation, received by one of the parties, respecting an infamous anonymous letter, which some base assassin has contrived to circulate, but of

which, we are happy to state, it is now satisfactorily ascertained, the party suspected had not even the remotest knowledge" (June 18, 1816).

38. Charles Ferdinand, duc de Berri, married Caroline Ferdinande Louise on June 17, 1816.

39. Lady Melbourne refers to the marriage of William Frederick, second duke of Gloucester of the fifth creation (1776-1834), to his first cousin Mary, fourth daughter of George III, on August 13, 1816. "Yesterday the Prince Regent held a Court at Carlton House," the *Morning Chronicle* reported, "for the purpose of receiving the Address of Congratulation upon the Marriage of the Princess Mary with the Duke of Glocester &c." (August 14, 1813). The couple lived at Gloucester House, Piccadilly.

40. Princess Sophia (1777-1848), sister of George III.

41. Augustus William Clifford Foster and his wife, Elizabeth Townshend.

42. Lady Byron. This letter challenges the assumption that Byron did not communicate with Lady Melbourne after his separation from Annabella. Rumours of letters sent to Lord Byron from Lady Melbourne would surely have reached Annabella through Caroline Lamb or Lady Melbourne's servants. Byron learned news of his wife through Hobhouse, his closest friend, and others.

43. Lady Melbourne hopes that Lord Byron, who had become more friendly with Madame de Staël, does not give Rocca (de Staël's lover) cause for uneasiness. De Staël offered to serve as a liaison between Byron and his wife in order to facilitate a reconciliation (Marchand, *Portrait* 249).

44. Madame Nareskin [Narischkine] is listed among the guests at a grand dinner party given by the Prince Regent on October 20, 1816 to celebrate Prince Gotchakoff and Count Witgenstin upon their arrival in England. Other guests included the Prince and Princess Esterhazy, the duke de Bourbon, the marquis of Headfort, the Count and Countess Lieven, Mons. de Niemame, Mons. Prefell, Count Pamella, Count Fernan Nun-Duide, Lord Fife, Sir Henry and Lady George Wellesley, Lord W. Gordon, Lord St. Helens, Sir Benjamin Bloomfield, and Mons. Politieu. After tea and coffee, the Countess of Lieven, described as a finished musician, played on Kirkman's newly invented patent octave grand piano-forte (*Morning Chronicle,* October 21, 1816).

45. But what can one go to see at Oxford?

46. Matvei Ivanovich, Count Platov.

47. The physician Sir Henry Halford, who had treated Judith Milbanke for erysipelas and asthma in January 1816 (Mayne, *Life* 332). The erysipelas caused Lady Noel to lose some of her hair, and Byron once stole the wig that she used to conceal this condition—a prank that did nothing to endear him to his mother-in-law.

48. Annabella was close friends with Caro George Lamb.

49. The famous beauty Anne-Francoise-Aimée de Franquetot de Coigny, who was also known as duchess de Fleury.

50. I saw Mrs. Berry and her old father, who went to Marseilles, or perhaps into the next world.

51. George Adam, Count von Staremberg (1724-1807), was the Austrian ambassador in London.

52. Lady Melbourne was prophetic. *Timon of Athens* opened on October 28, played seven times, and was abandoned. The season of 1816-17 was the "dullest" Kean endured (Hillebrand).

53. Lady Melbourne may have read the following, which appeared under "Marriage in High Life" in the *Morning Chronicle* of October 25, 1816: "John G. Lambton, sq. Member for Durham, is about to lead to the Hymeneal altar the beautiful and accomplished Lady Louisa Grey."

54. The "Law Suit" Lady Melbourne refers to in 1816 may be related to her brother's financial troubles which, according to his daughter, very nearly landed him in "Gaol" in April of that year. Judith Milbanke refers to the "recent failures of the Durham and Sunderland Banks [which] have swept away *many thousands*" (Elwin, *Wife* 327). In 1804, Ralph Milbanke was forced to sell his properties in Northumberland at a considerable loss. Banks were failing and he could not obtain a mortgage. In 1812, Ralph Milbanke chose not to offer himself as a candidate for Durham because of the financial strain of election expenses (Elwin, *Wife* 76; 325).

PART VII

The Making of a Diplomat, 1817~1818

𝒥n 1816 Caroline George, George Lamb's wife, had an affair on the continent with Henry Brougham. Always concerned with propriety, Lady Melbourne commented on the embarrassment caused by Brougham's delayed arrival back in England in the House of Commons (April 3, 1817). Further speculation about the couple was created by George's decision to rent out his marital home. By the end of 1817, however, Caroline had returned from the continent and the two were reconciled (November 14, 1817).

Lady Melbourne continued to write to Annabella, but the meetings between them became less frequent. On one occasion, Annabella even visited London without informing her aunt. "What a Naughty undutiful Neice you are, never to have written me a Line," Lady Melbourne wrote (April 21, 1817). Matters had not improved much by November, when she did not know where to direct a letter to Annabella (November 14, 1817).

On November 5, 1817, Princess Charlotte died while giving birth to a still-born boy. In a letter to her son George, Lady Melbourne gave a moving account of the princess' last hours (December 2, 1817). She maintained her contacts at Carlton House, for she still hoped the prince would advance Frederick's diplomatic career. In a letter to her son, in fact, Lady Melbourne described how she tried to find out what Castlereagh had in store for Frederick by quizzing Mr. Tyrwhitt, private secretary to the Prince Regent (December 2, 1817).

The Melbournes moved regularly between Brocket Hall and Whitehall, and the *Morning Chronicle* dutifully charted their peregrinations. Lord Melbourne complained loudly of a cold he caught during one of these journeys, but Lady Melbourne suffered from the more serious complaint of rheumatism. She rode her horse despite the discomfort. "It did my stomach good and if I can get down by Christmas day, & stay a M[on]th I shall be quite well," she wrote to Frederick (December 16, 1817). She wished she had set out for the country six weeks ago, she explained, because the cold "comes on gradually & one don't mind it, though after all London is the Coldest" (December 23, 1817).

The move to the country may have been fatal. By mid-January, Lady Melbourne was treated by Dr. Warren for a bilious condition "& Rheumatism upon strain'd & weaken'd Muscles" (January 16, 1818). Despite her illness, she was consoled by the fact that her son William had finally found a place in Parliament after a four-year hiatus. He was M.P. for Peterborough (1816-19) and was taking a greater interest in public affairs than he had previously. Emily and Lord Cowper were nearby during Lady Melbourne's final days, having returned from their European tour. Still, her son Frederick's lapses in letter writing were painful to her, and in a rare confession of weakness she indicated something of her loneliness: "Why have I no Letters from you deast[.] it is very tormentant" (January 30, 1818).

Lady Melbourne died on April 6, 1818. Frederick returned to England in August, looking "old and *world-beaten*, but still handsome," according to Hary-O (August 21, 1818; Surtees 122). William Lamb wrote the following note to Henry Fox, the warden at Melbourne Hall: "I have to inform you of the Melancholy event of Lady Melbourne's decease, which took place this morning—her end was tranquil & free from pain, but the suffering of her illness had been great—you will communicate this sad intelligence to Mr. Middleton & all at Melbourne."

Lady Melbourne to Caroline George Lamb (45547, f.31-33)

[After 3 April 1817]

I was very sorry to receive a Letter from you of yᵉ 3ᵈ April fᵐ Florence
written under such evident marks of Violent irritation. I do not however intend to
answer you in yᵉ same Stile, but to try yᵉ effect of a plain Statement ~~of facts
towards dispelling the mist with which you seem to be surrounded~~,[1] ~~& if it should~~[2]
appear to you that you see any crossness in what I shall say I beg you will look
upon it as wholly non-intentional, as all I ~~mean or~~ wish to prove is that yr friends
have ~~all along~~ ^always^ & do now mean to act, with yᵉ same affection & kindness
towards towards you as they ~~always have~~ ^have hitherto^ done & which you have
always received in the same manner till this unfortunate *friendship* began,[3] & ~~then~~
^at that time^ you always ~~all along~~ ^were^ pattern ~~of~~ ^for^ amiable quiet feelings
coolness of Judgment, ~~& being perfectly~~ right headedness. That all these qualitys
should have given way, to mis-Statements ^& false representations^ is wonderful—
& that they must be strangely perverted you will allow yourself when you consider, that advice given you by, your oldest most affᵗᵉ & Sincere friends should have
not only been received by you as an Affront, but been yᵉ cause of yʳ immediately
determining to act directly contrary to ~~what~~ certainly ~~was~~ prompted by yᵉ best
motives, & even to afflict by so doing a person who loves you ~~you~~ so tenderly by
this you see I mean the Duchess who certainly has proved her love for you too
much to admit of any doubt—to her I Spoke openly & according to circumstances
which only people *here at yt time* could judge of—& I thought that it would have
been of great advantage if you had delay'd your appearance here for a Mᵗʰ or two
longer when Mʳ. B[rougham] left[.] [Y]ou can not be known to people here. They
only judge ~~of~~ from his arrival ~~here~~ which was not till Febʸ after having been
expected ever since yᵉ beginning of Term where his not appearing caused great
Wonder & from that time till a day or two before the intended opening of Parlᵗ
people were busied in guessing the cause of this delay, & his most intimate friends

were the most clamorous, & often have~~ing~~ I heard their Observations repeated, that a Man embarked in Politicks ought not to be in Love[.] [W]hen I say I often heard y^t Speech it was only repeated to me by one—or two of y^r most intimate friends who are ye only persons to whom I have ever talk'd on the subject—now from ye Middle of Feby to y^e *Middle* of April is but two M^ths not long enough certainly to admit a hope of all this being forgotten—Tho' four or five M^ths might have had y^t effect— I[t] seems to me that all the ~~sorts of~~ reports you mention must cease the instant you arrive & ~~therefore~~ ^for that reason^ they are of so little consequence that it was not worth while to come a day sooner on that account—& in fact M^r B[rougham] has to answer for them all for had he not followed you abroad none of these reports would have existed[,] but it seems to be his system to condemn every thing your friends do—& to think himself exempt from all blame, it is very odd that he should have ye power to persuade you to be of y^t ^y^e same^ opinion & I could not believe it was so untill I received y^r last Letter—neither you nor him I think could be really Angry at those who are so much interested about you; for not approving of his ~~conduct towards~~ ^attention to^ you or of y^r being brought before the Publick in ye way you have been by his attentions—their ~~conduct~~ ^feelings^ have been governed by their affection so they have all acted in the way they thought most likely to be to y^r advantage he ought to feel this & to be obliged to them, instead of reviling & abusing them—if his Love is at all like what love ought to be preferring the happiness & ~~welfare~~ of ye person you love to your own—& sacrificing all y^r feelings to them ~~for that purpose~~ for I do not call a Mad passion Love—

 As to your House I always supposed you & George had settled what was to be done before you went away—you seem to forget what I have so often stated but which is nevertheless perfectly true—that none of us have ever had any conversations with G[eorge] on this Subject, what his thoughts Sentiments or intentions are may be known to you but they are not to us as ye most inflexible Silence ~~but provoked been kept to no~~ ^has been maintained^ for what I know to ye whole but I do not believe that there was ye least intention of keeping you abroad by letting y^r House——when you first left England you know Clifford's[4] intentions were to return at the end of this Summer—& all Georges fears appeared then that the D^{ss} should wish & y^t you should not be able to resist her entreaty to keep you & not allow of y^r returning with him, but which reason I have always remonstrated y^t he made Clifford *promise* not to return without you but as this was only to be at ye en[d] of ye Summer he s^d he should let his House till next Christmas for y^t if you returned in Septr we should probably be at Brocket or that you & he might go some where, till the House was at liberty—when he was assisting in <da^{se}>. ye D[uchess] of Devonshire wrote to me to know if he still intended to let his House by ye desire of Ld Tavistock, & I was oblig^d to write to G[eorge] for information he told me that Weston had orders to let it & knew ye terms & I wished to have it for a longer time to which G would not agree, she afterwards let it to another person—& here you must allow me to observe upon what you say, I shall wait for letters to tell me where I am to go[5] but certainly it is rather foolish to have no idea of its being let with you away while there are Hopes and houses to be let in every Autumn

There was a time you would not have ask'd y^t question when we were in Town—why ye difference Now? it is all worthless—we are ye same

---

Lady Melbourne to Lady Byron (Lovelace 376)

[April 21, 1817]

The Lady Byron
Frognell
Hampstead

Dear Annabella —

what a Naughty undutiful Neice you are, never to have written me a Line
to inform me of your being within my reach, when you know how happy I always
am to see you—I met L^y Barrington[6] accidentally Yesterday Mor^g who informed me
of your present residence, & I should have gone to you to scold you for allowing
me to hear it from a third person if I had not been afraid of missing you, & if you
will be gracious enough to let me know at what times you are likely to be found at
home I shall be most happy to call upon you —I hope to hear that Ada is in perfect
health

> Y^rs most affec^ly
> E Melbourne

21st April 1817

Lady Melbourne to Emily Cowper (45549, f.242)

[July? 1817?][7]

D^st Emily— Dawson I believe has often painted the Lights of ye House, he takes
them off & can paint them in a Shed, but the Wood work of the House for which
there must be a sort of Scaffold & the lights that are fix'd I think were done by the
Painters but it seems to me not near so often as you mention, however it may always
be seen when it is much wanted, & then a little paint is necessary & saves the Wood
and Carpenters do a great deal of painting[.] I think they generally have 7 or 8 p^ds
worth of Paint & <Wd> from Town every Year & Dawson about 3 or four but very
small part of what goes to ye Carpenter is for ye Garden—sometimes they do the
Frames in the <Milan> Ground but I will be more particular when I can look over
ye papers & Glasses Bill, or if you should go over to B[rocket] H[all] Dawson would
tell it you—this is a famous day for ye Country & I hope ye Weather will now be
finer—I went to ye Concert at L^y Hertfords[8] last Night[.] the P[rince]. immediately

attack'd me for a Dinner—<plan> it for Sunday. I have sent him a note to ask if ye Bessb^ghs & Morpeths will be agreable to his R.H. You never saw so odious a place so few people I knew—there was L^y Shelly ashamed of being [manuscript ends]

(45549, f.243, fragment)

which I am sure Thomas is too idle ever to do. but as I think he must be poor & saddled with my Chambermaid Betsy who is idle—pray give him a present from me of a couple of Pounds and tell him I sent it to him as I heard he was out of place

Here's a courier has been kept these three hours for Em to pack up her rosaries? and I'm found at last to interefere & cant allow him ever to sign his name so I finish further, she'll be three quarters of an hour yet, let me do what I can.

Lady Melbourne to Frederick Lamb (HRO)

24th Oct^r,

1817

D^st Frederic

I have two letters of yours to answer and no time to do it in,—first I enclose the receipts for Mince Pies—the Quantity set down is what we make here. I can not think you will want so much, as on Christmas day & new Y^rs day we give them to all the House—this receipt alltogether makes 84 p^d. I lessened it last year as we used to have between a hundred & twenty or thirty p^ds made & we did quite as well. I really think one half would do for you—however that['s] as you like—I dont think on ye receipt that it is express'd that every thing must be minced quite small & mix'd together with great care that it may not be in *Lumps* of one Sort of thinness and then patted down in some Crockery or Earthen ware and <tied> over closely to keep it good, & it will keep 4 or 5 M^ths. There is also the receipt for the pastry, & you must tell him the Shape & Size you like—this pastry is for the Large flat Pies I conceive you mean to describe—& which French Cooks have no idea of & if you dont take the trouble to describe it he will mix all the minced meat into a large Pye—like a Perigord or Strasbourg Pye—I have got the money f^m Snow⁹ now & will pay y^r Bills & send you the receipts by next Post—I dont care how many Commissions you give me, & now I can send *any thing* to M^r. Bidwell who is now returned to Town after an Absence of 2 or 3 M^ths. I have written to him to ~~tell~~ ^send^ you ye Embassy to China,¹⁰ which by ye bye seems to me by ye extracts in ye News papers to be a very flippant arrogant production for a young Man, & quite in ye Stile of ye Canning Statesmen,¹¹ how absurd not to settle before they went whether they would go thro' ye ceremonies which they knew would be required— & after all I think *quand on est a Rome, il faut faire comme on fait a Rome*¹²———I have just done up your Seal & sent it to Mr Bidwell, & also your Flannel. 24 y^ds in two parcels 12 y^ds in each. A piece runs to near 80 y^ds & by these parcels you may judge of the *Volume* of it. it would have required three Bidwells to manage & send it, if you want more let me know. You will find this very fine & so Woolly that you can feel no threads which I reckon the great perfection of flannel—I send the Bill perhaps you'll think it dear but it is cheap for such fine flannel—Your tricot I must have more time to chuse & wont send it unless I think it exactly what you mean— as to ye Dresden Linnen I am much obliged but am not much in want of *very fine* Table Linnen however if you have an Opportunity I should like you to enquire what a Table Cloth 4 y^ds long and three Yards Wide would cost of good Linnen, fine to be sure but not Superlatively So—& what this Napkins would be p^r Doz to suit it—our yard is three foot—or 36 In^c—I don't know y^r Measure but the french foot & the In^c are both longer than ours I believe—at least I know their foot contains 13 of our In^c. The Brussells y^d. is only two thirds of ours— ———perhaps you may make something out by this

28th Oct 1817

Dearest Fred—in my last I really had not ye grace to thank you about the Horse ride that I forgot it but I had so many other things to say—I should not like to ride so tall a Horse, it is very uncomfortable & I have always rode low Horses. Jersey was ye tallest I ever had & kinder being rough is ye only fault I have with my Mare—she really carrys me very well, I can't say of her as you do of y^rs that she never made a false Step—but she never has fall'n with any one & particularly not with L^d M—which somehow or another all Horses do, that have y^t inclination but do believe how much I am obliged to you, her Brother[13] whom you mention was sold soon after you went, as he cut so much on ye road but if you ever see a clever strong Active low Horse, continue to try him & if he is safe & good temper'd I always think all ye rest may be brought about by good treatment & quiet riding— When I sent the last Letter I wrote you I sent M^r. Bidwell y^r Seal & the Flannel in two parcels—& I had before wrote to him about sending Mr. Ellis's Book———

Yesterday I went about the Tricot to what they tell me is one of ye first shops now in London for Gentlemen's dress & I found what you wish'd for & the Man assured me the finest that could be made, & which they had done for ye Marquis of Abercorn & had it made on purpose—I have ordered two pieces, which I concluded were to make 2 p^rs pantaloons it is very dear less the <87> a Y^d—The Man promised to send it here this Morn^g & if he does it shall go to M^r. B, & if not, next post day—remember this is not bought at a trumpers Cable Shop for cheapness, but a very fine Shop—& when I was there y^t Man took it into his head to sell me a Pelisse, & produced Some of the most beautiful Cloth I ever Saw made of Saxon Wool, which he says is the finest in ye World Much Superior to Merins[14]—& he Says the Landgrav of these has ye finest flock known of this Sort of Sheep—the Cloth was 28^d p^r y^d—now as I never heard of these Sheep I am curious about them & I wish you would give me some information if you can get it—Ben King is come home looks fat well & in good Sp^ts, he dined here Yesterday, & is gone to Hatfield to day, he enquired much about you, & longs to go & see you from y^e. Acc^t I gave him of your comfortable way of Living—he travelled from Florence with Bob Smith,[15]— so now its all bob Smith,—who has seen you somewhere Lately—I find f^m him that L^y. G.W. makes a most amazing fuss about the dullness of M—& that they would not be Surprised if she was to return with her Brother for a short time. This I can not believe but he adds that their Hearts & Souls are set upon going to Vienna—& that it is thought by their friends that the Duke will be able to do that for them— you know one always *finds* out a great deal f^m this same B[en]- K[ing]-[.] I send you a long Letter from Emily, so that I shall say nothing about her, W^m & C[aroline] are not yet come from Brighton. The wine is come & p^d for, but they say it must stand 3 M^ths before it can be Bottled—Y^r- draft was 60 L. & the expense into the Cellar in ye Casks is 40—5—0 which all together supposing each run 15 Doz[en] will be 3-6- 6 p^r Doz^n—& something more, but ye wise Men say it will only run 14 Doz—how- ever altogether it will come cheap I think not more than 6^s a Bottle—it was Aglue de Gramont—I remember I wrote S^t. Jules by mistake——I must put off till next post answering all the other parts of your Letter, as I must go out[.] we are come back to London. Em & L^d C[owper]- come ye beg^n of November & I hope we shall even go into ye Country. L^d M[elbourne] sends his Love God bless you D^st Frederick

Aff^ly y^rs,

EM

I must add a Story about ye King of France which I think almost better as being more liberal than most things one has heard of ye last—S^r. F Burdett's son[16] in a drunken frolick went into ye Streets of Paris calling out vive L'empereur & other abuse of ye present—he was taken up and put in prison, & this *made* prodigious noise—& told to ye King who s^d Oh that's an unfortunate young man who has late- ly had a Severe blow to his Head, it must be in consequence of that; he must be liberated—& this was done Accordingly—& no mention has been made of it, in ye French papers—God bless you dearest Frederic there is no news Stirring L^d M[elbourne] sends his love

Aff^ly y^rs,

EM—

I send y^r receipts by this post, & as this tricot is just come I enclose ye Letter remember & tell y^r cook that she <said> for ye Mince Pyes must be hashed very fine by itself & the other things by themselves—& then put together & minced & minced together over & over again. I think y^t was not fully explained in ye receipt

don't you remember when you were a boy that you had an odd erruption which came out in large red blotches and that Sal Volatile[17] cured you, a Teaspoonful taken in Water twice or three times a day. This you might try but not push it too far, as it impoverishes the Blood—

Lady Melbourne to Lady Byron (Lovelace 92, f.111-12)

14th Nov^r

1817

Dear Annabella

I am writing to L^y Noel & shall add a few lines to You to say that I am very happy to hear so good an Acc^t of you & of Ada & that I should have made some enquirys long ago, had I known where you were, or how to direct a Letter to you

We have had a most melancholy time here since ye untimely fate of P^ss Charlotte[18]—for very unluckily, Emily & Ld Cowper had settled to be in Town just now on their way, to some of their Friends house, where they had intended to go;

this had kept us here, & upon this melancholy event all their Visits were postponed & we have all remained here, where the greatest gloom has taken place for all ranks of persons feel it as a personal Misfortune to themselves

There are Several people in Town but nobody meets, as every one wishes to avoid even ye Appearance of a party—George & Mrs Lamb are with us till their House is at Liberty & I am sure you will be glad to hear, y^t she looks & is quite well & has recover'd Some embonpoint[19]—when she arrived fm the continent She was terribly thin, but now, looks better than when she set out—

I hope you intend to pass some time in Town this Winter & that I shall have an Opportunity of making an Acquaintance with my great Neice

If you should come either in Decr or January, I hope you will visit me at B.H.[20] where I flatter myself I shall pass both those Months—L^d M[elbourne] begs to be kindly remember'd & believe me

Aff^ly y^rs.

EMelbourne

Lady Melbourne to Frederick Lamb (HRO F73/ELb)

Decr 2^d, 1817

D^st Fred

as I wrote last post I must confess that I was not going to write to you to day but y^r Letter (the last parts of it the 25th) has altered my determination, & I must thank you for it by ye return of ye post—I think in my last I gave you an Acc^t- of Clarke's Sermons,[21] I will now tell you of another, but I cannot recollect ye Mans name; he prayed to God to comfort & assist a Father depriv'd of his only Child & having no hope of Future Progeny, which must send his Grey Hairs to ye Grave in Sorrow—Ld G. who writes me this, adds, what a waste of Money there has been in Ten Guinea Wages—it is now known by yᵉ proclamation that Par[liamen]ᵗ meets the 27ᵗʰ Janʸ & it is positively said that it will be disolved the 25ᵗʰ March following——I perfectly agree with you about yᵉ probability of a quarrel for yᵉ reasons you assign altho' at present there are no Symptoms. I approve of yʳ reasoning very much & think that is yᵉ proper way affairs should be happened—I can not give you or your Doctor any Satisfatory Acc'ᵗ about yᵉ poor Pss for I have not heard her death Accounted for, & I believe the Medical people themselves are puzzled[.] You shall have Croft's Acc'ᵗ to a lady soon afterwards for yʳ Doctor—from yᵉ first of her being taken ill *there* appear'd a great Sluggishness—nothing came forward. The pains seem'd to do no good, when she lay down or Sat down no pains came on, but only when she was walking about. She was not ill, & the labour came on ^well only^ so Slowly that *I believe* there was no question of arresting it. When she was brought to bed Crofts found what we call here an *Hour* glass Seizure coming on, & on that Acc'ᵗ forced away, what should have come away naturally—this Hour glass Seizure I don't know how to explain except that it is a contraction which the Shape of an Hour Glass will explain.²² After this, she was perfectly well, & in two Hʳˢ they gave a most favourable Accᵗ—& all Sign'd it, Crofts went into yᵉ next room as P Leopold²³ came into his & was dissuading ^Dr.^ *Sims*²⁴ from going to Town so Soon, (which has always made me Suspect he was not quite Satisfied) when yᵉ Prince came in & told him the Pss wanted him, he went, she sᵈ, I am happiest when you are bye me, he answer'd then I will not leave you all Night; he then felt her Pulse & found it so feeble that he gave her Brandy & Water & sent for Bayley²⁵ who came, and desired more Brandy to be given, & this they did repeatedly for 2 Hʳˢ & 1/2 till she expired, having just before ask'd if there was danger, they sᵈ no & beg'd her to be composed she Answer'd so & Bayley who held her hand, said she's gone—This is a melancholy detail, but I believe it to be very correct—There is a report of Something being wrong in the formation of those parts, but I don't know if it is true or not,——I wonder there never has been a report publish'd of yᵉ report of yᵉ Physicians about yᵉ Morning after death—I believe it to have been a peculiar case and of those which happen once in a thousand times & as to exhaustion many Women have been four & five days in labour & done well————if I hear any other Acc't from good Authority you shall have them——certainly some Vessel may have given way internally & I should think that most probable but they dont say so; what ever it was, they were not aware of the danger——I must finish.

	[L.s.d.]
Mss. Campbell	5.13.0
Fox for Tricot	3.4.0
Map of Rivers	0.9.0
	9.7.0

Rec'd of Miss Inn.

	10.3.0
	9.7.0
	16.0

You made a mistake in ye bill for Tricot, as you stated it to be 4 L, & this has left me with 16 in hand agst ye next payt. you may want me to make——I enclose you a Bill fm Mss Campbell for fifteen yds of flannel which I have sent in two parcels to the foreign office & I think you will find it softer than the last, which I had chosen in preference as being warmer, by being a little thicker which I thought you might like better but I hope you will find this more to your taste; it is 6d a yd dearer——

I have sent to ye foreign Office; also, the Map of the Rivers which I hope you will receive Safe——now I have done with business dearest Fred & must for yr amusement tell you a matrimonial conversation between Ld. & Ly Worcester[26]——you have heard of Miss Foote, it was sd yt she had insisted on a Settlement of 500 per Annum & it was also stated that Miss Foote's father used to sell a famous sort of blacking for shoes. Ld W[orcester] on coming into the room was greeted with Well Worcester you have done it to day your shoes are better black'd than ever quite beautifull——he retorted if you plague me about the blacking of my Shoes, I'll talk to you about Francis Russell. Aye said she——but I don't give him 500 a Year.

In walking Yesterday I met S^r T[homas] Tyrrwhit,^27 well he s^d, I have not been at Offenbach[.] This time the Bird was flown. Oh I s^d, I suppose it was when he went to the Baths of Baden—says he, I think he'll have a step soon, where s^d I, after humming & hawing & evidently knowing nothing of the matter, in a low Whisper he s^d—I don't think L^d S[tewart].^28 will go back[.] Oh I said I think he will[;] he has behaved *too well* to be displaced well he s^d I am sure he's (Fred) is very high in their opinion, indeed the P[rince]- told me he would in time make a most distinguishd Minister—isn't this so like ye twaddle of a foolish courtier[.] I went home & Ben King came to me, I began laughing at what had passed between S^r T[yrwhitt] & me & telling it him—to my Surprise he put on a very important look & s^d he has no chance of that,—Lord I s^d, I know y^t, besides L^d. Stewart will go back. Oh but if he did not he has no chance, y^t is promised—what! I said to S^r. <N> Wellesly^29 he Nodded a Yes, not daring Speak it. Oh I s^d there are fifty people wanting it & here it ended, but you see they think themselves sure,—& I would rather *bet* they'll be bit—God help you dearest Fred I go to Panshanger^30 tomorrow to stay there 3 or 4 days before they go to Middleton where I shall not go but remain here to get things to Brocket to be ready for them when they return as they are to come there. I mean to ride—as much as I can for I have not been quite well lately. My stomach has been out of sorts & I expect that it will cure me, I have also got a good deal of Rheumatism in my Knee which makes me think of you as you always complain of it, I believe it always comes whenever there has been a Strain, George & Caro are returned from H^d house & he will read loud and puzzles me so[.] God help you. L^d. M[elbourne] would send his love but is fast Asleep upon the opposite Couch—Ever D^st Fred

Most aff^ly y^rs,

EM

8th Dec^r
1817

Lady Melbourne to Frederick Lamb (45546, f.222)

16th Dec^r, 1817

Dear Fred,

I write you a few Lines to day merely that you may not say I am imitating y^r idleness, for I have really nothing to tell you, but that Em[ily] & Ld Cowper are going to Middleton and we are return'd to London and that we have order'd the Waggon up on Friday sent to move some plate and that L^d M[elbourne] is as cross as <parson> on that Acc^t—& says he shall be ill all ye time he is in the Country— how very unlucky that he should have had a violent pain in his face all the time he was at Panshanger[. He] caught cold I believe on the way down for there was no other reason for his having it and warmth cured it in two days. I took a rheuma- tism with me and have brought it back. I rode my Mare the first day which was very fine and she went delightfully but ye next it froze quite hard and was so Slippery I could not venture, & so it was the 3^d, & ye 4th we came back. There's my History, it did my stomach good and if I can get down by Christmas day, & stay a M[on]th I shall be quite well—They have at Middleton M^r. & L^y Elizth Fielding—L^d & L^y Worcester Ld Glengall & L^d E Butler, F[rancis] Russell &, M^r. Luttrell[31]—Fred <Brying>[32] has just been here and we agreed y^t we did not think this a tempting list, for we should be puzzled what to do with our Eyes, where ever they look'd someone would say how satirical you are—y^{re} inclined to quiz every body—what did you mean by looking at me at dinner &c. &c.— —

don't you think this is true—perhaps you would think it good fun—& so should I perhaps for one day, if I could drop amongst them without the trouble of going. Ben King is in town & going to Brocket to morrow the fool is so heated with ye amiable reception Caroline has given him y^t when she writes to entreat him to come into ye Country and bring Bob <Smith> he don't see the *Sit* of ye note but thinks it is pour ses beaux yeux & tells people that he thinks she has good quali- ties—this out of my hearing. I shall have my revenge, no doubt. I hope she will try to play him some d- trick—I hear it is reported at Paris that Ld Clare is to marry Miss Seymour. it may be true, but I doubt it because Ld Clare and Miss Fitzherbert[33] were living very much together & I think people will surmise it,—however, she may like him altho' the Sizes do not agree—I shall be sorry as it is just what a young smart Gen^e would prefer—a Man of Fashion, & a decided Tory, & a great deal of fun will be Spoil'd as this same Cuyler[34] finds the dandy of the desert such a thorn in his Side, that I am sure he dreams of him and his attentions to her every Night—& thinks he sees her look & fancies she passes a Secret when it is much more likely she should do anything in Secret than that—You can not think what fun this was to me last Winter, & I shall be sorry if I am cut Loose of it this Winter——Fordwych[35] is coming here to day for ye hollidays: I cannot say how much I love y^t boy—so Natural so unassuming & pleasant & affectionate so clever at his Books—I never saw any thing like him. George is also at home and has done very well at ye India college where he has been ye last quarter at the examinations which take place every quarter, he got two prizes, one for *French* & one for Classics & was second for Mathematics & Bengalese. This in a class of Eleven. I am ye more pleased as Caroline is always so ill natur'd to him, & prophesied he would not get thro' the common business

Aff^ly y^rs EM

—L[ord] M[elbourne]'s love,

Note on envelope:

Your razors are come back by now reaching you I hope & desired, & all ye parcels I had to send except a Stilton Cheese which I shall now send in a day or two
[The Honorable Frederick Lamb, Frankfort]

Lady Melbourne to Frederick Lamb (45546, f.224)

23d December 1817

Dst Fred   I am laughing at all yr. projects for boring me which have completely failed—when I came home yesterday Morg I was presented with yr Letters
& a Card of Mr St. G36—who had call'd with them when I was out—Ld M[elbourne]
was much distress'd at his not having given in ye place of his residence upon his
Card, & was dying to go & see him. This Morng he call'd again but being accustom'd to foreign Hours, I had not left my address and George Foster knew better
than to let a stranger in to Ld M[elbourne], so here was another failure, & Ld.
M[elbourne]. having slept upon it was no longer so anxious to see him altho' he left
his directions this time, however he is now going to see him but as he will not be
there till near five I think foreign Hours will have sent Mr St G out to Dinner, & he
will leave a note which I have given him to say how sorry I am that we leave Town
to morrow, but hope to see him at my return—we are really going to spend our
Christmas in the country and to remain till the meeting of Parlt—Your messages to
the <Duke> & Sir G Robinson shall be duly given & yr Secret duly kept, tho' I was
told of ye last of ye two Benedricks this month—Emily & Ld Cow stay at Middleton
& do not come till the end of the Week—the whole World have been there—my
Rheumatism is somewhat better perhaps riding will cure it, but I am afraid here's a
hard frost beginning, it is terrible to be in ye Country when ye *Weather* is so cold,
we should have been there 6 Weeks ago & then it comes on gradually & one don't
mind it, though after all London is the Coldest——This is a Short Letter Dearest
Fred but I am in ye midst of packing & will write a longer one to Em—I have sent
in an office Frank as [it]37 was too heavy—by ye bye I can not get you I think a
good Stilton & I think better not send a bad One—The Cheesemongers say they

have not ripened kindly. last Summer was so cold I do not wonder at it—but this is yᵉ first that I could not find one to send you

Affˡʸ yʳˢ EM— —Fordwich says he

hopes <all> is well—

[The Honorable Frederick Lamb/&c &c &c Frankfort]

Lady Melbourne to Frederick Melbourne (45546, f.226)

Melbourne Hall

16ᵗʰ Janʸ,

1818

Dearest Frederick,

Emily wrote to you last Friday & I intended to have done the same last Tuesday but being in yᵉ Country I miss'd the day & forgot to write on the Monday—We are now come to Tuesday, & Emily has sent me a Letter for you from Panshanger for the post—I have been going on with Mr. Lucas whose Medicines certainly did me some good but so very slowly that I determin'd to come to Town & having found Farquhar ill, I have seen Warren,[38] & am now under yᵉ influence of some of his large doses,—as he says my complaint is Bilious & Rheumatism upon strain'd & weaken'd Muscles—I was cupp'd[39] on my knee at Brocket but the only use I have as you found from it has been such Soreness & tenderness that I can hardly tell whether I have any pain in it, or not, yᵉ other being so much more troublesome

I think in one of my Letters I mentioned to you some hints that had been given me about Cuyler's intending to reward a person—so I think I added if this be done I shall believe it & time will show—are you up to it? I have only been in Town 2 days, & have seen Nobody as my Rheumatism is too painfull to allow me to chat with dandy's—but Mr D came to me last Night & says y[t] y[e] app[t] you see in y[e] Newspapers of Sir W[m] Knighton[40] to one of y[e] Situations in Cornwall causes much Awk[ss] as he is in Dorsetshire Manor & in a line that seems to me [to] lack app[ts]—what will our *Friend be.*   I suppose he'll have y[e] next because of y[e] sort—as at least expect it——you have of course read Hone's trial & will not read L[d] Sefton's Letter[.][41] poor Man he is very ill in Lancashire—another sort of event is also much y[e] topic of conversation—I mean where a Lady is concerned—& Wme de Roz[42] who has taken himself off to Paris[.] I don't believe he was to blame except that he talk'd—a prevailing System among young Men now. She is a pretty girl, but like her family is Mad, I can't bear their having allowed of this Publicity instead of sending her away into y[e] Country & hushing it up—God Bless you Dearest Frederick Most aff[ly] y[rs],

EM

L[d] M sends a thousand loves to you[43]

[The Honorable Frederic Lamb, Frankfort]

Lady Melbourne to Frederick Lamb (HRO)

[January 23, 1818]

D[st] Frederic

on Tuesday last I had pen ink & paper lying before me & s[d] twenty times, I am going to write to Fred—& it ended in my finding it 1/2 past five before

I suspected it was four[.] in my last I wrote you word I was under Warren's care, & I really am much the better in Health—& I am convinced if I could go out I should be quite well but yᵉ Rheumatism continues, & yᵉ pain of it not to be endured. I have better Nights and yᵉ pain is greater in the day when I don't move, but then I get the fidgets & must move, altho yᵉ consequence is an Acute pain in my knee or Thigh or down my Leg. Next post I hope I shall be able to write You a better account, & so says Warren for he is attacking this pain with all his Skill—

    <Nurky> is in town without her & dines here frequently—he had seen Lᵈ Stewart where he has been, who sᵈ he should go to Vienna, forthright—he has been at Brighton with the Prince who has given him a Lodge upon some of yᵉ Forests, & he told Nʸ he intended to lay bye out of his Sallary 500 pᵉʳ An for 4 or 5 Yʳˢ which would make it a very comfortable habitation.—

    I have a remonstrance to make you from Lᵈ Melbourne who is really quite uneasy at yʳ not having written lately. You can not think how much he talks about it. Therefore convey news. Mʳˢ. Damer is just come in & was received with—I must finish my Letter—she desires her love to you—God bless you, Dˢᵗ Fred—

                Mst affˡʸ Yʳˢ

                EM

23ᵈ Janʸ

1818

[The Honᵇˡᵉ/Frederic Lamb/ &c. &c. &c./Frankfort]

Lady Melbourne to Frederick Lamb (HRO)

30th Jan^y

1818

Dearest Frederic:

There never was so Stupid a meeting of Par^t—there seems to be nothing to
do. W^m says the real difficulties of ye country begin to appear—although the
Speeches are all fill'd with its prosperity.

I am still unwell & in pain but I think I walk better to day than I have
done yet, & with less pain. Emily and Ld Cow come to town & the Children are all
well.—Why have I no Letters from you dea^st[.] it is very tormentant—you told me
once that when you did not write, you were as much plagued about it as I was—
but this is no consolation to me—who only want to hear from you & not to
plague you

L^d M[elbourne] has got a touch of ye gout but I hope it will only be a touch
as it seems going off but it has made him very low—George is at last quite out of
Drury Lane, & his Successor chosen Yesterday—what do you think of L^d.
Yarmouth.⁴⁴ They had a dinner at Kinnairds Yesterday where there were Narns &
Colman⁴⁵ y^e [torn text] to know something of Lord Y[armouth]'s future intentions
declared afterwards that he was the same Ld Burleigh—God bless you Dearest
Frederick L^d M[elbourne] sends his Love—& believe me

most aff^ly y^rs.

EM

Lady Melbourne to Frederick Melbourne (45546, f.228)

17th Feb^{ry} [1818]

Dearest Fred

I can not get rid of these pains I have had them very bad this last Week to day they seem to be a little quieter—nothing appears to take hold of them and do ye least good but some Sedative Medicines & that is only temporary & makes me heavy & drowsy all day

I have been tired by ingesting—all sorts of things[.] I think I told you of this Indian Oil, then the tincuary of laudanum then ye plants ground, next I shall try y^r Spirits of Wine

I do not hear many things now and cannot go Pumping about but I heard the other day that it was very unlikely that ye beautiful flowers should carry the point; there are many objections here and besides it is very unlikely that in these times they should like to show that it is such a Sinecure—these are the reasonings of the people here & so may be all set aside, & the more so because they are just

L^d. Stewart is going back[.] the P[rince]- has given him a Lodge upon The Forest of Dun[;] he told some person that it was no grand palace now but that he should buy up 300 p^d a y^r while he stay'd at Vienna & as he should remain there 5 or Ten y^{rs} it would just make the Sum that would make this Lodge *Beautifull*

There has been a most disagreeable report about here lately and the most absurd that can be conceived to gain universal belief—It was s^d the D^{ss} of D[evonshir]^e is turn'd Catholic & from a remord de conscience confes'd that, the Child of which the D^{ss} lay in, died, & she put one of her own in its place; nothing can be more foolish than crediting one word of it. This was [the] time when the D[uches]s lay in near Paris & when as much fuss was made about it as if she had been a Queen and as much patheuse—, God bless You dearest Fred I must finish & L^d M[elbourne]'s love[.] he is much better and I might almost say quite well for he has only a little Weakness left—I hope to send you good Acc^{ts} of myself soon most aff[ectionate]ly Drst Fred

Yrs

EMelbourne

Lady Melbourne to Frederick Lamb (45546, f.230)

18th Feby 1818

Dearest Frederick

I have at last had the Satisfaction of hearing from you as yr. letter of the 26th of Jany arrived two days ago—I told Warren yr caution about Spirits of wine & he sd that was ye most sensible prescription he ever heard a Gentleman make & he was afraid he must have suffered a great deal in acquiring his knowledge[.] he always flatters himself—that he has cured the inflammation about me & that only ye aching remains but I shall prove his error to him to day as some Rygrathee Oil which I tried last night has added to ye pain[.] do you know no cooling embrocation[?] If you do send me the receipt—My Stomach is better but ye pain is not to be endured at times[.] My gout is going off—and so is Lord Melbourne—by ye bye Perhaps Ld Cowper's Doctor says you gave him a commission for <Heidle's> cases & etc.—which he sent you but they cost 16L 8d more than you gave him & that the Bill was in the inside of ye Parcel—& he wants me to pay him—Shall I—? The Weather is colder than you can conceive White frost & no Sun—poor Sir Walter can not recover—I must finish Dearest Frederick so God bless you—Ld M[elbourne]'[s] Love & I am most affecly yrs

EM

What do you say abroad of our marriage I wish I could send you a letter I rec'd this morning from Ld E[gremon]t

Lady Melbourne to Frederick Lamb (HRO)

[March 13, 1818]

My Dst dear Fred

Emily is gone out of Town for 2 or 3 days & promis'd me to write to you before she went but as Ladys do not always keep their word I send you a few lines. I am in great pain & go into a Warm Bath twice a day, which they assure me does great good tho' I do not think it does—my pain is in my thigh, my knees & down my Leg & into my Foot which is & sometimes I wish'd not unlike the Gout but my Thigh & my knee are the painful points & prevent my putting Myself in a State of ease to write with any comfort—I had written this ye other day but Emily having call'd and told me she wrote to you I did not send it—she does not come back till to morrow[.] There never were such Storms & a number of Trees blown down not large nor in View I hope———W^m made a Very fine Speech ye other Night[.] The matter is another case[.] He made B^{m46} very Angry I believe but I don't know much about it— God bless you Dst Fred[.] if I could write a Word that I was released from the pain I should be very happy most aff^{ly} y^{rs},

EM

Friday

13 March

1818

William Lamb to Henry Fox (Melbourne 234/6/15)

[April 6, 1818]

I have to inform you of the Melancholy event of Lady Melbourne's decease, which took place this morning—her end was tranquil & free from pain, but the suffering of her illness had been great—you will communicate this sad intelligence to Mr. Middleton & all at Melbourne.

[6 April, 1818, Whitehall]

William Lamb, 2nd Viscount Melbourne[47] *to Lady Noel Byron (Lovelace 376)*

Whitehall

[Saturday] March 6, 1830

My Dear Lady Byron

      I find your note upon my return from the Country, Whither I Went early this Morning—I am truly sorry to hear of your being so unwell—The More I think of the Matter,[48] the More I am anxious that it should be settled if possible, by Moore's[49] Making such a retraction as would render any publication upon your part unnecessary—I come to this Conclusion disinterestedly, & solely upon Consideration of what appears to me would be the best for all parties, & particularly for you—for as to myself, tho' I do not care much about the Matter, yet I own I feel so much remains of resentment, as would make me rather glad than otherwise of any thing which should tend to unmask his real Character & show it in its true Colours—I do not know any better way of effecting the above object, than that of communicating with Moore through Ld Holland, & for that purpose if you approve it, I will ask L^d H to go down to see you, which I have no doubt he will readily do, or if you feel yourself unequal to such an interview I will Speak to him upon the matter myself, tho' I think it would be better, that you should see him, because you can explain & impress upon him your own peculiar feelings more strongly, than I should be able to do—Let me know which of these Courses you prefer—

                      Yours faithfully & affectionately,

                      Melbourne

William Lamb, 2nd Viscount Melbourne to Lady Noel Byron (Lovelace 92, f.120)

The Lady Byron
Hanger Hill.
Whitehall

[Thursday] March 18, 1830

My dear Cousin

I found your note here yesterday Evening, upon my return from Brocket—I met L^d & Lady Holland at dinner & the latter said to me have you heard how handsomely little Moore has behaved in offering to bind up Lady B^s Statement with his second edition—I answered that I had heard of the offer from you—& asked her whether it had been made directly from Moore to you or through Ld Holland—She said the latter & added, not that he (Moore) means to retract any thing he has written, but that he thinks that both Parties have a right to be heard—I just tell you this in order that you may be aware of the manner, in which this offer is considered & represented—Ld Holland said nothing to me upon the subject nor I to him—I should like to know the exact terms in which the offer has been conveyed to you, as they might make some difference in my opinion, but upon the whole I should rather incline to that which appears to be from our view namely that you should pursue your own course, leaving him of course at liberty to pursue his & to insert the Statement in his second edition, if he thinks proper—Were you to acquiesce in his proposal, it seems to me that it would appear as if you were perfectly satisfied with his Conduct & would be upon the Whole, as you express it, forming a junction with him which strikes me as being of doubtful policy—at the same time the matter requires to be well considered, as he has many friends amongst those, whose good opinions are worth preserving, & your conduct in this Matter will be subjected to very severe, & even hostile Scrutiny & observation—

The Weather yesterday was very Mild—I hope it has done you & Ada good—

Yours affectionately

Melbourne

Notes: Part VII

1. These words are crossed out lightly with a single horizontal line.
2. The last four words, necessary to preserve the meaning of the sentence, are mistakenly crossed out as well.
3. Caro George's affair with Henry Brougham, which took place in Italy and the south of France in April 1817. Frederick Lamb wrote about Brougham in scathing terms even before the affair began.
4. Augustus William Clifford Foster.
5. The remainder of this sentence is written between the lines.
6. Possibly the wife of the bishop of Durham, Shute Barrington.
7. This letter is undated but is placed in the British Museum file before the July letter from Emily Cowper. The chronological sequence employed here follows that of the curators at the British Library.
8. Marchioness Isabella Hertford, a bluestocking, with whom the Prince of Wales had developed an infatuation in 1808 (Villiers 216).
9. Snow served as a banker for the Melbournes in their overseas transactions with Frederick.
10. Lady Melbourne is teasing her son. In 1816-17 Sir George Thomas Staunton served as the king's commissioner of the embassy to China.
11. George Canning's wit and venom made him a number of enemies. The fact that he was a supporter of Pitt did nothing to improve Lady Melbourne's opinion of him.
12. When one is at Rome, one must do as the Romans do.
13. The brother of the mare.
14. Merino: a breed of fine-wooled white sheep originating in Spain and widely popular, especially on the ranges of America and Australia.
15. Possibly Robert John Smith or Robert Percy Smith.
16. Robert Burdett, sixth baronet (1844), whose father was Sir Francis Burdett.
17. Sal Volatile: Ammonium carbonate; volatile salt.
18. Princess Charlotte died on November 6, 1817, five and one-half hours after giving birth to a still-born baby. Her death and the baby's broke the direct line of the English monarchs and eventually led to the accession of Queen Victoria.
19. *embonpoint:* plumpness of person, stoutness; derived from *en bon point,* in good condition.
20. Brocket Hall.
21. Possibly Adam Clarke, the Wesleyan divine and author, or Samuel Clarke, a disciple of Newton.
22. Richard Croft, Princess Charlotte's obstetrician, found her uterus contracting inertly; in the placental stage he had to "dilate an hourglass contraction to take the placenta away" (Corbett 37). In the ultraconservative phase of midwifery practiced after 1760, forceps were rarely used. The long second stage of the princess' labor makes it fortunate that Croft did not attempt a forceps delivery.

23. Charlotte's husband, Prince Leopold.

24. John Sims was consulting physician. Eardely Holland writes that it "seems astonishing that he was chosen as the consultant when there were in London such active and skilful men as David Davis, Merriman and John Ramsbotham. He was scarcely of the calibre to help Croft in his anxious duties.... when Sims arrived at Claremont he did not see Charlotte, and never entered the lying-in chamber until she was on the point of death" (Corbett 52). Corbett argues that following Croft's appointment, it would seem entirely reasonable for Sims to have been chosen, since he was Croft's senior colleague on the staff of the Surrey dispensary. At sixty-nine, Sims was too old to urge on Croft (Corbett 52).

25. Dr. Matthew Baillie served as physician-in-ordinary to Princess Charlotte in 1816-17. At that time he no longer practiced midwifery.

26. Henry Charles Somerset (1766-1835), marquis of Worcester, and his wife, the former Lady Charlotte Sophia Leveson-Gower.

27. Thomas Tyrwhitt was private secretary to His Royal Highness (Aspinall, *Correspondence* 3:250).

28. Possibly Charles William Stewart.

29. Henry Wellesley (1773-1847).

30. Panshanger was the Cowpers' estate.

31. Henry Charles Somerset, marquis of Worcester, and the former Lady Charlotte Sophia Leveson-Gower; Richard Butler, eleventh Baron Cahier, first earl of Glengal, and his wife, Emily; Major General Sir Edward Gerald Butler, lieutenant colonel in the 87th Foot (*BBI* 179:380), or Edmund Butler (1771-1846), earl of Kilkenny (*BBI* 371); Francis Russell, seventh duke of Bedford; and Henry Luttrell.

32. Frederick "Poodle" Byng.

33. Miss Fitzherbert was the Prince Regent's mistress and had been his wife.

34. Possibly General Sir Cornelius Cuyler, first baronet.

35. George Augustus Frederick, later Lord Fordwich, was Emily Cowper's son and Lady Melbourne's grandson. He was eleven years old at this time.

36. Possibly William Eliot, second earl of St. Germans.

37. Broken manuscript paper.

38. Dr. Richard Warren (1731-1797), physician to George, Prince of Wales.

39. See part III, note 68.

40. William Knighton had delivered up papers compromising to the Prince Regent. As a reward, the Regent appointed him to the auditorship of the duchies of Cornwall and Lancastor.

41. Lord Sefton's letter indicated his support in the amount of 100 guineas for William Hone, the radical publisher. In 1818 a number of trials took place for seditious libel against the government. These trials received much publicity in the London *Times* (January 16, 1816) and other papers, including the *Courier*. The *Times* took issue with the *Courier* in the case of Hone's trial and argued, rather improbably, that it was Hone's willingness to give up the publication of his satires that elicited Sefton's donation. The *Times* quoted the following extract from his letter: "I am happy," says his Lordship, "whatever may be the issue of my illness, to be able to mark my abhorrence of the tyrannical, vindictive, and persecuting spirit which was manifested on the late trials, my contempt for the spiteful imbecility which urged a continuance of them after the failure of the first, and my admiration of the intrepidity and ability of the individual who so triumphantly defeated the greatest and most dangerous conspiracy of the year 1817."

42. unidentified.

43. The last line of this letter appears at the top of the page.

44. Frances Charles, earl of Yarmouth.

45. The dramatist George Colman the younger (1762-1836).

46. The Prince Regent.

47. William Lamb succeeded to the viscountcy (1829) after his father's death in 1828. Augustus, his son, had died by 1842, when Frederick James became the third Viscount Melbourne.

48. Thomas Moore's life of Byron charged that Lady Byron's parents coerced her into the separation from her husband. Annabella contemplated publishing "Remarks" that denied this charge and Moore agreed to include them in the second edition (Mayne 317).

49. Thomas Moore (1779-1852), the Irish poet, and Byron's close friend and biographer.

APPENDIX A

Lady Melbourne's Letters to Henry Fox and
Transcriptions of Political Events

Lady Melbourne to Henry Fox (Melbourne X94/234/3/11)

[December 24, 1769]

Mr. Fox,

  Sir Peniston[1] desires you will send the Picture, that Hangs over the Chimney in the Dining Room at Melbourne to Sackville Street, by the first opportunity and begs you will see it Pack'd up very carefully. We intend sending another to supply the place. I am

Yr Humble Sev't

Eliz. Lamb

London, Decr. 24th
   1769

Lady Melbourne to Henry Fox (Melbourne 234/3/29)

[November 15, 1779]

Mr. Fox

  Ld Melbourne has sent four Greyhound Puppys which he desires you will send out to Walk about Melbourne or where you think they will be best taken care of. he also desires you will give the Man that comes with them one Guinea to bring him back. I hope you are quite well, & I am

Y^r Friend

EMelbourne

Novr 15th———1779

———————————

Lady Melbourne to Henry Fox (Melbourne 234/4/36)

[October 15, 1790]

M^r. Fox—

    We are much obliged to you for the finest Mutton—that ever was seen which arrived perfectly safe. Ld Melbourne has mislaid the account of the rent days you sent him, & wishes you would send him another—pray tear off the other side of this Sheet of Paper and give it to M^r. Burton

Y^{rs} EMelbourne

15th Octr. 1790

———————————

Lady Melbourne's Notes (45548, f.98-9; Airlie, IWS *19-21)*

[14 December 1792][2]

    written at ye beginning of the violent part of ye French revolution[3]

Whatever my principles may be you need not be afraid of my discussing them at your house I know how ill it will be received & shall therefore avoid it however angry I may sometimes be at hearing unqualified abuse of Men whose talents & general principles I must admire particularly when it comes from those who have neither talents nor principles but are guided in all their actions solely by selfishness

L^d E['s][4] opinions do not alarm me, I think his judgment generally good but on this

Subject he has always been a croaker—

The House of L^{ds} sat Yesterday till Eleven ye Commons till four[.] No division. There would have been a respectable minority in ye L^{ds} at least five—you will be surprized ~~at~~ ^some of^ ye opposition[5] M^r. Grenville at the head of them speaking much agst adminis^n.[6] Ld Milton & his Brother,[7] L^d G[eorge]. Cavendish[,][8] L^d E[dward] Bentinck[9] Ld Tichfield[10] not there. M^r. Brougham & Ld Wm Russell had been presiding in ye Mor^g at a parochial meeting.

The House met again to day & I understand Fox means to move another amendment on ye report[11][.] how can you know me so little as to suppose any thing could induce me even to accept, much more to ask a favor of ye present adm^n. I only wrote to L^d P[ortland][12] to thank him for his offer of the Lieutenancy but to decline it at the same time telling him I never would take it—I will never subject myself to ye caprice of a K[ing] & I might be hurried out for my political opinions as others have been—as to ye Militia I deferr'd giving him a positive answer till I see him[.] I should not have hesitated about accepting it as I had not been convinced y^t in every respect it would be disagreable to me & I could only be induced to do it from an assertion y^t in the present situation of affairs every body ought to stand forward particularly the Young ones & those whose keeping back might be attributed to their want of ardour in the cause, I therefore remain still in doubt urged on ye one hand by the wish to what I think I ought & on the other by the wish to avow what would be in every respect a disagreeable situation.——

You mistake me in supposing I am violent in my political opinions—at some moments I feel great apprehensions as to the effects of any change—my inclinations lead me to ye reformers, my aversions strengthen these inclinations—I see too with regret Men whom I always hoped would someday rescue the country from the arbitrary the oppressive the aristocratic Administration that now governs it— meanly playing second part and being the dupes by being the Cats paw of the very set of men their principles must make them detest (at least politically so) seeing all this I cannot help wishing a Speedy reform that will in some degree satisfy ye minds of ye people. I know the danger of any reform but I cannot help looking on a present moderate one as the only means of preventing a very Serious one soon. Opposition have lost their consequence whilst ye people had them to look to they flatter'd themselves the hasty stand of the present adminⁿ towards encreasing ye influence of the Crown would at least be checked if not Stopp'd; they can no longer have y^t hope for they see ye chiefs fighting Pitt's battles.

Lord Melbourne to Henry Fox ([Melbourne Collection, 234/3/38)

[no date]

Your letter announcing the Death of M^r. Burton gives me the greatest sadness. The more honest man I believe never existed and I am sure he had great attachment to my interest. You will be so good as to see that every thing at Melbourne goes on in the same way as when he lived. You must be fully acquainted with all my concerns, there and elsewhere. I can only for the present request that you will always be as regular and exact in the Business of the rents as you have allways been and as Mr. Burton's son has been used to attend I should like you to take him with you to them all and of course I shall pay his expenses

---

Lady Melbourne to Henry Fox (Melbourne 234/3/39)

[September 27, 1801]

M^r. Fox

Ld Melbourne desires you will send as much of the Melbourne rents as you can in cut Notes by the post as usual——he also desires you will pay the enclosed Bill to M^r. Robinson.

——EMelbourne

27th Sepr. 1801

Lady Melbourne to Henry Fox (Melbourne 234/4/64)

[November 16, 1802]

L^d. M[elbourne] returns you the receipt sign'd and desires you will pay Yourself—&
take the Money as proposed in y^r last Letter

Y^{rs}   EMelbourne

Ld Melbourne Yesterday agreed with Mr Rimington for ye Sale of ye Bolsterstone
Estate—at 35000—Timber included, which is exactly M^r. Blacks Valuation.

Whitehall
16th Nov^r

Lady Melbourne to Henry Fox (Melbourne 234/5/26)

[March 24, 1806]

Sir

L^d. Melbourne desires me to say that M^r. Cookney had written word to
remit William the Sum you mention, out of *the rents* but he did not mean that you
should send any part of <Wood> money which would have been a great inconvenience to him if he had not got the draft from William as the money was appropri-
ated to other purposes. M^r. Cookney will have written to you again by Lord
Melbournes orders & he begs you will follow the directions you will receive from
him.

Ld Melbourne desires you will send as much money as you can from
Melbourne in Bank Notes—The reason why L^d M[elbourne] wish'd that William
should receive his allowance from the different rents was to convenience him y^t he
might not have to wait for it till the Notting^{he} rents were paid, as they come in
so late, & therefore 700 ^L^ coming from them did not answer that purpose——
I enclose the receipt & am

Y^r H<u>ble</u> Servt

EMelbourne

Whitehall

March 24th 1806

Lady Melbourne to Henry Fox (Melbourne 234/5/29)

[July 26, 1806]

Mr Fox—

on the second of August two Gentlemen friends of Lord Melbournes will be at Melbourne & he desires that there may be some Beds well aired for them & that you will tell Mrs Howe to have some dinner ready for them I believe they will not stay more than a day—

The Gentlemans name is Mr Aylmer, & Mrs Howe must take care that they have every thing they can want

Y^{rs} ever

EMelbourne

26<u>th</u> July 1806

Lady Melbourne to Henry Fox (Melbourne 234/5/58)

Whitehall

13th Novr 1809

Mr. Fox

Lord Melbourne has desired me to send you the enclosed receipt, & also to inform you that he very much approves of the Farm late Surrender'd, being let to the person you recommend—who has had the management of Christopher Clarke's Farm for his Mother

I am Y^r H^{ble} Servt

EMelbourne

[M^r. Fox/Melbourne/Derby]

Lord Wellesley's Statement on His Resigning the Seals[13] *(45548, f.128-31v; Airlie,*
Whig 112-15)

[February 19, 1812]

L^d. Wellesley expressed his intention to resign, because his general opinions for a long time past on various important questions had not sufficient weight to justify him towards the Public, or towards his own Character in continuing in Office, and because he had no hope of obtaining from the Cabinet, (as then constituted) a greater portion of attention than he had already experienced.

Lord Wellesley's objections to remaining in the Cabinet, arose, in a great degree, from the *narrow* & imperfect scale, on which the efforts in the Peninsula were conducted. It was always stated to him by Mr. Perceval,[14] that it was *impracticable* to *enlarge* that system. The Cabinet followed Mr. Perceval implicitly. L^d. Wellesley thought that it was *perfectly practicable to extend* the Plan in the Peninsula & that it was neither safe nor honest towards this Country or the Allies to continue the present contracted scheme. No hope existed of converting Mr. Perceval, or any of his Colleagues; no alternative, therefore, remained for L^d. Wellesley but to resign, or to be the Instrument of a System, which he never advised, & which he could not approve.

L^d. Wellesley had repeatedly, with great reluctance, yielded his opinions to the Cabinet on many other important points. He was sincerely convinced by experience that, in every such instance, he had submitted to opinions more incorrect than his own, and had sacrificed, to the object of accommodation & temporary harmony more than he could justify in point of strict public duty. In fact, he was convinced by experience, that the Cabinet neither possessed ability, nor knowledge to devise a good plan; nor temper and discernment to *adopt* what he now thought necessary unless M^r. Perceval should concur with L^d. Wellesley. to Mr. Perceval's judgment, or attainments, L^d. Wellesley (under the same experience) could not pay any deference, without injury to the Public Service.

With these views and sentiments, on the   of January, L^d. Wellesley merely desired permission to withdraw from the Cabinet, not requiring any change in his own situation, and imploring no other favour than the facility of resignation.

This plain request was notified to the Prince Regent & to M^r. Perceval as nearly as possible at the same moment of time, with the expression of L^d. Wellesley's wish that the precise time of his resignation might be accommodated to the pleasure of his Royal Highness, & to the convenience of M^r. Perceval, as soon as the Restrictions should expire.

The P. R^t. received this notification with many gracious expressions of regret, & Mr. Perceval *in writing* used expressions of regret, & also of *thanks* for the manner, in which L^d. W[ellesley]. had signified his wish to resign.

Mr. Perceval *without* any comunication to L^d. W[ellsely]. instantly attempted to induce the P.R^t. to remove him before the expiration of the restrictions & repeatedly urged the attempt with great earnestness, severally proposing L^d. Castlereagh, Lord Moira,[15] & L^d. Sidmouth[16] or some of his party to supersede L^d. W[ellesley]., without an hour of delay. *Mr. P[erceval]. never gave any intimation* to L^d. W[ellesley]. of these proceedings, nor even of his wish for Lord W[ellesley].'s immediate retirement.

The P. R. still pressing L^d. W[ellesley]. to retain y^e. Seals, he submitted to His Royal Highness's comm^d. declaring at the same time his anxious desire to be liberated as soon as his R.H. should establish his Government.—

When it appeared, at the expiration of the restrictions that the P. R^t. intended to continue M^r. P[erceval].'s Government, L^d. W[ellesley]. again tendered the Seals to his R.H. with encreased earnestness: on that occasion, being informed, that H.R.H. was still at liberty, & was resolved to form his Cabinet, according to H.R.H. own views, and being *commanded to state his opinion* on the Subject, L^d. W[ellesley]. declared, that in his judgment, the Cabinet ought to be formed *first* on an intermediary principle respecting the Roman Catholic claims, equally exempt from the extremes of instant, unqualified concession, & of peremptory, eternal exclusion, and *secondly* on an understanding that the War should be conducted with adequate vigor. L^d. W[ellesley]. said that he personally was ready to serve *with* M^r. P[erceval] on such a Basis; that he never again would serve *under* P[erceval]. in any circumstances.

He said that he would serve under L^d. Moira or L^d. Holland on the proposed principle but that he desired no office, & entertained no other wish, than to be instrumental in forming such an Administration for the P R^t. as should be consistent with H.R.H.'s honor, conciliatory towards Ireland, and equal to the conduct of the War, on a scale of *sufficient extent*. He made no exception to any Prime Minister but M^r. P[erceval]., whom he considered to be incompetent to fill that office, although sufficiently qualified for inferior stations. He offered to act under any other person approved by H.R.H., but he stated that his own views rendered him much more anxious to resign instantly.

The P. R^t. commanded L^d. W[ellesley]. to continue until H.R.H. should have communicated with M^r. P[erceval]. through the L^d. Chancellor. L^d. W[ellesley]. stated, that such a communication must prove useless, but submitted to H.R.H. earnest desire; in two days afterwards, L^d. W[ellsley]. received through the L^d. Chancellor, the P.R^t.'s acceptance of his resignation, & accordingly delivered the Seals to H.R.H. on the 19th Feby 1812.

Letter of Lord Melbourne to Sophia Baddeley

Elizabeth Steele published The Memoirs of Sophia Baddeley *in 1782. She wrote of Lord Melbourne that "he was not the brightest man of the age, as his letters sent to Mrs. Baddeley at times will show; and he is one among many of the fashionable men of the age, who are acquainted neither with good grammar, nor orthography." Steele includes the following letter, among several others, as an example of Lord Melbourne's epistolary style.*

[1770-1774]

My dear Love,

      You can't conceive how unhappey I was, being disappointed at the happey-ness of seeing you, but I flatter myself you will be convinced that it was totally impossible for me, as I was obliged to go to the club with some ladies, who obliged me to play till after supper, when you know I couldnt be so happey to call on you on many accounts. My dear, I hope you will not be angry, as you know I have ever made a point not to disappoint you, which nothing that would hiner, should ever make me do; and if you knew how happy I am to see you, you will pity my being so unfortunate as not to see you half so much as I wish—I am just going into the country, shall retorn in the evenings, and am obliged to go with Lady Bellasyze, to Vauxhall; if, after your singing, you can come there, it will give me pleasure to see you. As I go to Bath on Wednesday next, I beg to be so happey as to see you at Pimlico tomorrow at nine 'clock. My dear love think of me, and be sure that any thing that hinders my seeing you, will ever give me pain. I send you ten thousand kisses.

"Melbourne."

"To Mrs. Baddeley." (Steele 1:201).

Mrs. Steele notes that *"This letter is a literal copy of his Lordship's: his other letters were equally ill spelt, &c. but I have taken the liberty to correct them, that they may not hurt the eye of the reader" (Steele 2:41).*

APPENDIX C

Unpublished Letter of the Prince Regent
to Lady Melbourne

Prince Regent to Lady Melbourne (45548, f. 109)

[30 Nov. 1803]

The invariable & boundless affection (if you will allow me to speak the truth) my ever dearest Lady Melbourne which is so strongly imprinted in my heart towards you, as well as the extreme desire I feel from the sincerity of my regard, & attachment to every Individual of your Family, would have made me most happy had it been in my power to have contrived to have offer'd William any thing worthy of his acceptance; but I am & have been so cruelly situated respecting the Duchy of Cornwall, that my hands are quite tied, & with sorrow to my self do I say it, must I am afraid continue so for a length of time. All this I will explain to you when we meet, as it is too long a topic for any Letter to contain. However rest assured of this, that whilst I live, I never will neglect an opportunity in which I can be of use to any of you or in which I can forward any wish of yours, or Melbournes, as you well know my ever dearest Friend, at least I hope so, that I can be depended upon, & that there is no one existing, who ever *was, is, or ever will* be so sincerely attached to You from the very bottom of their Heart & Soul

As your truly affectionate

George

Brighton
November 30th
1803.

P.S. You must forgive my not having written sooner, but I have been overwhelm'd with grief, & with business, arising from the late melancholy event; which though for the last two years almost hourly to be expected, & in some instances perhaps almost for *his* sake as well as of his Friends, to be wished; Still when the blow came, the recollection of his sincere attachment, & his many other excellent qualities made me after a friendship upwards of twenty years, feel it most severely.

APPENDIX D

Three Letters of Lord Grey to Lady Melbourne, Regarding the Appointment of Frederick Lamb to a Diplomatic Position in the Two Sicilies

The following letters are alluded to in Lady Melbourne's letter to the Prince Regent of February 4, 1811. Lord Grey made use of the confidential information to which he was privy in order to inform Lady Melbourne about the Prince Regent's true intentions regarding her son's diplomatic career.

(HRO D/Elb F9/1)
Howick February 23d 1811

My dear Lady Melbourne

      I received your very kind letter last night, & can assure you that I feel much flattered not only by your attention in communicating, but by your anxiety to know my opinion of Frederick's appointment. You know it is what I had desired for him if I had been placed in a situation to give it, 'till I was informed by you that you did not wish him to be sent abroad. As to the nature of the appointment, therefore there can be no doubt that I must think it one which it is highly creditable to him to accept. Nor do I see in the circumstances under which it has been offered, tho' coming from those of whom you would not have asked it, any thing that ought to have induced him to refuse it. On the contrary I decidedly concur in the opinion of those of his friends by whose advice he has acted. Lord Wm Bentinck being the Minister afforded I think an additional inducement. I have little personal knowledge of him, but what I hear even of his public conduct has given me the most favorable impression with respect to him, & from all I have heard from others, I believe him to be a most honorable & excellent Man. In short I have no doubt that Frederick will find his situation as pleasant as it can be made in the place to which he is going, which is not without its difficulties. But there will afford him a better opportunity of showing himself, & I am on every account glad that he has determined to go—

I was quite sure that you would take no measure that any fair person could blame, to procure this or any thing else, but I must add that from your account of what has passed it is impossible that the propriety of your conduct should not be universally acknowledged.

Indeed I have heard of it before, & with unqualified praise from the person from whom I received the information.

Many thanks for your kind inquiries. I wish I could answer them favorable, but I am still very unhappy about my poor Child. I do not think there is the least chance of my being able to return to Town this year—God Bless you—

Ever yrs. most faithfully,
Grey.

(HRO D/ELb F 9/2)
Pulman Square, Friday

Dear Lady Melbourne

I certainly had understood from William that an appointment in some of the Foreign Service would be what Frederic would like, & as he particularly mentioned Sicily I had, in my own mind, received for him the place of Sec.*y* of Legation there. I wish however, in consequence of what you say looking out for something else, tho' as I told you before it may be somewhat difficult at first. In the Foreign Office there is really nothing but appointments abroad, that I could at present propose to him. You may be assured, however, that I will do all I can, tho' the *If* which I before annexed to my promise, ought now to be written with a much sharper accent.

I certainly will not say a word to Lady Holland upon this subject. Indeed I am glad that she has given me an opportunity of knowing exactly what you wish, which I only beg you will never ask any apology for expressing to me with all the freedom of an old friend—

I am d^r. Lady Melbourne
ever yours, most respectfully
Grey.

(HRO D/Elb F9/3)
Confidential

Saturday

My dear Lady Melbourne

The *If* I wrote yesterday is now a certainty. There will be *no* change of Administration you will soon hear this from others, but till then don't say that you have heard it from me

Ever y^{rs}. affectionately,
Grey.

Notes: Appendices

1 . Peniston Lamb, Lady Melbourne's husband.
2. On December 13, 1792, the king opened the seventeenth Parliament of Great Britain with a speech that made reference to "seditious practices" and "a spirit of tumult and disorder" that "required the interposition of a military force in support of the civil magistrate." He charged that the riots and "tumult [were] encouraged by foreign countries" and called for an "augmentation of my naval and military force" in response. Debates in the House of Commons and the House of Lords responded to that speech. Members of the opposition charged that the seventeenth Parliament was illegal because it had been called within fourteen, rather than the customary forty, days. They also charged that George III's references to "tumult and disorder" were too vague to warrant an augmentation in military force.
3. At the beginning of the French Revolution, Lady Melbourne's gatherings included such Whig radicals as Charles Grey. Although typical of this political set who admired Voltaire, Jean Jacques Rousseau, and the Encyclopedists, Grey was horrified by the execution of the king of France (Airlie, *Whig* 18). During this time, Lady Melbourne copied the following letter, in which one of her guests, whose identity is unknown to us, apologizes for airing his disagreements with her more conservative lover, Lord Egremont.

4. Lord Egremont was a lifelong opponent of Catholic emancipation.

5. On December 13 there were relatively few members of Parliament present, perhaps because the session was called on such short notice. The following day, the opposition included fifty members, among them C. J. Fox, Charles Grey, R. B. Sheridan, Lord G. A. H. Cavendish, Lord Edward Bentinck, Lord John Russell, Lord William Russell, the earl of Wycombe, Viscount Milton, T. Erskine, Lionel Damer, T. Maitland, George Byng, William Hussey, John Crewe, William Baker, Dudley North, John Courtenay, John Shaw Stuart, Edward Bouverie, Thomas Grenville, R. Fitzpatrick, Samuel Whitbread, Joseph Jekyll, Thomas Whitmore, and W. H. Lambton. Brougham was not a member of the opposition on this occasion, though Thomas Grenville was.

6. This is an exaggeration, for on December 13 Thomas Grenville had voted for the king's proclamation asking for more military support to quell the country's "seditious spirit." The following day, Grenville said that he believed the danger to which "this country was exposed by a seditious spirit" had not been fully documented. He "had no reason to regret his vote," though he was satisifed with the loyalty shown by the people and saw "nothing . . . by any means quivalent to an insurrection. He was of the opinion that the state of the country was ill described by the proclamation." Grenville advocated the government continuing in a policy of neutrality towards France (Hansard 30:50).

7. John Damer (1720-1783) of Winterborne Came, near Dorchester, Dorset, and his brother Joseph Damer (1718-1798) (Valentine 1:236).

8. George Augustus Henry Cavendish.

9. Lord Edward Charles Cavendish.

10. William Henry Cavendish Bentinck, who was styled marquess of Titchfield until he became third duke of Portland in 1762.

11. This paragraph is omitted in Airlie's transcription (*Whig* 20). Fox's motion for an amendment to the king's report was defeated on December 13, 1792 (Hansard 30:59). On December 14 Fox continued to support the amendment, seconded by Sheridan (Hansard 30:60, 68). On December 15 he put forth an amendment to send a minister to Paris to treat with the provisional government of France and avoid a war (Hansard 30:80).

12. The writer of this letter means to distance himself from William Henry Cavendish Bentinck, third duke of Portland, who aligned himself with Pitt at this time.

13. Richard Colley Wellesley resigned as secretary of state for foreign affairs in 1812. He disapproved of the lack of military support offered to his brother, Sir Arthur Wellesley, during the Peninsular War and supported Catholic emancipation over the Prince Regent's objections. Lady Melbourne seems to have copied Lord Wellesley's statement on resigning the seals. She records his views so precisely as to belie the comments of previous biographers that her experience of life was "limited" (Cecil, *Young Melbourne* 31).

14. Spencer Percevel, who was prime minister at this time.

15. Francis Rawdon, second earl of Moira.

16. Henry Addington, first Viscount Sidmouth

Genealogical Tables
The Milbanke and Melbourne Families

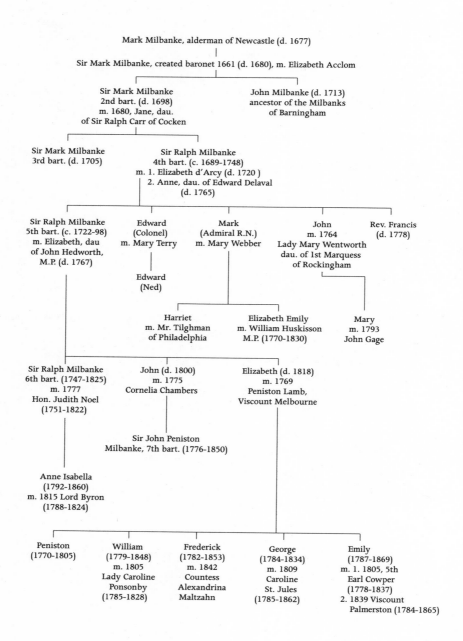

Mark Milbanke, alderman of Newcastle (d. 1677)

Sir Mark Milbanke, created baronet 1661 (d. 1680), m. Elizabeth Acclom

Sir Mark Milbanke
2nd bart. (d. 1698)
m. 1680, Jane, dau.
of Sir Ralph Carr of Cocken

John Milbanke (d. 1713)
ancestor of the Milbanks
of Barningham

Sir Mark Milbanke
3rd bart. (d. 1705)

Sir Ralph Milbanke
4th bart. (c. 1689-1748)
m. 1. Elizabeth d'Arcy (d. 1720)
2. Anne, dau. of Edward Delaval
(d. 1765)

Sir Ralph Milbanke
5th bart. (c. 1722-98)
m. Elizabeth, dau.
of John Hedworth,
M.P. (d. 1767)

Edward
(Colonel)
m. Mary Terry

Mark
(Admiral R.N.)
m. Mary Webber

John
m. 1764
Lady Mary Wentworth
dau. of 1st Marquess
of Rockingham

Rev. Francis
(d. 1778)

Edward
(Ned)

Harriet
m. Mr. Tilghman
of Philadelphia

Elizabeth Emily
m. William Huskisson
M.P. (1770-1830)

Mary
m. 1793
John Gage

Sir Ralph Milbanke
6th bart. (1747-1825)
m. 1777
Hon. Judith Noel
(1751-1822)

John (d. 1800)
m. 1775
Cornelia Chambers

Elizabeth (d. 1818)
m. 1769
Peniston Lamb,
Viscount Melbourne

Sir John Peniston
Milbanke, 7th bart. (1776-1850)

Anne Isabella
(1792-1860)
m. 1815 Lord Byron
(1788-1824)

Peniston
(1770-1805)

William
(1779-1848)
m. 1805
Lady Caroline
Ponsonby
(1785-1828)

Frederick
(1782-1853)
m. 1842
Countess
Alexandrina
Maltzahn

George
(1784-1834)
m. 1809
Caroline
St. Jules
(1785-1862)

Emily
(1787-1869)
m. 1. 1805, 5th
Earl Cowper
(1778-1837)
2. 1839 Viscount
Palmerston (1784-1865)

The Owners of Melbourne Hall

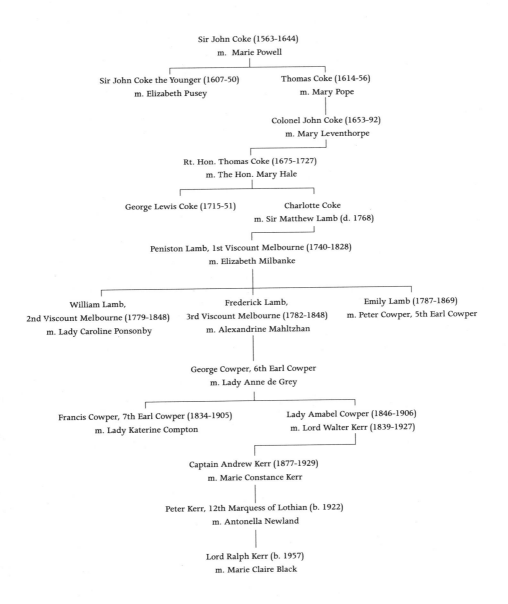

Sir John Coke (1563-1644)
m. Marie Powell

Sir John Coke the Younger (1607-50)
m. Elizabeth Pusey

Thomas Coke (1614-56)
m. Mary Pope

Colonel John Coke (1653-92)
m. Mary Leventhorpe

Rt. Hon. Thomas Coke (1675-1727)
m. The Hon. Mary Hale

George Lewis Coke (1715-51)

Charlotte Coke
m. Sir Matthew Lamb (d. 1768)

Peniston Lamb, 1st Viscount Melbourne (1740-1828)
m. Elizabeth Milbanke

William Lamb,
2nd Viscount Melbourne (1779-1848)
m. Lady Caroline Ponsonby

Frederick Lamb,
3rd Viscount Melbourne (1782-1848)
m. Alexandrine Mahltzhan

Emily Lamb (1787-1869)
m. Peter Cowper, 5th Earl Cowper

George Cowper, 6th Earl Cowper
m. Lady Anne de Grey

Francis Cowper, 7th Earl Cowper (1834-1905)
m. Lady Katerine Compton

Lady Amabel Cowper (1846-1906)
m. Lord Walter Kerr (1839-1927)

Captain Andrew Kerr (1877-1929)
m. Marie Constance Kerr

Peter Kerr, 12th Marquess of Lothian (b. 1922)
m. Antonella Newland

Lord Ralph Kerr (b. 1957)
m. Marie Claire Black

The Spencer and Poyntz Families

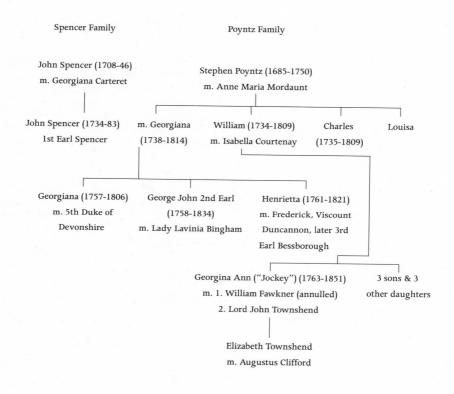

Spencer Family

John Spencer (1708-46)
m. Georgiana Carteret

John Spencer (1734-83)
1st Earl Spencer

Poyntz Family

Stephen Poyntz (1685-1750)
m. Anne Maria Mordaunt

m. Georgiana
(1738-1814)

William (1734-1809)
m. Isabella Courtenay

Charles
(1735-1809)

Louisa

Georgiana (1757-1806)
m. 5th Duke of
Devonshire

George John 2nd Earl
(1758-1834)
m. Lady Lavinia Bingham

Henrietta (1761-1821)
m. Frederick, Viscount
Duncannon, later 3rd
Earl Bessborough

Georgina Ann ("Jockey") (1763-1851)
m. 1. William Fawkner (annulled)
2. Lord John Townshend

3 sons & 3
other daughters

Elizabeth Townshend
m. Augustus Clifford

The Cavendish Family

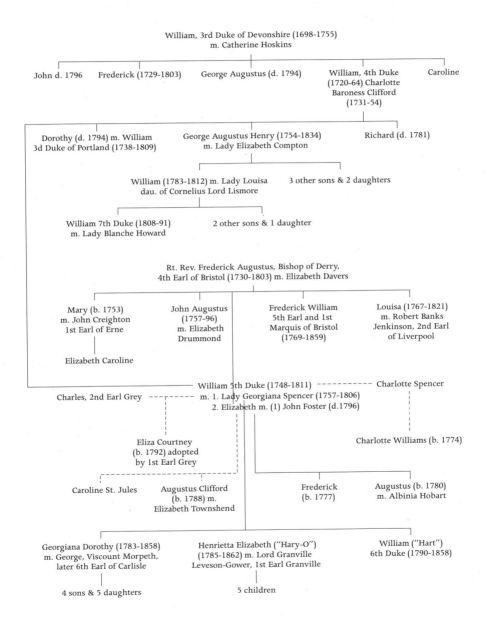

William, 3rd Duke of Devonshire (1698-1755)
m. Catherine Hoskins

John d. 1796   Frederick (1729-1803)   George Augustus (d. 1794)   William, 4th Duke (1720-64) Charlotte Baroness Clifford (1731-54)   Caroline

Dorothy (d. 1794) m. William 3d Duke of Portland (1738-1809)   George Augustus Henry (1754-1834) m. Lady Elizabeth Compton   Richard (d. 1781)

William (1783-1812) m. Lady Louisa dau. of Cornelius Lord Lismore   3 other sons & 2 daughters

William 7th Duke (1808-91) m. Lady Blanche Howard   2 other sons & 1 daughter

Rt. Rev. Frederick Augustus, Bishop of Derry, 4th Earl of Bristol (1730-1803) m. Elizabeth Davers

Mary (b. 1753) m. John Creighton 1st Earl of Erne   John Augustus (1757-96) m. Elizabeth Drummond   Frederick William 5th Earl and 1st Marquis of Bristol (1769-1859)   Louisa (1767-1821) m. Robert Banks Jenkinson, 2nd Earl of Liverpool

Elizabeth Caroline

William 5th Duke (1748-1811) - - - - - - - - - Charlotte Spencer
Charles, 2nd Earl Grey - - - m. 1. Lady Georgiana Spencer (1757-1806)
2. Elizabeth m. (1) John Foster (d.1796)

Eliza Courtney (b. 1792) adopted by 1st Earl Grey   Charlotte Williams (b. 1774)

Caroline St. Jules   Augustus Clifford (b. 1788) m. Elizabeth Townshend   Frederick (b. 1777)   Augustus (b. 1780) m. Albinia Hobart

Georgiana Dorothy (1783-1858) m. George, Viscount Morpeth, later 6th Earl of Carlisle   Henrietta Elizabeth ("Hary-O") (1785-1862) m. Lord Granville Leveson-Gower, 1st Earl Granville   William ("Hart") 6th Duke (1790-1858)

4 sons & 5 daughters   5 children

BIBLIOGRAPHY

ABBREVIATIONS

Manuscript sources cited in the text and notes have been identified by the abbreviations listed below. Books not listed below have been cited by the author's name and, where necessary, an abbreviated title. Full citations are given in the bibliography.

MANUSCRIPT SOURCES

45546–45549	Lamb Papers, British Library
Chatsworth	Chatsworth Archives
HRO	Hertford County Record Office
Huntington	Huntington Library
Lovelace	Lovelace Collection, Bodleian Library
Melbourne	Melbourne Hall Archives at Christie's (1993)
Murray	Murray Archives, John Murray Publishers
Yale	Osborn Collection, Yale University Library

BOOKS

BBI	Bank, David, and Anthony Esposito, eds. *British Biographical Index*.
Burke's	*Burke's Genealogical and Heraldic History of the Peerage, Baronetage, and Knightage*.
Chambers	Thorne, J. O., and T. C. Collocott, eds. *Chambers Biographical Dictionary*.
Columbia	*Columbia Encyclopedia*.

CDNB   *The Concise Dictionary of National Biography: From Earliest Times to 1985.*

CPW   Byron. *The Complete Poetical Works.*

DNB   *Dictionary of National Biography.*

Europa   *The Europa Biographical Dictionary of British Women.*

Hansard   *Hansard's Parliamentary Debates.*

Hary-O   Gower, Henrietta Elizabeth Leveson. *Hary-O. The Letters of Lady Harriet Cavendish, 1796-1809.*

LJ   Byron. *Letters and Journals.*

Peerage   *The Complete Peerage of England, Scotland, Ireland, Great Britain, and the United Kingdom.*

PPBD   *Private Papers of British Diplomats: 1782-1900.*

Manuscript Sources

British Library
Lamb Papers, 45546-45549. Lady Melbourne's letters to and from Lord Byron, William Lamb, George Lamb, Emily Lamb, Frederick Lamb, Henry Luttrell, the earl of Cowper, Annabella Milbanke, Ralph Milbanke, and Judith Milbanke.

Bodleian Library
Lovelace Papers. Letters to Annabella Milbanke, Lord Byron, Ralph Milbanke, and Judith Milbanke.

Christie's (1993)
Melbourne Papers. Letters to Henry Fox, Warden of Melbourne Estate.

John Murray's, 50 Albemarle Street
Murray Archives. Letters to Lord Byron; letters from Caroline George Lamb to Annabella Milbanke.

Hertford County Record Office, Hertfordshire
Hertford Record Office. Letters to Frederick Lamb and the Prince Regent; letters from Charles Grey to Lady Melbourne.

Huntington Library, Marino, California
Huntington Library. Letters to and from Mary Huskisson; letters to Thomas Grenille.

Osborne Collection, Yale University Library, New Haven
Osborne Collection. Letters to Charles Burney and Lady Bessborough.

Chatsworth, Devonshire House. Letters to Georgiana, duchess of Devonshire.

Pamphlets

Brocket Hall: Hatfield. A Catalogue of the Valuable Contents of the Mansion, For Sale by Auction on Wednesday, Thursday and Friday, March 7th, 8th and 9th, and Monday, Tuesday and Wednesday, March 12th, 13th and 14th, 1923, MESSRs. Foster: 54, Pall Mall, S.W.1, Panshanger Box 37, Hertford County Record Office.

Usher, Howard. *Femmes Fatales: Lady Melbourne and Lady Palmerston*. Derbyshire: Melbourne Hall, 1986.

————. *William Lamb, Lord Melbourne*. Derbyshire, Melbourne Hall, 1992.

Contemporary Newspapers and Journals

Lady Melbourne's movements from Brocket Hall to Whitehall were noted most frequently by the *Morning Chronicle*. *The Times* published her poetry and took delight in reporting the foibles of the aristocracy, as did *Town and Country*. Samuel Whitbread claimed that the *Morning Herald* and *Morning Post* were controlled by the government (*Morning Chronicle,* March 16, 1813, 2). Certainly those newspapers are more sympathetic to the Tories than was the Whig *Morning Chronicle*.

Gentleman's Magazine
Morning Chronicle
Morning Herald
Morning Post
London *Times*
Town and Country

Books and Articles

Airlie, Mabell. *In Whig Society, 1775-1818.* London: Hodder and Stoughton, 1921.

———. *Lady Palmerston and Her Times.* 2 vols. London: Hodder and Stoughton, 1922.

Arbuthnot, Charles. *The Correspondence of Charles Arbuthnot.* Edited by A. Aspinall. London: Royal Historical Society, 1941.

Arnold, Bruce. *The Art Atlas of Britain and Ireland: In Association with the National Trust.* London: Penguin, 1991.

Aspinall, Arthur, ed. *Correspondence of George, Prince of Wales,* 1770-1812. 8 vols. New York: Oxford University Press, 1980.

———, ed. *Lady Bessborough and Her Family Circle.* London: 1940.

———, ed. *The Letters of King George IV, 1812-1830.* 3 vols. Cambridge: Cambridge University Press, 1938.

———. *Lord Brougham and the Whig Party.* London: 1972.

Bank, David, and Anthony Esposito, eds. *British Biographical Index.* New York: K. G. Saur, 1990.

Battiscombe, *Georgina The Spencers of Althorp*. London: Constable, 1984.

Berry, Miss. *Journals and Correspondence of Miss Berry*. Edited by Lady Theresa Lewis. 3 vols. New York: AMS Press, 1971.

Bessborough, Earl of. *Lady Bessborough and Her Family Circle*. London: John Murray, 1940.

————. *Letters of Georgiana, Duchess of Devonshire*. London: John Murray, 1955.

Birkenhead, Sheila. *Peace in Piccadilly: The Story of Albany*. New York: Reynal & Company, 1958.

Blyth, Henry. *Caro—the Fatal Passion*. New York: Coward, McCann & Geoghegan, 1972.

Boyes, Megan. *My Amiable Mamma*. London: J. M. Taylor & Son, 1991.

Boyle, M. L. *Catalogue of the Portraits at Panshanger*. 1885.

Brewer's Book of Myth and Legend. Edited by J.C. Cooper. London: Helicon, 1992.

Brewer's Concise Dictionary of Phrase and Fable. Edited by Betty Kirkpatrick. London: Helicon, 1992.

Bryan's Dictionary of Painters and Engravers. Edited by G. C. Williamson. New York: Macmillan, 1904.

Buckingham, Duke of, and Richard Plantagenet Temple Nugent Brydges Chandos Grenville Chandos. *Memoirs of the Court of England during the Regency, 1811-1820*. 2 vols. London: Hurst and Blackett, 1984.

Burke's Genealogical and Heraldic History of the Peerage, Baronetage, and Knightage. Edited by Peter Townend. 105th ed. London: Burke's Peerage Limited, 1970.

Burney, Fanny. *The Journals and Letters of Fanny Burney*. Edited by Joyce Hemlow and Althea Douglas. 12 vols. Oxford: Clarendon Press, 1972.

Butlin, Martin. *Turner at Petworth: Painter and Patron*. London: Tate Gallery, 1989.

Byron, George Gordon. *The Complete Miscellaneous Prose: Lord Byron*. Edited by Andrew Nicholson. Oxford: Oxford University Press, 1991.

————. *The Complete Poetical Works*. Edited by Jerome J. McGann. 5 vols. Oxford: Oxford University Press, 1980-86.

————. *Letters and Journals*. Edited by Leslie A. Marchand. 12 vols. London: John Murray, 1973-95.

Calder-Marshall, Arthur. *The Two Duchesses*. New York: Harper & Row, 1978.

Calmet, Dom Augustin. *Dictionnaire Historique, Critique, Chronologique, Geographique et Litteral de la Bible, Enrichi de plus de trois cent Figures en taille-douce, qui represen tent les Antiquitez Judaiques*. 4 vols. Paris, 1730.

Cavendish, Georgiana, Duchess of Devonshire. *The Sylph*. 2 vols. Dublin: T. Lowndes, 1779.

Cecil, Lord David, *Lord M., or The Later Life of Lord Melbourne*. New York: The Bobbs-Merill Company, Inc., 1939.

————. *The Young Melbourne and the Story of His Marriage with Caroline Lamb*. London: Pan Books, 1948.

Chaloner Smith., John. *British Mezzotinto Portraits*. 5 vols. London: H. Sotheran & Co., 1878.

Charlotte, Princess. *The Letters of Princess Charlotte (1811- 1817)*. London: Home and Van Thel, 1949.

————. *Memoirs of the Late Princess Charlotte*. Edited by Robert Huish. London: T. Kelly, 1818.

Clowes, William Laird. *The Royal Navy: A History from the Earliest Times to the Present*. 7 vols. London: Sampson Low, Marston and Company, 1898.

Clubbe, John, "Byron's Lady Melbourne." *Byron Journal* (1984): 12:4-17.

Cobbett, William. *The Parliamentary History of England, from the Earliest Period to the Year 1803, from Which Last-Mentioned Epoch It Is Continued Downwards in the Work Entitled "Hansard's Parliamentary Debates."* London: T. C. Hansard, 1806.

Coke, Mary. "Journal of Mary Coke." Unpublished, in possession of Lord Home. Extracts quoted in Sheila Birkenhead, *Peace in Piccadilly*.

————. *The Letters and Journals of Lady Mary Coke.* Edited by Hon. James Archibald Home. 4 vols. Edinburgh: D. Douglas, 1889-96.

Columbia Encyclopedia. Edited by Barbara A. Chernow and George A. Vallasi. N.Y.: Houghton Mifflin, 1993.

Colvin, Howard. *A Biographical Dictionary of British Architects, 1600-1840.* London: John Murray, 1980.

The Complete Peerage of England, Scotland, Ireland, Great Britain, and the United Kingdom. 13 vols. London: Alan Sutton, 1982.

The Concise Dictionary of National Biography: From Earliest Times to 1985. 3 vols. New York: Oxford University Press, 1992.

Corbett, Henry Vincent. *A Royal Catastrophe: A Modern Account of the Death in Childbirth of Her Royal Highness the Princess Charlotte Augusta, Daughter of King George IV.* London: H. V. Corbett, 1985.

The Creevey Papers. Edited by John Gore. London: Folio Society, 1963.

Crompton, Louis. *Byron and Greek Love.* Berkeley: University of California Press, 1985.

Delany, Mrs. *Autobiography and Correspondence of Mary Granville, Mrs. Delany: With Interesting Reminiscences of King George the Third and Queen Charlotte.* Edited by Land Llanover. 6 vols. London: Richard Bentley, 1862.

Derry, John. *Charles, Earl Grey: Aristocratic Reformer.* Oxford: Blackwell Publishing, 1991.

Dictionary of National Biography. Edited by Sir Leslie Stephen and Sir Sidney Lee. Oxford: Oxford University Press, 1949-50.

Dijkstra, Bram. *Idols of Perversity: Fantasies of Feminine Evil in Fin-de-siècle Culture.* Oxford: Oxford University Press, 1986.

Elizabeth of England, Consort of Friedrich VI, Landgrave of Hesse-Homburg. *Letters of Princess Elizabeth of England, Daughter of King George III, and Landgravine of Hesse-Homburg, Written for the Most Part to Miss Louisa Swinburne.* London: T. F. Unwin, 1898.

Elwin, Malcolm. *Lord Byron's Wife*. London: Macdonald, 1962.

————. *The Noels and the Milbankes*. London: Macdonald, 1967.

Encyclopedia Britannica. 11th edition. 29 vols. Cambridge: Cambride University Press, 1910.

The Europa Biographical Dictionary of British Women: Over 1000 Notable Women from Britain's Past. Edited by Anne Crawford, Tony Hayter, Anne Hughes, Frank Prochaska, Pauline Stafford, and Elizabeth Vallance. Detroit: Gale Research, 1983.

Farington Diary by Joseph Farington, R.A. Edited by James Greig. 8 vols. London: Hutchinson & Co. 1924.

Foster, Vere, ed. *The Two Duchesses: Georgiana Duchess of Devonshire, Elizabeth Duchess of Devonshire (1777-1859)*. London: Blackie & Son Limited, 1898.

Gage, Deborah. "Firle Place, East Sussex." *Antiques* (June 1984):1326-30.

A General Biographical Dictionary. 8th edition. Edited by John Gorton. 3 vols. Boston: Mussey & Co. 1850.

George, Mary, ed. *Catalogue of Political and Personal Satires: Prints and Drawings in the British Museum*. Vols. 4-8. London: The Trustees of the British Museum, 1978.

Georgiana: Duchess of Devonshire. Edited by the earl of Bessborough. London: John Murray, 1955.

Gould, John. *Biographical Dictionary of Painters*. New ed. 2 vols. London: 1839.

Gower, Henrietta Elizabeth Leveson. *Hary-O. The Letters of Lady Harriet Cavendish, 1796-1809*. Edited by Sir George Leveson Gower. London: John Murray, 1940.

————. *Letters of Harriet, Countess Granville, 1810-1845*. Edited by Hon. F. Leveson Gower. London: Longmans, Green, and Company, 1894.

Graham, Peter W. *Byron's Bulldog: The Letters of John Cam Hobhouse to Lord Byron*. Columbus: Ohio State University Press, 1984.

————. *Don Juan and Regency England*. Charlottesville: University of Virginia Press, 1990.

Grand Larousse Encyclopedique. Edited by Pierre Larousse. 10 vols. Paris: Librairie Larousse, 1960-64.

Grand Dictionnaire Universel du XIXe Siecle. Edited by Pierre Larousse. 17 vols. Paris: Administration du Grand Dictionnaire Universel, 1867.

La Grande Encyclopedie, inventaire raisonne ds sciences, des lettres et des arts. 31 vols. Paris: Societe anonyme de la Grande Encyclopedie, 1900.

Granville, Granville Leveson-Gower, first earl, 1773-1846. *Private Correspondence of Earl Granville.* Edited by Castalia, Countess Granville. 2 vols. London: John Murray, 1916.

Graves, Algernon, and William Vine Cronin. *A History of the Works of Sir Joshua Reynolds.* 4 vols. London: H. Graves, 1899-1901.

Greville, Charles. *The Greville Memoirs: A Journal of the Reigns of King George IV, King William IV, and Queen Victoria.* Edited by Henry Reeve. 8 vols. London: Longmans, Green, and Company, 1888.

Grimm, Friedrich Melchior. *Correspondance littéraire, philosophique et critique, adressée à un souverain d'Allemagne (1753-1769).* 6 vols. Paris: Longchamps, 1813.

Hadfield, Charles. *British Canals: An Illustrated History.* London: David & Charles, 1974.

———. *The Canal Age.* New York: Frederick A. Praeger, 1968.

———. *The Canals of Southern England.* London: Phoenix House, 1955.

Hansard's Parliamentary Debates. London: T. C. Hansard, 1820.

Harrap's Standard French and English Dictionary. Edited by J. E. Manscon. London: George G. Harrap & Company, Ltd., 1934.

Harris, John. *Sir William Chambers, Knight of the Polar Star.* University Park: Pennsylvania State University Press, 1970.

Hawes, Frances. *Henry Brougham.* London: Jonathan Cape, 1957.

Herold, J. Christopher. *Mistress to an Age.* New York: Harmony Books, 1958.

Hibbert, Christopher. *King Mob: The Story of Lord George Gordon and the London Riots of 1780*. New York: World Publishing Company, 1958.

Hibbert, Christopher, and Ben Weinreb, eds. *The London Encyclopedia*. London: Macmillan, 1983.

Hillebrand, Harold Newcomb. *Edmund Kean*. N.Y.: AMS Press, 1966.

Holland, Elizabeth Vassall Fox, Lady. *The Journal of Elizabeth Lady Holland (1791-1811)*. Edited by the sixth earl of Ilchester. 2 vols. London: Longmans, Green & Co., 1908.

————. *The Spanish Journal of Elizabeth Lady Holland*. Edited by the sixth earl of Ilchester. London: Longmans, Green & Co., 1910.

Holland, Henry Richard Vassall, Baron. *Further Memoirs of the Whig Party*. New York: E. P. Dutton, 1905.

————. *Memoirs of the Whig Party During My Time*. 2 vols. London: Longman, Brown, Green, and Longmans, 1852-54.

Ilchester, Countess of, and Lord Stavordale. *The Life and Letters of Lady Sarah Lennox*. 2 vols. London, 1901.

Ilchester, Giles Stephen Holland Fox-Strangways, sixth earl of. *The Home of the Hollands*. London: E. P. Dutton, 1937.

Jack, Ian. *English Literature: 1815-1832*. Oxford: Clarendon Press, 1963.

James, Henry. *The Aspern Papers*. In *The Spoils of Poynton and Other Stories*. Edited and with an introduction by Louis Auchincloss. Garden City, New York: Doubleday, 1971.

Jenkins, Elizabeth. *Lady Caroline Lamb*. London: V. Gollancz, 1932.

Kerr, Philip W. "Melbourne Hall, Derbyshire: The Seat of Captain A. W. Kerr, R.N." *Country Life* (April 7 and 14, 1928) 63:492-99, 526-33.

Knight, Cornelia. *Autobiography of Miss Cornelia Knight, Lady Companion to the Princess of Wales*. 4th ed. 2 vols. London: W. H. Allen, 1861.

Knight, G. Wilson. *Lord Byron's Marriage: The Evidence of Asterisks*. London: Routledge and K. Paul, 1957.

Lamb, Caroline. *Glenarvon: A Facsimile Reproduction*. Edited and with an introduction by James L. Ruff. New York: Scholars' Facsimiles & Reprints, 1972.

Leslie, Charles. *Autobiographical Recollections*. Edited by Tom Taylor. Boston: Ticknor and Fields, 1860.

Leslie, Shane. *The Letters of Mrs. Fitzherbert*. London: Burns Oates, 1940.

———. *The Life of Mrs. Fitzherbert, and Connected Papers: Being the Second Volume of the Life of Mrs. Fitzherbert*. New York: Benziger Brothers, 1939.

Lever, Tresham, ed. *The Letters of Lady Palmerston*. London: John Murray, 1957.

Leveson Gower, Sir George, and Iris Palmer, eds. *Hary-O, The Letters of Lady Harriet Cavendish, 1796-1809*. London: John Murray, 1940.

Lieven, Princess de. *Letters of Dorothea, Princess Lieven, during Her Residence in London, 1812-34*. Edited by L. G. Robinson. London: Longmans, Green, and Co., 1902.

———. *The Lieven-Palmerston Correspondence, 1828-56*. Translated and edited by Lord Sudley. London: John Murray, 1943.

Lloyd, Stephen. *Richard and Maria Cosway: Regency Artists of Taste and Fashion, with Essays by Roy Porter & Aileen Ribeiro*. Edinburgh: Scottish National Portrait Gallery, 1995.

Low, Donald A. *That Sunny Dome: A Portrait of Regency Britain*. London: Dent, 1977.

Luttrell, Barbara. *The Prim Romantic*. London: Chatto & Windus, 1965.

Lyttleton, Lady. *The Correspondence of Sarah Spencer, Lady Lyttleton, 1787-1879*. Edited by the Hon. Mrs. Hugh Wyndham. New York: C. Scribner's Sons, 1912.

Marchand, Leslie. *Byron: A Biography*. 3 vols. New York: Alfred Knopf, 1957.

———. *Byron: A Portrait*. Chicago: University of Chicago, 1970.

Masters, Brian. *Georgiana: Duchess of Devonshire*. London: Hamish Hamilton, 1981.

Mayne, Ethel. *The Life and Letters of Anne Isabella, Lady Noel Byron*. New York: Charles Scribner's Sons, 1929.
———. *A Regency Chapter: Lady Bessborough and Her Friendships*. London: MacMillan & Co. Ltd., 1939.

Melville, Lewis, ed. *The Berry Papers: 1763-1852*. New York: John Lane, 1914.

Mitchell, Leslie. *Holland House*. London: Duckworth, 1980.

Moore, Doris Langley. *The Late Lord Byron: Posthumous Dramas*. Philadelphia: Lippincott, 1961.

Namier, Lewis, and John Brooke. *The House of Commons, 1754-90*. 3 vols. London: HMSO, 1964.

Newman, Bertrand. *Lord Melbourne*. London: Macmillan and Co., 1930.

O'Mahony, Charles K. *The Viceroys of Ireland*. London: J. Long, 1912.

Paine, James. *Plans, Elevations and Sections of Noblemen and Gentlemen's Houses*. 1767, 1783. Reprint. London: Gregg Press, 1967 [1767 and 1783].

Pange, Victor de, ed. *Le Plus Beau de Toutes Les Fetes: Madame de Staël et Elisabeth Hervey, Duchesse de Devonshire, d'apres leur correspondance inedite, 1804-1817*. Paris: Klincksieck, 1980.

———, ed. *The Unpublished Correspondence of Madame de Staël and the Duke of Wellington, 1815-1817*. London: Cassell, 1965.

Papers of British Cabinet Ministers: 1782-1900. London: Her Majesty's Stationery Office, 1982.

Papers of British Politicians, 1782-1900. London: Her Majesty's Stationery Office, 1989.

Parliamentary History of England, from the Earliest Period to the Year 1803, from Which Last-Mentioned Epoch It Is Continued Downwards in the Work Entitled, "The Parliamentary Debates." Edited by T. C. Hansard. London: T. C. Hansard, 1817.

Paston, George, and Peter Quennell. *"To Lord Byron": Feminine Profiles Based upon Unpublished Letters, 1807-1824*. London: John Murray, 1939.

Patterson, W. M. *Sir Francis Burdett and His Times*. 2 vols. London, Macmillan and Co., 1931.

Pearson, John. *The Serpent and the Stag*. New York: Holt, Rinehart, and Winston, 1984.

Penny, Nicholas. *Reynolds*. London: Royal Academy of Arts, 1986.

Ponsonby, John. *The Ponsonby Family*. London: Medici Society, 1929.

Priestley, J. B. *The Prince of Pleasure and His Regency, 1811-20*. London: Heinemann, 1969.

Private Papers of British Diplomats: 1782-1900. London: Her Majesty's Stationery Office, 1985.

Quennell, Peter, ed. *The Prodigal Rake: Memoirs of William Hickey*. New York: Dutton, 1962.

Sanders, Lloyd, ed. *The Melbourne Papers*. London: Longmans Green, 1890.

Sedgwick, Romney, ed. *The House of Commons, 1715-1754*. 3 vols. New York: Oxford University Press, 1970.

Sheridan, Richard Brinsley. *The Rivals*. In *The School for Scandal and Other Plays*. London: Penguin, 1988.

———. *School for Scandal*. New York: W. W. Norton, 1995.

Sichel, Walter. "Diary of Duchess of Devonshire." In *Sheridan, from New and Original Materials, Including a Manuscript Diary*. 2 vols. New York: Houghton, Mifflin, 1909.

Smiles, Samuel. *Memoir and Correspondence of the late John Murray*. 3 vols. London: John Murray, 1891.

Southey, Robert. *Letters from England*. Edited and with an introduction by Jack Simmons. 1807. London: Cresset Press, 1951.

Steele, Elizabeth, ed. *The Memoirs of Mrs. Sophia Baddeley, Late of Drury-Lane Theatre*. 6 vols. London: Statiners Hall, 1787.

Steffan, T. G., E. Steffan, and W. W. Pratt, eds. *Lord Byron: Don Juan*. London: Penguin, 1986.

Stephen, Leslie, and Sir Sidney Lee, eds. *Dictionary of National Biography*. 22 vols. London: Oxford University Press, 1917.

Stirling, A. M. W., ed. *The Letter-Bag of Lady Elizabeth Spencer-Stanhope*. London: 1939.

Stokes, Hugh. *The Devonshire House Circle*. London: Herbert Jenkins, Limited, 1917.

Strickland, Margot. *The Byron Women*. London: Peter Owen, 1976.

Stuart, D. M. *Daughter of England: A New Study of Princess Charlotte of Wales and Her Family*. London: Macmillan, 1952.

————. *Dearest Bess; the Life and Times of Lady Elizabeth Foster, afterwards Duchess of Devonshire, from Her Unpublished Journals and Correspondence*. London: Methuen, 1955.

Surtees, Viriginia, ed. *A Second Self: The Letters of Harriet Granville: 1810-1845*. London: Michael Russell, 1990.

Survey of London. Edited by F. H. W. Sheppard. 41 vols. London: Athlone Press, 1964.

Taylor, Basil. *George Stubbs*. London: Harper & Row, 1971.

Taylor, Tom. *Life of Sir Joshua Reynolds*. 2 vols. London: John Murray, 1865.

Thompson, J. M. *Napoleon Bonaparte*. Oxford: Basil Blackwell, 1952.

Thorne, J. O., and T. C. Collocott, eds. *Chambers Biographical Dictionary*. Edinburgh: W. & R. Chambers, 1985.

Thorne, R. G., ed. *The History of Parliament: The House of Commons, 1790-1820*. 6 vols. London: Secker & Warburg, 1986.

Tipping, H. Avray. "Brocket Hall, Hertfordshire: The Seat of Sir Charles Nall-Cain I." *Country Life* (July 4, 11, and 18, 1925) 58:16-22, 60-67, 96-103.

Torrens, William McCullagh. *Life of Lord Melbourne*. 2 vols. London: Macmillan and Co., 1878.

Usher, Howard. *The Owners of Melbourne Hall*. Derby: J. H. Hall, 1993.

Valentine, Alan Chester. *The British Establishment, 1760-1784: An Eighteenth-Century Biographical Dictionary*. 2 vols. Norman: University of Oklahoma Press, 1970.

Villiers, Margorie. *The Grand Whiggery*. London: J. Murray, 1939.

Voltaire. "Le Taureau Blanc." In *Contes Philosophiques*. London: Penguin, 1954.

Walpole, Horace. *The Letters of Horace Walpole, Fourth Earl of Orford*. Edited by Helen and Paget Toynbee. 16 vols. Oxford, Clarendon Press, 1903.

Ward, J. R. *The Finance of Canal Building in Eighteenth-Century England*. Oxford: Oxford University Press, 1974.

Wark, Robert Rodger. *Meet the Ladies; Personalities in Huntington Portraits*. San Marino, California: The Huntington Library, 1972.

White, Geoffrey. *The Complete Peerage of England, Scotland, Ireland*. 10 vols. London: St. Catherine Press, 1949.

Williamson, George C. *Daniel Gardner*. New York: John Lane, 1921.

Wilson, Harriette. *Memoirs Written by Herself 1825*. Reprint. 2 vols. London: E. Nash 1909.

Wraxall, Sir Nathaniel William. *Historical and Posthumous Memoirs of His Own Time*. 5 vols. London: Richard Bentley, 1836.

Wyndham, Maud Mary. *Correspondence of Sarah Spencer, Lady Lyttelton*. London: John Murray, 1912.

Young, Arthur. *A General View of the Agriculture of Hertfordshire*. London: Sherwood, Neely, and Johnes, 1813.

———. *A General View of the Agriculture of Sussex*. London: R. Phillips, 1808.

Ziegler, Philip. *Melbourne*. New York: Atheneum, 1976.

John James Hamilton, ninth earl of Abercorn (1756-1818), also known as Viscount Strabane and Viscount Hamilton, was a Tory M.P. for East Looe (1783-84) and St. Germains (1784-89). On October 15, 1790, he was created marquis of Abercorn. He married Catherine, eldest daughter of Sir Joseph Copley, in 1779. She died in 1791, and he married Lady Cecil Hamilton the following year. Hamilton became an earl's daughter by Royal Warrant (1789), which implies that she was the marquis' mistress before the death of his first wife (Wraxall 1:63-94). At his residence, George Lamb's play *Who's the Dupe?* was performed before the Prince of Wales; Peniston, Lady Melbourne's son, recited an epilogue "of his own composition"; and the Melbournes attended with the Sheridans and Lord Granville (January 25, 1803; *Hary-O* 48). In an undated letter, Frederick Lamb blamed his mother for her sycophantic behavior in returning to the marquis of Abercorn's residence after his previously shabby treatment of her (1803-5?; *HRO*).

Sir Robert Adair (1763-1855), an admirer of Lady Melbourne (1800-10), served as minister to Austria (1806-8) and plenipotentiary to Turkey (1808-9). He also served on a special mission to Belgium (1831-35) and Prussia (1835-36) (*PPBD* 1).

Henry Addington (1757-1844), first Viscount Sidmouth (1805), served as speaker of the House of Commons (1789-1801), prime minister and chancellor of the Exchequer (1801-4), lord president of the Council (January-July 1805, 1806-7, April-June 1812), lord privy seal (February-October 1806), and secretary for home affairs (1812-22).

Charles Bruce, third earl of (1682-1747) Ailesbury (1682-1747) married Caroline Campbell (1721-1803), daughter of the fourth duke of Argyll, in 1739. After Lord Ailesbury's death, Lady Caroline Campbell married Henry Seymour Conway in 1747 — before her first husband was even buried (Walpole *Index*: 307)

Tsar Alexander I (1777-1825), or Alexander Pavlovich, emperor of Russia (1801-25), alternatively fought and befriended Napoleon I, forming the coalition that defeated him (1813-15). His instrumental role in the occupation of Paris after the downfall of Napoleon (1814) made him a hero in London. At the Congress of Vienna (1814-15) he sought a Holy Alliance (1815) intended to bring about peace based on Christian love. In 1793 his grandmother had him married, unhappily, to Princess Louise of Baden-Durlach (Elizabeth Feodorovna). "The Emperor treats her with respect, but there is great mutual coldness between them," Granville Leveson-Gower wrote, after dancing with her in St. Petersburg. "It is doubtful on which side the coldness first began" (June 1805; G. L. Gower 2:78). The only child of the marriage died on May 12, 1808. Alexander had another child, who also died young, by Madame Narischkine (*Britannica*, 11th edition).

John Till Allingham (fl. 1799-1810) was the son of a wine merchant and trained as a lawyer. He wrote a number of farces, including *Fortune's Frolic* (1799), *'Tis All a Farce* (1800), *Marriage Promise* (1803), *Mrs. Wiggins* (1803), *Hearts of Oak* (1804), *Romantic Lover* (1806), *The Weathercock* (1806), *Who Wins?* (1808), and *Independence* (1809). The success of his musical farces depended, in part, on the abilities of Charles Mathews. Allingham died young from intemperate living. Lady Melbourne mentions seeing *The Weathercock* with Byron. In 1806, while a young boy, Byron directed and starred in a performance of this play at Southwell (Boyes 125). The play was first produced at Drury Lane in 1805 and "met with great approbation, and continues a favorite stock piece" (*BBI* 21:277; *DNB* 1:333).

Charles Arbuthnot (1767-1850) entered the foreign office (1793) and Parliament (1795). He served as secretary of legation in Sweden (1795-99) and on a mission extraordinary to Württemberg (1798). He was later appointed consul and charge d'affaires in Portugal (1800-1), envoy to Sweden (1802-4), ambassador at Constantinople (1804-7), joint secretary of the Treasury (1809-23), and chancellor of the duchy of Lancaster (1828-30). Arbuthnot was an intimate friend of the duke of Wellington (*PPBD*).

Lady Asgill (fl. 1802-8), née Jemima Sophia Ogle, was the daughter of Admiral Sir Charles Ogle. In 1790 she married Sir Charles Asgill, equerry to the duke of York. Admired by Lord Granville Leveson-Gower (G. L. Gower 1:334n), Asgill was a member of the duchess of Devonshire's circle and a friend of Madame de Coigny at Harrington House. "I am inclined to like her partly from her coaxing manners," Lady Bessborough wrote, but "she puts me quite out of patience with her coquetry and affectation," twisting herself "in ten thousand shapes to appeal to Lord Colleraine and Mr. Graham" (G. L. Gower 1:356).

William Assheton. *See* Harbour.

Augusta (1737-1813), duchess of Brunswick, was the sister of George III (1737-1813) (G. L. Gower 1:42).

Princess Augusta (1757-1831) was the daughter of George III.

Sophia Baddeley (1745-1786) was a Drury Lane actress and the mistress of Lady Melbourne's husband, Peniston Lamb. The daughter of Valentine Snow, late sergeant-trumpeter to His Majesty, she was known as Sophia Snow when she ran away from this tyrannical father who tried to teach her the harpsichord. Once in London, she married Robert Baddeley, an actor in Drury Lane, who brought her on stage in the part of Cordelia. Sophia Baddeley excelled in genteel comedy. She performed at Vauxhall, Ranelagh, playing the part of Mrs. Beverley in the *Gamester* alongside her husband, and gained royal recognition for her appearance with him in *The Clandestine Marriage*. Later she appeared as Lady Elizabeth Grey in *The Earl of Warwick* and as Louis Dudley in *The West Indian*. Baddeley separated from her husband in 1767. Her *Memoirs* (1782) were written by her close friend Elizabeth Steele and edited by Alexander Bicknell (*DNB* 1:855-56).

Matthew Baillie (1761-1823), the brother of Scottish poet and playwright Joanna Baillie (1762-1851), was physician extraordinary to George III and physician in ordinary to Princess Charlotte. Baillie studied medicine at Glasgow and Oxford (1773-80) and anatomy under William Hunter, his mother's brother, before inheriting his uncle's practice and lectureship. He was elected to St. George's Hospital in 1787 and took his M.D. degree in 1789. Respected as a morbid anatomist, Baillie was the first to define cirrhosis of the liver. In 1817 he no longer practiced midwifery, and he has been criticized for his passive role during most of Charlotte's days of labor. Lady Melbourne was also cared for by Baillie, who became a fellow of the College of Physicians and was considered "the most successful general physician in London during his last twenty years" (*Chambers* 82; Corbett).

Shute Barrington (1734-1826), bishop of Durham, was the brother of Samuel Barrington (1729-1800) and the son of John Shute, first Viscount Barrington. Educated at Eton, he attended Merton College, Oxford (1757) and served as chaplain-in-ordinary to George III (1760). His first wife was the only daughter of the second duke of St. Albans. After she died (1766), Barrington became bishop of Llandaff (1769) and married Sir William Guise's only sister. She inherited Guise's estates in Gloucestershire when her brother died in 1783.

This may be the same Lady Barrington mentioned by Lady Melbourne in a letter of April 21, 1817. Barrington later became bishop of Salisbury (1782) and Durham (1791). He published a number of religious works (*CDNB* 1:159; Elwin, *Noels* 449).

Charles Bragge Bathurst (1759-1831) was treasurer of the navy (1801-3), secretary at war (1803-4), master of the Mint (1806-7), chancellor of the duchy of Lancaster (1812-23), and president of the Board of Control (1821-22). In March 1815 his house was attacked for his support of the Corn Bill, which raised the price of bread (*Times,* March 11, 1815).

Charles-Juste de Beauvau (1720-1793) was marshal of France and second prince de Beauvau-Craon. Beauvau served in the siege of Prague (1742). He was later named lieutenant-general, then captain of the guards, and was distinguished for his service in the siege of Mahon (1756). He served as an aide de camp and contributed to the victory of Marshall de Broglie, served as governor of Languedoc (1765), and was noteworthy for his humanity in freeing Protestants who had been long detained for refusing to abdicate their religion. In 1782 he was called to the government of Provence and named marshal of France. He became a minister for five months in 1789 (*Grand Encyclopedie* 5:1078).

Francis Russell, fifth duke of Bedford (1765-1802), attended Trinity College, Cambridge (1780) and traveled abroad (1784-86). A supporter of Fox and of Whig principles, Bedford could trace his family's ancestry back to the earl of Bedford, the patron of Pym and the friend of Hampden, and he shared with this ancestor a "common horror for arbitrary power" (*DNB* 17:436). Accused of being sympathetic to "French principles," he protested against methods used in repressing the rebellion in Ireland. Bedford opposed the war against France, seceded from Parliament in 1796 with the Whigs in the House, and did not resume his place regularly until after a change of ministry (1801). Though he did not consider himself a party man, he was an important supporter of the Whigs and was sought out by Lady Melbourne, to whom he was attached.

Like Lord Melbourne, Bedford was a close friend of the Prince of Wales and supported him during his ill-fated marriage to Princess Caroline of Brunswick on April 8, 1795. "The Prince was so drunk that he could scarcely support him from falling," Lord John Russell wrote (*DNB* 17:436). A member of the original Board of Agriculture (1793) and the first president of the Smithfield Club (December 17, 1798), he established a model farm at Woburn with "every convenience that could be desired for the breeding of cattle and experiments in farming." His experiments upon the respective merits of the various breeds of sheep are recorded by Arthur Young in his *Annals of Agriculture* (1795).

John Russell, sixth duke of Bedford (1766-1839), was the second son of Francis Russell, marquis of Tavistock (1739-1767). His second wife was Georgiana, the fifth daughter of Alexander Gordon, fourth duke of Gordon. They were married on June 23, 1809, and had seven sons and three daughters. Russell was a parliamentary reformer and a member of the Society of Friends of the People, to which Sheridan and Erskine, Rogers and Whitbread, and Mackintosh and Grey belonged.

Henry Belasyse (d. 1802), second earl of Fauconberg, died on March 23, 1802 and left three daughters and coheirs: Lady Charlotte (b. 1767), who married Thomas Edward Wynne; Lady Anne (1760-1808), who married Sir George Wombwell; and Lady Elizabeth (1770-1819), who married Bernard Howard, Esquire, afterwards twelfth duke of Norfolk (1815), from whom she was divorced in 1794 when she married Richard, second earl of Lucan (G. L. Gower 1:335n). In a letter to Byron, Lady Melbourne describes Mr. Belasyse as a "very foolish, pompous person" and mentions that "L^y Charlotte Belasyse & L^y Lucan (Mr Howard's Mother) are Neices to Lord Melbourne" (October 19, 1814, *LJ* 4:217).

William Henry Cavendish Bentinck (1738-1809) was styled marquis of Titchfield until he succeeded his father, William Bentinck, as third duke of Portland in 1762. In 1766 he married Lady Dorothy Cavendish, daughter of William, fourth duke of Devonshire. Bentinck served as M.P. for Weobly, Herefordshire (1760). He became lord chamberlain of the household and privy councillor (1765) in Rockingham's first ministry (1765-66), opposed the North ministry (1770-82), and succeeded Rockingham as leader of the Whig Party (1782). For the next few years, he served as lord lieutenant of Ireland (1782), first lord of the Treasury (April-December 1783), and prime minister (1783). He joined forces with Pitt during the French Revolution, serving as home secretary (1794-1801) and lord-lieutenant of Nottinghamshire (1794), lord president of the Council (1801-5), and first lord of the Treasury (1807-10). As home secretary, Bentinck played an instrumental role in passing an Act of Union with Ireland (1798). When Pitt's friends returned to power (1807), he again became prime minister (1807-9). Lord Buckinghamshire noted that he was "essentially honourable and high minded . . . without any apparent brilliancy his understanding is sound and direct" (Valentine 1:163).

Lieutenant-General Lord William Henry Cavendish Bentinck (1774-1839) was commander-in-chief and minister to the Two Sicilies (1811-14).

Charles Ferdinand, duc de Berri (1778-1820), was the second son of Charles X. At the outbreak of the French Revolution, he fled with his father to Turin, fought under Condé against France, visited Russia, and lived in London and Edinburgh. In 1814 he returned to France and was appointed commander of the troops in Paris (1815). He married Caroline Ferdinande Louise (1798-1870), eldest daughter of Francis, who became king of the Two Sicilies. The marriage took place on June 17, 1816 at the Cathedral of Notre Dame (*Morning Herald,* June 22, 1816). After the Napoleonic wars, the marriage of the Berris seemed to take on a ritual significance. The *Morning Herald* reported that "the Duke and Duchess of Angouleme and Berri are descended in precisely the same degree from Louis XIV and Henry IV."

Henrietta Frances Bessborough (1761-1821) was a daughter of John, first Earl Spencer; the younger sister of Georgiana, duchess of Devonshire; and the mother of Lady Caroline Lamb. On November 27, 1780, she married Viscount Duncannon, who succeeded his father as third earl of Bessborough in March 1793. They had four children together. She was thirty-two, twelve years older than Lord Granville Leveson-Gower, when they met at Naples and began a brief affair and a lifelong correspondence (Surtees 307). Seven years later, she had two illegitimate children by Leveson-Gower: Harriette Stewart (1800-1852) and George Stewart (1804?-1870). Admired by Richard Sheridan, Lady Bessborough was thought by Lady Hester Stanhope to have "ten times more cleverness than her sister the Duchess" (G. L. Gower 1:xvii). Lady Bessborough's nickname for Lady Melbourne was "the Thorn."

Bingham. *See also* Lady Lucan.

Charles Bingham (1735-1799), first earl of Lucan, served as sheriff (1756) and as M.P. for County Mayo (1761-76). He was created Baron Lucan of Castlebar, County Mayo, in 1776 and earl of Lucan in 1795. In 1760 he married Margaret, the only daughter and coheir of James Smith, M.P. of Cannons Leigh, Devon. His two children were Richard, second earl of Lucan, and Lavinia. In 1781 his daughter married the second earl of Spencer and in 1794 his son married Lady Elizabeth Belasyse, formerly the wife of Bernard Edward Howard (later twelfth duke of Norfolk) (*Burke's* 1667).

Margaret Bingham (d. February 27, 1814), countess of Lucan, married Charles Bingham, baronet, in 1760. Daughter and coheir of James Smith, Lady Lucan was an amateur painter who copied works by Isaac (d. 1617) and Peter Oliver (1594?-1647), John Hoskins (d. 1665), and Samuel Cooper (1609-1672). She published a five-volume series of drawings relating to portraits, houses, tombs, and birds that appear in Shakespeare's plays. Her five children included Lavinia Spencer, who in 1781 married Earl Spencer, brother of the duchess of Devonshire, and Eleanor Margaret, who married Thomas Lindsay, Esquire. Louisa and Anne,

Lady Lucan's other daughters, both died unmarried. Richard, the second Earl Lucan, was her only son and heir (*DNB* 2:512-513).

Lady Blarney was the nickname sometimes used by Byron and Lady Melbourne when referring to Lady Bessborough, the mother of Caroline Lamb. Byron borrowed the name from the absurd society lady in Goldsmith's *Vicar of Wakefield* (*LJ* 2:185).

Gebhard Lebrecht Blücher (1742-1819), prince von Wahlstadt, was commander-in-chief of the Prussian army. He played an important role in defeating Napoleon at Leipzig and in Wellington's victory at Waterloo.

Stanislas-Jean Chevalier de Boufflers (1738-1815) was a French wit known for his sallies and repartee, which gave him the surname Pataud. He entered the seminary in 1759 and distinguished himself serving in the campaign of Hanover (1762). In 1765 he was recognized by Voltaire, to whom he addressed several poems. He was appointed colonel in 1776 and took the post of governor of Sénégal in 1785. He published *Poesie Fugitive* in 1782; *Libre Arbitre* in 1808; and *Essay on Men of Letters* in 1810. He regretted publishing this last work, which alluded to the Bonaparte family, because Napoleon sent his young child, le comte Elzear de Sabran, to Vincennes because of her liaisons with Madame de Staël. His other prose works include *Tamara* and *The Dervish (Grande Larousse)*.

Thomas Brand (1774-1851) of The Hoo, Kimpton Hertfordshire, served as M.P. for Helston (1807) and Hertfordshire (1807-19). He joined the Whig Club on June 6, 1797. Although Brand consorted with Whig society, he did not join Brooks' Club until March 9, 1815. A frequent guest of the Melbournes at Brocket, he was introduced to Lord Holland as "gentle in his manners, shy and not happy" (R. G. Thorne 3:248). Brand attended or was a warden at the *Crown and Anchor* reform dinner (1809) and was considered a moderate reformer and rather irreligious. Soon after his reelection as M.P. in 1812, Brand's mother, Lady Dacre, became ill. At first it seemed he would be forced to choose William Hale, his protégé, over William Lamb, the favorite candidate of the Whig hostesses, but the recovery of his mother enabled him to avoid this. Brand voted against the banknote bill (December 8, 1812) and supported the Princess of Wales, Catholic relief, and agricultural protection (1813-16) (R. G. Thorne 3:250).

Henry Peter Brougham (1778-1868), Baron Brougham and Vaux, was lord chancellor (1830-34) and joint founder (1802) of the *Edinburgh Review*. A harsh critic of Byron's *Hours of Idleness,* he later befriended Lady Byron, advising her against seeking a reconciliation with her husband. Lady Melbourne mentions his defense of Sir Henry Mildmay (December 1814) with admiration. Brougham's affair with Caroline George Lamb, Lady Melbourne's daughter-in-law, caused a scandal in 1816 when they were seen together in Italy. Hary-O noticed the flirtation in England long before he left, and commented that he had "that peculiar sort of ugliness which charms" (October 8, 1815; *Hary-O* 55). Brougham defended Queen Caroline during her husband's divorce proceedings and was a founder of London University. In 1819 he married Mary Anne Spalding, a widow with two children.

Charles Bruce. *See* Lord Ailesbury.

Robert Hobart, earl of Buckinghamshire (1760-1816), styled Lord Hobart (1793-1804), fourth earl of Buckinghamshire (1804), served as chief secretary for Ireland (1789-93), governor of Madras (1793-98), secretary of state for war and the colonies (1801-4), chancellor of the duchy of Lancaster (January-July 1805; May-June 1812), joint postmaster-general (1806-7), and president of the Board of Control (1812-16). Lady Melbourne mentions his duel with Thomas Hardy (June 29, 1816).

Sir (Thomas) Charles Bunbury (1740-1821) married Lady Sarah Lennox, daughter of the second duke of Richmond, in 1762. Their childless marriage was dissolved by Parliament in 1776. He served as M.P. of Suffolk for forty-three years (*Burke's* 408).

Robert Burdett (b. 1796), sixth baronet from 1844. In a cartoon of 1809 he is depicted receiving a lesson on the Magna Carta the day his father, Sir Francis Burdett, was arrested on charges of libel (George 5:11550)

Lord Burghersh. *See* John Fane.

Charles Burney (1726-1814), organist, composer, and musical historian, corresponded with Lady Melbourne, who alludes to his daughter, Fanny Burney.

Fanny Burney (1752-1840), later Madame d'Arblay, was the daughter of the composer and organist Charles Burney. She was associated with her father's famous friends, including David Garrick and Samuel Crisp. Burney was largely self-educated. Her first novel, *Evelina* (1778), was published anonymously, but she soon acknowledged its authorship and achieved literary prominence. Mrs. Thrale introduced her to literary society and Samuel Johnson visited her at the Thrales (1779-83). Burney became an intimate friend of Johnson and his circle. Her second novel, the social satire *Cecilia, or Memoirs of an Heiress* (1782), was followed by *Camilla, or, A Picture of Youth* (1796) and *The Wanderer* (1814). She became second keeper of the robes to Queen Charlotte (1786-91) and her experiences in the queen's household gave her insights into English culture and society. In 1793 she married General D'Arblay, a French émigré. She lived in France from 1802 until 1812.

Richard Butler (1775-1819), eleventh Baron Cahier, first earl of Glengal, married Emily, youngest daughter of James St. John Jeffreys, of Blarney Castle. He was raised to the earldom on January 22, 1816. His son was Richard Butler, Viscount Caher (1794-1858) of Caher Castle, County Tipperary (R. G. Thorne 4:347; *BBI* 179:19-22).

The Honorable Frederick "Poodle" Byng (1784-1871), wit and society dandy, was the fifth son of the fifth Viscount Torrington. He was called "Poodle" by Canning for his curly white hair and performed in theatrical amusements at the marquis of Abercorn's residence where the Cowpers, the Melbournes, and the Macdonalds were in attendance (December 1, 1805; *Hary-O* 134). Byng served as a clerk in the Foreign Office from 1804 until 1839. He married Catherine Neville, his mother's maid, and toward the end of his life was known as a "Regency remnant" (Surtees 301).

George Byng (1740-1812), fourth Viscount Torrington (1750), was minister plenipotentiary at Brussels (1783-92). Lady Mary Coke remembered the extravagance of Lord and Lady Torrington in Brussels, and his debt to the duke of Portland (Walpole 33:210 n.8).

John Byng (1743-1813), fifth Viscount Torrington (1812), was an army officer and diarist (Walpole 33:210). His brother, George Byng, was said to have caused John's financial ruin.

Robert Byng (fl. 1798-1818) was the son of George Byng, fourth Viscount Torrington (1740-1812), and the brother of the first earl of Strafford. In 1798 Lady Bessborough defended him against Lord Granville Leveson-Gower, who charged that he and Adair were fools. "Bob Byng is . . . very good natur'd and . . . as good as . . . your acquaintainces whom you would be very angry to have call'd fools" (G. L. Gower 1:222). Lady Melbourne mentions him as a visitor at Brocket Hall in 1817.

George Gordon Noel, sixth Baron Byron (1788-1824). Lord Byron began his affair with Lady Melbourne's daughter-in-law, Caroline Lamb, in the spring of 1812. Lady Melbourne pursued a correspondence to end this affair and agreed to propose marriage on Byron's behalf to her niece, Annabella Milbanke, who rejected him in 1812 but accepted him in the fall of 1814. In the intervening years, Byron had an affair with his half-sister,

Augusta Leigh, and with a number of other women. Lady Melbourne became his chief confidante during these years. Creevy repeats the uncorroborated rumor that Lady Melbourne "extended her amours so late in life as to entrap Ld Byron" (September 29, 1825; *Creevey* 244).

Miss Campbell, formerly sub-governess, was not liked by Princess Charlotte, but "gradually, by 'diffidence and delicacy' won the Princess over" (Stuart, *Daughter of England* 207). She was one of her attendants at Cranbourne Lodge and, later, at Weymouth.

Lady Caroline Campbell (1721-1803) was the daughter of the fourth duke of Argyll. She married Charles Bruce, third earl of Ailesbury, in 1739. The widowed Campbell married the Honorable Henry Seymour Conway in 1747 and the couple had a daughter, Anne Damer, who became a close friend of Lady Melbourne's (Walpole 25:360).

George Canning (1770-1827), born outside of aristocratic circles, was regarded as a brilliant opportunist by many of his contemporaries. His sarcasm and arrogance, as displayed in the Tory *Anti-Jacobin,* often earned him more contempt than admiration. After becoming M.P. for Newport, Isle of Wight (1794) and president of the Board of Control (1799), he served his first term as foreign secretary (1807-9). Canning insisted that Lord Castlereagh, the war secretary, be removed because of his disastrous handling of the Walcheren expedition. In 1809 they fought a duel and Canning was wounded in the thigh. As a result of this incident, his political career was interrupted for many years, during which time he served as M.P. for Liverpool (1812), ambassador to Portugal (1814-16?), president of the Board of Control (1816-21), and M.P. for Harwich (1822). After Castlereagh's suicide he served as foreign secretary once again (1822-27). Canning became prime minister in 1827, the year in which he died.

Frederick Howard, fifth earl of Carlisle (1748-1825), was chancery guardian to Byron but did not introduce him to the House of Lords and was attacked in *English Bards and Scotch Reviewers.* His tragedy, *The Father's Revenge* (1783), was praised by Johnson and Walpole, and his *Tragedies and Poems* was issued in 1801. A friend of Charles James Fox and George Selwyn, Carlisle served as treasurer of the household (1777), head of the commission to treat with Americans (1778), president of the Board of Trade (1779), viceroy of Ireland (1780-82), and lord steward (1782-83). He opposed Pitt on the regency question (1788-89). In February 1780 he was appointed lord-lieutenant of East Riding of Yorkshire. In October of that year he succeeded John Hobart, second earl of Buckinghamshire, as lord-lieutenant of Ireland. He surrendered his position at the Board of Trade (December 1780) and arrived in Dublin at the close of that month, taking William Eden, afterwards Lord Auckland, as his chief secretary. He is mentioned as a dancing partner of Lady Melbourne's at the French ambassador's ball (1773).

Lady Carrington was the wife of Robert Percy Smith.

Lord Carrington. *See* Robert Percy Smith.

Lord Edward Charles Cavendish (1744-1819), son of the second duke of Portland, was M.P. for Carlisle (1768-74) and Nottinghamshire. In 1782 he married the eldest daughter of Richard Cumberland, Esquire (*BBI* 97:129). He is mentioned as not present during the vote on the king's amendment in 1792.

George Augustus Henry Cavendish (1754-1834), third son of William Cavendish (1720-1764), was styled Lord George Cavendish until 1831, when he was created Baron Cavendish and earl of Burlington. In 1782 he married Elizabeth, only daughter of Charles Compton, seventh earl of Northampton. He served as M.P. for Knaresborough (1775-80), Derby Borough (1780-96), and Derbyshire (1797-1831). Cavendish opposed the North ministry (1780; 1783), voted against Shelburne's peace terms (1783), and served as L.L.D. of Cambridge (1811) (Valentine 1:236).

Giuseppe Ceracchi (1760-1801). Born in Corsica, Ceracchi was nine when he left his country with his father to escape French domination. He studied sculpture in Rome and had attained a certain reputation when Bonaparte's presence in Italy led him to embrace his cause. He executed a bust of the general and returned to Rome after the departure of the French army. In 1798 he took an active role in the insurrectionist movement that Championnet brought to Rome, leaving at the same time as the French. He arrived in Paris in 1799, expecting Bonaparte to make his fortune. Bonaparte did nothing for him, forgetting his former compatriot despite numerous petitions. Ceracchi joined with Demerville, Arena, Diana, and Topino-Lebrun in an unsuccessful plot to assassinate the first consul in the lobby of the opera and was hanged (*Grand Dictionnaire* 3:743).

Sir William Chambers (1723-1796) was architect of Melbourne House, Piccadilly, where Lady Melbourne lived before trading her residence with the duke of York and Albany (1791). After the Duke of York sold the building, it was enlarged and reconstructed by Henry Holland and A. Copland as the Albany Chambers (1803-4), and was the bachelor residence of Byron, Canning, Macaulay, and others. Chambers was recommended to Lord Bute as a suitable architectural tutor to the Prince of Wales, afterwards King George III. He began his professional training at J. F. Blondel's École des Arts in Paris, where he met the leaders of French neoclassicism in the 1760s and 1770s. In 1750 he set out for Italy, spending five years in Rome and other cities. In 1763 he published *Plans, Elevations, Sections and Perspective Views of the Gardens and Buildings at Kew in Surrey,* based on the Dowager Princess's commission for the grounds of her house at Kew. He exhibited at the Society of Arts (1761-68) and brought about the foundation of the Royal Academy of Arts, where he exhibited from 1769 to 1777. He designed Somerset House and numerous other commissions. Chambers' architectural style was a combination of French neoclassicism and English Palladianism, and he remained unsympathetic to what he called "Attic Deformity" or to the Gothic style. His *Dissertation on Oriental Gardening,* published in 1772, was an attack on the bare style of landscape gardening associated with "Capability" Brown. Chambers' pupils and assistants included James Gandon, Edward Stevens, John Yenn, Thomas Hardwick, and Robert Brown. His daughter Cornelia married Lady Melbourne's brother, John Milbanke, in 1775 (Colvin 204-6).

Princess Charlotte (1796-1817) was the only child of the future George IV and Caroline of Brunswick. Her six-month engagement to Prince William of Orange was broken off in June 1814, much to the annoyance of the Prince Regent. In 1816 Charlotte married Prince Leopold of Saxe-bourg, who later became first king of Belgium.

Giovanni Battista Cipriani (1727-1785), the Italian historical painter and engraver, was born in Florence. He received instruction from an English painter, Ignazio Hugford, before studying in Rome for three years (1750-53). In 1755 he accompanied Sir William Chambers and the sculptor Joseph Wilton to London, where his drawings, engraved by Bartolozzi, became extremely popular. He was a member of the St. Martin's Lane Academy and a foundation member (1768) of the Royal Academy, where he exhibited from 1769 to 1783. Cipriani studied design in the duke of Richmond's gallery in Privy Garden, Whitehall. He illustrated a number of books and married an English woman in 1761, settling in Hammersmith (*DNB* 4:364-65).

John Fitzgibbon, Lord Clare (1792-1851), succeeded his father as second earl of Clare in 1802. Upon leaving England in 1809, Byron left him his library. The poet apostrophizes him in "Childish Recollections" as Lycus (lines 287-99).

Adam Clarke (1762-1832), Wesleyan divine, was the author of a *Bibliographical Dictionary* (8 vols., 1802-6) and a well-known edition of the Scriptures (8 vols., 1810-26).

Samuel Clarke (1675-1729), a disciple of Newton, was rector of St. James' Westminster from 1709. He was accused of Arianism in 1714. Clarke believed moral laws could be deduced from logical necessity. Byron mentions him favorably in a letter to Edward Daniel Clarke (June 17, 1813; *LJ* 3:63).

Lady Clermont (1733-1820), Frances Cairnes Murray, was married in 1752 to William Henry Fortescue. She was a friend of Marie Antoinette, and the Clermonts often attended the court of Versailles. This is possibly the woman who had an abortion after an affair with an apothecary, an incident mentioned in the duchess of Devonshire's letter of 1778, when Lady Melbourne was at Tunbridge Wells (1778).

Lord Clermont (1722-1806), William Henry Fortescue, was created baron (1770), viscount (1776), and earl of (1777) Clermont. He was a close friend to Charles James Fox and the Prince of Wales, who accidentally shot Clermont (1787) on a hunting trip and made him a gentleman of the bedchamber. His house was in Berkeley square. Wraxall wrote, "I have scarcely ever known a man more fitted for a companion of kings and queens, than was Lord Clermont" (2:340-45). Lady Melbourne mentions him in a letter describing the panic created by rumors of a French invasion (1780).

Augustus Clifford. *See* Augustus William Clifford Foster.

Madame de Coigny (1758/9-1832), or Louis Marthe de Conflans, married (1775) the marquis de Coigny, eldest son of François Franquetot, duc de Coigny. Before the French Revolution she was friends with Marie Antoinette and was known in Parisian society for her wit and caustic tongue. While an émigré in London (1801), she was a friend to Georgiana, duchess of Devonshire, and Lauzun, duc de Biron. Her daughter, Antoinette, was called "Fanny" and married (1805) General Sebastiani, who died at Constantinople (1807) (G. L. Gower 1:177).

Anne-Francoise-Aimée de Franquetot de Coigny (1769-1820), only child of the comte de Coigny, was a famous beauty also known as the duchess de Fleury. Her first husband was André-Hercule-Marie-Louis de Rosset de Rocozel de Perignan, marquis, duc de Fleury, whom she married in 1784 and divorced in May 1793. Her second marriage was to Claude-Philibert-Hippolyte de Mouret, comte de Montrond. She was divorced from him in 1802 and was known thereafter as Mme Aimée de Coigny (October 8, 1792; Walpole 11:181). Lady Melbourne's daughter mentions her in a letter of October 25, 1816.

Thomas Coke (1675-1727) was the son of John Coke (d. 1692), from whom he inherited the mansion and estate of Melbourne in Derbyshire. Educated at New College, Oxford, he sat in Parliament as a member for Derbyshire (1698-1710) and for the rotten borough of Grampound (1710-14). Politically he was a Tory and a supporter of Harley, but he retained the court post of vice-chamberlain, to which he was appointed in 1707, throughout the reign of George I. His designs for the monuments at Melbourne indicate that he was also an amateur architect. At Melbourne, with the assistance of Henry Wise, he laid out a formal garden that is one of the best surviving examples of its kind in the country (Colvin 228).

George Colman (1762-1836) the younger, son of George Colman the elder, was a dramatist. He attended Westminster (1772), Christ Church, Oxford (1779), and Aberdeen University (1781). Colman wrote or adapted more than twenty-four dramatic pieces, including the comedies *The Heir at Law* (1797) and *John Bull* (1803). He served as manager of the Haymarket theater (1789-1813) and published coarse comic poems (1797-1820). A judicious examiner of plays (1824-36), he later became involved in litigation and debt. He sometimes used the pseudonym of Arthur Griffinhoofe. *Random Records* is his autobiography (1830) (*CDNB* 1:614; *DNB* 4:849).

Benjamin Constant (1767-1830), the French novelist and politician, published his master-piece *Adolphe* in 1816. In her letter to Annabella of June 29, 1816, Lady Melbourne praises this novel, which deals with Constant's relationship with Madame de Staël and also captures the flavor of his early romance with Madame de Charrière, who was twenty-seven years his senior. At first a harsh critic of Bonaparte, Constant was expelled from the tribunate in 1802. Disappointed when the Bourbon monarchy was restored, he reconciled himself to the Napoleonic Empire of the Hundred Days under the influence of Madame Récamier.

Field-Marshal Lord Henry Seymour Conway (1719-1795) was a nephew of Sir Robert Walpole and the father of Anne Damer. He served in Flanders and was present at the battles of Dettingen, Fontenoy, and Culloden. Conway served under Prince Ferdinand of Brunswick, opposed the continuance of the war against the United States, and served as governor of Jersey (1772-95). In 1747 he married Caroline, the widow of Charles Bruce, earl of Ailesbury (also Aylesbury and Alisbury), and the only daughter of Lieutenant-Colonel John Campbell, afterwards fourth duke of Argyll (G. L. Gower 1:78).

Maria Cosway (1759/60-1838), née Maria Hadfield, was born in Florence. She studied music and painting, copying works in the Uffizi Gallery and the Pitti Palace. In 1781 she married Richard Cosway and the couple kept a fashionable studio and salon in Berkeley Street and at Shomberg House in Pall Mall after 1784. Maria Cosway painted a portrait of Georgiana, duchess of Devonshire, bursting from the clouds. She also painted Lady Melbourne's son George, in the allegorical manner of the day, as *The Infant Bacchus* (Lloyd 25).

Richard Cosway (1742-1821), the famous miniaturist, was a companion of the Prince Regent's. Born at Tiverton, he studied art in London and painted numerous miniatures of fashionable women, including Mrs. Fitzherbert. Cosway painted Lady Melbourne's portrait for the Prince Regent.

Madame Cottins (1770-1807) wrote five novels, including *Claire d'Albe* (1799), *Malvina* (1801), and *Elisabeth ou les Exiles de Siberie* (1806). Her moral thoughts and reflections were published in London (1820). One of her lovers was J. de Vaines. Cottins is rumored to have committed suicide (*Grande Larousse*). Lady Melbourne compared Lady Caroline Lamb to a heroine from one of Cottins' novels (September 29, 1812).

Emily Cowper. *See* Emily Lamb.

Peter, fifth earl of Cowper (1778-1837), succeeded his bachelor brother George Augustus to the earldom (February 12, 1799). He married Lady Melbourne's daughter Emily (July 20, 1805) at Melbourne House, Whitehall. Cowper suffered from a melancholy disposition. Augustus Foster described him as a "discontented rich man, because with all the idea that he ought to be happy he never is so" (April 13, 1802; Foster 174). Cowper did go on to Rome, however, and wrote to tell of his encounter with Lady Elizabeth Foster's father, the eccentric Lord Bristol (December 28 [1802]; 45549, f.3).

Anne Crewe (1748-1818), née Frances Anne Greville, was the daughter of Fulke Greville. She married John Crewe, of Crewe Hall in Chesire, whose income of £10,000 a year enabled her to preside over a salon in Grosvenor Street. There she entertained the same set of friends that assembled at Devonshire House. Crewe was compared with the duchess of Devonshire as early as 1772 and has been described as "a less daunting presence than Lady Melbourne." Fanny Burney thought the "form of her face . . . exquisitely perfect" (Masters 47).

Richard Croft (1762-1818), accoucheur, served as obstetrician to the duchess of Devonshire and, more than two decades later, to Princess Charlotte. He was trained by Denman, whose assistant he became, whose daughter he married, and whose practice he inherited. Croft followed Denman's principles, laid out in *An Introduction to the Practice of Midwifery* (1788), which advocated letting nature take its course and discouraged the use of instruments in facilitating labor. Princess Charlotte died on November 6, 1817, five and one-half hours after giving birth to a stillborn baby. Her death broke the direct line of the English monarchs, resulting in the accession of Queen Victoria. Croft was unjustly vilified for the death of the popular princess who, it was thought, might have been saved by a timely forceps delivery. He committed suicide from guilt over the incident. "I cannot imagine an obstetrician who suffered more cruel misfortune, more undeserved criticism nor more false accusations," Henry Vincent Corbett argues in *A Royal Catastrophe* (37).

Sophia Susanna Curzon (1758-1782), third sister of Judith Milbanke, married Nathaniel Curzon on August 11, 1777.

Louis-Joachim D'Arnheim (1781-1834), the German poet who traveled in Germany and neighboring regions, married the sister of his friend Clement Brentano (1811). In 1810 Lady Bessborough described him at Chiswick leading a group "waltzing every night and all night long." He "seems the best humour'd person in the world and most obliging, but like every other of the same description, born to be laugh'd at" (G. L. Gower 2:355-56). His principal works include popular songs, which he edited with Brentano under the title *Des Knaben Wunderhorn* (Heidelberg, 1806- 8) (*Columbia*).

Robert Charles Dallas (1754-1824). Dallas' sister Henrietta Charlotte married George Anson Byron, the poet's uncle. Dallas had already written poetry, a tragedy, and two novels when Byron met him in 1808. He served as Byron's literary agent, arranging for the publication of *English Bards* by Cawthorn and the first two cantos of *Childe Harold* with John Murray. Byron gave him the copyrights to these manuscripts and additional money. On February 20, 1814, Lady Melbourne praised Dallas for admitting this in the newspaper when critics charged Byron with collecting royalties (*LJ* 1:274).

Anne Seymour Damer (1749-1828), a close friend of Lady Melbourne's, was a sculptress and painter. The daughter of Henry Conway, she married John Damer (June 14, 1767), eldest son of Joseph Damer, Lord Milton (afterwards earl of Dorchester), and heir to a fortune of £30,000 a year. Lady Melbourne mentions how Damer shot himself at the Bedford Arms, Covent Garden (August 15, 1776). His wardrobe was sold for £15,000 and his widow was left with a jointure of £2,500 a year. Damer's work in stone includes busts of Lady Elizabeth Foster (afterwards duchess of Devonshire), Lady Melbourne, George III, George IV, Admiral Nelson, Mrs. Siddons, the Princess of Wales, Miss Berry, and—for the British Museum—herself. On the peace of Amiens, Josephine, as wife of the first consul, invited Damer to Paris and introduced her to Napoleon. Damer gave Napoleon a bust of Fox during the "hundred days." Napoleon presented her with a diamond snuffbox with his portrait, now in the British Museum.

Horace Walpole compared Damer's sculptures to those of Bernini and praised her knowledge of Latin and Greek. He granted Strawberry Hill to her for life, along with a legacy of £2,000 with which to maintain it. She lived there until 1811, gave popular garden parties, and surrounded herself with a coterie of friends, especially the Berrys. In 1800 she produced *Fashionable Friends,* a comedy by Miss Berry. Damer recited the epilogue, written by Joanna Baillie, and it was performed, unsuccessfully, at Drury Lane (April 22, 1802). In 1818 she bought York House, Twickenham (*DNB* 5:451).

John Bligh, fourth earl of Darnley (1767-1831) was among those who supported the Corn Bill. His house was attacked by rioters in March 1815 (*BBI* 118:272-77, 304:69).

Thomas Davison (1744-1794) of Blakiston assumed the additional surname of Bland (1786) when he inherited Kippax Park from his cousin, the sister of Sir Hungerford Bland, last baronet of that name. Davison is mentioned by Lady Melbourne as someone interested in renting the house at Halnaby (1770-80). He married Jane Meynell (1776) and their son, Thomas Davison Bland of Kippax Park, was one of the trustees of Lady Byron's marriage settlement (Elwin, *Wife* 57).

John Dawson (1744-1798) was a close friend of the Noels. On January 1, 1778, he married Lady Caroline Stuart, daughter of the third earl of Bute. Dawson succeeded his father as second Viscount Carlow in 1779 and became earl of Portarlington in 1785 (Elwin, *Noels* 65).

Pierre De Vaux (1705-1788) was born in Puy-en-Velay in 1705; he died in Grenoble (1788). He served successively in Italy, distinguished himself in the defense of Prague, Fontenoy, and in sieges of Tournay and Brussells. Named lieutent general in 1759, he forced Prince Ferdinand to end the siege of Goettingue and, in 1769, ended the Corsican revolt in two months. In 1783, he was appointed General (*Grand Dictionnaire* 15:818).

Edward, twelfth earl of Derby (1752-1834), served as lord-lieutenant of County Lancaster. He was married first (1774) to Elizabeth, only daughter of the sixth duke of Hamilton and Brandon, and second (1797) to Eliza, the celebrated actress who died in 1829 (*Burke's* 776).

Elizabeth, Lady Derby (1755-1797) was the daughter of the duke of Hamilton and the Irish beauty Elizabeth Gunning. She married Edward, twelfth earl of Derby in 1774, at the age of nineteen (Masters 74).

Georgiana Poyntz, duchess of Devonshire (1757-1806), married the fifth duke of Devonshire in 1774. She campaigned for Fox in the Westminster election of 1784 and had a child by Charles Grey in 1791. She was one of Lady Melbourne's closest friends.

William, fifth duke of Devonshire (1748-1811), was the husband of Georgiana, duchess of Devonshire. His wife complained of his coolness in *The Sylph*. The duke had two children by Elizabeth Foster, whom he later married and who became the next duchess of Devonshire.

William, sixth duke of Devonshire (1790-1858). Born on May 21, 1790, he was the first legitimate son of Georgiana, duchess of Devonshire. His disputed birth is mentioned by Lady Melbourne in a letter to her son Frederick on February 17, 1818.

Lady Douglas and **Sir John Douglas** made a deposition to the effect that the Princess of Wales had an illegitimate child by Sir Sydney Smith in 1802 (Villiers 272).

Lord Dudley. *See* John William Ward.

Sir George O'Brien Wyndham, third earl of Egremont (1751-1837), was the close friend and lover of Lady Melbourne. He was reputed to be the father of William and Emily Lamb. Egremont was a great art patron, cultivating the careers of William Turner, John Flaxman, and others. Raised to the peerage at the age of twelve, he protested Lord North's American policy and rejected Shelburne's motion in favor of economic reform. Egremont proposed restrictions on the power of the Prince of Wales as Regent (1789). Charles Greville admired his political ability, and Fox consulted him for his opinions on India. He became increasingly conservative and was a consistent opponent of Catholic emancipation. Appointed to a seat at the Board of Agriculture (August 31, 1793), he later became lord lieutenant of Sussex (1819-35) and was a leading figure in London society before retiring to Petworth. His proposed marriages to Lady Mary Somerset in 1774 and Lady Charlotte Maria Waldegrave (afterwards the duchess of Grafton) in 1780 did not take place, reputedly because of Lady Melbourne.

 The following poem, which summarizes Egremont's virtues, appears to have been written by a contemporary:

> Heedless of pomp, to art and science dear,
> Lord of the soil, see EGREMONT appear;
> Firm in attachment to his native land,
> No foreign feeling guides his fostering hand;

In judgement sound, in contemplation calm,
To gifted Britain still he gives the palm;
To pining genius still he points the way,
And merit ushers to the blaze of day

(Butlin 105)

John Scott, first earl of Eldon (1751-1838), the English lawyer and politician, served as M.P. (1782), knight and solicitor-general (1788), and lord chancellor (1801-27). He supported the Corn Bill and opposed Roman Catholic emancipation, abolition of the slave trade, and reform of the House of Commons.

William Eliot (1767-1845), second earl of St. Germans (1823), served as secretary of legation in Prussia (1791-93) and secretary of embassy in the Netherlands (1793-95).

Elizabeth (1770-1840), princess of England and landgravine of Hesse-Homburg, was the seventh child and third daughter of George III and Queen Charlotte. In 1795 she designed a series of pictures titled *The Birth and Triumph of Cupid*. Elizabeth involved herself in philanthropic work, patronizing literary artists and attending her father during his periods of mental illness. On April 7, 1818, she married Phillip Augustus Frederick, hereditary prince of Hesse-Homberg (*DNB* 6:658).

Margaret Mercer Elphinstone (1788-1867), comtesse de Flahault, Viscountess Keith, Baroness Nairne, was the daughter of Admiral Lord Keith. Her uncle, William Ada, adviser to the Regent, introduced her to Princess Charlotte, with whom she struck up an intimate friendship. The two entered into a confidential correspondence, and Elphinstone was thought to have betrayed Princess Charlotte's secrets to the Prince Regent. On June 20, 1817, she married the comte de Flahault, aide-de-camp to Bonaparte, who took refuge in England during the restoration of the Bourbons. She had hoped to marry the sixth duke of Devonshire (Surtees 303) and had once invited Byron to Tunbridge Wells, shortly after he met Caroline Lamb (July 29, 1812; 2:183n).

Thomas Erskine (1750-1823), first baron, lord chancellor, was born in Edinburgh and graduated from Trinity College, Cambridge (1776). He was immediately successful as an advocate, defending Captain Baillie, lieutenant-governor of Greenwich Hospital, for libel (1778). He also defended Admiral Lord Keppel (1779) and Lord George Gordon (1781). In 1783 Erskine was king's counsel and M.P. for Portsmouth. Unsuccessful as a parliamentary orator, he sympathized with the French Revolution, joined the "Friends of the People," and defended clients during the political prosecutions of 1793-94. He accepted a retainer from Tom Paine and thus forfeited the attorney-generalship, which he had held since 1786, to the Prince of Wales. Erskine's other clients included John Frost (1793), Thomas Hardy (1794), Horne Tooke (1794), and James Hadfield (1800). In 1802 he was appointed chancellor to the Prince of Wales. He was raised to the peerage in 1806, but resigned the following year. Erskine was invested with the Order of the Thistle (1815) on the death of Lord Lothian. Lady Melbourne charged him with apostasy for accepting such a ministerial honor (Murray 1:297; *DNB* 6:853-58).

John Fane (1759-1841), tenth earl of Westmoreland, received his M.A. from Cambridge (1778), where he befriended Pitt. He later became joint paymaster-general (1789), member of the Privy Council (1789), and lord-lieutenant of Ireland (1789-95). Fane restrained his opposition to Catholic emancipation out of deference to Pitt. His first wife was Sarah Anne, only daughter and heiress of Robert Child, the London banker. He eloped with her in May 1782 and succeeded in reaching Scotland, where the marriage took place. Most of Robert Child's property was left to the eldest daughter by this marriage, Lady Sarah Sophia Fane, who married the earl of Jersey. Lady Westmoreland, who bore six children, died in 1793. Seven years later, the earl married his second wife, Jane, the daughter and coheiress of R. H. Saunders, M.D. By her he had three sons and one daughter. His second wife and six of his children survived him (*DNB* 6:1040-41).

John Fane (1784-1859), eleventh earl of Westmoreland, was known as Lord Burghersh (1784-1841) until he succeeded his father, John Fane, tenth earl of Westmoreland. He founded the Royal Academy of Music (1823) and served in the militia in a number of capacities. Burghersh was aide-de camp to the duke of Wellington and took part in the battle of Talavera in 1809. In 1810 he served in the third dragoon guards in Portugal. Burghersh was named privy councillor (1822) and went to Naples to congratulate Francis I on his accession to the throne of the Two Sicilies (1825). His wife was Priscilla Anne Fane. (*DNB* 6:1040-41).

Priscilla Anne Fane (1793-1879), countess of Westmoreland, was the fourth child of William Wellesley-Pole, third earl of Mornington. She married John Fane (who was then Lord Burghersh and afterwards eleventh earl of Westmoreland) on June 26, 1811. An accomplished linguist and a distinguished artist, she exhibited six figure pieces in the Suffolk Street Exhibition (1833-57) and sent two scriptural subjects to the British Institution (1842-57). Fane painted Anne, countess of Mornington, surrounded by her three distinguished sons: Richard, marquis of Wellesley; Arthur, duke of Wellington; and Henry, Baron Cowley. Lady Melbourne attended a party of hers on March 24, 1813 (*DNB* 6:1043).

Lady Sarah Sophia Fane (1785-1867), afterwards Villiers, countess of Jersey, was the eldest daughter of John, earl of Westmoreland, K.G., and his first wife, Sarah Anne, the daughter and sole heiress of Robert Child of Osterley Park, Middlesex. She married George Villiers, fifth earl of Jersey, on May 23, 1804 (*BBI* 389:411). Fane was a mistress of the Prince of Wales and was one of the few to support Byron publicly after his separation from his wife (*BBI* 1228:49).

Sir Walter Farquhar (1738-1819) cared for Lady Melbourne during the final stages of her rheumatism. He studied under Claude Nicolas le Cat, the celebrated anatomist and surgeon at Rouen. Educated at King's College, Aberdeen, before graduating he served in Lord Howe's expedition against Belle Isle (1761). Farquhar obtained the degree of M.D. from Aberdeen on January 29, 1796. Created a baronet in March of that year and appointed physician in ordinary to the Prince of Wales, he rapidly obtained a high place in the profession. His patients included many persons of rank and influence, and he was physician to Pitt during the prime minister's final illness. By 1813 Farquhar had partially withdrawn from practice. Though able and successful, he made no contributions to medical science or literature (Wraxall 2:72).

Charles Ferdinand. *See* duc de Berri.

John Finlayson (1730?-1776?), an engraver, worked in London. He received a premium from the Society of Arts in 1773 and died about three years afterwards. He engraved several portraits in mezzotint, including Reynolds' portrait of Lady Elizabeth Melbourne and a portrait of the duchess of Gloucester, as well as historical subjects. Finlayson also engraved paintings by Francis Cotes (1725-1770) and John Zoffany (1733-1810) (*Bryan's* 2:167).

John Fitzgibbon. *See* Lord Clare.

Alleyne Fitzherbert. *See* Lord St. Helens.

Maria Anne Fitzherbert (1756-1837) was the daughter of Walter Smythe and the mistress and then wife of the Prince Regent. She was married first to Edward Weld of Lulworth Castle (1775) and second to Thomas Fitzherbert of Swynnerton (1778). She lived at Richmond after the death of her second husband in 1781. In December 1785 she was married at her house before witnesses to George, Prince of Wales, with whom she lived until 1803. She was recognized by the royal family in spite of the Royal Marriage Act and the Act of Settlement, which made the marriage illegal on account of the minority of the prince and the Roman Catholic religion of Fitzherbert. Fox's denial in Parliament that the ceremony had taken place was privately repudiated by the prince.

Lady Flahurter, or Madame de Flahaut, was an attendant to Princess Charlotte (Stuart, *Daughter of England* 291).

Comtesse de Flauhault. *See* Margaret Mercer Elphinstone.

William Henry Fortescue. *See* Lord Clermont.

Sir Augustus John Foster (1780-1848), first baronet (1831), was the son of Lady Elizabeth Foster by her husband, John Thomas Foster. He was an unsuccessful suitor of Annabella Milbanke, Byron's future wife (Mayne, *Life and Letters* 31), and an admirer of Caroline Lamb (Blyth 63). Foster served as secretary of legation to the United States (1804-8) and Sweden (1808-10; in charge 1808, 1809-10), and as minister to the United States (1811-12), Denmark (1814-24), and Sardinia (1825-40).

Augustus William Clifford Foster (1788-1877) was the illegitimate son of the fifth duke of Devonshire and Lady Elizabeth Foster. He was born in Rouen while the duke was married to Georgiana, duchess of Devonshire. Foster entered the navy in 1838 and was created a baronet that same year. He married Elizabeth Townshend, sister of the fourth Marquis Townshend (Masters 297).

Elizabeth Foster (1759-1824), née Lady Elizabeth Hervey and later duchess of Devonshire (1809). Georgiana, duchess of Devonshire, first met Elizabeth Foster and her sister, Lady Erne, on May 22, 1782. Foster had recently separated from her husband, a womanizing gambler named John Thomas Foster. She was without financial support and without custody of her two children, Frederick, born in 1777, and Augustus, born in 1780. Foster's father, the eccentric earl of Bristol, would not support her financially (Masters 95) and encouraged his daughter to return to her husband. Georgiana's sympathy was aroused and she invited "Bess," as Foster preferred to be known, to stay with her and her husband at Plympton. Foster's great beauty appealed to the duke. She dispelled the gloom that hung over the Devonshire marriage and seems to have played an important role in facilitating the birth of Georgiana's first child, who was conceived in October 1782. Biographers have suggested that a ménage à trois occurred between "Canis," "Racky," and the "Rat," as they called themselves. To avoid scandal, Foster was appointed governess to the duke's illegitimate daughter, Charlotte Williams. Foster left England on December 29, 1782 and traveled throughout Europe with Charlotte.

Foster's affair with the duke seems to have begun in earnest upon her return to England (1783). On two subsequent occasions, she traveled abroad to conceal pregnancies. With the assistance of her brother, who posed as her husband, she gave birth to Caroline St. Jules in Italy on August 16, 1785. Four years later, she had no reason to keep her next pregnancy a secret from Georgiana. She gave birth to the duke of Devonshire's first son, Augustus William James Clifford, on May 26, 1788 in Rouen. Following Georgiana's death in 1806, Foster married the fifth duke. After his death in 1811 she lived abroad (*LJ* 5:270; (Masters 150 and passim).

Charles James Fox (1749-1806) served in Parliament from the age of nineteen, before becoming junior lord of the Admiralty and a junior lord of the Treasury. A scholar with erudition in five languages, he could quote Cicero, Tacitus, Virgil, and Shakespeare. Fox could hardly be called a "man of the people," and though he supported the American revolution he did so in part to embarrass the ministry. "I am for maintaining the independency of Parliament, and will not be a rebel to my King, my country, or my own heart, for the loudest huzza of an inconsiderate multitude," he wrote.

Georgiana, duchess of Devonshire, praised Fox's "amazing quickness in seazing any subject, he seems to have the particular talent of knowing more about what he is saying and with less pains than anyone else" (August 14, 1777; Masters 55).

Francis II (1768-1835), the last of the Holy Roman emperors, declared himself emperor of Austria in 1804. After a brief alliance with France, he joined the Russians and Prussians and defeated Napoleon in the battle of Leipzig (1813).

Frederick-William III (1770-1840) succeeded his father, Frederick-William II, in 1797. At first neutral toward Napoleon, the king declared war (1806) and, after the defeats of Jena and Auerstadt, fled into East Prussia. Restored by the victory of Leipzig (1813), in the Treaty of Vienna (1815) he negotiated for recovery of possessions west of the Elbe.

Francis Joseph Gall (1758-1828). Lady Melbourne first mentions Gall's book in a letter to Byron on March 24, 1813. In a letter to Annabella on May 25, 1814, she again alludes to this Austrian anatomist and founder of phrenology who devoted his life to studying the nervous system, especially the brain. Gall collaborated with his favorite pupil, John Caspar Spurzheim (1776-1832), producing a four-volume work and atlas that appeared between 1810 and 1819. He demonstrated that the nerve fibers exist in the white matter of the brain and showed that mental processes occur in specific portions of it. His Vienna lectures on "cranioscopy," or phrenology, offended religious leaders and were condemned by the Austrian government in 1802. Three years later he was forced to leave the country (*Columbia*). Though mocked for his involvement in phrenology, he was honored in France and also in England and the United States, where Spurzheim carried his teachings (*Chambers* 1257).

Daniel Gardner (1750-1805), the English portrait painter, studied at the Royal Academy and was patronized by Reynolds. His portraits in oil and crayon were successful and he retired early from practice. Gardner exhibited only once at the Royal Academy (1771). He painted Lady Melbourne, the duchess of Devonshire, and Anne Damer as the three witches from *Macbeth*. At least two different versions of this painting exist. Thomas Watson engraved a number of his portraits, including *Mrs. Gwyn and Mrs. Bunbury (the Horneck sisters) as the Merry Wives of Windsor* (*Bryan's* 2:215-16; *DNB* 7:870-71).

Sir William Garrow (1760-1840), baron of the exchequer, was called to the bar on November 27, 1783. He served as attorney-general to the Prince of Wales (1806) and later became solicitor-general in Lord Liverpool's administration (June 27, 1812). Elected to the borough of Eye, Garrow became attorney-general (May 4, 1813) and replaced Sir Richard Richards as chief justice of Chester. The following year (1814), Lady Melbourne criticized him for exaggerating the injustice done to his client, Lord Roseberry, in his civil suit against Sir Henry Mildmay. Mildmay was charged with criminal conversation with Roseberry's wife.

George IV was the father of Lady Melbourne's fourth son, George (1784). Their affair lasted from 1780 until 1785 and subsided into a lifelong friendship. It was at his urging that Lady Melbourne swapped homes with the prince's brother, the duke of York, in 1792. The two lovers exchanged paintings of one another, and a Reynolds' portrait of George IV when Prince of Wales can still be found at Brocket Hall. As Prince Regent, George IV was a close friend of Lady Melbourne's husband, appointing him first gentleman of the bedchamber (1783-96) to the Prince of Wales; lord of the bedchamber (1812-28); and a peer of the realm (1816). He tried to appoint William Lamb to the Treasury Board in 1812, which William turned down, and made nominal efforts to advance Frederick Lamb's diplomatic career.

George Germain (1770-1836) was the younger son of Lord George Sackville Germaine (1716-1785) and may have carried Sackville as an honorary title. His brother was the fashionable Regency figure and lifelong bachelor Charles, fifth duke of Dorset (1767-1843). George Germain married Harriet Pearce.

Lord George Sackville Germaine (1716-1785), "scarecrow of the Whigs," served as secretary of war and was attacked by Fox (1777) for his conduct in allowing General Burgoyne, a friend of Fox, to surrender. Years earlier, after the Battle of Minden, he had been tried for cowardice and was court-martialed. Fox made use of the incident to embarrass Germaine (Villiers 26), but Germaine survived the attack. He was created Viscount Sackville in 1782 by George III as a public gesture in response to Whig efforts to abandon the war (*DNB* 7:1110-14).

Sir Vicary Gibbs (1751-1820) was solicitor general (1805-6) and M.P. for Totnes (1804-6), Great Bedwyn (1807), and Cambridge (1807-29). He attended Eton and King's College, Cambridge (1770), where he was distinguished as a Latin and Greek scholar. Gibbs later became attorney-general, lord chief-baron, and chief justice of the common pleas. He made his reputation defending Horne Tooke in 1794 (*Chambers* 556; *CDNB* 2:1136).

Daniel Giles (1761-1831) of Youngbury, near Ware in Hertfordshire, was M.P. for East Grinstead (1802-7) and St. Albans (1809-12). He was the only son of Daniel Giles of Youngsbury, director of the Bank of England, and Elizabeth Messman. He received his B.A. (1781) and M.A. (1784) from Hertford College, Oxford and was called to the bar in 1784. Giles opposed the convention of Cintra (February 21, 1809), the militia completion bill (March 24, 1809), the conduct of the Scheldt expedition (1810), and the imprisonment of Gale Jones (1810). His vote in favor of parliamentary reform (May 21, 1810) and his objections to the Regency proposals (January 23, 1811), the Irish secretary's treatment of the Catholics (February 22, 1811), and the militia enlistment plan were consistent with Whig positions. In 1809 he did not object to giving up his seat to one of Lord Melbourne's sons. By 1812, however, he had gained some popularity and warned Lady Melbourne, who now wanted his seat for William, that he did not mean to relinquish it, as he did not hold it "as a mere tenant for another" (Airlie, *Whig* 120-25). In 1812 Giles supported economic reform, was placed on the civil list committee but did not participate, and voted with the opposition on Ireland and for Catholic relief. He did not expect to win the contest at St. Albans that same year and was, in fact, defeated by a ministerialist. His Whig colleague Halsey led him in the poll. Giles did not seek reelection (R. G. Thorne 4:23-24).

Lord George Gordon (1751-1793). The Gordon Riots (1780) were named after the third and youngest son of the third duke of Gordon. Educated at Eton, he entered the British navy and earned the rank of lieutenant (1772). Seven years later, he organized and led the Protestant association that was formed to secure the repeal of the Catholic Relief Act (1778). He led a mob that marched on the houses of Parliament to present a petition against this act

(June 2, 1780). The mob burned Newgate, opened other prisons, and destroyed the houses of Lord Mansfield and Sir John Fielding. Two thousand criminals soon joined the mob, destroying the King's Bench prison and New Bridewell. They threatened the bank before being quelled by twenty thousand troops. Three hundred people were killed; 192 rioters were convicted and 25 executed. Gordon was arrested on a charge of high treason. He was defended by Thomas Erskine and acquitted on the grounds that his actions were not treasonable (*DNB* 8:197-98).

Lord William Gordon (1744-1823) was the lover of Lady Sarah Lennox, who gave birth to their child in 1768, when she was married to Sir Charles Bunbury. The following year Lennox left her husband to live with Gordon, but she soon returned to Bunbury (Elwin, *Noels* 434). Gordon vowed never to return to England, but did so in 1774. He was a libertine, a gambler, and, from 1781, a "conventional husband." Dependent on his brother (fourth duke of Gordon), he supported Sandwich and addressed Parliament on the militia (1779), his only reported speech (Valentine 1:372-73).

Lord Granville Leveson-Gower (1773-1846), first Earl Granville, was a diplomat and the third and youngest son of Granville Leveson-Gower, first marquis of Stafford. Known as the "Adonis" of his day, he entered Christ Church, Oxford (1789), where his friendship with Canning led to an introduction to Pitt. Gower became M.P. for Lichfield (1795-99) and Staffordshire (1799-1815), lord of the Treasury (1800), privy councillor (1804), and ambassador-extraordinary at St. Petersburg (1804-5). He was created Viscount Granville (1815) and served as minister at Brussels (1815) and ambassador at Paris (1824-41). In 1833 he was created Earl Granville and Baron Leveson of Stone (*DNB* 11:1028-29). A Tory by virtue of his family connections, he conducted a lengthy correspondence with Lady Bessborough and became a kind of bridge between the Whigs and Tories. His affair with Lady Bessborough led to the birth of two children. In 1809 he married Harriet Granville, or Hary-O, the youngest daughter of Georgiana, duchess of Devonshire.

Comte de Gramont (1789-1855). Antoine-Heraclitus-Genevieve-Agenor (later duc de Guiche) served in the English army in Portugal and Spain, accompanying the duc d'Angouleme, who named him lieutenant general (1823). He followed Charles X to Cherbourg and Ecosse (1830), returning to France in 1833. He was asked to testify in the court-martial trial of Colonel Quentin but did not come to England in time to be useful. Lady Melbourne speculated that he was made an English captain by the Prince Regent, possibly to keep him from testifying in this trial.

Lady Harriet Granville (1785-1862), or Hary-O, was the youngest daughter of Georgiana, duchess of Devonshire and the fifth duke of Devonshire. Her older sister was Lady Georgiana Morpeth (1783-1858). Hary-O grew up at Devonshire House with Augustus Clifford and Caroline St. Jules, the illegitimate offspring of the duke of Devonshire and Lady Elizabeth Foster. In December 1809 she married Sir Granville Leveson-Gower, the lover of her aunt, Lady Bessborough. She disliked Lady Melbourne and referred to her as "La Vecchia" ([Autumn, 1814]; Surtees 66).

George Grenville. *See* George, Baron Nugent.

Richard Temple-Nugent-Brydges-Chandos-Grenville (1776-1839), second marquis of Buckingham (1813), first duke of Buckingham and Chandos (1822), was M.P. for Buckinghamshire (1797-1813), vice-president of the Board of Trade and joint paymaster-general (1806-7), and Lord Steward (1830) (*PPBD* 103).

Thomas Grenville (1755-1846) was the second son of George Grenville of Wolton, Bucks and Elizabeth, daughter of Sir William Wyndham. He graduated from Christ Church, Oxford (1771) and Lincoln's Inn (1774), serving as minister to Paris (1782), Vienna (1794), and Berlin (1798-99); president of the Board of Control (1806); and first lord of the Admiralty (September 1806-April 1807). Grenville was M.P. for Buckinghamshire (1779-84; 1813-18), Aldeburgh (1790-96), and Buckingham (1796-1810). His opposition to the Tory government cost him his seat (1784) and estranged him from his family, but he remained loyal to the opposition. Grenville resented attempts by Burke, Windham, and Lord Loughborough to bring the conservative Whigs in closer alignment with the ministry and to adopt a more aggressive military policy. He rejected resolutions to seek "offensive war" against France, which would "provoke distress and inflame the people." Anxious to keep on good terms with Fox, he voted for Fox's amendment to the address (December 13, 1792) as an indictment of the government's internal policy. Lady Melbourne mentions this in her letter of December 14, 1792. Due to her friendship with Thomas Grenville, Lady Melbourne was consulted by Emily Huskisson and others who sought to obtain promotions for their children in the navy.

Charles Grey (1764-1845), second earl, was educated at Eton and Cambridge. He served as Whig M.P. for Northumberland (1786), led the impeachment of Warren Hastings, and helped found the Society for the Friends of the People (1792). Grey led the Whigs in their temporary secession from Parliament (1794), denouncing the Union of England and Ireland (1798). In 1806 he gained the title of Lord Howick and was appointed lord of the Admiralty, becoming foreign secretary and leader of the House of Commons at Fox's death. He carried through an act abolishing the African slave trade (1806), opposed renewal of the war (1815), condemned the bill against Queen Caroline (1820), and supported the commercial policy of Huskisson. The government he formed in 1830 sought peace, retrenchment, and reform, but the Reform Bill did not pass until three versions were produced (June 1832) (*Chambers*; *DNB* 620).

Sir Henry Halford (1766-1844), first baronet, was physician to George III, George IV, and William IV. In 1813 he helped identify the body of Charles I at Windsor *(Chambers)*. Halford treated Judith Milbanke for erysipelas and asthma in January 1816 (Mayne, *Life and Letters* 332).

John James Hamilton. *See* Abercorn.

John Hanson (d. 1841), Byron's solicitor and business agent, was introduced to Mrs. Byron by an Aberdeen friend. Hanson took over the management of the Newstead and Rochdale estates from 1798, when George Gordon Byron became the sixth baron. Lady Melbourne blamed him for delaying Byron's marriage to her niece, Annabella Milbanke (*LJ* 1:275).

Harbour. Possibly William Assheton (1766-1821), M.P. for Ludgershall (1790-96) and Plympton Erle (1807-10). His brother was Edward Harbour. Lady Melbourne mentions him as a visitor in 1805.

George Harcourt. *See* George Granville Venables Vernon.

John Harcourt (d. 1825) was M.P. for Ilchester (1785; 1790-96) and Leominster (1812-18; 1819-20). He lived in Hanover Square, joined the Whig Club (March 7, 1785), and voted with the Foxite opposition (1790). Harcourt opposed Pitt's Russian policy (April 12, 1791) and voted for Fox's amendment to the address (December 13, 1792). He was in the minority against the war with revolutionary France on June 17, 1793 and opposed it steadily afterwards, voting against the restriction of civil liberty in England (January 5 and 23, 1795) (R. G. Thorne 2:150).

Lady Elizabeth Hardwicke (d. 1858), daughter of the fifth earl of Balcarres, married (1782) Philip Yorke, third earl of Hardwicke, (*Burke's* 1246). She ran a private theatrical company (Berry 2:502) and Byron described her as "a very superior woman" (March 20, 3:252; *LJ* 4:103).

Sir Charles Hardy (1716?-1780) the younger was an admiral and the son of Vice-Admiral Sir Charles Hardy. He entered the navy as a volunteer on board the *Salisbury,* commanded by Captain George Clinton (February 4, 1730-31); served as third lieutenant of the *Swallow* (1737); and was appointed to the *Augusta* (1738); the *Kent* (1739); and the *Rupert's Prize* (June 9, 1741). Hardy later became governor of New York (1755), admiral of the blue (1770), governor of Greenwich Hospital (1770), and M.P. for the borough of Portsmouth (1774). In 1779 he commanded the Channel fleet, Viscount Augustus Keppel having resigned when French and Spanish ships were invading on July 9. Hardy was to resume command of the fleet when he died of an apoplectic fit at Portsmouth on May 18, 1780 (*DNB* 8:1236-37).

Sir Thomas Masterman Hardy (1769-1839) was a British sailor closely associated with Nelson, whom he served as flag-captain at the Battle of Trafalgar (1805). He was created baronet in 1805 and governor of Greenwich Hospital from 1834. Hardy fought a duel with Lord Buckinghamshire (June 16, 1816) as a result of a dispute at Almack's Balls. In 1822 his wife, Lady Hardy, applied to Byron to escape James Wedderburn Webster's advances in Italy (Marchand, *Biography* 3:1045).

Jane, Countess Harrington (d. 1824), was the daughter and coheir of Sir John Fleming, Baronet, of Brompton Park. She married Charles Stanhope, third earl of Harrington (1753-1829), on May 23, 1779 (*Burke's* 1152). She was a lady of the bedchamber and friend of the queen. In 1804 she served as representative of Queen Charlotte and presented the queen's Royal Volunteers in the rotunda at Ranelagh, delivering a speech on the occasion. Her husband was a friend to the royal family and the duke of York (*BBI* 1031:399).

Hary-O. *See* Lady Harriet Granville (1785-1862).

Sir Gilbert Heathcote (1773-1851) was fourth baronet and M.P. for Lincolnshire (1796-1807) and Rutland (1812-41). He was married first (August 16, 1793) to Katherine Sophia, eldest daughter of John Manners of Grantham Grange, Lincolnshire, and second (August 10, 1825) to Mrs. Eldon of Park Crescent, Marylebone. His eldest son (Gilbert John, fifth baronet) by the first marriage was created Lord Aveland in 1856 and married Clemintina Elizabeth Drummond, Baroness Willoughby de Eresby (1827) (*Farington* 4:252). Heathcote voted with the opposition in the House of Commons and did "honour to the party of English country gentlemen" (*BBI* 535:191). In 1841 he won the Derby with Amato (*BBI* 535:190-94).

Lady Heathcote (fl. 177?-1825), née Miss Katherine Sophia Manners, married Gilbert

Heathcote in 1793.

Lady Elizabeth Hervey. *See* Elizabeth Foster.

Lord Hervey (1730-1803), fourth earl of Bristol, attended Corpus Christi College, Cambridge (1754). He was the eccentric father of Elizabeth Foster, duchess of Devonshire. Trained for the bar, he took holy orders and became an avid art collector.

Robert Hobart. *See* earl of Buckinghamshire.

John Cam Hobhouse, Baron Broughton (1786-1869). Born at Bristol, Hobhouse attended Westminster School and Trinity College, Cambridge, where he became close friends with Byron and his traveling companion. The son of a mother who was a dissenter, Hobhouse founded the Whig Club at Cambridge. He was in Paris in May 1814 when Louis XVIII entered the capital. He was best man at Byron's wedding. In 1816 Hobhouse visited Byron at Villa Diodati, near Geneva, and they visited Venice and Rome together. On Byron's orders, he tried to retrieve the poet's letters from Lady Melbourne's family after her death in 1818. The following year, he lost an election contest with George Lamb by 4,465 votes to 3,861. His pamphlet, *A Trifling Mistake,* led to his being charged with a breach of privilege and sentenced to Newgate on December 14, 1819. He defeated George Lamb the following year and delivered his maiden speech in May 1819. On Hobhouse's advice as one of several executors, Byron's memoirs were destroyed after the poet's death in 1824 (*DNB* 9:941-42).

Henry Holland (1745-1806) was the eldest son of the successful Georgian architect Henry Holland (1712-1785). In 1771 he became the partner of Lancelot Brown, landscape gardener. His first architectural commission was Brooks' Club (1776-78) at 60 St. James Street, and he received numerous others from the Whig aristocracy whom he met there. Holland's patrons included the fifth duke of Bedford, for whom he remodeled Woburn, and the Prince of Wales, for whom he designed the interior of Carlton House. "The Gallic sympathies of the Whig circle into which Holland was introduced were reflected in the French influence which is apparent in his architecture" (Colvin 424). In 1787 he added the portico and domed entrance hall for the home of Frederick, duke of York (formerly Fetherstonhough, afterwards Melbourne, and now Dover House, Whitehall) (*Survey of London* 14:60-64; 92-93).

Thomas Hope (1770?-1831). Lady Melbourne suggested that Byron attend a party given by Hope's wife, Louisa Beresford, in March 1813. Byron admired Hope's best-known work, *Anastasius, or Memoirs of a Greek Written at the Close of the Eighteenth Century,* which appeared anonymously in 1819 (8 vols.). *Blackwood's* assumed Byron was the author. Byron told the countess of Blessington that he wept bitterly upon reading *Anastasius* for two reasons—first, that he had not written it; and second, that Hope had (Smiles 2:74-76). Hope settled in England in 1796, when Holland was occupied by France. He collected ancient paintings and sculpture. A French artist, Dubost, satirized him in a caricature called *Beauty and the Beast* (*DNB* 9:1221-23).

Frederick Howard. *See* fifth earl of Carlisle.

Elizabeth Huskisson, *See* Milbanke-Huskisson, Elizabeth Emily.

William Huskisson (1770-1830) was educated privately in Paris and appointed secretary to the Treasury under Pitt (1804-5) and Portland (1807-9). He resigned with Canning (1809), publishing *Depreciation of the Currency* (1810) the following year. Huskisson spoke frequently on the corn laws and bank restriction (1816) and served as a member of the finance committee (1819), as treasurer of the navy (1823-7), and as president of the Board of Trade (1823-27). He was a consistent advocate of free trade and served on the committee on agricultural distress (1821), defeating Londonderry's proposed relief loan (1822). A colonial secretary and leader of the House of Commons under Goderich and Wellington (1827), he resigned on the question of the redistribution of disfranchised seats (1828). Huskisson supported Catholic emancipation (1828) and additional representation for Leeds, Liverpool, and Manchester (1829) (*CDNB* 2:1529). William Lamb thought him the best statesman of his day and was influenced by his views on free trade. Huskisson married Elizabeth Emily, younger daughter of Admiral Mark Milbanke, who survived him (*DNB* 10:328).

Robert Banks Jenkinson (1770-1828), earl of Liverpool, was a liberal Tory whose views on finance included liberalizing the tariff. He entered Parliament in 1790 and served as a member of the India Board (1793-96), as master of the Royal Mint (1799-1801), and as foreign secretary (1801-4). In 1801 he negotiated the unpopular Treaty of Amiens. Created Lord Hawkesbury in 1803 and earl of Liverpool in 1807, he served as home secretary on Pitt's return to power in 1804-6 and again in 1807-9. Jenkinson served as secretary for war and the colonies under Perceval (1809-12). As prime minister, his administration lasted for nearly fifteen years (1812-27). He has been viewed as a reactionary for coercive measures at home, his increase of duties on corn, and his treatment of Poland, Austria, Italy, and Naples (*DNB* 10:748-52).

Edmund Kean (1789-1833), the English actor, first appeared as Shylock (January 26, 1814) but was associated with the title role of *Othello*. He introduced a naturalistic style of acting, relying on agility rather than on the declamatory style of John Philip Kemble (1757-1823). Kean joined Samuel Jerrold's company at Sheerness, Kent for ten years, marrying a fellow thespian, Mary Chambers (1808). His performance as the archvillain in Philip Massinger's *New Way to Pay Old Debts* was so convincing that it sent Lord Byron into convulsions. Contemptuous of distinctions in rank, Kean lost his popularity when he was successfully sued for adultery with the wife of a city alderman (1825) (*Chambers*).

Lord Edward, duke of Kent (1767-1820) entered the army and proved himself a severe disciplinarian. In 1818, ridding himself of Madame St. Laurent, he married Victoria Mary Louisa, widow of the prince of Leiningen. He corresponded with Robert Owen, the socialist, and had a daughter, the future Queen Victoria.

Ellis Cornelia Knight (1757-1837), authoress. Her mother was a friend of Reynolds' sister, and Knight became friendly with members of the Johnson circle. Shortly after the death of her mother, she was placed under Lady Hamilton's protection and discouraged the unwelcome advances of Lord Nelson. In 1805 she became a companion to Queen Charlotte, whom she offended by exchanging this position for a similar one in the household of Princess Charlotte. In July 1814, the princess' refusal to marry the Prince of Orange led the Prince Regent to dismiss all of her attendants, including Knight. Lady Melbourne wrote of this matter to George Lamb (July 13, 1814).

Sir William Knighton (1776-1836). Born in Devonshire, he studied medicine under his uncle, Dr. Bredall, a surgeon of Tavistock, and at Guy's Hospital, London, receiving his M.D. from the University of Aberdeen (April 21, 1806). Knighton served as assistant surgeon in Royal Navy Hospital, attended Marquis Wellesley as his physician in his embassy to Spain, and returned with him in October 1809. Wellesley recommended him to the Prince of Wales, and Knighton became one of the prince's physicians. He was soon created baronet (1812). When his friend Sir John Macmahon died, Knighton became his executor. He delivered into the Prince Regent's hands papers from Macmahon's estate that were compromising to the Regent. As a reward, he was appointed to the auditorship of the duchies of Cornwall and Lancastor. A shrewd adviser to George IV on financial matters, he attended him on the continent (1821) and was appointed private secretary to the king and keeper of the privy purse, succeeding Sir Benjamin Bloomfield. Knighton gave up practice on September 11, 1822. He oversaw the prince's estate after his death on January 26, 1830 (*DNB* 11:270-72).

Caroline Lamb (1785-1828), novelist, married Lady Melbourne's son William Lamb, afterwards Viscount Melbourne, at the age of sixteen. She was the only daughter of the third earl of Bessborough and Lady Henrietta Frances Spencer. Lamb lived in Italy (1788-94) during her mother's illness. She published *Glenarvon* (1816), which satirized members of Lady Melbourne's immediate circle. The novel was translated into Italian (1817) and republished as *The Fatal Passion* (1865). Her notorious affair with Byron (1812) led to Lady Melbourne's correspondence with the poet. In 1819 she canvassed in Westminster for her brother-in-law, George Lamb, and published *A New Canto,* which was a response to Byron's *Don Juan.* She followed the advice of Ugo Foscolo in writing a less scandalous second novel, *Graham Hamilton* (1822), followed by *Ada Reis: A Tale.* The long-awaited separation from her husband was finally achieved in 1824. After Lady Melbourne's death (1818), she lived at Brocket Hall, Hertfordshire, with her father-in-law and her son George Augustus Frederick Lamb (1807-1836). She died at Melbourne House, Whitehall, at the age of forty-two. Some of her poems were collected in Issac Nathan's *Fugitive Pieces and Reminiscences of Lord Byron . . . also Some Original Poetry, Letters and Recollections of Lady Caroline Lamb* (1892) (*Europa* 245).

Caroline George Lamb (1785-1862), or "Caro-George," was the illegitimate daughter of Elizabeth Foster by the fifth duke of Devonshire, Georgiana's husband (Elwin, *Noels* 13). She lived at Devonshire House and was known as Caroline St. Jules until she married George Lamb, Lady Melbourne's fourth son, in 1809. Caro-George was close friends with her half-sister, Harriet Granville ("Hary-O"), and with Lady Byron. She had a protracted affair and friendship with Henry Brougham, which led to tortuous letters from Lady Melbourne. Her dislike for Lord Byron and his friend, John Cam Hobhouse, is evident in her correspondence (Lovelace).

Emily Lamb (1787-1869), the future Countess Cowper and Viscountess Palmerston, was the daughter of Lady Melbourne and the wife first of Lord Cowper (1805) and subsequently of John Henry Temple, third Viscount Palmerston (1839). Her father was presumed to be Lord Egremont (Usher, *Owners* 3). Emily was a leading political hostess of the nineteenth century and a practical businesswoman with a cosmopolitanism gained, in part, from her frequent trips abroad. She often urged her brother William to separate from his wife Caroline and was a fierce defender of her brothers and the family name. Emily had two sons: George Augustus Frederick, later Lord Fordwich, born 1806, and George Spencer Cowper, born 1816.

Frederick James Lamb (1782-1853), Baron Beauvale (1839), third Viscount Melbourne (1848), was Lady Melbourne's third son. He was born at Melbourne House, Piccadilly.

Educated at Eton (1791-99) and then at Glasgow from ages seventeen to twenty-one, he received his M.A. from Trinity College, Cambridge in 1803. He entered the army that year as a cornet in the Royal Horse Guards. Lady Melbourne used her influence with the Prince Regent to assist her son's diplomatic career. Frederick held numerous diplomatic appointments, including secretary of legation in the Two Sicilies (1811-13), secretary of embassy in Austria (1813-15), minister ad interim (1814), and minister to Bavaria (1815-20). He also served on a special mission to the Germanic Confederation (1817) and as minister to the Germanic Confederation (1817-24), minister to Spain (1825-28), ambassador to Portugal (1827-28), and ambassador to Austria (1831-41). In 1842 he married Countess Alexandrina Maltzahn, who was forty years younger than him (*Hary-O* 305) (*PPBD* 37).

George Lamb (1784-1834), Lady Melbourne's fourth son, was reputedly the son of the Prince Regent. He wrote the play *Whistle for It,* which was ridiculed by Byron, and translated Catullus. Lamb opposed John Cam Hobhouse in the election of 1819.

Matthew Lamb (d. 1738) was the grandfather of Peniston Lamb, Lady Melbourne's husband. He was a Southwell attorney (Tipping 58:20), whose chief job was managing the legal business and estate agency of the Cokes. His first son entered the church and became bishop of Peterborough; his second entered the legal profession and profited from his uncle, Peniston Lamb, who reached a lucrative practice as a successful pleader "under the bar." Peniston Lamb had no children and made his nephews his heirs when he died in 1738. The younger Matthew Lamb not only carried on his uncle's practice, but had his share of his uncle's fortune—estimated at £100,000—which enabled him to marry the daughter of his father's main employer (Tipping 58:20).

Sir Matthew Lamb (1705?-1768), Lady Melbourne's father-in-law, was a successful usurious lawyer at Lincoln's Inn and the confidential adviser of Lord Salisbury and Lord Egremont. In 1740 he married Mrs. Charlotte Coke, sister and heir of George Lewis Coke and daughter of Thomas Coke, vice-chamberlain to Queen Anne (*Peerage* 8:635). He purchased Brocket Hall from the Reade family in 1746 (Usher, *Owners* 30) and, according to his grandson, the second Lord Melbourne, "did the Salisburys out of some land." The widow of the first marquis of Salisbury charged that the rise of the Lamb family was from the plunder of the earls of Salisbury (Sedgwick 2:196). Lamb served in Parliament representing Stockbridge (1741-47) and Peterborough (1747-68). He became a baronet on January 17, 1755 and died on November 5, 1768, leaving a million pounds in property, money, and investments (Sedgwick 195-96).

Peniston Lamb (d. 1734), uncle of Matthew and Robert Lamb, built a flourishing lawyer's business and left his fortune, as well as his chambers in Lincoln's Inn, London to his nephew Matthew. His wealth was believed to be £100,000, which went mainly to Matthew as residual legatee. Matthew's brother, Robert, followed a career in the church and later became bishop of Peterborough (Usher, *Owners*, 29).

Sir Peniston Lamb (1745-1828), second baronet, first Viscount Melbourne (Irish Peerage) of Brocket Hall, Hertfordshire and Melbourne Hall, Derbyshire, was Lady Melbourne's husband. He was M.P. for Ludgershall (1768-84), Malmesbury (1784-90), and Newport, Isle of Wight (1790-93). Lamb had two sisters, Charlotte and Anne. Charlotte married Henry, the second earl of Fauconberg, in 1766 and Anne died unmarried in 1768. Lamb purchased one of two seats that belonged to the well-known rotten borough of Ludgershall and was maintained there by George Selwyn. A Whig who rallied to the government in wartime, he succeeded to the baronetcy and became first Lord (1770) and then Viscount (1781) Melbourne in the Irish peerage. He voted silently with Lord North and was rewarded for his allegiance by the title of Baron Melbourne of Kilmore in the Irish peerage. Through his wife's influence, he was appointed first gentleman of the bedchamber (1783-96) to the Prince of Wales and a lord of the bedchamber (1812-28) until his death. "George the Third," remarks Mr. Dunckley, "used his prerogative in one country as a means of governing another. Not for all his fortune would Sir Peniston Lamb have been allowed at that time to win a British peerage" (Torrens 1:6). Lady Melbourne used her influence to procure her husband an English title in 1815, when he became Baron Melbourne of Melbourne in the county of Derby.

Throughout the American war, Lord Melbourne supported the ministers. He continued to vote with the Tories after 1795, even as his wife became a prominent Whig hostess. Melbourne defended the prince (January 16, 1784), acted in opposition to Pitt (May 17, 1790), and met with Whigs at Burlington House to consider whether to support the proclamation against seditious writings and democratic conspiracies. He voted against Pitt on the Oczakov question on April 12, 1791, and supported the repeal of the Test Act in Scotland. As one of the Portland Whigs, he was known to be a supporter of the Prince of Wales. The prince terminated Melbourne's household services in 1795, though Lady Melbourne assured him her husband would serve without a stipend. He was restored to his former position in 1812. "The Duke of Portland failed to secure peerage promotion for Melbourne in August 1794 concealing the fact that the Prince of Wales was Melbourne's sponsor." On two separate occasions, an Irish earldom was sought for him by the prince, once during Pitt's administration (1800) and once during Lord Grenville's (1806). Melbourne only received his title when the prince was Regent (1815) (R. G. Thorne 4:358).

Peniston Lamb (1770-1805), the eldest son of Lady Melbourne, attended Eton (1781-86) and traveled abroad (1787-88). His brother William remembered that "he was a man of high honor, and scrupulously exact in his dealings . . . had he lived, he would have . . . afforded a model of what ought to be the conduct of an English gentleman" (R. G. Thorne 4:357). Peniston was admitted to Brooks' Club on April 1, 1790. He became M.P. for Newport, Isle of Wight (1793-96), replacing his father, who had purchased the seat for him for the remainder of that Parliament. As a yeomanry officer in the Hertfordshire militia (1794), he was otherwise engaged and rarely attended Parliamentary sessions. He did not seek reelection in 1796, but opposed William Baker in 1802 and won, becoming M.P. for Hertfordshire (1802-5). Sheridan noted that it was a "puzzle to know which of the 13 parties in the House of Commons he belonged to, so strange an amalgamation of Court and Club, Foxite and Ministerial, has never been dished up to Parl't from any county in England" (R. G. Thorne 4:357). William remembered him as a loyal supporter of William Pitt (R. G. Thorne 4:357). When Peniston died he was thirty-five and still unmarried, although he had had an affair at Colwick, Nottingham with Mrs. Musters, who was invited by Lady Melbourne to his deathbed.

William Lamb (1779-1848), second Viscount Melbourne, English statesman, and prime minister to William IV and to Queen Victoria, was Lady Melbourne's son by Lord Egremont. He attended Eton (1788-96), Trinity College, Cambridge (1796-99), the University of Glasgow (1799-1801), and Lincoln's Inn (1797), before being called to the bar in 1804 (R. G. Thorne 4:359). Lord Melbourne, his legal father, bought him a seat at Leominister for 2,000 guineas, instigated by the duke of Norfolk and Lord Kinnaird. Afterwards he served Parliament in a number of capacities, at Haddington Burghs (1806-7), Portarlington (1807-12), Peterborough (1816-19), Hertfordshire (November 29, 1819-26), Newport, Isle of Wight (April 24-29, 1827), and Bletchingley (May 7, 1827-July 22, 1828). He served under Canning as chief-secretary of Ireland (1827) and retained the post under Goderich and Wellington. Succeeding his father as second Viscount Melbourne (Ireland) and second baron (United Kingdom) on July 22, 1828, William served as home secretary with the Whigs (1830-34) and as prime minister on two separate occasions (July 16-November 14, 1834; April 18, 1835-August 30, 1841). He introduced Queen Victoria to her duties in 1837 and in 1841 passed the seals of office to Peel (Torrens 1:5; R. G. Thorne 4:359-64).

John George Lambton (1792-1840), first earl of Durham, served as Whig M.P. for Durham (September 1813) until he became a peer in 1828. He supported mediation on behalf of Norway (May 12, 1814), opposed the second reading of the Corn Bill (March 1815), condemned Canning's appointment as ambassador extraordinary to Lisbon (May 1817), and led the opposition in the first reading of the Indemnity Bill (March 1818). Lambton denounced the government for the Manchester massacre (October 21, 1819), forwarded a proposal for parliamentary reform (April 17, 1821), and supported the Canning and Goderich administration. He hoped to pass the Reform Bill by an unlimited creation of peers and was violently opposed in this action by Lord Grey (December 1831). Appointed ambassador extraordinary and minister plenipotentiary to St. Petersburg (July 5, 1835-37), he later became governor-general of the British provinces in North America (February 1838) and was abandoned by the ministers who appointed him. In January 1812 he married Harriet Cholmondeley, who died in July 1815. In December 1816 he married Lady Louisa Elizabeth Grey, eldest daughter of Charles, second earl Grey, by whom he had two sons. Lady Melbourne mentions this marriage in a letter of October 25, 1816 (*DNB* 11:463).

Lady Lansdowne, formerly Lady Louisa Emma Fox-Strangways, was the fifth daughter of Henry Thomas, second earl of Ilchester. Henry Petty-Fitzmaurice, third marquis of Lansdowne (1780-1863), had two sons by her, the second of whom succeeded him as marquis of Lansdowne. Her husband was a moderate Whig and she was a Whig hostess. Twenty years after the death of Fox, the Whig party "appeared to exist only in the drawing-rooms of Lansdowne, Devonshire, and Holland House" *(DNB* 15:1014-17). Lord Lansdowne entertained at Bowood Park, near Calne in Wiltshire (Delany 2:223) and at Lansdowne House.

Edward Law (1750-1818), first Baron Ellenborough (1802), was attorney-general (1801-2), lord chief justice (1802-18), and chancellor of the Exchequer (January-February 1806).

Augusta Leigh (1783-1851) was the daughter of Byron's father by his first wife, Amelia d'Arcy, Baroness Conyers, the divorced wife of Francis, marquis of Carmarthen (later fifth duke of Leeds). Raised by her grandmother, Lady Holderness, she began corresponding with Byron in 1804. Leigh married her first cousin, Colonel George Leigh, in 1807, a match that Lady Melbourne helped to arrange. In 1813 Byron confessed his passion for Augusta to Lady Melbourne, who distrusted her afterwards and referred to her as Byron's "corbeau noir." Lady Melbourne thought that the poet's marriage to her niece, Annabella Milbanke, might distract Byron from this affair with his half-sister. Biographers have been divided over whether Byron and Augusta had an illegitimate daughter, Medora, in 1814 (*LJ* 1:273).

Charles Lennox. *See* third duke of Richmond.

Lady Sarah Lennox (1745-1826) was the daughter of Charles, second duke of Richmond.

Having declined a proposal from the fifteenth earl of Erroll, she married Sir Charles Bunbury in 1762. On December 19, 1768, Lennox gave birth to a daughter by Lord William Gordon. The following year she left her husband to live with her lover (Elwin, *Noels* 434). She soon returned to Bunbury, although their childless marriage was dissolved by Parliament in 1776 (Elwin, *Noels* 42, 442). Lennox later married the Honorable George Napier.

Prince Leopold I (1790-1865), first king of the Belgians (1831- 65), served with the allies against Napoleon (1800-15). In 1816 he married Charlotte, the only child of the future King George IV of Great Britain. His rival for Charlotte's hand was William of Orange, the choice of the Prince Regent. The young couple lived away from the court at Claremont near Esher, having refused an official residence in London (Corbett 7). Charlotte died in 1817, but Leopold continued to reside in England until 1831. He declined the Greek crown in 1830 and accepted the office of king of the Belgians in 1831. Leopold helped strengthen the nation's new parliamentary system and signed commercial treaties with Prussia (1844) and France (1846). As a leading figure in European diplomacy, he maintained Belgian neutrality during the Crimean War (1853-56). He was the ancestor of Leopold III (1901-1983), the king who abdicated in favor of his son.

M. G. "Monk" Lewis (1775-1818) was the author of *The Monk* (1796) and a friend to William Lamb during Lamb's visit to Scotland. Educated at Westminster and Christ Church, Oxford, he served as attaché to the British embassy at The Hague (1794) and as M.P. for Hindon (1796-1802). He brought out the *Castle Spectre* at Drury Lane (1798) and made Walter Scott's acquaintance (1798), visiting his West Indian property in order to arrange for proper treatment of the slaves (1815-16; 1817-18). Lewis died at sea on his way home. His writings influenced Scott's early poetical efforts. Some of his numerous dramas and tales were translated from the German.

Earl of Liverpool. *See* Robert Banks Jenkinson.

William Lowther (1757-1844), first earl of Lonsdale of the second creation, succeeded his third cousin, James Lowther, earl of Lonsdale, as Viscount Lowther by special patent in 1802. He was created earl of Lonsdale in 1807. Lowther was the well-known patron of Wordsworth (*CDNB* 2:1839).

Lucan. *See also* Bingham.

Elizabeth, Lady Lucan married Bernard Howard, Esquire, afterwards twelfth duke of

Norfolk. She divorced him in 1794 to marry Richard, second earl of Lucan (Bingham), in 1804 (Gower 1:335, 489). Her marriage to the earl of Lucan, styled Lord Bingham (1764-1839), also ended in divorce. "How extraordinary after giving up the world for each other and living happily near ten years!" Lady Bessborough wrote. "At the end of that time they went to Brighthelmstone, where he had the gout. She took to racketing and neglected him; he grew low spirited and scolded her. Incessant wranglings ensued, mix'd up with accusations of flirtation on one side and stinginess on the other" (G. L. Gower 1:489). Lady Melbourne served as an arbitress during this separation. The earl of Lucan left one of his children in her care and the other with Lady Duncannon. Lady Charlotte Belasyse and Lady Lucan were nieces to Lord Melbourne.

Henry Luttrell (1765?-1851), poet, wit, and diner-out, was a biological son of the second Lord Carhampton. He and his close friend George Nugent, who was believed to be his half-brother, were known as "the Albanians" (Surtees 306). Luttrell published *Lines Written at Ampthill-Park, in the Autumn of 1818* (1819) and *Advice to Julia: A Letter in Rhyme* (1820), a witty poem admired by Byron (Jack 579-80). He traveled with Lady Melbourne's son-in-law, Lord Cowper, and wrote many long letters to Lady Melbourne describing Italy and southern France shortly after the Peace of Amiens (1802). Luttrell admired Lady Melbourne. "When you see Lady Melbourne," he wrote to Cowper, "keep me alive in her recollection. I like her, as we are told we should love God, with all my heart, mind and strength" (Strickland 101).

James MacDonald (1784-1832) was M.P. for Tain Burghs (1805-6), Newcastle-under-Lyme (1806-12), Sutherland (1812-16), Calne (1816-31), and Hampshire (1831-32). He was married first to Elizabeth Sparrow (1805) and then to Lady Sophia Keppel (1819), daughter of William Charles, fourth earl of Albemarle. MacDonald opposed the convention of Cintra (1809), was in opposition on the Scheldt question (1810), opposed sinecure places (1810), and supported Catholic emancipation at every opportunity. He joined the nonpartisan Grillion's Club at Canning's suggestion. In 1817 he and Abercromby were Lord Lansdowne's protégés (R. G. Thorne 4:487-89). A cousin of Granville Vernon, he is possibly the same MacDonald mentioned by Lady Melbourne (January 20-21, 1805) as a visitor who appeared at Whitehall in the company of Luttrell. In 1819 he sponsored George Lamb's candidacy for Westminster in Romilly's place (Thorne 4:489).

Charles Manners. *See* fourth duke of Rutland.

Sir James Mansfield (1733/4?-1821) served as M.P. for Cambridge University (1779-84), solicitor-general (September 1780-April 1782; November-December 1783), chief justice of Chester (1799-1804), and chief justice of the common pleas (1804-14). He prosecuted Lord George Gordon in February 1781 and convicted the spy De la Motte of high treason. Mansfield was knighted in May 1804 (Aspinall, *Correspondence* 5:313).

Melbourne. *See* Lamb.

Godfrey Meynell had three daughters, one of whom, Jane, was a close friend and neighbor of Judith Milbanke's in Durham and North Riding. In 1776 Jane married Thomas Davison (1744-1794) of Blakiston. Their son, Thomas Davison Bland, was a trustee in Lady Byron's marriage settlement (Elwin, *Noels* 57).

Elizabeth [Hedworth], Lady Milbanke (d. 1767), daughter of John Hedworth of Chester Deanry (1683-1747), was Lady Melbourne's mother. She was the wife of Ralph Milbanke, fifth baronet. In 1755 Hedworth sat for Sir Joshua Reynolds (Graves and Cronin 2:638).

John Milbanke (d. 1800), Lady Melbourne's older brother, was architect and contractor of His Majesty's Works. His son, afterwards Sir John Milbanke, seventh baronet (1776-1850), married Eleanor, the daughter of Julius Hering. Lady Melbourne tried to extricate the couple from debt.

Judith Milbanke (1751-1822), née Judith Noel, was the mother of Annabella Milbanke. She married Lady Melbourne's brother, Ralph, in 1777. An ardent Whig, she supported her husband's parliamentary efforts in Durham. Provincial and somewhat judgmental, Judith Milbanke limited her association with Lady Melbourne after she learned of her sister-in-law's affairs with Lord Egremont and the Prince Regent in the 1780s. She was also protective of her only daughter, Annabella, and blamed Lady Melbourne for defending Byron during the separation proceedings. Judith Milbanke inherited the name Noel, from her father Sir Edward Noel, baronet, which Byron later adopted through his wife.

Admiral Mark Milbanke (1725?-1805) was one of Lady Melbourne's uncles (the others were Colonel Edward Milbanke, Reverend Francis Milbanke, and John Milbanke). He was third of the six sons of the fourth baronet by his second wife, Anne Delaval. He married Mary Webber and had two daughters: Harriet, who married an American named Tilghman, and Elizabeth Emily, who married William Huskisson (1770-1830), the cabinet minister (Elwin, *Noels* 13, 61).

Milbanke entered the navy in 1737, serving as lieutenant (1744). He was promoted to command the *Serpent* (1746) and served as commissioner to Morocco (1759) and as rear-admiral of the white (1779). He sat on the court martial of Admiral Keppel, was vice-admiral of the blue (1780), port-admiral at Plymouth (1783-86), commander-in-chief in Newfoundland (1790-92), admiral (1793), and commander-in-chief at Portsmouth (1799-1803) (*CDNB* 2:2027). Milbanke attended the Academy at Portsmouth, completing his education under Admiral Thomas Smith. Biographers praise his integrity and note that he rose on his own merits, despite powerful family ties with the marquis of Rockingham (in 1764 his brother John married Lady Mary Wentworth, daughter of the first marquis of Rockingham). Milbanke distinguished himself as captain of the Guernsey, cruising the Mediterranean, and on an embassy to Morocco, where he refused to take his shoes off to enter a mosque. He relieved Rear Admiral Parker as commander-in-chief of ships at Plymouth, and also commanded a squadron in the North Seas at Portsmouth (*BBI*:67).

Sir Ralph Milbanke (1722-1798), fifth baronet, was the father of Lady Melbourne and the husband of Elizabeth Hedworth.

Ralph Milbanke (1747-1825), sixth baronet, was the eldest son of Sir Ralph Milbanke and the brother of Lady Melbourne. In 1777 he married Judith Noel, daughter of Sir Edward Noel, baronet, who succeeded as Baron Wentworth in 1745. Milbanke assumed the surname of Noel in 1815. His portrait was painted by Reynolds in February 1757 and March 1779 (Graves and Cronin 3:636). He served as Whig M.P. for the county of Durham (1790-1812) and succeeded to the baronetcy on January 8, 1793. Milbanke owned estates centered at Halnaby Hall and in Durham near Seaham (Elwin, *Wife* 16).

Elizabeth Emily Milbanke-Huskisson (1770-1830) was the daughter of Admiral Mark Milbanke (1725?-1805) and Mary Webber and the cousin of Lady Melbourne. She married William Huskisson (1770-1830) and the two were frequent guests at Melbourne House.

Lord Moira (1754-1826). Francis Rawdon-Hastings, second earl of Moira, was an intimate friend of the Prince of Wales. He supported the prince's right to assume full legal power during George III's illness. A powerful orator in the House of Lords, he inherited estates from his maternal uncle, the earl of Huntington, and succeeded his father as the second earl of Moira (1793). Appointed adjutant-general of the British forces in America (1778), Moira distinguished himself at Bunker Hill and as commander under Cornwallis at the battle of Camden (1780). On April 25, 1781, with an inferior army, he defeated the American general Nathanael Greene at Hobkirk's Hill. Upon his return, he was captured by the French and created Baron Rawdon (1783). He joined the opposition party (1789), supporting the Prince of Wales' cause on the regency question (1789). He assumed the additional name of Hastings (1790), succeeded as Irish earl of Moira (1793), commanded an expedition to Brittany (1793), and led the reinforcements for the duke of York in Flanders (1794). Moira spoke against Irish Union (1799). In 1803 he was appointed general and also commander-in-chief in Scotland. He was appointed master-general of the ordnance (1806-7), resigning when his party fell. Moira served instead as governor-general of British India (1812-22). Created first marquis of Hastings (1817), he established British supremacy in Central India (1817-18) and secured the cession of Singapore (1819). He was appointed governor of Malta (1824), but died on board the *Revenge* in Baia Bay (*DNB* 9:117-22). In a letter of October 15, 1813, Lady Melbourne mentions Moira's examination of doctors, which took place in connection with the Prince Regent's efforts to divorce his wife.

John Hamilton Mortimer (1741-1779), the historical painter, was born at Eastbourne and studied under Thomas Hudson, at the duke of Richmond's sculpture gallery, and under Cipriani and Reynolds. In 1770 he won an award for the best historical painting, *St. Paul Converting the Britons,* which established his reputation (*Bryan's* 1:374). He executed a ceiling in Brocket Hall, Hertfordshire for Lord Melbourne; the design of *The Elevation of the Brazen Serpent* for the great window in Salisbury Cathedral; and some stained glass for Brasenose College, Oxford. In 1775 Mortimer married Jane Hurrell, a farmer's daughter (*DNB* 13:1026).

Joachim Murat (1767-1815) served under Bonaparte in Italy and Egypt and rose to be general of division (1799). He married Bonaparte's sister and was proclaimed king of the Two Sicilies as Joachim Napoleon. On October 13, 1815, after Napoleon's overthrow, he was court-martialed and shot.

Princess Narischkine (1782-1854), Madam Nareskin, or Marie Narischkin, was the Polish-born wife of Dimitri Narischkine, a member of the princely family to which Peter the Great's mother belonged (Lieven, *Letters* 6). She was only fifteen when appointed maid of honour (1797). A woman of remarkable beauty, she was the mistress and confidante of Alexander I. Her relations with the emperor, by whom she had a daughter who died early, were an open secret (G. L. Gower 1:507n). Her arrival in England was noted by the *Morning Herald* when she attended a party given by Lady Tyrwhitt Jones on July 18, 1814. She was in the country as early as March of that year. Lady Melbourne describes her visit to London and Oxford.

Noel. *See also* Milbanke.

Thomas Noel (1745-1815) was the brother of Judith Milbanke and thus the brother-in-law of Lady Melbourne's brother. He became second Viscount and tenth Baron Wentworth at the death of his father on October 31, 1774, inheriting Kirkby Mallory in Leicestershire. Judith Milbanke inherited the Noel name in 1815 (Elwin, *Noels* 16).

George, Baron Nugent (1788-1856), or George Grenville, of Gosfield Hall, served as M.P. for Buckingham (1810-12) and Aylesbury (1812-32; 1847-50). Grenville was the second son of George Grenville, first marquis of Buckingham, and Lady Mary Elizabeth Nugent. He succeeded to his mother's Irish peerage in 1813 (Surtees 307). A loyal Whig of liberal inclinations after 1815 (R. G. Thorne 4:88), he was the author of *Portugal* (1812), an epic poem (Aspinall, *Lady B* 209). He was said to be a half-brother to Henry Luttrell. Together they were known as "the Albanians." Lady Charlotte Bury described him as a "fat fubsy man very like a white turkey cock, a good musician and sings correctly" (Surtees 307).

Richard Nugent. *See* Richard Temple-Nugent-Brydges-Chandos-Grenville

Eliza O'Neill (1791-1872), later Lady Becher, was born in Drogheda, County Louth. The Irish actress appeared in her father's theater and in Belfast and Dublin before she was engaged at Covent Garden in 1814. That year, she appeared as Juliet in Shakespeare's play, as Mrs. Teazle in Sheridan's *School for Scandal,* and as Belvidera in Otway's *Venice Preserved (Morning Herald,* October 6 and 14). Though less noble, she was considered a worthy successor to Sarah Siddons. O'Neill retired from the stage (December 18, 1819) to marry William Becher, Irish M.P. for Mallow.

Lady Ossulstone, née Corisande Sophie Leonice Helene Armandine, was the daughter of the Antoine, duc de Grammont. She married Charles Augustus (Bennet), earl of Tankerville, who was called Lord Ossulstone.

Lady Oxford (1772-1824), Jane Scott, married Edward Harley, fifth earl of Oxford, in 1794. She soon devoted herself to the cause of reform and took various lovers, including Sir Francis Burdett, Lord Archibald Hamilton, Lord Gower, Arthur O'Connor, and Lord Byron, who was sixteen years younger than her when they met. The Oxfords traveled on the Continent, visiting Paris (1802), Italy (1803), Vienna (1804), and Dresden (1804), before returning to Eywood, Herefordshire (1804). Henry Bickersteth, who served as their traveling physician, later married (1835) Lady Oxford's daughter, Lady Jane Harley. From 1804 until 1813, the Oxfords remained in England, and between 1809 and 1813 Lady Oxford formed part of the entourage of the Princess of Wales, who was separated from her husband. In 1813 the Oxfords returned to Italy, residing in Naples (1813-14), where they remained in close touch with Murat and his court. Lord Oxford was arrested in Paris on his way to England, in order to search for evidence of any conspiracy between him and Napoleon (December 1814). Lord Oxford sought to obtain English support for Murat as king of Naples (*Farington* 7:276). Lady Oxford wrote letters to Hobhouse expressing her own support for this lost cause (Patterson 1:100 and passim).

Lord Oxford (d. 1848). Byron's affair with Lady Oxford was the subject of a number of his letters to Lady Melbourne. He referred to Lord Oxford as "Potiphar." In Italy, Lord Oxford met William Jones Burdett, through whom he formed his subsequent friendship with Sir Francis Burdett. Oxford shared Burdett's views on Ireland. The Oxfords and Burdett were caricatured in the famous cartoon of Gillray on the "New Morality." Burdett holds a placard that reads "Glorious Acquittal, Arthur O'Connor, dedicated to Lady Oxford."

James Paine (1717-1789), who studied under Mr. Thomas Jersey and at St. Martin's Lane Academy, worked on Nostell Priory. Working at a transitional time in architectural style from the Burlington school of George II to that of Robert Adam, he designed or altered nearly thirty country houses in the northern counties, including Alnwick, Chatsworth, Kedleston (where he was superseded by Robert Adam in 1767), Sandbeck, and Worksop. From 1746 onwards, he designed Melbourne House, Whitehall (1754-58), Brocket Hall, Hertfordshire (c. 1760-75), Thorndon Hall, Essex (1764-70), and Wardour Castle, Wilts (1770-76). The Whitehall house was designed by Paine for Sir Matthew Fetherstonhaugh and was known afterwards as Melbourne (1792) and now Dover House. The portico and entrance were added by Henry Holland, who also rebuilt the west front. At Melbourne House (now Albany), Piccadilly, Paine designed (1773) chimney-pieces for the first Lord Melbourne. One of these was removed in 1803 and is now at Renishaw Hall, Derbyshire. Brocket Hall is one of the few surviving structures wholly designed and completed by him (Tipping 58:21). In deference to the picturesque school of "Capability" Brown, Paine rebuilt Brocket Hall, Hertfordshire (1760-75) on an old site for Sir Matthew Lamb and his son, Sir Peniston Lamb, preserving the old walling and part of the interior court of a quadrangular building (Tipping 58:20). He also designed the bridge in the park (1772-74) and the entrance screen and lodges (c. 1770-75) (Colvin 611).

John Henry Temple, third Viscount Palmerston (1784-1865), served as William Lamb's foreign secretary (1834; 1835) and later as premier (1855-57; 1859-65) (Ziegler, appendices 1 and 2). He was the second husband of Emily Lamb and the father, perhaps, of four of the children conceived during her first marriage, to Lord Cowper.

Dr. George Pearson (1751-1828), the physician, was also chemist to St. George's Hospital. He received his doctor's degree in 1773 and studied under Dr. Fordyce at St. Thomas's Hospital in 1774. His discoveries in smallpox vaccination were not recognized by Parliament, and Dr. Jenner received credit instead (*BBI* 860:116).

Spencer Perceval (1762-1812) served as solicitor-general (1801- 2), attorney-general (1802-6), chancellor of the Exchequer and of the duchy of Lancaster (1807-12), and prime minister (1809-12) *(DNB* 15:821-27).

Matvei Ivanovich, Count Platov (1757-1818), was born at Azov and served in the Turkish campaign (1770-71). In 1801 Alexander I named him "hetman of the Cossacks of the Don." He took part in campaigns against the French (1805-7), pursued them during their retreat from Moscow (1813), defeating Lefebvre at Altenburg, and gaining a victory at Laon.

George Ponsonby (1755-1817) was the leader of the opposition in the Commons from 1808. He studied at Trinity College, Cambridge and became M.P. for Wicklow (1776), Inistioge (1783-97), and Galway (1798). Called to the Irish bar (1780), he became chancellor of the Exchequer under the duke of Portland (1782). Ponsonby supported the cause of Catholic emancipation. He retired from political life (1797), but returned to resist the act of Union. He became M.P. for County Wicklow (U.K.) (1801), County Cork (1806-7), and Tavistock (1808), as well as lord chancellor of Ireland on formation of the Fox-Grenville ministry (1806), retiring within a year (*DNB* 16:82-84).

Lady Powis (fl. 1755), a macaroni rake, spent a great deal of her estate in frequent losses at cards. She was the wife of William Herbert, third marquis of Powis (*BBI* 1230:438). He died on September 11, 1772, while her son was a minor (*Post,* July 10, 1776). Lady Mary Coke frequently refers to Lady Powis' losses at cards, which, "in spite of attempts to be prudent, were excessive" (Coke, *LJ* 4:426, 429; Coke, "Journal" December 7, 1776, November 26, 1777, June 1-30, 1778, November 10, 1780, September 9, 1782) (Walpole 32:109).

Colonel Dick Quentin. The court-martial proceedings against Colonel Quentin of the 10th Hussars began on October 17, 1814. He was tried on four counts: first, that on January 10 he did not take sufficient precautions to ensure the security of the corps during foraging duty in the south of France; second, that the day after the battle of Orthes (February 28, 1814), he abandoned his duty as commanding officer; third, that he behaved similarly during the Battle of Tolouse on April 10, 1814; and fourth, that he allowed a relaxed system of discipline in the regiment, which earned a rebuke from the commanding officer, the duke of Wellington. Quentin was found guilty of a part of the first charge, acquitted of the second and third charges, and found guilty of "the undisciplined state of the Regiment," but the duke of Wellington's censure was seen as "sufficient reprehension of such misconduct." The sentence closed by censuring the officers of the regiment for "want of cooperation with their Commanding Officer." The Prince Regent regretted the lack of discipline in the corps, but also criticized those officers who had complained about it. He asked that "they should all deliver up their Swords, and be dispersed into other Regiments." Lady Melbourne faulted the Regent for his high-handed dismissal of the officers of the corp (London *Times*, November 11, 1814). On December 15, 1815, Lord Egremont spoke on Quentin's behalf in the House of Lords, perhaps at Lady Melbourne's prompting.

George Augustus Henry Anne, second Baron Rancliffe (1785-1850), succeeded his grandfather as fourth baronet in 1806. He served as equerry to the Prince of Wales and as a Whig M.P. On October 15, 1807, he married Lady Elizabeth Mary Forbes (d. February 1852), eldest daughter of the sixth earl of Granard by Selina Frances, daughter of the first earl of Moira (*Burke's* 1891). See Lady Melbourne's letter of July 7, 1813.

Charlotte Rawdon (1769-1834) married Hamilton Fitzgerald in 1814. She and Lady Ailesbury were Lord Moira's sisters (Aspinall, *Correspondence* 3:448).

Francis Rawdon. *See* Lord Moira.

Biaggio Rebecca (1735-1808), a Florentine artist, designed the frescoes at Melbourne House, Piccadilly.

Charles Lennox, third duke of Richmond (1734-1806), graduated from Leyden University (1753) and joined the army, distinguishing himself in the battle of Mindin (1759). Appointed lord of the bedchamber in 1760, he resigned after a quarrel with George III, with whom he was in frequent conflict. Richmond served as lord lieutenant of Sussex (1763) and ambassador to Paris (1765). He opposed Chatham's election (1766), supported the cause of the American colonists (1770), and favored annual parliaments, manhood suffrage, electoral districts (1783), and parliamentary reform (1782-83). After 1785 he became a zealous courtier and almost fought a duel with Lord Lansdowne (1787) when the latter accused him of apostasy on the issue of parliamentary reform. He later favored (1795) Union with Ireland, though he had opposed it previously (1779); Lansdowne's charge was not without justification. Richmond also condemned the peace of 1802 as humiliating. Lady Melbourne described going to one of his private theatricals, a fad that reached the height of its vogue from 1770 until 1790 (Sir Watkin Williams Wynn also had a theater at Wynnstay). The duke of Richmond's theater at Richmond House, London, was constructed out of two rooms by Wyatt in 1787 and held about 150 spectators. Thomas Greenwood provided the scenery. Richmond married (1757) Lady Mary Bruce, the only child of Charles, third earl of Ailesbury and fourth earl of Elgin, and his third wife, Lady Caroline Campbell. She died on November 5, 1796 (*DNB* 11: 923-27).

Frederick John Robinson (1782-1859), first Viscount Goderich (1827), first earl of Ripon (1833), served as under-secretary of state for war and the colonies (January-September 1809), lord of the Admiralty (1810-12), vice-president of the Board of Trade (1812-18), joint paymaster-general of the forces (1813-17), president of the Board of Trade and treasurer of the navy (1818-23), chancellor of the Exchequer (1823-27), secretary of state for war (1827; 1830-33), prime minister (1827-28), lord privy seal (1833-34), president of the Board of Trade (1833), and president of the Board of Control (1843-46). He married Lady Sarah Hobart, eldest daughter of the earl and countess of Buckinghamshire. In March 1815 Robinson's house was damaged in the riots over the corn laws (*Morning Herald,* September 1, 1814). He dined at Melbourne House with Robert Adair.

George Robinson was a friend of Lady Melbourne's and an assistant at Whitehall.

Samuel Rogers (1763-1855), the poet, was also a banker in his father's firm in Cornhill, London. He contributed to *Gentleman's Magazine* (1781) and published *Pleasures of Memory* (1792), which achieved popularity. When his father died (1793), he inherited a comfortable income and began collecting art. Rogers was a generous and influential patron to men of letters, many of whom were indebted to his influence or personal generosity. He printed privately (1808) and later published (1810) a fragmentary epic on *Columbus,* and also published other poems, including *Human Life* (1819) and *Jacqueline,* which was printed with Byron's *Lara* (1814). He declined the laureateship in 1850.

Sir Samuel Romilly (1757-1818), a follower of Rousseau and Bentham, reformed the criminal code and favored Catholic emancipation and the abolition of slavery. He defended Lady Byron in the separation proceedings (1816) and committed suicide when his own wife died (*CDNB* 3:225).

Henrietta Elizabeth (Bouverie), countess of Rosslyn (1771-1819), was the widow of the first earl, who as Lord Chancellor Loughborough had been present at Charlotte's christening. Lady Rosslyn did not get along with Princess Charlotte, who referred to her as "Old Famine" and thought her "as detestable an old lump o' bones as ever was" (Stuart, *Dearest Bess* 207).

Sir William Rowley (1761-1832), second baronet, of Tendring Hall, Suffolk, served as M.P. for Suffolk (1812-30). He sat on the corn trade committee from April 7, 1813. His house in Welbeck Street was attacked by the London mob because of his support of the Corn Bill in 1815 (R. G. Thorne 5:59).

Russell. *See also* Bedford.

Francis Russell (1788-1861), marquis of Tavistock, of Woburn Abbey and Oakley, Bedfordshire, was made seventh duke of Bedford in 1839. He was M.P. for Peterborough (1809-12) and Bedfordshire (1812-32). Elizabeth, duchess of Devonshire, described him as a man everyone likes, "very gentlemanlike and pleasing, but wastes good parts and sense originally from being neglected in his youth and getting into bad attachments to women. He has made himself a mere jockey and dawdler." Russell supported parliamentary reform and visited John Cam Hobhouse when the latter was imprisoned in Newgate on December 16, 1819. Like Hobhouse, he felt that the Whigs were insincere about reforming Parliament (R. G. Thorne 4:61-63). Lady Melbourne mentions his affair with Lady Worcester (December 2, 1817).

William Russell (1740-1818), merchant and reformer, was engaged in export trade from Birmingham to Russia, Spain, and the United States. He advocated political measures of reform, including the repeal of the Test and Corporation Acts. In 1792 he retired, traveling in America and Europe (*CDNB* 3:2613). On the settlement of Joseph Priestley at Birmingham (1780), Russell, who was a member of Priestley's congregation, became Priestley's generous supporter and intimate friend. The dinner of July 14, 1791, which led to the Birmingham riots, was mainly promoted by Russell. On the third day of the riots, Russell's house at Showell Green was burned by the mob. He went up to London with his family, arriving on July 18, and at an interview with Pitt obtained assurance that the government would indemnify the sufferers (*DNB* 17:488-89).

Charles Manners, fourth duke of Rutland (1754-1787). Known as Lord Roos (1760-70) after his brother's death and styled marquis of Granby (1770-79), Manners was educated at Eton (1762-70) and Trinity College, Cambridge (1771-74). He served as M.P. (Whig) for Cambridge University (1774-79) and as lord lieutenant of Leicestershire (1779-87).

Appointed knight of the garter (October 3, 1782), Manners served as lord steward of the household (1783), with a seat in Lord Shelburne's cabinet; as lord privy seal (1783-84); and as lord lieutenant of Ireland (1784-87). Though he opposed taxing the American colonies (1777) and moved, with Fox and Burke, for the restoration of peace in America, he later joined Pitt and the Tories. The duke of Leinster wrote that "provided he gets his skin full of Claret, he cares little about anything else" (*DNB* 12:932). Manners created a record for dining out unequalled by any subsequent viceroy (O'Mahony 191). In 1775 he married Mary Isabella, youngest daughter of the fourth duke of Beaufort. They were considered the "handsomest couple in Ireland" (*DNB* 12:932). Lady Mary Isabella Somerset was a rival—in both politics and fashion—to Georgiana, duchess of Devonshire. Reynolds painted her portrait four times, the first of which (1780) was destroyed in a fire at Belvoir (1816).

Lady Susan Ryder (1772-1838), née Lady Susan Leveson-Gower, was the daughter of the earl of Harrowby and the granddaughter (through her mother) of Granville Leveson-Gower, first marquis of Stafford. In 1795 she married Dudley Ryder (1762-1847), afterwards earl of Harrowby, and in 1817 she married Lord Obrington, who became Lord Fortescue. Lady Melbourne teased Byron that Ryder was his "former favourite" (letter of January 31, 1815), but he denied this (Aspinall, *Correspondence* 3:358).

Lord George Sackville. *See* Lord George Sackville Germaine.

St. Germans. *See* William Eliot.

Lord St. Helens (1753-1839), Alleyne Fitzherbert, served as minister at Brussels (1777-82) and France (1782-83); envoy to Russia (1783-87) and Holland (1789-90); and ambassador to Spain (1790-94), Holland (1794-95), and Russia (1801-2). He was plenipotentiary to Denmark (1801-2) and Sweden (1801-2), before being elected to the Irish (1791) and then the British (1801) peerage (Aspinall, *Correspondence* 2:54, 492, 910).

Mrs. Barbara St. John was the daughter of Colonel Bladen and the sister of the countess of Essex. She married Major-General Henry St. John (d. 1818), second son of Viscount St. John, colonel of the Herefordshire Regiment of Foot. Her husband was promoted to general (1797) and served as M.P. for Wootton Bassett (1761-84; 1802).

The duchess of Salisbury (d. 1835) was the wife of James, first marquis of Salisbury (1748-1823), lord chamberlain to George III (1783-1804). She was a rival to the duchess of Devonshire during the famous 1784 Westminster election, when the duchess of Devonshire was recruited to campaign on behalf of Fox. In a cartoon of the 1780s she is depicted as a mistress of the duke of Bedford. She resided at Hatfield House and died there in a fire in the west wing (*Burke's* 2155).

John Scott. *See* first earl of Eldon.

Lord Sefton (1772-1838). William Philip (Molyneux), second earl of Sefton, did not graduate from Oxford where he matriculated on April 25, 1789. An advanced "Liberal" in politics, he served as M.P. for Droitwich (1816-31). Sefton married Maria Margaret (d. 1851), daughter of the sixth Baron Craven, and had four children. In 1777 the duchess of Devonshire described him as "the most disagreeable and noisy of fools," and his wife as "the soonest affronted and the soonest appeased" (White 2:593). As M.P. Sefton could carry more votes than any unofficial man of his day. "His natural parts were excessively lively," Greville wrote, "but his education had been wholly neglected. His father stamped upon him his hideous form, but, with it, his sharp and caustic wit. . . . having sought for amusement in hunting, shooting, racing, gaming, . . . he plunged with ardour into politics" (White 2:593).

Richard Brinsley Sheridan (1751-1816), the British dramatist, orator, and Whig politician, married Elizabeth Linley (1773). A close friend of the duchess of Devonshire's, he was also an intimate in Lady Melbourne's circle and an admirer of Lady Bessborough. *The Rivals* was produced at Covent Garden (January 17, 1775) and was followed by *St. Patrick's Day* and *The Duenna*. Lady Melbourne alludes to *The Rivals* in a letter to Byron at the time of his marriage, for there were several similarities between Byron and Falkland. Sheridan's greatest work, *School for Scandal* (1777), made use of Lady Melbourne and the duchess of Devonshire as models. It was followed by *The Critic* (1779), his last work. The following year he began a political career, assisted by the duchess of Devonshire. Sheridan served as M.P. for Middlesex and delivered several memorable speeches during the trial of Warren Hastings; these, however, were never recorded.

John Sims (1749-1831) was a botanist and physician at the University of Edinburgh (1774), where he received his M.D. In 1776 he moved to London, where he was admitted licentiate of the Royal College of Physicians (1779). He became physician to the Surrey dispensary and to Princess Charlotte (*Memoirs of the Late Princess Charlotte* [London: 1818], 579). Sims edited Curtis' *Botanical Magazine* (1801-26) and, with Charles Konig, *Annals of Botany* (1805-6). He was a fellow of the Royal Society and one of the original fellows of the Linnean Society (*DNB* 18:281-82).

Robert Smith (1752-1838) of Bulcote Lodge, Nottinghamshire, served as M.P. for Nottingham (1779-97). He was the third, but first surviving, son of Abel Smith, a Nottingham banker. Smith married twice: on July 6, 1780, to Anne, the daughter of Lewyns Boldero Barnard of South Cave, Yorkshire; and on January 19, 1836, to Charlotte, daughter of John Hudson of Bessingby, Yorkshire. He succeeded his father (1788) and was created Baron Carrington (July 11, 1796). A patron of Pitt, Smith subscribed £20,000 to the loyalty loan (1797) and was promoted to an English peerage a year later (R. G. Thorne 5:199-201).

Robert John Smith (1796-1868) was the only son of Robert Smith, first Baron Carrington, and his first wife.

Robert Percy Smith (1770-1845) of Savile Row, Middlesex, was Baron Carrington by his first wife. Educated at Eton (1782-88) and King's College, Cambridge (1789), he served as M.P. for Grantham (1812-18) and Lincoln (1820-26). He was the eldest son of Robert Smith and Maria Ollier and the brother of Sydney Smith. On December 9, 1797, Smith married Caroline Maria, daughter and coheir of Richard Vernon of Hilton Park, Staffordshire, with whom he had two sons and two daughters. He contributed to George Canning's *The Microcosm*. A friend of Lord Holland and Ward, he altered the corn laws (1814-15) and supported Catholic relief. Lady Bessborough referred to him as "Bobus" Smith in a letter of September 9, 1811 (G. L. Gower 2:395).

Lord Fitzroy Somerset (1788-1855) was military secretary to the duke of Wellington during the Peninsular War and at Belgium. Somerset was wounded at Busaco on September 27, 1810 and at Waterloo, where his right arm was amputated in June 1815. He served as lord of the Admiralty, but soon resigned. He later served as secretary of embassy at Paris (1814-19) and as minister plenipotentiary (January-March 1815). Somerset was sent on special embassies to Madrid (1823) and St. Petersburg (1826) and served as M.P. for Truro (1818-20; 1826-29).

Henry Charles Somerset (1766-1835), marquis of Worcester, served as M.P. for Monmouth (1788-90), Bristol (1790-96), and Gloucestershire (1796-1803). On May 16, 1791, he married Lady Charlotte Sophia Leveson-Gower, the daughter of Granville Leveson-Gower, first marquis of Stafford (R. G. Thorne 5:225)

Henry Somerset (1792-1853), marquis of Worcester, served as M.P. for Monmouth (1813-31; 1831-32) and Gloucestershire West (1835). Educated by Reverend Walter Fletcher at Dalston, Cumberland and at Westminster (1805), he graduated from Christ Church, Oxford

(1809). He married Georgiana Frederica (July 25, 1814), daughter of Henry Fitzroy, fourth son of Charles Fitzroy, first Baron Southampton. His second marriage was to Emily Frances (June 29, 1822), the half-sister of his first wife and the daughter of Charles Culling Smith. Somerset succeeded his father as the seventh duke of Beaufort on November 23, 1835. He joined the 10th Hussars (1811), then under the command of Quentin Dick, and it was at this time that he became the attentive lover of Harriette Wilson. His father, desperate to separate him from Wilson, arranged for his appointment as aide-de-camp to the duke of Wellington (1812-14) during the Peninsular War. He subsequently became lieutenant in the 7th Hussars (1815). Somerset was lord of the Admiralty (1815-19) and served in a variety of military capacities (1819). A ministerialist, he voted against Catholic emancipation (May 21, 1816; 1817; 1819). He turned evidence against Wilson to deny her the annuity Somerset's father had promised (R. G. Thorne 4:224-25).

Georgiana, Countess Spencer (1737-1814), or Lady Spencer, was the mother of Georgiana, duchess of Devonshire.

Madame de Staël (1766-1817). Born in Paris as the daughter of a finance minister, Jacques Necker, Madame de Staël married (1786) the Baron de Staël-Holstein (1742-1802), a bankrupt Swedish ambassador. She had two sons (1790; 1792) by Narbonne, and a daughter (1797) by B. Constant. She separated from her husband to protect her fortune (1798). The fall of her father during the French Revolution led her to leave Paris for Coppet (September 1792). In England, she met Fanny Burney (1793), "but their friendship was cut short because Madame de Staël's politics and morals were considered undesirable by good society in England." She joined her husband at Coppet in May 1793, and established an important salon under the Directory. Her liaison with Benjamin Constant, who influenced her interest in German culture, began in 1794 and lasted fourteen years.

De Staël's works include *Delphine* (1802), *Corinne* (1807), and *DeL'Allemagne* (1810), which was the result of a tour though Germany. Napoleon ordered the destruction of this last work, which celebrated German culture, on the grounds of its being "un-French." On July 15, 1817, Emily Cowper wrote to her mother from Frankfurt, Germany: "I have been reading M de Stael's account of *L'Allegmagne* again it is so exact and so true that I do not wonder they abuse her and are so angry at it" (45549, f.217). In 1811 de Staël secretly married Albert de Rocca, an Italian officer who fought for the French. She traveled to Austria in May 1812 and, after visiting Russia, Finland, and Sweden, arrived in England in June 1813. She was accompanied by her husband, who August Schlegel, her friend of seven years, nicknamed Rocca Caliban (Herold 415). Rocca was intensely jealous of Benjamin Constant, whom he challenged to a duel on April 18 and May 10. De Staël kept the birth of the couple's retarded baby a secret. She never fully recovered her health after her pregnancy (Herold 417), suffering from the effects of opium, grief (over the death of her son, Albert, in a duel), and emotional exhaustion.

Lady Hester Stanhope (1776-1839) was the eldest daughter of Charles, third Earl Stanhope (1753-1816). From 1803 until his death in 1806, she resided with and served as secretary to her uncle, William Pitt. Grieved by the deaths of her brother Major Stanhope and of Sir John Moore, whom she loved, she left England (1810) and settled on Mount Lebanon (1814), adopting Eastern customs and gaining a reputation among Arab tribes as a prophetess. She published her travels and memoirs in six volumes.

George Adam, Count von Staremberg (1724-1807), was the Austrian ambassador in London.

Sir George Thomas Staunton (1781-1859), second baronet (1801), served as the king's commissioner of embassy to China (1816-17).

Sir Charles William Stewart (1778-1854), afterwards General Vane, first Baron Stewart (1814), third marquis of Londonderry (1822), served as minister to Prussia (1813-14); plenipotentiary to the congresses of Chatillon, Paris, and Vienna (1814-15); and ambassador to Austria (1814-22). He worked closely with Lady Melbourne's son Frederick Lamb.

Robert Stewart (1769-1822), second marquis of Londonderry, was also known as Lord Castlereagh. He was the chief Irish secretary (1797) who worked for Pitt's Act of Union between England and Ireland and served as president of the Board of Control (1802) and as war minister (1805-6; 1807-9). Stewart organized the coalition against Napoleon (1813-14) and represented England at congresses in Chatillon and Vienna (1814-15), Paris (1815), and Aix-la-Chapelle (1818). Detested by Byron and many of his contemporaries, he is largely credited with the forty-year peace that followed Napoleon's capture. Stewart did much to further the career of Lady Melbourne's son, Frederick Lamb, who accompanied him to Vienna as secretary of embassy in Austria (1813-15; minister ad interim 1814).

Charles Stuart (1779-1845), Baron Stuart de Rothesay (1828), was secretary of legation in Austria (1801-4), secretary of embassy in Russia (1804-8), charge d'affaires in Austria (1805-6), on special missions to Spain (1808-9) and Austria (1809), minister to Portugal (1810-14) and France (1814), ambassador to the Netherlands (1815) and France (1815-24), ambassador on special missions to Portugal (1825) and Brazil (1825-26), and ambassador to France (1828-31) and Russia (1841-44).

Charles Maurice de Talleyrand-Perigord (1754-1838), prince of Venevento. The French statesman was educated for the clergy and became Abbot of St. Denis (1775) and agent-general to the French clergy (1780). He attacked the clergy to which he nominally belonged, urging the confiscation of church property, and was excommunicated in 1791. In 1792 he was sent to London to offer peace terms to Pitt. After a brief exile, he became foreign minister under the Directory (1797). Talleyrand helped to consolidate Napoleon's power as consul for life (1802) and as emperor (1804). He helped to destroy Great Britain's European coalition (1805) and organized the Confederation of the Rhine (1806). He opposed the invasion of Russia and deserted Napoleon in 1814. As minister of foreign affairs under Louis XVIII, he negotiated treaties that gave France the boundaries of 1792. Talleyrand was Louis-Philippe's chief adviser at the July revolution (*Chambers* 605).

Henry John Temple. *See* third Viscount Palmerston.

George Tierney (1761-1830), the Whig politician, was educated at Eton and Peterhouse, Cambridge. Having risen from the mercantile class, he was shunned by the aristocratic Whigs and could not rise until their death or retirement. He opposed Pitt's policies in 1797 and continued attending the house on the withdrawal of Fox and his party in 1798, deeply offending them. That same year, he fought a duel with Pitt, who had accused him of obstruction. He became treasurer of the navy in Addington's ministry (1802) and president of the Board of Control (1806-7). Tierney led the Whigs (1817-21) after the death of George Ponsonby (1817). He joined Canning as master of the Mint and quit office with Goderich (1828) (*DNB* 19:865-67).

Torrington. *See* Byng.

Edward Venables Vernon (1757-1847) (afterwards Vernon-Harcourt) was bishop of Carlisle (1792) and afterwards archbishop of York. He married Lady Anne Leveson-Gower, daughter of Granville Leveson-Gower, first marquis of Stafford, and had two sons, George Granville Venables Vernon and Granville Venables Vernon.

George Granville Venables Vernon (1785-1861) was a friend of John William Ward and the son of Edward Venables Vernon. His brother was Granville Venables Vernon. He attended Westminster (1798) and Christ Church, Oxford (1803). His first marriage (March 27, 1815) was to Lady Elizabeth Bingham (d. September 9, 1838), the daughter of Richard Bingham, second earl of Lucan. His second marriage (September 30, 1847) was to Frances Elizabeth, the widow of John James Waldegrave of Navestock, Essex. He took the name of Harcourt, his father having succeeded to the estates of William Harcourt, third Earl Harcourt (January 15, 1831). In 1809 Vernon criticized the ministry's handling of the convention of Cintra, the Scheldt question, and the imprisonment of Sir Francis Burdett. In 1810 he voted for parliamentary reform, but sought an alliance with Canning at the instructions of Lord Leveson-Gower. Vernon disliked the "pure . . . Whiggism" of Grey and was less radical than his brother, Granville Vernon, who joined him in the house (1815). His cousin James MacDonald also adhered to the Whigs. Vernon described his interview with Bonaparte at Elba, which Lady Melbourne recounts in her letter of January 11, 1815 (R. G. Thorne 5:450).

John William Ward (1781-1833), first earl of Dudley of Castle Dudley, Staffordshire (1827), fourth Viscount Dudley and Ward (1823), received his master's degree from Oxford in 1813. He served as secretary of state for foreign affairs (1827-28). A society wit accused of apostasy by Byron for making an alliance with Canning, he was a frequent guest of the Melbournes and of William Lamb. Byron joked about Ward's apostasy in a famous jest. When asked how much it would take to "re-Whig" Ward, the poet responded that "he must first, before he was *re-whigged*, be re-*warded*" (*LJ* 3:227). Byron planned a trip to Holland with Ward, but the trip was cancelled because Ward was suddenly called to Scotland (*LJ* 3:176). Along with George Canning and Hookham Frere, Ward was a dining companion of Byron's and a contributor to the *Anti-Jacobin* and the *Quarterly Review* (Marchand, *Portrait* 156). In the latter capacity, he reviewed Sam Rogers' *Columbus* in March 1813 (*LJ* 3:62). Harriette Wilson remembers him as a pedant, repeating Greek and Latin verses to himself (Wilson 250) and his friend, Luttrell. Ward was a Tory M.P. for Downton (1802), Worcestershire (1803), Petersfield (1806), Wareham (1807), Ilchester (1812), and Bossiney (1819-23). A member of the Durham party (that is, the followers of John George Lambton, first earl of Durham), he sought, with George Vernon, an alliance of Whigs and Tories under Canning.

Dr. Richard Warren (1731-1797) was physician to George, Prince of Wales (Aspinall, *Correspondence* 3:1026).

Thomas Watson (1743-1781), the engraver, was apprenticed to an engraver on plate. He worked "in the dot manner, but afterwards became very successful in mezzotint" (*Bryan's* 5:338). He kept a print shop in Bond Street with W. Dickenson, exhibiting at Spring Gardens in 1775. His engravings of Lady Melbourne, Warren Hastings, and Georgina, Countess Spencer (after Reynolds) represent his more esteemed work (*Bryan's* 5:338).

Lady Frances Webster was the wife of James Wedderburn Webster, a philandering, foolish, and vain husband. In letters to Lady Melbourne, Byron described his flirtatious conduct with Frances Webster as a reprisal for James Webster's boasts about his wife's virtue. The couple was later separated, and Frances Webster flirted with the duke of Wellington and other military officers shortly after Wellington's defeat of Napoleon at Waterloo (September 18, 1815; *LJ* 4:312n).

Sir Godfrey Vassal Webster (1788-1836) was the son by the first marriage of the Whig Hostess Lady Holland (Ziegler 51). He had an "affair" with Lady Melbourne's daughter-in-law, Caroline Lamb (November 6, 1812; *LJ* 2:241).

James Wedderburn Webster (b. 1789) married Lady Frances Annesley, the daughter of Arthur, first earl of Mountnorris and eighth Viscount Valentia. Byron's letters to Lady Melbourne recount his flirtation with Lady Frances when he visited the Websters at Aston Hall in 1813 (*LJ* 2:287).

Henry Wellesley (1773-1847), first Baron Cowley (1828), served as secretary of legation in Sweden (1792-95); minister to Spain (1810-11); and ambassador to Spain (1811-22), Austria (1823-31), and France (1835; 1841-46).

Lady Wellesley (d. November 7, 1816) was the wife of Richard Colley Wellesley, second earl of Mornington. Her full name was Hyacinthe Gabrielle and she was the illegitimate daughter of Christopher Fagan, chevalier in the French service. She had three sons and two daughters before her marriage. In a letter to Caroline Lamb, Lady Melbourne alludes to Lady Wellesley's compromised reputation.

Richard Colley Wellesley (formerly Wesley; 1760-1842), styled Viscount Wellesley (1760-81), second earl of Mornington (1781), and Marquis Wellesley (1799), was M.P. for Bere Alston (1784-86), Saltash (1786-87), New Windsor (1787-96), and Old Sarum (1796-97). He later served as ambassador to Spain (1809) and as foreign secretary (1809-12). Wellesley was the brother of Arthur Wellesley, the duke of Wellington, and of Henry Wellesley and William Wellesley-Pole. Lady Melbourne transcribed his letter of resignation from Perceval's administration (appendix A).

Arthur Wellesley, first duke of Wellington (1769-1852), was the fourth son of Garrett Wellesley. He became a major-general (1802), was chief-secretary for Ireland (1807-9) during a tumultuous period, and commanded forces sent to the Peninsula. He was superseded by Sir Harry Burrard, but resumed command in Portugal (1809) and was disturbed by the lack of reinforcements (1810). Created marquis of Wellington (1812), he was assigned the task of reconciling King Ferdinand and the Spanish *liberales*. He returned to England, where he was named duke of Wellington (1814), and served briefly as ambassador at Paris (1814) before attending the Congress of Vienna (1815). With the assistance of Blücher he defeated Napoleon, and he persuaded Blücher not to make reprisals on the French capital. In 1817 he was given Apsley House and Strathfieldsaye by the nation (*CDNB* 3:3166-68; *DNB* 20:1081-115).

Westmoreland. *See* Fane.

Francis Wheatley (1747-1801) designed gardens at Brocket Hall and collaborated with John Hamilton Mortimer on the saloon ceiling, finishing it after Mortimer's death (Tipping 58:98). Wheatley was well known for his *Cries of London* series (Airlie, *Palmerston* 5, 7).

Samuel Whitbread (1758-1815) was a leading member of the House of Commons and the son and heir of the eminent brewer. Born in 1758 and educated at Eton and St. John's College, Cambridge, he toured Europe and married the daughter of Sir Charles (afterwards Earl) Grey. He served as M.P. for Steyning and Bedford. An active member of the opposition, he often voted independently of party. Whitbread was a highly effective critic of Pitt and the war with France. He is best remembered for conducting the impeachment proceedings against Lord Melville (1805). Suffering from nervous exhaustion, he committed suicide while manager of Drury Lane theater (*CDNB* 3:3196-97).

Watkin Williams (1783-1856), or Sir Henry Watkin Williams Wynn, was envoy to Saxony (1803-6) and minister to Switzerland (1822-23), Württemberg (1823-25), and Denmark (1824-53) (*PPBD* 380).

Sir Robert Thomas Wilson (1777-1849), military hero and governor of Gibraltar, was instrumental in assisting Count Lavalette's escape from Paris. Lady Melbourne refers to this incident in her letter to Annabella of January 19, 1816.

Marquis of Worcester. *See* Henry Somerset.

Sir George O'Brien Wyndham. *See* earl of Egremont.

Sir Watkin Williams Wynn (1772-1840), fifth baronet, served as M.P. for Bemires (1794-96) and Denbighshire (1796-1840).

Frances Charles, earl of Yarmouth (1777-1842), afterwards third marquis of Hertford, married Maria Fagniani in 1798. He was a notable figure at the court of the Prince Regent and was the model for Thackeray's marquis of Steyne in *Vanity Fair* and for Disraeli's Monmouth in *Coningsby* (April 19, 1806; G. L. Gower 2:188; Marchand, *Biography* 3:71n). Lady Melbourne mentions him in a letter to Frederick Lamb (January 30, 1818) and Harriette Wilson described him as "*au fait* on every subject one can possibly imagine, especially drawing, horse-riding, painting, profligacy or morals; religion of whatever creed" (Wilson 1:287). He had a large collection of miniatures by well-known artists.

Charles Philip Yorke (1764-1834). Educated at Harrow and St. John's College, Cambridge (1781), Yorke spoke frequently in opposition to Pitt, but defended the Copenhagen expedition (1808) and stifled inquiry into the Walcheren expedition (1810), which made him unpopular in the press. His windows were smashed for attacking the liberty of the press (1810) during the arrest of Burdett and for supporting the Corn Bill (1815). He was distrusted and disliked by the Prince Regent (1811). Yorke served as secretary of war (1801-3), secretary of state for home affairs (1803-4), and first lord of the Admiralty (1810-12).

INDEX

Bingham, Lavinia. *See* Spencer, Lavinia
Bingham, Louisa, 416
Bingham, Margaret, 416-17
Bingham, Richard (second earl of Lucan), 324,
    339n.26, 415, 416, 417, 449, 465
Birmingham riots, 458
Biron, duc de (Lauzin), 423
Blacher, Gebhard Lebrecht, 295, 417, 467
Black, Mr., 118, 377
Blackwood's, 441
Bladen, Colonel, 91n.17, 459
Bland, Sir Hungerford, 427
Bland, Thomas Davison, 427, 450
Blarney, Lady. *See* Bessborough, Lady
    Henrietta Frances
Blessington, countess of, 441
Bligh, John. *See* Darnley, fourth earl of
Blondel, J. F., 422
Bloomfield, Benjamin, 340n.44, 443
Bolsterstone, 37
Bonaparte. *See* Napoleon
Bonaparte, Caroline, 112n.2
Bonaparte, Joseph, 65n.72, 106, 112n.2,
    113nn.22-23
Bonaparte, Josephine, 426
Botanical Magazine, 460
Boufflers, Stanislas-Jean de, 73, 92n.26, 417
Bourbon, duc de, 340n.44
Bouverie, Edward, 389n.5
Bouverie, Henrietta Elizabeth. *See* Rosslyn,
    countess of
Bowman, 90
Bowood Park, 447
Boyce, Susan, 51, 297n.3
Boyle, M. L., 61n.21
Bradford, Orlando, first earl of, 200n.118
Brand, Thomas, 294, 304n.80, 417
Bredall, Dr., 442
Brentano, Clement, 338n.14, 426
Briggs, Mr., 86, 89
Bristol, Lord. *See* Hervey, Lord
British Institution, 61nn.15-16, 430
Brocket, Sir John, 61n.13
Brocket Hall, 13, 70, 135, 182, 278, 343, 347, 348,
    357, 445; Thomas Brand visits, 304n.80; 417;
    entertains Brougham, 54-55; Robert Byng
    visits, 419; Byron invited, 146, 155n.91;
    Lady Byron invited, 354; proximity to Lord
    Cowper at Panshanger, 40; garden, 35; George
    IV portrait, 434; during Gordon riots, 25;
    history of, 61n.13; illness at, 358, 361;
    Caroline Lamb's residence, 443; purchased by

Matthew Lamb, 444; Peniston Lamb nursed,
    98; William Lamb's view of, 197n.63; visited
    by Edwin Landseer, 27; Lawrence painting of
    Emily and Harriet, 64n.64; *Maternal Affection*, 29; decorations by Lady
    Melbourne, 16-17; ceiling by John Mortimer,
    452; architect James Paine, 454; visit by Lord
    Henry Petty, 46; rent days, 87; theatricals at,
    20; garden and ceiling by Francis Wheatley,
    467; **8-11**
Broglie, Marshall de, 414
Brooks' Club, 62n.25, 66n.88, 417, 440, 446
Brougham, Henry Peter, 417-18; advises Princess
    Charlotte, 181; and French Revolution, 375,
    389n.5; affair with Caroline George Lamb,
    54, 57, 96, 343, 345-46, 370n.3, 418, 443;
    critic of William Lamb, 67n.99; defends
    Mildmay, 158, 192, 203nn.164-65, 204n.167;
    out of office, 48; **58**
Broughton, Baron. *See* Hobhouse, John Cam
Brown, Lancelot "Capability," 422, 440, 454
Brown, Robert, 422
Browne, Philip, 201n.132
Bruce, Mr., 277, 298n.15
Bruce, Charles. *See* Ailesbury, third earl of
Bruce, Lady Mary, 91n.8, 457
Bruce, Michael, 311, 337n.2
Brunswick, duchess of, 413
Buckingham, Lord. *See* Grenville, George;
    Villiers, George
Buckinghamshire, countess of, 457
Buckinghamshire, earl of, 457
Buckinghamshire, second earl of. *See* Hobart,
    John
Buckinghamshire, Lady, 22
Buckinghamshire, Lord (Robert Hobart), 415,
    418, 439
Bunbury, Sir (Thomas) Charles, 71, 418, 436, 448
Burdett, Sir Francis, 67n.99, 301n.60, 303n.71,
    304n.79, 352, 370n.16, 418, 453, 454, 465,
    468
Burdett, Robert, 352, 370n.16, 418
Burdett, William Jones, 454
Burges, Sir James Bland, 304n.83
Burghersh, Lord. *See* Fane, John (1784-1859)
Burgoyne, General, 435
Burke, General, 100
Burke, Edmund, 1, 437, 459
Burleigh, Lord, 364
Burlington, earl of. *See* Cavendish, Lord George
    Augustus Henry
Burney, Charles, 78-79, 418

67n.97, 414, 422

Carrington, Baron, 461. *See also* Smith, Robert Percy

Carrington, Lady, 182, 421

Carrington, Lord. *See* Smith, Robert Percy

Castlereagh, Lord. *See* Stewart, Robert

Catalani, Madame Angelica, 121, 151n.26

Catesby, Robert, 202n.140

Catullus, 444

Caulaincourt, 197n.57

Cavendish, Lady Dorothy, 415

Cavendish, Lord Edward Charles (Lord Edward Bentinck), 375, 389n.5, 421

Cavendish, Lord George Augustus Henry, 92n.30, 375, 389n.5, 421

Cavendish, Lady Harriet. *See* Granville, Lady Harriet (Hary-O)

Cavendish, William, 421

Cawthorn, 426

Cecil, Lord David, 62n.37

Ceracchi, Giuseppe, 30, 63n.44, 421

Chambers, Cornelia. *See* Milbanke, Cornelia

Chambers, Mary, 442

Chambers, Sir William, 16, 33, 197n.64, 421-22

Championnet, 421

Charles, Francis. *See* Yarmouth, earl of

Charles, William, 449

Charles I, 116, 438

Charles IV (Spain), 44, 65n.71

Charles X, 415, 436

Charlotte, Princess, 58-59, 67nn.100-1, 155n.89, 157, 178, 180-82, 200n.102, 200nn.111-13, 343, 353-54, 355-56, 370n.18, 371nn.23-25, 413, 420, 422, 425-26, 429, 432, 442, 448, 458, 460, **60**

Charlotte, Queen, 419, 429, 439, 442

Charriäre, Madame de, 339n.35, 424

Chatham, 456

Child, Robert, 430, 431

Chippendale, Thomas, 16

Cholmondeley, Harriet, 447

Churchill, Winston, 200n.123

Cicero, 433

Cipriani, 16, 17, 422, 452

Clairmont, Claire, 57, 67n.102

Clare, Lord (John Fitzgibbon), 359, 422

Clarke, 354

Clarke, Dr., 155n.95

Clarke, Adam, 370n.21, 422

Clarke, Christopher, 378

Clarke, Edward Daniel, 423

Clarke, Samuel, 370n.21, 423

Claughton, Thomas, 117, 149n.6

Clermont, Mrs., 273

Clermont, Lady (Frances Cairnes Murray), 23, 73, 423

Clermont, Lord (William Henry Fortescue), 73, 423

Clifford, Mrs. *See* Townshend, Elizabeth

Clifford, Augustus. *See* Foster, Augustus William Clifford

Clint, G., *Sir George O'Brien Wyndham,* **22**

Clinton, Captain George, 439

Clowes, William, 92n.23

Cobbett, Lady, 102

Coigny, duc de (François Franquetot), 423

Coigny, Madame de, 56, 412, 423

Coigny, marquis de, 92n.38, 423

Coigny, Anne-Francoise-Aimé de Franquetot de, 334, 340n.49, 423

Coke, Charlotte (mother of Lord Melbourne), 60n.3, 444

Coke, George Lewis, 444

Coke, John, 423-24

Coke, Lady Mary, 20, 21, 23, 27, 419, 455

Coke, Sir Thomas, 17, 61n.12, 423-24, 444

Coke family, 17, 62n.24, 444

Colemores, 92n.38

Coleridge, E. H., 59

Coleridge, Samuel Taylor, *Christabel,* 308, 327, 339n.30

Colleraine, Lord, 412

Colman, George, 364, 424

Compton, Charles, 421

Compton, Elizabeth, 73, 92n.30, 421

Condé, 415

Conflans, Louis Marthe de. *See* Coigny, Madame de

Constant, Benjamin, 328, 339nn.35-36, 424, 462-63; *Adolphe,* 308, 328, 339n.35

Conway, Caroline, 424

Conway, Henry Seymour, 91n.5, 92n.28, 411, 420, 424, 426

Conyers, Baroness. *See* d'Arcy, Amelia

Cookney, Mr., 89, 105, 118, 296, 377

Cooper, Samuel, 416

Copland, A., 421

Copley, Catherine, 411

Copley, Sir Joseph, 411

Corbett, Henry Vincent, 426

Corn Bill, 287-88, 301n.60, 303n.68, 303-4nn. 71-73, 304nn.76-77, 304n.79, 414, 427, 429, 447, 457, 458, 461, 468

corn riots, 274, 297n.2, 289, 291, 303n.68,

69; affair with Charles Grey, 32-33, 53, 63nn.47-48, 64n.53; marriage of, 20; portraits of, 19, 425, 434, 466; *The Sylph,* 4, 24-25, 31, 428; **16, 18-20, 32**
Devonshire, fourth duke of (William), 415
Devonshire, fifth duke of (William), 20, 25, 31, 32-33, 44, 62n.27, 63n.45, 64n.53, 64n.67, 64n.70, 69, 72, 112n.14, 300n.40, 309, 334, 428, 432-33, 437, 443, **34**
Devonshire, sixth duke of (William), 299n.30, 428, 429
Diana, 421
Dibdin, Mr., 337n.3
Dick, Quentin (Quintin), 140, 153nn.64-65, 303n.68, 462
Dickenson, W., 465
Dighton, R., *George Lamb,* **50**
Dilettanti Club, 15
Disraeli, 468
Distiller's Company, 299n.27
Dorchester, earl of. *See* Milton, Lord
Dorset, Charles, fifth duke of, 23, 25, 297n.1, 435
Douglas, Lady, 149n.3, 152n.46, 428
Douglas, Mr., 276, 283
Douglas, Sir John, 152n.46, 428
Dover House, 63n.52, 454. *See also* Melbourne House, Whitehall
Downman, John, *Ralph Milbanke,* **55;** *Judith Milbanke,* **56**
Doyle, Colonel Francis Hastings, 199n.96
Doyle, Selina, 177, 199n.96
Drummond, Clemintina Elizabeth, 439
Drury Lane, 3, 44, 112n.10, 148, 156n.107, 192, 297n.3, 309, 334, 337n.3, 364, 412, 413, 427, 448, 467
Dubost, 441
Dudley, first earl of. *See* Ward, John William
Duncannon, Lady. *See* Bessborough, Lady Henrietta Frances
Duncannon, Viscount. *See* Bessborough, third earl of
Dunckley, Mr., 445
Durham, first earl of. *See* Lambton, John George

East India Company, 303n.68
Eden, George, 49, 66n.90, 198n.79, 202n.143
Eden, William, 66n.90, 421
Edinburgh Review, 417
Edleston, John, 155n.102
Edmeades, Thomas, 152n.47
Edward, Lord. *See* Kent, Lord Edward, duke of
Egerton, Sir Philip Grey, 61n.22

Edgeworth, Maria, 57
Egremont, third earl of (Sir George O'Brien Wyndham), 1, 428-29; and canals, 70; and Princess Charlotte, 181; on Corn Bill, 301n.60; on French Revolution, 374, 388nn.3-4; as horse breeder, 64n.56; father of Emily Lamb, 27, 443; father of William Lamb, 24, 27, 36, 37, 62n.30, 446; father of twins, 23; affair with Lady Melbourne, 3, 23, 24, 26-27, 35, 36, 69, 136, 155n.103, 366, 428, 450; advises Lady Melbourne on agriculture, 17, 35; and Peninsular War, 44-45; defends Colonel Quentin, 201n.132, 456; patron of Turner, 64n.57; **22**
Eldon, first earl of (John Scott), 281, 291, 300n.34, 429
Eldon, Mrs., 439
Elgin, third earl of. *See* Ailesbury, third earl of
Eliot, William, 371n.36, 429
Elizabeth, Princess, 181, 429
Ellenborough, first Baron. *See* Law, Edward
Ellis, Mr., 351
Elphinstone, Margaret Mercer, 181, 429
Elwin, Malcolm, 151nn.28-29, 151n.30, 302n.64, 338nn.11-12, 338n.19
Erne, Lady, 432
Erroll, fifteenth earl of, 448
Erskine, Thomas, 280, 299n.27, 389n.5, 415, 429-30, 436
Essex, Lady, 76, 91n.17, 93.39, 459
Essex, Lord, 92n.29
Esterhazy, Prince, 340n.44
Esterhazy, Princess, 197n.61, 340n.44
Evans, Mr., 75

Fagan, Christopher, 466
Fagniani, Maria, 468
Fairford, Lady, 76, 93n.39
Fane, Jane, 430
Fane, John (1759-1841), 430, 431
Fane, John (1784-1859), 430
Fane, Priscilla Anne, 430-31
Fane, Sarah Anne, 430, 431
Fane, Lady Sarah Sophia, 430, 431
Farquhar, Sir Walter, 97, 98, 112n.4, 361, 431
Fauconberg, second earl of. *See* Belasyse, Henry
Fauconberg, Lady, 14
Fawkes, Guy, 185, 202n.140
Fenwick, Dr., 47
Feodorovna, Elizabeth. *See* Louise of Baden-Durlach, Princess
Ferdinand, King, 112n.1, 467

William Chambers, 422; and Princess Charlotte, 180-81, 200n.102, 429; and Lord Clermont, 423; and Richard Cosway, 425; possible nickname by Anne Damer, 197n.59; death of, 443; and duchess of Devonshire, 28, 31, 47, 63n.47, 65n.77, 69; divorce of, 152n.46, 152n.50, 428; and Lord Egremont, 23; and Erskine, 430; marriage to Maria Fitzherbert, 2, 28, 62n.37, 67n.97, 371n.33, 431-32; assassination attempt on George III, 36-37; and Prince Gotchakoff, 340n.44; and Lady Hertford, 92n.38, 370n.8; and Henry Holland, 440; arranges house swapping, 33, 63n.50, 63-64n.52; and Sir William Knighton, 442-43; father of George Lamb, 27-28, 91n.18, 444; godfather of George Lamb, 27; spoofed by George Lamb, 66n.90; and death of Peniston Lamb, 40; and William Lamb, 66n.78, 371n.46; and Count Lavalette, 337n.2; and Prince Leopold I, 448; affair with Lady Melbourne, 2, 3, 13, 27-30, 40, 52, 62nn.32-34, 69, 72, 91n.18, 155n.89, 434, 450; breakfast with Lady Melbourne, 149n.5; plans dinner with Lady Melbourne, 348-49; visits Lady Melbourne, 183, 201n.130; and Lord Melbourne, 15, 82-83, 445; and Lord Moira, 451-52; and physicians, 371n.38, 371n.40, 438, 465; political favors of, 52-53, 58, 66nn.90-92, 82-83, 92, 93n.47, 95, 102, 108-10, 112n.5, 112n.17, 155n.89, 182-83, 343, 357, 363, 365, 384-85, 386, 434, 437, 442, 444, 445-46; portraits of, 29, 155n.89, 426, 434, and Dick Quentin, 201nn.131-32, 202-3nn.154-55, 456; affair with Mary Robinson, 62n.36; and Madame de Staâl, 48, 281; and Tyrwhitt, 371n.27; and Wellesley, 380-81, 389n.13; and Whitehall, 44-45; and marriage of William Frederick, 340n.39, 44-45; and Charles Yorke, 468; **29**

Germain, George, 194, 278, 279, 297n.1, 434-35

Germaine, Lord George Sackville, 194, 297n.1, 434-35

Gibbs, Sir Vicary, 182, 435

Giles, Daniel (father of Daniel Giles), 435

Giles, Daniel (1761-1831), 96, 111, 182, 435

Gillray, 454

Glenbervie, Lord, 297n.10, 300n.45

Glengal, Lord. See Butler, Richard

Glorious Revolution, 20, 61n.20

Gloucester, duchess of, 330, 431

Gloucester, duke of, 48, 330, 340n.39

Gloucestor, Lord, 193

Goderich, 441, 446, 447, 464. *See also* Robinson, Frederick John

Godoy, 44, 65n.71

Goldsmith, Oliver, 196, 417

Gordon, duchess of, 39, 64n.63

Gordon, third duke of, 436

Gordon, fourth duke of (Alexander Gordon), 415, 436

Gordon, Lord George, 429, 435-36, 450

Gordon, Lord William, 76, 340n.44, 436, 448

Gordon riots, 25, 69, 91n.21, 435

Gosford, Lady, 186

Gotchakoff, Prince, 340n.44

Gower, Lord Granville Leveson- (youngest son of Granville Leveson-Gower, first marquis of Stafford), 436, 465; and Robert Adair, 419; correspondence and affair with Lady Bessborough, 35, 38, 41-42, 64n.67, 64n.69, 92n.35, 298n.15, 412, 416; marriage of, 437; and Madame Narischkine, 197n.61; **49**

Gower, Granville Leveson- (first marquis of Stafford; Lord Stafford); apostasy of, 280, 299n.23; father of Lady Anne Leveson-Gower, 464; grandfather of Lady Susan Ryder, 459

Grafton, duchess of. *See* Waldegrave, Lady Charlotte Maria

Graham, Mr., 103, 412

Graham, Maria, 300

Grammont, duc de (duc de Guiche), 183, 201n.131, 453

Gramont, comte de, 436-37

Granard, sixth earl of, 456

Granby, marquis of, 458

Grant, 98

Granville, Lady Harriet (Hary-O), 37, 38, 41, 43-44, 45, 64n.60, 64n.67, 64n.69, 66n.87, 66n.95, 343, 418, 436, 437, 443

Granville, Lord, 411

Greene, General Nathanael, 452

Greenwich, Lady, 20

Greenwood, Thomas, 457

Grenville, 76

Grenville, George, 43, 437, 453, 455. *See also* Nugent, George

Grenville, Richard Temple-Nugent-Brydges-Chandos-, 144, 437

Grenville, Thomas, 2, 92n.37, 96, 101-3, 113n.18, 157, 375, 389nn.5-6, 437, 466

Greville, Charles, 428, 460

Greville, Frances Anne. *See* Crewe, Anne

Greville, Fulke, 425

Grey, Earl, 337n.2

339n.34, 343, 347-48, 353-54, 368-70, 424, 432, 433, 443, 450, 467; birth of child, 51, 274, 337n.1; courtship by Byron, 47-48, 49-50, 115, 123-24, 150n.21, 151nn.27-28, 194-95nn.1-2, 300n.42, 419; marriage to Byron, 50-52, 157, 183, 185, 188, 199n.86, 200n.125, 201-2nn.136-38, 203n.157, 273-74, 297n.6, 298n.17, 297, 301n.59, 338n.19, 438, 440, 447; marriage settlement, 304n.83, 427, 450; separation from Byron, 51, 59, 154n.76, 199n.96, 274, 301n.58, 302n.65, 304n.83, 307, 312-13, 337-38n.9, 312-19, 326, 339n.27, 340nn.42-43, 372n.48, 417-18, 431, 450, 457; **54**

Milbanke, Cornelia, 16, 422

Milbanke, Colonel Edward, 450

Milbanke, Eleanor, 70, 84-85, 450

Milbanke, Lady (Elizabeth Hedworth), 14-15, 60n.3, 450, 451

Milbanke, Elizabeth. *See* Melbourne, Lady

Milbanke, Elizabeth Emily. *See* Milbanke-Huskisson, Elizabeth Emily

Milbanke, Reverend Francis, 450

Milbanke, Harriet, 450

Milbanke, John (uncle of Lady Melbourne), 451

Milbanke, John (brother of Lady Melbourne), 14, 16, 60n.3, 70, 83-85, 93n.48, 193, 422, 450, **1**

Milbanke, Sir John (nephew of Lady Melbourne), 70, 75, 84-85, 450

Milbanke, Judith (Lady Noel), 14, 33, 51, 65n.80, 66n.85, 69, 79-82, 91n.1, 92n.38, 93n.44, 177, 179, 183, 186, 191, 194, 199n.96, 275, 283, 292, 307, 309, 312, 314, 315-16, 319, 320, 322, 327, 333, 335, 337-38n.8, 338n.13, 338n.17, 340n.47, 340n.54, 353, 372n.48, 426, 427, 438, 450-51, 453, **56**

Milbanke, Admiral Mark, 91n.15, 441, 450, 451-52

Milbanke, Sir Ralph (father of Lady Melbourne), 14, 60n.3, 450, 451, **1**

Milbanke, Ralph (brother of Lady Melbourne), 14, 51, 65n.80, 69-70, 79-81, 91n.1, 177, 179, 183, 184, 188, 191, 194, 199n.96, 274, 275, 282, 283, 292, 3041n.83, 312, 314, 315, 317, 320-21, 331, 333, 335, 336, 337-38nn.7-8, 338n.12, 338nn.18-19, 339n.27, 340n.54, 372n.48, 427, 450, 451, **55**

Milbanke-Huskisson, Elizabeth Emily, 101-2, 112-13nn.16-19, 183-84, 201n.131, 202n.138, 289, 437, 441, 450, 451

Mildmay, Sir Henry, 158, 193, 203n.164, 204n.173, 418, 434

Millar, Professor John, 36

Mills, Samuel Gillam, 152n.47

Milton, Lord (Joseph Damer), 21-22, 71, 91n.6, 375, 389n.5, 389n.7, 426

Moira, Lord (Francis Rawdon), 137, 152n.47, 380-81, 451-52, 456

Molyneux, William Philip. *See* Sefton, Lord

Montgomery, Mary Milicent, 186, 202nn.143-44

Montmorence, Anne, duc de, 60n.2

Montrond, comte de, 423

Moore, Mr., 282

Moore, Doris Langley, 198n.70

Moore, Sir John, 113n.23, 463

Moore, Thomas, 57, 59, 67n.96, 280, 338n.19, 368, 369, 372nn.48-49

Morning Chronicle, 66n.90, 158, 197n.44, 201n.136, 203n.165, 337n.2, 339n.27, 340n.39, 340n.53, 343

Morning Courier, 157, 167, 371n.41

Morning Herald, 191, 339-40n.37, 416, 452

Morning Post, 21, 152n.46, 157, 197n.51, **21**

Mornington, countess of (Anne), 433

Mornington, second earl of. *See* Wellesley, Richard Colley

Morpeth, Georgiana, 156n.108, 437

Morpeths, 349

Morris, John, 303n.68, 303n.70

Mortimer, John Hamilton, 17, 452, 467

Mountnorris, first earl of (Arthur), 466

Mouret, Claude-Philibert-Hippolyte de, 423

Murat, Joachim, 95, 112n.2, 281, 300n.37, 452, 454

Murray, Frances Cairnes. *See* Clermont, Lady

Murray, John, 67n.101, 152n.45, 156n.112, 198n.76, 309, 426

Musters, Mrs., 40, 446

Napier, George, 448

Napier, Sarah, 22, 27

Napoleon Bonaparte, 3, 30, 39, 40, 43, 45, 48, 49, 56, 63n.44, 64n.59, 65n.72, 65n.79, 95, 112n.2, 113n.22, 197n.57, 276, 290, 295, 297n.8, 297n.11, 308, 328, 334, 339n.35, 412, 417, 421, 424, 426-27, 429, 433, 448, 452, 454, 462, 463, 464, 465, 466, 467

Nareskin, Madam. *See* Narischkine, Madame

Narischkine, Madame, 197n.61, 308, 332, 340n.44, 412, 452

Narischkine, Dimitri, 452

Narns, 364

Nathan, Issac, 443

Necker, Jacques, 462

Strabane, Viscount. *See* Abercorn, marquis of
Strafford, first earl of, 112n.6, 419
Stuart, Lady Caroline, 427
Stuart, Charles, 463-64
Stuart, John Shaw, 389n.5
Stubbs, George; *The Milbanke and the Melbourne Families*, 14, 60n.3, 1
Surrey, earl of (Howard), 184, 201n.134

Tacitus, 433
Talavera, Battle of, 45, 65n.72, 95, 113n.21, 113n.23, 430
Talbots, 76
Talleyrand-Perigord, Charles Maurice de, 40, 183, 464
Tamworth, Lady, 87, 88
Tamworth, Lord, 87
Tankerville, earl of. *See* Ossulstone, Lord
Tavistock, Lord, 347
Tavistock, marquis of. *See* Bedford, fifth duke of; Russell, Francis (1788-1861)
Taylor, Mr., 78
Temple, John Henry. *See* Palmerston, third Viscount
Thackery, 468
Thomas, Henry, 447
Thompson, Mr., 148
Thrale, Mrs., 418
Tichfield, Lord. *See* Bentinck, William Henry Cavendish
Tierney, George, 48, 67n.99, 181, 200nn.131-32, 464
Tilghman, Harriet, 103, 113n.19, 450
Tilghman, Mr., 113n.19, 450
Times, 30, 34, 62n.37, 137, 152n.49, 155n.107, 200n.131, 303n.68, 303n.70, 371n.41
Titchfield, marquis of, 415
Toby, 98
Tomkins, Mr., 303n.68
Tomkins, P. W., *Francis, Fifth Duke of Bedford*, **40**
Tooke, Horne, 430, 435
Topino-Lebrun, 421
Torrens, William McCullagh, 197n.63
Torrington. *See* Byng
Tour, Madame de la, 15
Tour, Mr. la, 100
Townshend, Elizabeth (Mrs. Clifford), 308, 333, 340n.41, 432
Townshend, fourth Marquis, 432
Trafalgar, 112n.14, 101, 439
Trafford, Mr., 75, 77
Turner, William, 26, 35, 428; *Fighting Bucks*, 35;

The Forest of Bere, 35, 64n.57
Tyrwhitt, Sir Thomas, 343, 357, 371n.27

Upton, Mr., 87

Vaines, J. de, 425
Valentia, Viscount. *See* Mountnorris, first earl of
Van Nost, 61n.12
Vane, General. *See* Stewart, Sir Charles William
Vanneck, Miss, 62n.35
Vanneck, Sir Joshua, 62n.35
Varegas, 113n.23
Vernon, 45
Vernon, Edward Venables, 26, 464
Vernon, George Granville Venables, 65n.72, 276, 297n.11, 464-65
Vernon, Granville Venables, 449, 464, 465
Vernon, Richard, 461
Victoria, Queen, 3, 13, 200n.112, 370n.18, 426, 442, 446
Victoria Mary Louisa, 442
Villiers, countess of Jersey. *See* Fane, Lady Sarah Sophia
Villiers, George (Lord Buckingham), 328, 339-40n.37, 431
Villiers, Marjorie, 154n.65, 154n.75, 154nn.77-78
Virgil, 433
Vitoria, Battle of, 65n.72
Voltaire, 92n.26, 120, 155n.73, 280, 298n.21, 388n.3, 417
Vyse, Edward, 303n.68, 303n.71

Walcheren expedition, 420, 468
Waldegrave, Lady Charlotte Maria, 26, 428; **24**
Waldegrave, Frances Elizabeth. *See* Bingham, Frances Elizabeth
Waldegrave, John James, 465
Waldegrave sisters, 26, **24**
Wales, Prince of. *See* George IV
Wales, Princess of. *See* Caroline, Queen
Walpole, Horace, 13, 20, 21, 23, 26, 62n.35, 420, 427
Walpole, Sir Robert, 424
Ward, John William (first earl of Dudley), 98, 119, 144, 148, 154n.81, 156n.108, 166, 195n.16, 332, 461, 464, 465
Warren, Sir John, 101
Warren, Dr. Richard, 32, 59, 344, 361, 371n.38, 363, 366, 465
Waterloo, Battle of, 304n.81, 417, 461, 466
Watson, Samuel, 61n.12
Watson, Thomas, 61n.16, 434, 465-66

Webber, Mary, 450, 451
Webster, Lady Frances ("Phryne"), 49, 117,
    155n.97, 155nn.100-2, 162-63, 195nn.6-7,
    195n.15, 196n.28, 199n.90, 466
Webster, Sir Godfrey Vassal, 45-46, 96, 107,
    113n.24, 115, 466
Webster, James Wedderburn ("Sir Brilliant"),
    117, 147, 148, 155n.97, 155n.101, 195n.6,
    195n.14, 439, 466
Wedgwood, Josiah, 196n.31, 290
Weld, Edward, 431
Wellesley, Marquis. See Wellesley, Richard
    Colley; Wellington, first duke of
Wellesley, Viscount. See Wellesley, Richard
    Colley
Wellesley, Arthur. See Wellington, first duke of
Wellesley, Garrett, 467
Wellesley, Lady George, 340n.44
Wellesley, Henry, 340n.44, 357, 431, 466
Wellesley, Lady (Hyacinthe), 113n.25, 466
Wellesley, Richard Colley, 2, 107, 108, 379-81,
    389n.13, 431, 442, 466
Wellesley-Pole, William, 430, 466
Wellington, first duke of (Arthur Wellesley), 3,
    45, 65n.72, 95, 106, 158, 182, 183, 200n.123,
    389n.13, 412, 417, 430, 431, 441, 446, 456,
    461, 462, 466, 467
Wentworth, Baron. See Noel, Sir Edward; Noel,
    Thomas
Wentworth, Lady Mary, 451
Westall, R., Lord Byron, **53**
Westminster Abbey, 18, 33
Westmoreland, countess of. See Fane, Priscilla
    Anne
Westmoreland, tenth earl of. See Fane, John
    (1759-1841)
Westmoreland, eleventh earl of. See Fane, John
    (1784-1859)
Westmoreland, Lady, 46, 139, 430
Westmoreland, Lord, 56
Weston, 347
Weymouth, 200n.111, 420
Wheatley, Francis, 16, 467
Whitbread, Samuel, 137, 152n.50, 181, 182,
    389n.5, 415, 467
Whitehall. See Melbourne House, Whitehall
Whitmore, Thomas, 389n.5
Whitworth, Lord, 66n.91
William IV, 438, 446
William of Orange, Prince, 58, 61n.20, 178, 181,
    200n.102, 200n.112, 422, 442, 448
Williams, Lady, 190

Williams, Charlotte, 25, 63n.45, 69, 433
Williams, Watkin, 283, 467
Williamson, George C., 61nn.22-23
Willoughby de Eresby, Baroness. See Drummond,
    Clementina Elizabeth
Wilmot, Mr., 332
Wilsford, 37
Wilson, Harriette, 37-38, 44, 64n.61, 299n.31,
    462, 465, 468
Wilson, Sir Robert Thomas, 311, 312, 337n.2,
    337n.6, 467
Wilton, Lord Grey de, 61n.22
Wilton, Joseph, 422
Windham, 437
Winnington, Thomas, 61n.13
Wise, Henry, 17, 424
Witgenstin, Count, 340n.44
Wolves Club, 337n.3
Wombwell, Sir George, 415
Woollatt, Mr., 294
Worcester, Lady. See Leveson-Gower, Lady
    Charlotte Sophia
Worcester, marquis of. See Somerset, Henry;
    Somerset, Henry Charles
Wordsworth, William, 448
Wraxall, Nathaniel, 19, 92n.38, 423
Wray, Cecil, 63n.42
Wyatt, 457
Wycombe, earl of, 389n.5
Wyndham, Elizabeth, 437
Wyndham, Sir George O'Brien. See Egremont,
    third earl of
Wyndham, Sir William, 437
Wynn, Sir Henry Watkin Williams. See Williams,
    Watkin
Wynn, Sir Watkin Williams, 457, 468
Wynne, Thomas Edward, 415

Yarmouth, earl of (Frances Charles), 364, 468
Yenn, John, 64n.52, 422
York, duchess of, 33, 48, 196n.24
York, Frederick, duke of, 2, 33, 61n.11, 63nn.50-
    52, 66n.92, 182, 196n.24, 197n.64, 200n.112,
    412, 421, 434, 439, 440, 452
York House, 33, 63-64n.52, 37. See also
    Melbourne House, Whitehall
Yorke, Charles Philip, 291, 303n.72, 468
Yorke, Philip, 439
Young, Arthur, 3, 35, 64n.55, 414

Ziegler, Philip, 17, 112n.17
Zoffany, John, 431